Costing Human Resources

Costing Human Resources:
The Financial Impact of Behavior in Organizations

Fourth Edition

Wayne F. Cascio
University of Colorado at Denver

 **South-Western College Publishing**
Thomson Learning™

Australia • Canada • Denmark • Japan • Mexico • New Zealand • Philippines
Puerto Rico • Singapore • South Africa • Spain • United Kingdom • United States

*Costing Human Resources: The Financial Impact of Behavior in Organizations,
4e,* by Wayne Cascio

Acquisitions Editor: John Szilagyi
Developmental Editor: Linda Chaffee
Marketing Manager: Joseph A. Sabatino
Production Editor: Anne Chimenti
Manufacturing Coordinator: Sandee Milewski
Cover Design: Paul Neff Design/Cincinnati
Cover Photography: © 1999 PhotoDisc
Production House: UpperCase Publication Services, Ltd.
Printer: WebCom

Printed in Canada
1 2 3 4 5 02 01 00 99

For more information contact South-Western College Publishing,
5101 Madison Road, Cincinnati, Ohio, 45227, or find us on the Internet at
http://www.swcollege.com

For permission to use material from this text or product, contact us by
- telephone: 1-800-730-2214
- fax: 1-800-730-2215
- web: http://www.thomsonrights.com

Library of Congress Cataloging-in-Publication Data
Cascio, Wayne F.
    Costing human resources : the financial impact of behavior in
  organizations / Wayne F. Cascio. -- 4th ed.
       p. cm.
  Includes bibliographical references and index.
  ISBN 0-324-00709-4
  1. Labor costs--Accounting. I. Title.
HF5681.L2 C37   1999
658.15'53--dc21

                               99-049457

This book is printed on acid-free paper.

For Joe

My most important asset

P R E F A C E

Over the past 40 years or so, a large amount of literature on the general subject of costing human resources (HR) has accumulated. Much of that literature has developed in three fields—accounting, economics, and psychology—and much of it is unknown to academics and practicing managers alike.

Although methods for costing HR activities are available, I believe that much of what we do in the human resource management field remains generally misunderstood and underestimated by the organizations we serve. In part, we in the field are responsible for this state of affairs because much of what we do is evaluated only in statistical or behavioral terms, if at all. Like it or not, *the language of business is dollars, not correlation coefficients.*

Consider a familiar example: An organization hires a consultant to develop a new selection program because its current program is affecting protected groups adversely, and the organization fears a lawsuit. The consultant develops a more valid selection procedure that eliminates the problem, and the organization is happy because it stays out of court. It would be even happier, however, if it knew that the more valid procedure would net another $250,000 per year in increased productivity and fewer post-hire failures.

It is now possible to estimate the dollar value of HR programs in a number of key areas, and *Costing Human Resources* examines nine of them. I make no attempt to be comprehensive, but some of the methods in this book are versatile enough to be applied in areas that the book does not address specifically.

I have thoroughly enjoyed writing this book—in no small part because the more I researched applicable methods for costing human resources, the more comfortable I felt about the ability of practicing managers to contribute to their organizations by assigning relatively accurate dollar amounts to their activities. Indeed, I am now fully confident that on the basis of results achieved—results that are measured in dollars—HR management can compete successfully for resources with the managers of other functional business areas.

The fourth edition of *Costing Human Resources* includes several major changes, including the addition of two completely new chapters. Chapter 4 examines the high cost of mismanaging human resources, including the costs of investigating and litigating single-plaintiff and class-action lawsuits on unfair discrimination, and the economic consequences of ineffective management of people. Chapter 7 is a new chapter on the strategic and financial effects of work–life programs, and it includes a model to guide managers charged with making the business case for such programs. As in other chapters, actual company examples show how this can and has been done.

Most of the features of the previous editions have been retained, but they have been updated to reflect new research findings. Some of these include:

- Intellectual capital as a framework for integrating HR costing measures and as a new way of strategic thinking (Chapter 1).
- New company examples illustrating the causes of, costs of, and methods for dealing with employee turnover and absenteeism (Chapters 2 and 3).
- Extensive coverage of the costs, benefits, types, and program-evaluation issues associated with worksite health-promotion programs, plus company-level evaluations of such programs (Chapter 5).
- Inclusion of the Sears Roebuck & Co. research showing cause–effect relationships among employee attitudes, customer satisfaction, and profits (Chapter 6).
- Thorough treatment of the Raju-Burke-Normand model of utility analysis along with examples of its application (Chapter 8).
- Fully updated alternative methods for estimating the dollar value of a one-standard-deviation difference in criterion level (SD_y) and comparative research on the methods (Chapter 9).

- Examination of the utilities of competing predictors that differ in adverse impact, how to deal with risk and uncertainty in utility analysis, and how to maximize the impact of utility analysis on decision makers (Chapters 10 and 11).
- Improved treatment of costing procedures for proposed or ongoing HR development programs, including effect-size estimation (Chapter 11).
- Updated treatment and examples of alternative competitive strategies, and methods for linking effective HR management to profits (Chapter 12).

As in previous editions, an instructor's manual accompanies the fourth edition of *Costing Human Resources,* and includes complete solutions to all end-of-chapter problems in the text. The manual is available on disk (ISBN 0-324-00710-8) from your South-Western College Publishing representative or at *www.management.swcollege.com.* The text can be used in university-level courses in HR management, either as a supplement to or in conjunction with other textbooks. Practicing HR managers and consultants will also find this book to be valuable.

Acknowledgments

I would like to acknowledge trial attorneys Evelyn Becker and Tony Crouse for their assistance in developing and critiquing material in Chapter 4, and Dr. Dana Friedman, senior vice president of Bright Horizons Family Solutions, for helping me to understand the strategic and financial implications of work–life programs (Chapter 7). Their help was invaluable.

Finally, I would like to thank those at South-Western College Publishing who worked hard to make this edition possible: executive editor John Szilagyi; editorial assistant Linda Chaffee, who patiently managed the revision process; and production editor Anne Chimenti. I am grateful for their efforts.

Wayne F. Cascio

THOMSON LEARNING
DISTRIBUTION CENTER
7625 EMPIRE DRIVE
FLORENCE, KY 41042

TIM W. MEEKMA 800 590-9951 X879

SHIP TO: jon werner
U Of WI White CBMG
Management Department
800 W Main Street
WHITEWATER WI 531900000

SALES SUPPORT

Date	Account	Contact
01/18/00	698144	13

WAREHOUSE INSTRUCTIONS

SLA: 7   BOX: Staple

LOCATION	QTY	ISBN	AUTHOR/TITLE
K-26F-004-20	1	0-324-00709-4	CASCIO COSTING HUMAN RESOURCES 4E

INV# 25980866SM
PO# 15902259
DATE: / /
CARTON: 1 of 1
ID# 4766220

PRIME-INDUCT
-SLSB

VIA: UP

PAGE 1 OF 1

BATCH: 0882492
002/007

C O N T E N T S

Chapter 3

The Hidden Costs of Absenteeism and Sick Leave   59

Chapter 4

The High Cost of Mismanaging Human Resources   83

PART II   Costing EAPs and Worksite Health-Promotion Programs,
Attitudes, and Work–Life Programs   107

Chapter 5

Costing the Effects of Employee Assistance and Worksite Health-Promotion Programs   109

Chapter 6

The Financial Impact of Employee Attitudes   139

Chapter 7

The Strategic and Financial Effects of Work–Life Programs   163

PART III   HR Programs: A Return-on-Investment Perspective   187

Chapter 8

Utility: The Concept and Its Measurement   189

Chapter 9

Estimating the Economic Value of Job Performance   219

Chapter 10

Valid Selection Procedures Can Pay Off   253

Chapter 11

Estimating the Costs and Benefits of Human Resource Development Programs   285

Chapter 12

Linking Effective Human Resources Management to Profits   315

Appendix A

Appendix B

Index   351

The Costs and Benefits of Human Resources

Human resource (HR) management activities —those associated with the attraction, selection, retention, development, and utilization of people in organizations—commonly are evaluated in behavioral or statistical terms. Behavioral measures include measures of the reactions of various groups (top management, HR specialists, applicants, or trainees), of what individuals have learned, or of how their behaviors have changed on the job. Statistical measures include ratios (for example, accident frequency or severity); percentages (for example, labor turnover); measures of central tendency and variability (for example, mean and standard deviation of cash register shortages and surpluses); and measures of correlation (for example, validity coefficients for selection programs). The need to evaluate HR management (HRM) activities in *economic* terms, however, is becoming increasingly apparent. In the current climate of rising costs for labor, energy, and raw materials, operating executives justifiably demand estimates of the expected costs and benefits of HR programs. Developing such measures requires an interdisciplinary approach that incorporates information from accounting, finance, economics, and behavioral science. This book attempts to present such an approach in several key areas that are relevant to HR programs.

Economic measures can help senior executives assess the extent to which HR programs are consistent with and contribute to the strategic direction of an organization. All too often, unfortunately, HR professionals have been accused of being out of touch with the strategic direction

1

of their organizations, of being isolated and parochial. Consider one chief executive officer's (CEO's) appraisal of the field:

> HR professionals have been getting by focusing on the day-to-day. They need to develop a broader and farther-reaching vision and understand where their organization is headed and how they can help steer the company in that direction. (Leonard 1998, p. 85)

To be sure, many HR managers caught up in the wave of mergers, acquisitions, and restructurings that characterized the 1990s have adopted a more strategic orientation out of necessity. Today, more and more HR executives sit on top executive councils, where they understand how markets work in general and how their own organizations compete for business so they make meaningful contributions to strategic business decisions. They have embraced successfully the challenges to think and to act like businesspeople, and they are being treated as full partners with other members of top management (Ulrich 1998).

CEOs also want their HR officers to contribute to bottom-line success. Research has shown over and over that carefully designed, valid HR programs pay off. HR managers will benefit by taking advantage of methods now available for demonstrating this contribution. Says Robert McDonald, CEO of the North American Division of Standard Chartered Bank in New York:

> When it comes to the bottom line, I would say that HR generally has been a bit out to lunch. . . . But their understanding of the bottom line has improved over the past few years, and I do believe that most HR executives are striving to better understand how their decisions and actions can truly affect the bottom line. (Leonard 1998, p. 83)

This book identifies some of the key areas to consider in demonstrating the costs and benefits of human resource programs, but first let us distinguish the current approach to costing human resources from its predecessor, human resource accounting.

HUMAN RESOURCE ACCOUNTING

There are no generally accepted accounting procedures for employee valuation (Johanson et al. 1998; Roslender 1997). The first major attempt at such valuation was made by the R.G. Barry Corporation of Columbus, Ohio. Barry's 1967 annual report described the company's inauguration of human resource accounting (HRA) procedures as a first step in developing sophisticated measurement and accounting procedures to enable the company to report accurate estimates of the worth of the organization's human assets. Under the following five categories, Barry accumulated costs in individual subsidiary accounts for each manager: recruiting and acquisition; formal training and familiarization; informal training and informal familiarization; experience; and development. A full description of the nature of expenses analyzed is given by Woodruff (1970). Costs were amortized over the expected working lives of individuals (or sometimes shorter periods), and unamortized costs (for example, when an individual left the company) were written off.

That is the *historical-cost* approach to employee valuation (that is, expenses actually incurred). It is an *asset model* of accounting in that it measures the organization's investment in employees. For external reporting—to inform interested parties of the financial position and the results of a company's operations, with emphasis on performance measurement—that model is widely viewed as most appropriate (Morrow 1997; Tsay 1977). The historical-cost approach is relatively objective; it permits comparisons of levels of human resource investment on a basis consistent with the accounting treatment of other assets, and it seems a fair matching of benefits exhaustion with expense in particular time periods (Brummet, Flamholtz, & Pyle 1968).

The method is not without its disadvantages, however, as Baker (1974) has noted. First, historical-cost valuation is based on the false assumption that the dollar is stable. Second, deleting and writing off abortive expenditures involve a great deal of subjectivity. Third, because the assets valued are not salable there is no independent check of valuation. Finally, this approach measures only costs to the organization; it ignores completely any measure of the value of the employee to the organization. Hence, the soundness of the investment in human resources is not directly indicated.

In view of the shortcomings of the historical-cost approach, it seems prudent to examine other bases of valuation that might provide supplemental information. Those fall broadly into three categories: replacement cost, present value of future earnings, and present value to the organization (that is, profit contribution).

Replacement Cost

One alternative to measuring the historical cost of an employee is to measure the cost of replacing that employee. According to Flamholtz (1985), replacement costs include recruitment, selection, compensation, and training costs (including the income foregone during the training period). An example of the replacement-cost approach was presented by Flamholtz, Searfoss, and Coff (1988). Flamholtz (1971) pointed out that it is easier in practice to estimate replacement cost than market value, and the former might therefore be adopted as a surrogate measure of the latter.

On the other hand, it could be argued just as plausibly that substituting replacement for historical cost does little more than update the valuation, at the expense of importing considerably more subjectivity into the measure (Turner 1996; Scarpello & Theeke 1989; Baker 1974). Also, replacement-cost valuation may lead to upwardly biased estimates because an inefficient firm may incur greater costs (Steffy & Maurer 1988). Finally, one might question the usefulness of such a measure. The principal actions in which those data would be relevant would be in dismissing and replacing staff. Most organizations make such decisions too infrequently to make it worthwhile to build into the accounting system the regular production of replacement-cost data on all employees.

Present Value of Future Earnings

Lev and Schwartz (1971) proposed an economic valuation of employees based on the present value of future earnings, adjusted for the probability of employees' deaths. To determine this value, the organization establishes what an employee's future contribution is worth to it today. That contribution can be measured by its cost or by the wages the organization will pay the employee. The measure is an objective one because it uses widely based statistics such as census income returns and mortality tables. The measure is severely limited, however, because it assigns a value to the *average* rather than to any specific group or individual. The organization does not benefit by monitoring the efficiency of its investment in employee development because the investment has little or no impact on the present valuation of future earnings.

Baker (1974) pointed out three other faulty assumptions underlying this method. If the present value of future earnings is regarded as a fair appraisal of the individual's economic worth to an organization, then (1) subject to any profit expectancy built into the discount rate applied (because worth is equal to future cost), the employing organization is indifferent as to whether it pays the cost to obtain the value (that is, whether it retains the employee); in either case it comes out even. (2) Insofar as earnings exclude fringe costs, the organization is indeed better off without this resource. (3) Consequently, the value of past recruitment and employee development is zero in (1) or is negative assuming (2).

Value to the Organization

The value of a professional athlete's services is often determined by how much money a particular team, acting in an open competitive market (the free agent draft), is willing to pay him or her. In fact, this approach is quite common among British football clubs (Morrow 1996). An analogous approach might also be taken in other types of organizations. Hekimian and Jones (1967) proposed that where an organization had several divisions seeking the same employee, the employee should be allocated to the highest bidder, and the bid price should be incorporated into that division's investment base. On the surface this approach has merit, but in practice the opportunities to use it are relatively rare. If the objective is to evaluate opportunity costs (that is, the potential profit lost by failing to take the optimal course of action in a given situation), then the appropriate inclusion in the investment base is the highest unsuccessful bid. Moreover, the soundness of the valuation depends wholly on the information, judgment, and impartiality of the bidding divisions.

An alternative aggregate-valuation approach has been proposed by Hermanson (1964). It involves establishing the net present value of expected wage payments (discounted at the economy rate of return on owned assets for the latest year) and applying to this a weighted efficiency ratio (the rate of income on owned assets for all firms in the economy). As noted earlier, use of such broadly based statistics appears to diminish the precision of the calculations in general and incorporates unrelated risk factors into the efficiency-ratio calculation. Moreover, human resources so valued would apparently subsume all other intangible assets of a goodwill nature.

Advocates of HRA make a compelling case for this kind of measurement, but they tend to forget that dollar values cannot always be attached to the information that is collected. Thus, HRA may be of much more limited application than is commonly supposed (Baker 1974). Perhaps the major limitation of these approaches to HRA is that they reflect only inputs and not effectiveness. They are *human asset accounting* models that focus exclusively on investments in people (inputs); they ignore completely information about the output those resources produce.

In view of the conceptual and methodological limitations of human asset models, Pyle (1970) suggested that HRA be extended to compute returns on assets and returns on investments. That approach properly compares input and output measures but still fails to distinguish between individual and group effects that produce variability in output. The search continues for a single, limited-criterion measure for HRA (see Dobija 1998), but it is unrealistic to expect that such a measure will be developed (Turner 1996; Tsay 1977). Consider the following summary comments from reviewers of the HRA literature regarding the value and feasibility of HRA data. Following the implementation of two "action research projects" involving the creation of new information systems in organizations, Mirvis and Lawler (1983) noted

> Most organizations do not want to make a public accounting of how well they manage people and, more to the point, . . . they do not want to be held accountable for it. (p. 175)

Following their review of the HRA literature, Ferguson and Berger (1985) wrote

> As tempting as it is to try to establish a balance sheet value for a firm's human assets, such attempts are probably doomed; at this point it is not possible to calculate a figure that is both objective and meaningful. (p. 29)

After they reviewed more than 140 articles and several books on human resource accounting, Scarpello and Theeke (1989) concluded

> At the theoretical level, HRA is an interesting concept. If human resource value could be measured, the knowledge of that value could be used for internal management and external investor decision making. However, until HRA advocates demonstrate a valid and generalizable means for measuring human resource value in monetary terms, we are compelled to recommend that researchers abandon further consideration of possible benefits from HRA. (p. 275)

An analysis of seven case studies (Johanson 1998) concluded that most managers in most studies hold positive attitudes toward HRA. However, HRA tends not to be used as part of the actual management control process—a fact consistent with a finding by Roslender and Dyson (1992) that HRA largely has failed to develop in the way of practical applications.

An alternative approach focuses on attaching dollar estimates to the behavioral outcomes produced by working in an organization. Criteria such as absenteeism, turnover, and job performance are measured using traditional organizational tools, and costs are estimated for each criterion. For example, in costing labor turnover, dollar figures must be attached to separation, replacement, and training costs. That method, which measures not the value of the individual but the economic consequences of his or her behavior, assesses behavior in terms that are taken seriously by most decision makers—those of dollars. That approach, termed an *expense* model of HRA (Mirvis & Macy 1976), is the approach to costing human resources taken in this book and will be developed further in the next section.

COSTING EMPLOYEE BEHAVIORS

The general idea of costing human resources is not a new one. A classic article by Brogden and Taylor (1950) addressed the potential for developing on-the-job performance criteria expressed in dollars. They noted

> The criterion should measure the contribution of the individual to the overall efficiency of the organization. . . . It centers on the quantity, quality, and cost of the finished product. Such factors as skill are latent—their effect is realized in the end product. (pp. 139, 141)

The contribution each employee makes is not related to the size of a firm's investment in that employee, but it is directly related to how each person works and what is produced.

What is different in the general costing approach is the quantification in financial terms of a set of common behavioral and performance outcomes. Standard cost-accounting procedures are applied to employee behavior. To accomplish this, the cost elements associated with each behavior must be identified and their separate and independent dollar values computed. Costs can be conceptualized in two ways. One reflects *outlay costs* (for example, materials used in training new employees) versus *time costs* (for example, supervisors' time spent orienting the new employees). A second distinguishes among *fixed, variable,* and *opportunity costs.* Fixed costs (for example, salaries) are incurred independently of production rate; variable costs (for example, sales commissions) are those that rise as the production rate rises. Opportunity costs reflect what the organization might have earned had it put the resources in question to another use. Other examples of these costs include the overtime cost incurred because of absenteeism (a variable cost); the salary and benefits for personnel who replace the absentees (a fixed cost); and the profit lost during the replacement process (an opportunity cost). These distinctions are important because only variable costs are related directly to behavior. Fixed costs are incurred regardless of behavioral occurrences, and opportunity costs are realized only if some employees put their free time to productive use while others do not (Macy & Mirvis 1976).

For an organization there are distinct costs associated with each behavior, but in most organizations those costs are unknown. People interested in uncovering such costs can rest assured of four things: it can be done; it does not take a great deal of extra work to do so; a valid business reason exists for doing it; and they will be recognized and rewarded for their efforts.

Contrary to common belief, all aspects of HRM (including morale) can be measured and quantified in the same manner as any operational function. Although that is technically true, qualitative assessment of critical features of the HRM system, such as the degree to which any proposed HRM program fits with the strategic direction of a business, is no less important.

In summary, an organization might use HRA asset models to reflect its investment in employees—models that assess the value of employees, treating them as capitalized resources (that is, the economic concept of human capital). In contrast, an organization might use HRA expense models to measure the economic effects of employees' behavior. The latter are particularly useful in attempts to account for intellectual capital—the subject of the following section.

INTELLECTUAL CAPITAL

Commercial enterprises have always been valued according to their financial assets and sales, their real estate holdings, or other tangible assets. That valuation basis made great sense in the industrial age, but it makes less sense in the information age, which is characterized by dynamism and innovation. The service sector, in particular, has few visible assets. What price does one assign, for example, to creativity, service standards, or unique computer systems? All of that is intellectual capital—knowledge, information, intellectual property, experience—that can be put to use to create wealth (Stewart 1997). Microsoft Corporation is one example of a firm with a prodigious supply of intellectual capital.

The total market value of Microsoft (the number of shares outstanding times the price per share) was about $412 billion in mid-1999, but the total value of all of its physical assets (buildings, equipment, furniture) was only about $24 billion (U.S.). What accounts for this difference of roughly $388 billion? The answer is its intellectual assets—anticipated revenues from existing and new software products, customer relationships, brand equity (the premium customers will pay to acquire a brand-name product instead of a generic one), databases, organization structure, and overall organizational capability.

Is Microsoft an unusual example? Hardly. Leif Edvinsson, director of intellectual capital for Skandia Assurance and Financial Services (AFS), the Swedish financial services company, estimates the ratio of the value of intellectual capital to the value of physical and financial capital as between 5:1 and 16:1. Values this large convey an important lesson: ignore those assets at your peril. To date, however, there is no clear agreement in the accounting profession about how to account for them (Johanson et al. 1998).

The implication of all of this is that traditional financial statements are less illuminating with respect to the assets that create wealth than they were in the past. Intangible assets such as brand names, intellectual capital, patents, copyrights, and expenditures for research and development now generate an increasing amount of wealth for firms. The shift to a knowledge-based economy has created entirely different categories of assets, so-called "soft" assets, that are not recognized in financial statements. Information is the essence of these soft assets.

The Information Revolution

It is no exaggeration to say that the information revolution is reinventing business, economic life, and society. Just as the industrial revolution caused wrenching changes in the nature of work and in the attitudes and habits of workers, the information revolution will transform everything it touches—and it will touch everything.

Day by day, the information economy continues to expand. Just look at the growth of the computing, communications, and entertainment industries. As Thomas Stewart notes in his influential book, *Intellectual Capital* (1997), every country, every company, and every individual depends increasingly on knowledge—patents, processes, skills, technologies, information about customers and suppliers, and experience. No force can stop, or even slow, the revolution that is going on all around us. Knowledge has become the fundamental ingredient of what we make, do, buy, and sell. As a result, managing it—finding and growing intellectual capital, storing it, selling it, sharing it—has become the most important economic task of individuals, businesses, and nations.

What does this "new-wave" trend toward maximizing the payoff from intellectual assets imply for HR costing and accounting? It suggests a new way of strategic thinking, rather than a technical approach about "how to put people on the balance sheet."

Valuing Intellectual Capital

The first firm to attempt to account for its intellectual capital was Skandia AFS, in a supplement to its 1994 annual report. The firm emphasized that the supplement should be viewed "as a way of describing the otherwise intangible dimensions of the operations, and not as an attempt to create added value in the likes of the emperor's new clothes." Working with Hubert Saint-Onge of the Canadian Imperial Bank of Commerce, and building on earlier work by Karl Erik Sveiby, Edvinsson of Skandia developed a framework, called the Skandia Navigator, to conceptualize otherwise intangible dimensions. He did so in the belief that it is not possible to manage intellectual capital unless one can locate it in places in the company that are strategically important and where management can make a difference. The Navigator helps to focus attention on where to look.

According to the Navigator, intellectual capital in a company can be found in one or more of three places: its people, its structures, and its customers. Thus, intellectual capital comprises human capital, structural capital, and customer capital.[1] Although each is intangible, and reflects the knowledge assets of a company, each can be measured and targeted for investment. More importantly, each represents something that managers and investors can understand. Let us now define each of those terms.

Human capital represents the knowledge, skill, and capability of individual employees to provide solutions to problems that customers think are important. Notice that last phrase: "problems that customers think are important." This is an "outside-in" approach in which leading customers define a firm's strategy, as opposed to an "inside-out" approach whereby an insular group of top executives defines it. The relevance and significance of human capital is a fundamental tenet among leading thinkers about the twenty-first century economy ("The Twenty-First Century Economy" 1998). Human capital, like the other types, becomes important to a business in the context of a strategy or purpose. It matters because it is the source of innovation and renewal (Stewart 1997).

Sharing, transporting, and enabling human capital—that is, leveraging it—requires other structures or organizational capabilities. Thus, *structural capital* consists of everything that remains when the employees go home, including databases, customer files, software manuals, trademarks, and organizational structures (Skandia AFS 1994).

Customer capital is the value of an organization's relationships with the people with whom it does business, including suppliers. It is in relationships with customers that intellectual capital turns into money, as is the case with brand equity. Thus, Coca-Cola, the world's most valuable brand name, is worth about $39 billion. But customer capital also shows up in complaint letters, renewal rates, cross-selling, referrals, and the speed with which phone calls are returned. It is manifest in learning, access, and trust (Stewart 1997). When Boeing was designing its 777 jet airplane, it made special efforts to seek input from suppliers and customers, including frequent fliers and airline crews. As a result, the aircraft has received almost universal acclaim from passengers, pilots, and crews for its state-of-the-art features. Customer capital is critical to Boeing as it is to many other firms.

Measuring Intellectual Capital

A variety of measures assess each component of intellectual capital, but this field is still too new to proclaim any set of measures as definitive. Each company needs to think through its own sources and uses of intellectual capital, experiment with alternative measures, and then choose those that make the most sense in terms of its strategic direction. The following three principles should guide a company in deciding what to measure (Stewart 1997).

1. *Keep it simple.* Try for no more than three measures each of human, structural, and customer capital, plus one number that provides a broad view of the whole.
2. *Measure what is strategically important.* Neither 3M Company nor Hewlett-Packard Company attempts to assign a dollar figure directly to its human capital, but because both employ innovation as a strategy to compete for business in the marketplace, both track the percentage of sales generated by new products. That is one measure of innovativeness, a measure of human capital.

3. *Measure activities that produce intellectual wealth.* HR professionals should resist the temptation to focus only on what is measurable—activities and costs (Pfeffer 1997). Focus instead on measuring factors that meet real organizational needs, such as the turnover rate among high-performing knowledge workers who are not easily replaced.

It is understandable that HR professionals want to develop and use measures of human capital. Those efforts are the focus of this book. As we have seen, however, intellectual capital encompasses more than just human capital. Although it is beyond the scope of this book, firms should develop a set of measures like those that follow to produce a comprehensive picture of intellectual capital.

Human Capital Measures

Measures of Innovation. Years ago, 3M established as a goal that at least 25 percent of its annual sales would come from products less than four years old. As an even better strategy, a firm might compare gross profit margins from new products to gross profit margins from old ones. Genuine innovation should command a premium.

Measures of Employee Attitudes. After eight quarters of experimentation, retailer Sears, Roebuck and Co. found that employees' attitudes about the job and the company are the two factors that predict their behavior toward the customer. That behavior, in turn, predicts the likelihood of customer retention and customers' recommendations of Sears to others—two factors that, in turn, predict financial performance. The lesson here is that no matter how good your merchandise is, you won't get satisfied customers without a trained, literate, and motivated workforce with decision-making authority. The right workforce, coupled with high-quality products, creates customer satisfaction, and that produces superior financial performance (Rucci, Kirn, & Quinn 1998).

Measures of Tenure, Turnover, Experience, and Learning. These are indices of a company's "inventory" of knowledgeable employees. To quantify that inventory, Canadian Imperial Bank of Commerce uses "competency maps" to display the skills people need to move along career paths. The maps describe the abilities that customers expect from people they deal with at the bank: familiarity with its product line, a knowledge of accounting, selling skills, expertise in credit analysis—about four dozen in all. Obviously, because the range and depth of knowledge expected from a teller differs from that of a branch manager or loan officer, the maps help employees to understand the difference between what they can do now and what customers expect them to be able to do. Employees themselves are expected to take the initiative to learn what they need to do their jobs now, and what they will need to progress over time (Stewart 1997).

Customer Capital Measures

There are many ways to measure customer satisfaction. HR professionals might participate as members of a cross-functional team to develop measures of *customer retention rate, brand equity,* and *customer satisfaction.* Sears has tied customer satisfaction to performance management for individual employees. Here's how that process works (Rucci et al. 1998). Cash registers in each retail store randomly print out a special coupon along with customer receipts in a small percentage of transactions. With 468 million transactions per year at Sears registers, it's not hard to generate a statistically reliable sample, even for an individual sales associate. The coupon says that if you agree to call a toll-free number in the next week and answer prerecorded questions by pressing buttons on your telephone keypad Sears will take $5 off your next purchase. Because each call is linked to a particular transaction, For the first time, Sears is able to collect meaningful data on individual sales associates, and concurrently assess customer satisfaction. In the context of HR management, such data can be especially helpful in the performance-management process and in providing true 360-degree feedback to employees from supervisors, peers, subordinates, and customers.

Structural Capital Measures

To determine if a company's systems are helping or hindering its people in serving its customers better, consider such measures as suggestions made versus suggestions implemented, time-to-market (how long it takes to develop and introduce new products or services), and databases at estimated replacement cost.

As an overall measure of a company's intellectual capital, compare market value to book value. Market value is what a company is worth in the stock market—price per share multiplied by the number of shares outstanding. Book value, which can be found in every annual report, is the equity portion of a company's balance sheet, what's left after all debt is accounted for. The assumption is that everything left in the market value after accounting for the fixed assets must be intangible assets. As we noted earlier, if the total market value of Microsoft is $412 billion, while the total value of all of its physical assets (buildings, equipment, furniture) is $24 billion, then its intellectual capital is $388 billion.

Although there are advantages to that measure (for example, interest rates and stock market conditions generally affect all firms in an industry equally), there are offsetting disadvantages that should be noted. For example, if the stock market drops, does that mean that a firm's intellectual capital has dropped as well? If a company trades for less than its book value (as sometimes happens), does that mean that the company has no intellectual assets? Finally, it is important to note that both book and market values are usually understated. We know this because takeovers (friendly or unfriendly) almost always cost a premium over a firm's market capitalization. Perhaps, instead of looking at the raw numbers that reflect market-to-book values, we should compute the *ratio* of market-to-book values. Doing so permits comparisons to competitors and to industry averages.

Numerous measures might be computed but each is useful only if it passes two tests: (1) it allows management to evaluate year-to-year performance (to assess progress toward goals), and (2) it permits company-to-company comparisons. Admittedly passing both tests is difficult but, if such comparison data were available, the field of HR costing and accounting would expand its visibility in a quantum fashion.

To create a coherent picture that integrates the various measures of human, structural, and customer capital, Stewart (1997) suggests that a firm consider using a "radar" chart, an intellectual capital (IC) navigator such as the one shown in Exhibit 1–1. Start with a circle, like that on a radar screen, and include as many lines radiating from the center as there are items to measure. Mark each axis with a relevant scale (for example, ratios or percentages). Zero is placed normally at the center of the chart, but some scales, such as the turnover rate among knowledge workers, are reverse-scored with zero on the outside of the axis where the axis crosses it.

For each scale, the firm's goal should be on the rim of the circle. For example, for market-to-book ratio, put –0.5 at the center, and put whatever is best-in-class for the industry (for example, +2.0, +6.0) on the rim of the circle. The firm should plot where it is on each scale, and then connect the dots. The result is an irregular polygon that is relatively easy to interpret. What is inside the polygon is what you have; what is outside it is what you want. As a graphic expression of a firm's

EXHIBIT 1-1   *Intellectual Capital Navigator*

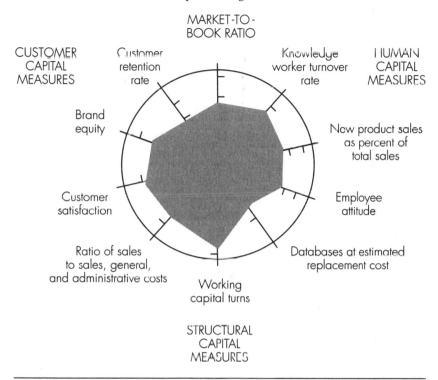

Source: Adapted from *Intellectual Capital* by Thomas A. Stewart (p. 246). Copyright © 1997 by Thomas A. Stewart. Used by permission of Doubleday, a division of Random House, Inc.

distribution of intellectual capital, the navigator does several things: (1) it tells a firm where it is now, and (2) it shows where the firm should be going. To assess progress over time, the navigator makes it possible to compare year-to-year charts. Finally, the navigator can serve as a diagnostic tool. For example, in Exhibit 1-1 notice the relatively high scores on customer satisfaction and brand equity and the mediocre score on customer retention. Decision makers might ponder why this is so—a connection that might not have been so obvious without a graphic display, such as the navigator provides.

Armed with a set of measures such as those, we can focus management decisions and investments into areas of intellectual capital (human, structural, and customer capital) that will have the greatest payoff for the firm. As a way to assess human capital, HR costing represents a new way of thinking strategically. Boudreau (1998) has noted that measures of HR costs and benefits can serve a variety of purposes: as catalysts for change, to enhance the credibility of the HR function, to persuade others to support investments in human resources, and to improve the quality of HR decisions. Such measures make HR strategy persuasive because they link behavioral outcomes to the strategic direction of the firm.

PLAN OF THE BOOK

The intent of this book is to consider some important areas where costs can be attached to HR activities, to identify important cost elements, and to show how they may be combined to yield valid cost estimates. A great many words have been written on those topics, and integrating that information is essential to developing practical costing procedures. The payoff from such procedures may be enormous.

In part I, we will consider procedures for costing employee decisions to quit and to be absent and the high cost of HR mismanagement. The high costs of turnover and absenteeism have been recognized for some time, but few managers are aware of the costs of investigating and litigating employment discrimination lawsuits or of the effect that such negative publicity has on a company's stock price (see chapter 4).

In part II, we will examine the costs and benefits of employee assistance programs (EAPs) and worksite health promotion programs (chapter 5), the financial impact of employee attitudes (chapter 6), and work–life programs (chapter 7). Although EAPs and worksite health promotion programs have been popular for some time, the economic benefits accruing from them are not determined easily. In chapter 5, therefore, we will consider the methods used to determine those programs' relative costs and benefits and the outcomes resulting from them. Employee attitudes may affect how an employee behaves on the job; the financial impact of such attitudes can be measured, and dollar estimates assigned to targeted improvements in job attitudes. We will consider those issues in chapter 6. Many organizations have adopted work–life programs, but few have assessed the economic outcomes of such programs. Chapter 7 will show how such outcomes can be estimated.

In part III, we will direct considerable attention to the concept of utility or overall worth, so that managers of human resources can adopt a return-on-investment perspective with respect to personnel selection, job performance measurement, and training and development efforts (chapters 8 through 11). Finally, in chapter 12, we will consider evaluation of the entire HR function, using qualitative and quantitative measures.

Wise decisions about HR programs demand a knowledge of their costs and benefits. Such a view encompasses issues of program design, implementation, and evaluation in both tangible (dollar) and intangible terms, but such a view is essential. Comprehensive assessment requires that the HR system be viewed as a network of interacting components.

EXERCISES

1. Discuss the advantages and disadvantages of the historical cost, replacement cost, and present value of future earnings approaches to employee valuation.
2. How are HRA expense models different from HRA asset models?
3. Discuss the concept of intellectual capital. What is it? What does it comprise? How can it help managers and investors?

REFERENCES

Baker, G.M.N. (1974). The feasibility and utility of human resource accounting. *California Management Review 16*(4), 17–23.

Boudreau, J. W. (1998). Strategic human resource management measures: Key linkages and the Peoplescape model. *Journal of Human Resource Costing and Accounting 3*(2), 21–40.

Brogden, H. E., Taylor, E. K. (1950). The dollar criterion—applying the cost accounting concept to criterion construction. *Personnel Psychology 3*, 133–154.

Brummet, R. L., Flamholtz, E., Pyle, W. (1968). Human resource accounting: A challenge for accountants. *Accounting Review 43*, 217–224.

Dobija, M. (1998). How to place human resources into the balance sheet? *Journal of Human Resource Costing and Accounting 3*(1), 83–92.

Ferguson, D. H., Berger, F. (1985). Employees as assets: A fresh approach to human-resources accounting. *Cornell H.R.A. Quarterly 25*(4), 24–29.

Flamholtz, E. G. (1971). A model for human resource valuation: A stochastic process with service rewards. *Accounting Review 46*, 235–267.

Flamholtz, E. G. (1985). *Human Resource Accounting.* San Francisco: Jossey Bass.

Flamholtz, E. G., Searfoss, D. G., Coff, R. (1988). Developing human resource accounting as a decision support system. *Accounting Horizons* 2, 1–9.

Hekimian, J. S., Jones, C. H. (1967). Put people on your balance sheet. *Harvard Business Review* 45(Jan.–Feb.), 107–113.

Hermanson, R. H. (1964). *Accounting for Human Assets.* East Lansing, MI: Bureau of Business and Economic Research.

Johanson, U. (in press). Why the concept of human resource costing and accounting does not work: A lesson from seven Swedish cases. *Personnel Review.*

Johanson, U., Eklov, G., Holmgren, M., Martensson, M. (1998). *Human Resource Costing and Accounting Versus the Balanced Scorecard: A Literature survey of experience with the concepts.* Stockholm: School of Business, Stockholm University.

Leonard, B. (1998). What do CEOs want from HR? *HRMagazine* 43(12), 80–86.

Lev, B., Schwartz, A. (1971). On the use of the economic concept of human capital in financial statements. *Accounting Review 46,* 103–112.

Macy, B. A., Mirvis, P. H. (1976). Measuring the quality of work life and organizational effectiveness in behavioral-economic terms. *Administrative Service Quarterly 21,* 212–226.

Mirvis, P. H., Lawler, E. E. III. (1983). Systems are not solutions: Issues in creating information systems that account for the human organization. *Accounting, Organizations, and Society 8,* 175–190.

Mirvis, P. H., Macy, B. A. (1976). Human resource accounting: A measurement perspective. *Academy of Management Review 1,* 74–83.

Morrow, S. (1996). Football players as human assets. Measurement as the critical factor in asset recognition: A case study investigation. *Journal of Human Resource Costing and Accounting 1*(1), 75–97.

Morrow, S. (1997). Accounting for football players. Financial and accounting implications of "Royal Club Liégois and others v. Bosman" for football in the United Kingdom. *Journal of Human Resource Costing and Accounting 2*(1), 55–71.

Pfeffer, J. (1997). Pitfalls on the road to measurement: The dangerous liaison of human resources with the ideas of accounting and finance. *Human Resource Management 36*(3), 357–365.

Pyle, W. C. (1970). Human resource accounting. *Financial Analysts Journal 10*(Sept.), 68–78.

Roslender, R. (1997). Accounting for the worth of employees: Is the discipline finally ready to respond to the challenge? *Journal of Human Resource Costing and Accounting 2*(1), 9–26.

Roslender, R., Dyson, J. R. (1992). Accounting for the worth of employees: A new look at an old problem. *British Accounting Review 24*, 311–329.

Rucci, A. J., Kirn, S. P., Quinn, R. T. (1998). The employee-customer-profit chain at Sears. *Harvard Business Review 76*, 82–97.

Scarpello, V., Theeke, H. A. (1989). Human resource accounting: A measured critique. *Journal of Accounting Literature 8*, 265–280.

Skandia AFS. (1994). *Visualizing Intellectual Capital: Supplement to Skandia's 1994 Annual Report*. Stockholm: Author.

Steffy, B. D., Maurer, S. D. (1988). Conceptualizing and measuring the economic effectiveness of human resource activities. *Academy of Management Review 13*, 271–286.

Stewart, T. A. (1997). *Intellectual Capital*. New York: Doubleday.

The twenty-first century economy. (1998). *Business Week* (Aug. 31), 58–146.

Tsay, J. J. (1977). Human resource accounting: A need for relevance. *Management Accounting 58*, 33–36.

Turner, G. (1996). Human resource accounting—whim or wisdom? *Journal of Human Resource Costing and Accounting 1*(1), 63–73.

Ulrich, D. (1998). A new mandate for human resources. *Harvard Business Review 76*, 124–134.

Woodruff, R. C. Jr. (1970). Human resources accounting. *Canadian Chartered Accountant 97*, 156–161.

ENDNOTE

1. This book focuses on an important aspect of human capital, namely, the economic consequences of employee behavior.

PART I
Costing Employee Turnover, Absenteeism, and Human Resource Mismanagement

The High Cost of Employee Turnover

Turnover rates and costs for many organizations are unacceptably high. Turnover rates are widely available and easily calculated. For example, a monthly turnover rate may be computed by the following formula:

$$\frac{\Sigma \text{ turnover incidents}}{\text{average workforce size}} \times 100$$

where Σ means "sum of." Typical monthly turnover rates, as reported by the Bureau of National Affairs, are shown in Exhibit 2–1. As that graph indicates, the average monthly rates by year are approximately 1 percent. This represents an average annual turnover rate of about 12 percent of the workforce for all employers. Turnover can represent a substantial cost of doing business. As an example, consider the results Corning Glass Works found when it tallied *only* its out-of-pocket expenses for employee turnover, such as interview costs and hiring bonuses. That number, $16–$18 million annually, led to investigations into the causes of the turnover, and in turn to new policies on flexible scheduling and career development.

Indeed, the fully loaded cost of turnover—not just separation and replacement costs, but also an exiting employee's lost leads and contacts, the new employee's depressed productivity while he or she is learning, and the time co-workers spend guiding him or her—can easily cost 150 percent or more of the departing person's salary (Branch 1998). Merck & Company, the pharmaceutical giant, found that turnover costs 1.5 to

EXHIBIT 2.1   *Employee Turnover (Median Percent of Workforce)*

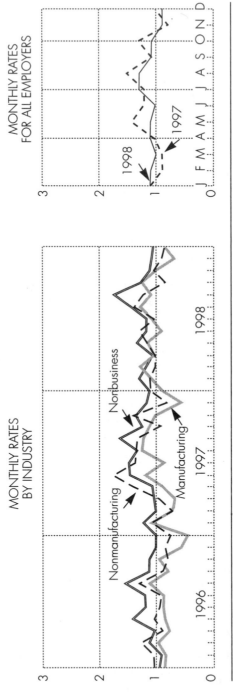

Source: BNA's job absence and turnover report—4th quarter 1998. Reprinted with permission from *Bulletin to Management* (BNA Policy and Practice Series), Vol. 50, No. 10, Part II (March 11, 1999). Copyright 1999 by The Bureau of National Affairs, Inc. (800-372-1033) <http://www.bna.com>

2.5 times the annual salary paid for it, depending on the job (Solomon 1988). That compares quite closely with results reported in the *Journal of Accountancy,* namely, that the cost of turnover per person ranges from 93 percent to 200 percent of an exiting employee's salary, depending on the employee's skill and level of responsibility (Johnson 1995).

It is unfortunate that many organizations are unaware of the actual cost of turnover. Without such information, management may be unaware of the need for action to prevent controllable turnover and may not develop a basis for choosing among alternative programs designed to reduce turnover. Thus a recent nationwide survey by Kepner-Tregoe, Inc., found that employee turnover is a growing problem that cuts across all U.S. industries, jobs, and regions. Disturbingly, 52 percent of managers and 64 percent of workers said that top management has not initiated any programs to reduce turnover in their organizations ("U.S. Employers" 1998).

Organizations need a practical procedure for measuring and analyzing the costs of employee turnover, especially because the costs of hiring, training, and developing employees are now viewed as investments that must be evaluated just like other corporate resources. The objective in costing human resources is not only to measure the relevant costs, but also to develop methods and programs to reduce the costs of human resources by managing the more controllable aspects of those costs.

Turnover is defined as any departure beyond organizational boundaries (Macy & Mirvis 1976). Turnover may be voluntary on the part of the employee (for example, by resignation) or involuntary (for example, requested resignation, permanent layoff, retirement, or death). Some reasons for leaving, such as "another job that offers more responsibility," "returning to school full time," or "improved salary and benefits," are more controllable than other reasons, such as employee death, chronic illness, or spouse transfer. Once the costs of employee turnover are known, therefore, an organization must determine which of those costs are reasonably controllable and focus attention on reducing them.

Remember, however, that not all turnover is bad, and expecting any one program to eliminate turnover completely is unrealistic. Some mistakes in selection are unavoidable, and employee turnover, to the extent that it is concentrated on erroneous acceptances into the organization, can have a cleansing effect by making room for new employees whose abilities and temperaments better fit the organization's needs. Other employees may have burned out, reached a plateau of substandard performance, or developed such negative attitudes toward the organization that their continued presence is likely to have harmful effects on the motivation and productivity of their co-workers. Here again, turnover can be beneficial. In contrast to those passive noncontributors, a few active noncontributors may willfully violate organizational rules concerning, for example, drug or alcohol abuse at work, fighting, or stealing company property. Turnover among those people also is likely to have a salutary effect on organizational health and productivity.

Thus, the organization must determine what kinds of turnover are harmful and then attempt to reduce them by redesigning jobs to enhance opportunities for responsibility and decision making, providing better working conditions, improving salaries and benefits, or clarifying and opening up promotional opportunities. More will be said on these issues later, but first we need to develop procedures for identifying and measuring turnover costs.

IDENTIFYING AND MEASURING TURNOVER COSTS

The general procedure for identifying and measuring turnover costs is founded on the premise that in measuring turnover, the organization must consider three major, separate cost categories: separation costs, replacement costs, and training costs (Smith & Watkins 1978). In addition, it must consider the difference in dollar-valued performance between those leaving and their replacements. For each of these categories, we shall first present the relevant cost elements and formulas and then provide numerical examples to illustrate how the formulas are used. The "pay rates" referred to in each category of costs refer to "fully loaded" compensation costs—direct pay plus the cost of benefits.

Separation Costs

Exhibit 2–2 presents the key cost elements and appropriate formulas that apply to separation costs. Those include exit interviews (S_1); administrative functions related to termination, such as deletion of the exiting employee from payroll, personnel, and benefits files (S_2); separation pay, if any (S_3); and unemployment tax, if applicable (S_4). Thus:

$$\text{Total Separation Costs } (S_T) = (S_1) + (S_2) + (S_3) + (S_4)$$

The cost of exit interviews comprises two factors: the cost of the interviewer's time (preparation + actual interview time) and the cost of the

EXHIBIT 2-2 *Measuring Separation Costs*

Cost Element	Formula		
Exit interview (S_1)	= cost of interviewer's time cost of terminating employee's time	= (time required prior to interview + time required for the interview) = time required for the interview	× interviewer's pay rate during period × weighted average pay for terminated employees	× number of turnovers during period × number of turnovers during period
Administrative functions related to termination (S_2)	= time required by HR dept. for administrative functions related to termination	× average HR dept. employee's pay rate		× number of turnovers during period
Separation pay (S_3)	= amount of separation pay per employee terminated	× number of turnovers during period		
Unemployment tax (S_4)	= (unemployment tax rate − base rate)	× [[($7,000 × number of employees earning at least $7,000) + (weighted average earnings if <$7,000) × (number of employees earning <$7,000)]]	+ unemployment tax rate	× [$7,000 or weighted average earnings if <$7,000] × number of turnovers during period

Source: Cascio, W. F. (1989). *Managing Human Resources: Productivity, Quality of Work Life, Profits* (2nd ed.). New York: McGraw-Hill. Copyright © 1989 McGraw-Hill. Used with permission.

terminating employee's time (time required for the interview × weighted average pay rate for all terminated employees). That latter figure may be calculated as follows:

$$\text{weighted average pay rate per terminated employee} = \frac{\Sigma\,(\text{pay rate}_i \times \text{number of employees terminated at pay rate}_i)}{\text{number of employees terminated during the period}}$$

Times for exit interviews may be estimated in either of two ways (because those data are not recorded routinely): time a random sample of exit interviews over the course of some period, say three months, or interview a representative sample of managers who conduct exit interviews regularly and develop an average or weighted average of their estimated times.

Each organization should specify exactly what administrative functions relate to terminations and the time required for them. Each of those activities costs money, and the costs should be documented and included when measuring separation costs.

Separation pay, for those organizations that offer this benefit (it is not legally required under the Fair Labor Standards Act), can usually be determined from the existing accounting information system. Most lower-level employees receive one week of pay for each year they worked for a company ("Take my job, please" 1996). Mid-level executives with median salaries of $60,000 per year can expect three or more weeks of severance pay for each year worked. CEOs with employment contracts may receive two to three years of salary (Alderman 1996; "Work Week" 1996).

In all states, employers' unemployment tax rates (applied, for example, to the first $7,000 of each employee's earnings) are based upon each employer's history of claims. Organizations with fewer claims for unemployment benefits are subject to a lower unemployment tax than are organizations with more unemployment claims. That increase in unemployment tax resulting from an increased incidence of claims is an element of separation costs.

In practice, high turnover rates that lead to high claims for unemployment compensation by former employees increase the cost of unemployment tax in two ways. First, the state increases the employer's tax rate (called the "penalty" in this instance). Second, the employer must pay additional, regular unemployment tax because of the turnovers. For example, consider a 100-employee firm with a 20 percent annual turnover rate (that is, 20 people). The total increase in unemployment tax is computed in the following manner.

Penalty:
(new tax rate – base rate) × [$7,000 × (100 + 20)]
= (5.4% – 5.0%) × [$840,000] = $3,360

Additional Unemployment Tax Resulting from Turnover:
(new tax rate) × ($7,000 × number of turnovers during period)
= (5.4%) × ($7,000 × 20) = $7,560

Total Additional Unemployment Tax:
$3,360 + $7,560 = $10,920

What about the incremental costs associated with social security taxes? Those costs should be included only if the earnings of workers who leave exceed the taxable wage base for the year. Thus, in 1998 the taxable wage base was $68,400 and the tax rate was 7.65 percent. If an employee earning $40,000 per year left after six months, the employer paid tax only on $20,000. If it took one month to replace the departing employee, the replacement earned five months' wages or $16,666. Thus the employer incurred no additional social security tax because the total paid for the position for the year was less than $68,400. However, if the employee who left after six months was a senior manager earning $150,000 per year, the employer would already have paid the maximum tax due for the year for that employee. If a replacement worked five months (earning $62,500) the employer then incurred additional social security tax for the replacement.

A final element of separation costs that should be included, if possible, is the cost of decreased productivity resulting from employee terminations. That may include the decline in the productivity of an employee prior to termination or the decrease in productivity of a work group of which the terminating employee was a member. Unfortunately, in many situations, unless an ongoing productivity-measurement program is functioning, computing that cost is simply too difficult and expensive to justify expending resources for its measurement.

Let us now compute separation costs over one year for Wee Care Children's Hospital, a 200-bed facility that employs 1,200 people. Let's assume that Wee Care's monthly turnover rate is 2 percent. That rate represents 24 percent of the 1,200-person workforce per year, or about 288 employees. From Exhibit 2–2 we apply the following formulas (all costs are hypothetical).

Exit Interview (S_1)

interviewer's time = (15 min. preparation + 45 min. interview) × \$19/hour interviewer's pay rate × 288 turnovers during the year
= \$5,472

terminating employee's time = 45 min. interview time × \$17.82/hour weighted average pay rate[1] × 288 turnovers during the year
= \$3,849.12

total cost of exit interviews = \$5,472 + \$3,849.12
= \$9,321.12

Administrative Functions (S_2)

S_2 = time to delete each employee × HR specialist's pay/hour × number of turnovers during the year
= 1 hour × \$18.50 × 288
= \$5,328

Separation Pay (S_3)

Suppose Wee Care Children's Hospital has a policy of paying one week's separation pay to each terminating employee. Using the weighted average pay rate of the 288 terminating employees as an example, \$17.82/hour × 40 hours/week = \$712.80 average amount of separation pay per employee terminated.

Total Separation Pay = \$712.80 × 288
= \$205,286.40

Unemployment Tax (S_4)

Let us assume that because of Wee Care's poor experience factor with respect to terminated employees' subsequent claims for unemployment benefits, the state unemployment tax rate is 5.4 percent, as compared with a base rate of 5.0 percent. Let us further assume that turnovers occur, on the average, after four and a half months (18 weeks). If the weighted average pay rate of terminating employees is \$17.82 per hour, then the weighted average earnings per terminating employee exceed \$7,000.

The dollar increase in unemployment tax incurred because of Wee Care's poor experience factor is, therefore:

$$(5.4\% - 5.0\%) \times [\$7,000 \times (1,200 + 288)]$$
$$= (0.004) \times [\$7,000 \times 1,488]$$
$$= \$41,664 \ \{penalty\} + (5.4\%) \times (\$7,000 \times 288)$$
$$= \$108,864 \ \{additional \ tax\}$$
$$Total \ increase = \$41,664 + \$108,864$$
$$= \$150,528$$

Now that we have computed all four cost elements in the separation-cost category, total separation costs ($\Sigma S_1, S_2, S_3, S_4$) can be estimated. That figure is:

$$S_T = S_1 + S_2 + S_3 + S_4$$
$$= \$9,321.12 + \$5,328 + \$205,286.40 + \$150,528$$
$$= \$370,463.52$$

Replacement Costs

Costs incurred by an organization in replacing a terminated employee are defined as replacement costs. Exhibit 2-3 shows the cost elements and the formulas for estimating them. As the exhibit indicates, there are eight categories of replacement costs:

1. communication of job availability
2. pre-employment administrative functions
3. entrance interviews
4. testing
5. staff meetings
6. travel/moving expenses
7. post-employment acquisition and dissemination of information
8. employment medical examinations

The costs of communicating job availability will vary by type of job and targeted labor market. Depending on the methods used in recruitment, those costs may range from the cost of a classified advertisement in a local newspaper to employment agency fees borne by the employer (see Cascio 1998, chapter 11). Typically those costs can be obtained from existing accounting records. However, to the extent that this communication process

EXHIBIT 2–3   *Measuring Replacement Costs*

Cost Element	Formula
Communicating job availability (R_1)	$=$ [advertising and employment agency fees per termination $+$ (time required for communicating job availability $\times$ HR dept. employee's pay rate)] $\times$ number of turnovers replaced during period
Pre-employment administrative functions (R_2)	$=$ time required by HR dept. for pre-employment administrative functions $\times$ average HR dept. employee's pay rate $\times$ number of applicants during period
Entrance interview (R_3)	$=$ time required for interview $\times$ interviewer's pay rate $\times$ number of interviews during period
Testing (R_4)	$=$ (cost of materials per person $+$ cost of scoring per person) $\times$ number of tests given during period
Staff meeting (R_5)	$=$ time required for meeting $\times$ (HR dept. employee's pay rate $+$ dept. representative's pay rate) $\times$ number of meetings during period
Travel/moving expenses (R_6)	$=$ (average travel cost per applicant $+$ average moving cost per new hire) $\times$ number of new hires
Post-employment acquisition and dissemination of information (R_7)	$=$ time required for acquiring and disseminating information $\times$ average HR dept. employee's pay rate $\times$ number of turnovers replaced during period
In-house medical examinations (R_8)	$=$ [(time required for examination $\times$ examiner's pay rate) $+$ cost of supplies used] $\times$ number of turnovers replaced during period
OR	
Contracted medical examinations (R_9)	$=$ rate per examination $\times$ number of turnovers replaced during period

requires considerable time from HR department employees, the cost of their time should also be included in replacement costs.

Administratively, several tasks are frequently undertaken in selecting and placing each new employee—for example, accepting applications, screening candidates, and checking references. Those procedures can be expensive. For example, a simple background investigation that includes verification of last educational degree, a check with the last two employers, a five-year criminal check, and verification of the social security number costs only about $100. However, an extensive check that includes the previous items plus interviews with previous employers, teachers, neighbors, and acquaintances can run $10,000 or more. The time required to perform those activities is not documented routinely by organizational information systems, but the methods described earlier for estimating exit interview time requirements may be applied in determining the time necessary for pre-employment administrative functions.

Virtually all organizations use entrance interviews to describe jobs, to communicate employee responsibilities and benefits, and to make some general assessments of candidates. The costs incurred when completing entrance interviews result from the length of the interview, the pay rates of interviewers involved, and the number of interviews conducted. It is clear that links exist between valid selection procedures and reduced turnover. If decision makers are to make sound cost/benefit decisions regarding elements of the selection process, those costs (and benefits) must be documented. This chapter focuses on costs; chapter 10 will detail the benefits to be derived from the use of valid selection procedures.

Many firms use pre-employment testing of one sort or another—for example, aptitude, achievement, drug, and honesty testing. To account properly for the costs of these activities, consider the costs of materials and supplies as well as the cost of scoring the tests. The costs of materials and scoring for aptitude, achievement, and honesty tests are often less than $25 per candidate. Although the actual cost of drug testing is roughly $17 to $25 for a simple screening test, the fully loaded cost is closer to $85 to $100 when set-up costs are considered (Harris & Heft 1993). Confirming a positive test with more accurate equipment—a step recommended by most specialists—costs an additional $50 to $75 (Wessel 1989). After adjustment for inflation, the cost to confirm a positive test was $70 to $105 in 1999.

For some classes of employees, especially top-level managers or other professionals, a meeting may be held between the HR department and the department holding the vacant position. The estimated time required for this meeting multiplied by the sum of the pay rates for all attendees provides a measure of this element of replacement costs.

Travel and moving expenses can be extremely costly to organizations that pay those costs. Travel costs for candidates from a local labor market are minimal (bus and subway fare, parking, tolls), but travel costs for candidates who must fly in and stay in a hotel can average over $1,500. Moving expenses can cover a range of cost elements from mortgage differentials, lease-breaking expenses, company purchase of the old house, costs of moving personal effects from the old to the new location, closing costs, hook-up fees for utilities, and more. Fully loaded moving costs average about $45,000 (Auerbach 1996).

The seventh category of replacement costs is post-employment acquisition and dissemination of information. Pertinent information for each new employee must be gathered, recorded, and entered into various subsystems of a HR information system (for example, employee records, payroll files, benefits records). If an organization offers flexible, cafeteria-style benefits, an HR specialist could spend considerable time in counseling each new employee about those benefits. Managers must estimate the time required for this overall process for each replaced employee, and then multiply it by the wage rates of HR department employees involved. To compute the total cost of acquiring and disseminating information to new employees, multiply this cost by the number of turnovers.

Pre-employment medical examinations are the final element of replacement costs. The extent and thoroughness, and therefore the cost, of such examinations vary greatly. Some organizations do not require them at all, some contract with private physicians or clinics to provide this service, and others use in-house medical staff. If medical examinations are contracted out, the cost can be determined from existing accounting data. If the examinations are done in-house, their cost can be determined based on the supplies used (for example, X-ray film, laboratory supplies) and the staff time required to perform each examination. If the new employee is paid while receiving the medical examination, then his or her rate of pay should be added to the examiner's pay rate in determining total cost. The following text estimates replacement costs for a one-year period, based on Exhibit 2–3, for Wee Care Children's Hospital.

Job Availability (R₁)

Assume that fees and advertisements average $350 per turnover, that three additional hours are required to communicate job availability, that the HR specialist's pay rate is $18.50 per hour, and that 288 turnovers are replaced during the period. Therefore:

$$R_1 = [\$350 + (3 \times \$18.50)] \times 288 = \$116{,}784$$

Pre-employment Administrative Functions (R₂)

Assume that pre-employment administrative functions to fill the job of each employee who left require five hours. Therefore:

$$R_2 = 5 \times \$18.50 \times 288 = \$26{,}640$$

Entrance Interview (R₃)

Assume that, on the average, three candidates are interviewed for every one hired. Thus, over the one-year period of this study, 864 (288 × 3) interviews were conducted. Therefore:

$$R_3 = 1 \times \$18.50 \times 864 = \$15{,}984$$

Testing (R₄)

Assume that aptitude tests cost $8 per applicant for materials, another $8 per applicant to score, and that as a matter of HR policy Wee Care uses drug tests ($35 per applicant) as part of the pre-employment process. The cost of testing is therefore:

$$R_4 = (\$16 + \$35) \times (288 \times 3) = \$44{,}064$$

Staff Meeting (R₅)

Assume that each staff meeting lasts one hour, that the average pay rate of the new employee's department representative is $26 per hour, and that for administrative convenience such meetings are held, on average, only once for each three new hires (288 ÷ 3 = 96). Therefore:

$$R_5 = (\$18.50 + \$26) \times 96 = \$4{,}272$$

Travel/Moving Expenses (R₆)

Assume that Wee Care pays an average of $65 per applicant in travel expenses, and that moving expenses of $45,000 are incurred, on average, for only one of every eight new hires. Therefore:

$$R_6 = [\$65 \times (288 \times 3)] + (\$45{,}000 \times 36)$$

$$= \$56,160 + \$1,620,000$$
$$= \$1,676,160$$

Post-employment Acquisition and Dissemination of Information (R_7)

Assume that two hours are spent on these activities for each new employee. Therefore:

$$R_7 = 2 \times \$18.50 \times 288 = \$10,656$$

Pre-employment Medical Examination (R_8 and R_9)

Assume that if the medical examinations are done at the hospital (in-house) each one will take one hour; the examiner is paid $40 per hour; X-rays, laboratory analyses, and supplies cost $85; and 288 examinations are conducted. Therefore:

$$R_8 = [(1 \times \$40) + \$85] \times 288 = \$36,000$$

If the examinations are contracted out, let us assume that Wee Care will pay a flat rate of $150 per examination. Therefore:

$$R_9 = \$150 \times 288 = \$43,200$$

Wee Care decides to provide in-house medical examinations for all new employees, so total replacement costs (R_T) can now be computed as the sum of R_1 through R_8:

$$R_T = \$116,784 + \$26,640 + \$15,984 + \$44,064 + \$4,272 +$$
$$\$1,676,160 + \$10,656 + \$36,000$$
$$R_T = \$1,930,560$$

Training Costs

In virtually all instances, replacement employees must be oriented and trained to a standard level of competence before they assume their regular duties. As we will see in chapter 11, that training often involves considerable expense to an organization. For the present, however, assume that replacement employees are either placed in a formal training program, assigned to an experienced employee for some period of on-the-job training, or both. The cost elements and computational formulas for this category of turnover costs are shown in Exhibit 2–4. The three major elements of training costs are informational literature, instruction in a formal training program, and instruction by employee assignment.

The cost of any informational literature provided to replacement employees must be considered a part of orientation and training costs. Unit costs for those items may be obtained from existing accounting records. Multiplying the unit costs by the number of replacement employees hired during the period yields the first cost factor in determining training costs.

New employees may also be involved in a formal training program. The overall cost of the training program depends on the costs of two major components: costs associated with trainers and costs associated with trainees. An organization incurs 100 percent of the costs associated with training replacements for employees who leave, but the cost associated with trainers depends on the extent to which formal training is attributable to turnover. Because it is unlikely that the *total* cost of a training program can be attributable solely to turnover, managers must determine the proportion of training costs that arises from turnover, and that which results from other factors, such as planned expansion of the workforce. For the sake of simplicity, the costs of facilities, food, and other overhead expenses have not been included in these calculations.

Instead of or in addition to instruction in a formal training program, new employees may also be assigned to work with more experienced employees for a period of time or until they reach a standard level of competence. The overall cost of that on-the-job training must be determined for all replacement employees hired during the period because it is an important element of training costs.

Notice that in Exhibit 2–4 the cost of reduced productivity of new employees while they are learning is not included as an element of overall training costs. That is not because such a cost is unimportant. On the contrary, even if an organization staffs more employees to provide for a specified level of productivity while new employees are being trained, the cost of a decrease in the quantity and quality of goods or services produced is still very real. Less experienced employees may also cause an increase in operating expenses by their inefficient use of supplies and equipment. All such costs are important, and when they can be measured reliably and accurately they should be included as an additional element of training costs. The same is true for potential productivity gains associated with new employees. Such gains serve to offset the costs of training.

EXHIBIT 2-4 *Measuring Training Costs*

Cost Element	Formula
Informational literature (T_1)	= cost of informational package × number of replacements during period
Instruction in a formal training program (T_2)	= [length of training program × average pay rate of trainer(s) × number of programs conducted] + [average pay rate per trainee × total number of replacements trained during period × length of training program × proportion of training costs attributed to replacements]
Instruction by employee assignment (T_3)	= number of hours required for instruction × [(average pay rate of experienced employee × proportional reduction in productivity due to training × number of experienced employees assigned to on-the-job training) + (new employee's pay rate × number of instructions during period)]

Source: Cascio, W. F. (1989). *Managing Human Resources: Productivity, Quality of Work Life, Profits* (2nd ed.). New York: McGraw-Hill. Copyright © 1989 McGraw-Hill. Used with permission.

In many organizations, however, especially those providing services (for example, credit counseling, customer services, patient care in hospitals), the measurement of these costs or gains is simply too complex for practical application.

The following text estimates the total cost of training employee replacements at Wee Care. Using the formulas shown in Exhibit 2–4, Wee Care estimates the following costs over a one-year period.

Informational Literature (T₁)

If the unit cost of informational literature is $14, and 288 employees are replaced, the total cost of informational literature is:

$$T_1 = \$14 \times 288 = \$4,032$$

Instruction in a Formal Training Program (T₂)

New employee training at Wee Care is conducted ten times per year, and each training program lasts 40 hours (one full week). The average pay for instructors is $35 per hour; the average pay rate for trainees is $15.50 per hour; and of the 576 employees trained on the average each year, half are replacements for employees who left voluntarily or involuntarily. The total cost of formal training attributed to employee turnover is

$$
\begin{aligned}
T_2 &= (40 \times \$35 \times 10 \times 0.50) + (\$15.50 \times 288 \times 40) \\
&= \$7,000 + \$178,560 \\
&= \$185,560
\end{aligned}
$$

Instruction by Employee Assignment (T₃)

To ensure positive transfer between training program content and job content, Wee Care assigns each new employee to a more experienced employee for an additional week (40 hours). Experienced employees average $24 per hour, and their own productivity is cut by 50 percent while they are training others. Each experienced employee supervises two trainees. The total cost of such on-the-job training for replacement employees is

$$
\begin{aligned}
T_3 &= 40 \times [(\$24 \times 0.50 \times 144) + (\$15.50 \times 288)] \\
&= 40 \times (\$1,728 + \$4,464) \\
&= 40 \times \$6,192 \\
&= \$247,680
\end{aligned}
$$

Total training costs now can be computed as the sum of T_1, T_2, and T_3:

$$T_T = \$4{,}032 + \$185{,}560 + \$247{,}680 = \$437{,}272$$

Performance Differences Between Leavers and Their Replacements

A final factor to consider in tallying net turnover costs is the uncompensated performance differential between employees who leave and their replacements. We will call this *difference in performance (DP)*. DP needs to be included in determining the net cost of turnover because replacements whose performance exceeds that of leavers reduce turnover costs, and replacements whose performance is worse than that of leavers add to turnover costs.

To begin measuring *DP* in conservative, practical terms, compute the difference by position in the salary range between each leaver and his or her replacement. Assume that performance differentials are reflected in deviations from the midpoint of the pay grade of the job class in question. Each employee's position in the salary range is computed as a "compa-ratio"; that is, salary is expressed as a percentage of the midpoint of that employee's pay grade. If, for example, the midpoint of a pay grade is $50,000 (annual pay), an employee earning $40,000 is at 80 percent of the midpoint. Therefore, his or her compa-ratio is 0.80. An employee paid $50,000 has a compa-ratio of 1.0 (100 percent of the midpoint rate of pay), and an employee paid $60,000 has a compa-ratio of 1.2 because he or she is paid 120 percent of the midpoint rate of pay. Compa-ratios generally vary from 0.80 to 1.20 in most pay systems (Milkovich & Newman 1999).

To compute *DP*, use the following formula:

$$DP = \sum_{i=1}^{n} (CR_l - CR_r)MP_i$$

where *DP* is difference in performance between leaver and replacement, $\sum_{i=1}^{n}$ is summation over all leavers and their replacements; CR_l is the compa-ratio of the leaver; CR_r is the compa-ratio of the replacement; and MP_i is the annual rate of pay at the midpoint of the pay grade in question. Consider the following example:

$$CR_l = 0.80 \quad CR_r = 1.0 \quad MP_i = \$50{,}000$$
$$DP = (0.80 - 1.0) \times \$50{,}000$$

$$DP = (-0.20) \times \$50,000$$
$$DP = -\$10,000$$

DP is therefore *subtracted* from total turnover costs because the firm is gaining an employee whose performance is superior to that of the employee who was replaced.

If the compa-ratio of the leaver was 1.0, that of the replacement was 0.80, and the paygrade midpoint was \$50,000, then $DP = \$10,000$. These costs are *added* to total turnover costs because the leaver was replaced by a lesser performer.

Why are differences in performance assumed to covary with differences in pay? Actually, this assumption is true only in a perfect labor market (Hirschey & Pappas 1998). In a perfectly competitive labor market, every worker earns the marginal revenue product accrued to the firm from his or her labor. Thus the firm is indifferent to workers whose compa-ratios are 0.80, 1.0, or 1.20 because each worker is paid exactly what he or she is "worth."

Perfectly competitive labor markets exist for many entry-level jobs (for example, management analysts), but labor markets are often imperfect above the entry level because workers develop what economists call "firm-specific human capital" (Becker 1964). Workers who have specific job knowledge that is valued by their firms (for example, in banking, automobiles, computers) tend to command higher wages. Yet their value is reflected only partly in their higher wages. Wages reflect what economists call "opportunity costs," or the value of a worker's second-best employment opportunity. Competitors are able only to offer a wage that reflects the economic value of a worker to *them*. Therefore, opportunity costs and the wage rates paid to valued employees tend to reflect only the portion of a worker's economic value that is easily transferable from one employer to another (that is, "generic" value). The portion of an employee's value that is not easily transferable, the firm-specific component, typically is reflected only partially in employee wages, if at all. Thus the economic value of workers with firm-specific human capital is above their wage (opportunity cost) level, but can be assumed to be proportionate to that wage. If an employee with substantial amounts of firm-specific human capital leaves the firm and is replaced by a worker who lacks such firm-specific human capital, the replacement will receive a lesser wage. However, if a poor performer leaves and is replaced by a worker with more human capital, albeit non–firm-specific, then the replacement will receive a higher wage than the leaver (Lazear 1998). The difference in pay between leavers and their replacements thus represents an indicator, although an imperfect one, of the "uncompensated performance differential" due to firm-specific human capital, and it must be considered when determining the net costs of turnover.

The assumption that excess value to the firm is a function of wages paid and that excess value and wages covary in a linear (straight-line) fashion is conservative. In practice, the relationship can be curvilinear (positive or negative), but for our purposes the conservative assumption of a linear relationship between excess value and wages is appropriate.

For Wee Care, assume that the net DP = +\$150,000. On average, therefore, the firm hired slightly poorer performers than it lost. The following equation, which uses the four major components of employee turnover, represents the total cost of employee turnover:

$$\text{Total Cost of Turnover} = S_T + R_T + T_T + DP$$

where S_T is total separation costs; R_T is total replacement costs; T_T is total training costs; and DP is net differential performance between leavers and their replacements. For Wee Care, the total cost of 288 employee turnovers during a one-year period was

$$\$370,463.52 + \$1,930,560 + \$437,272 + \$150,000 = \$2,888,295.52$$

This represents a cost of \$10,028.80 for each worker who left the hospital.

The purpose of measuring turnover costs is to improve managerial decision making. That is, once turnover figures are known, managers have a more realistic basis for choosing between current turnover costs and instituting some type of turnover-reduction program, such as increased compensation and non-wage benefits, job enrichment, realistic job previews, and expanded recruitment and selection programs. The final section of this chapter examines this issue in greater detail.

MONITORING AND MANAGING TURNOVER

In managing turnover, the firm's goal should be to retain employees who are valuable to the organization in terms of overall performance and replaceability (Dalton, Todor, & Krackardt 1982). Taken together, performance and replaceability have an important bearing on the consequences of turnover for an organization, as shown in the performance-replaceability strategy matrix in Exhibit 2–5.

Although turnover may be voluntary or involuntary, we will focus on voluntary turnover, much of which is controllable. Turnover may be

EXHIBIT 2-5 *The Performance-Replaceability Strategy Matrix*

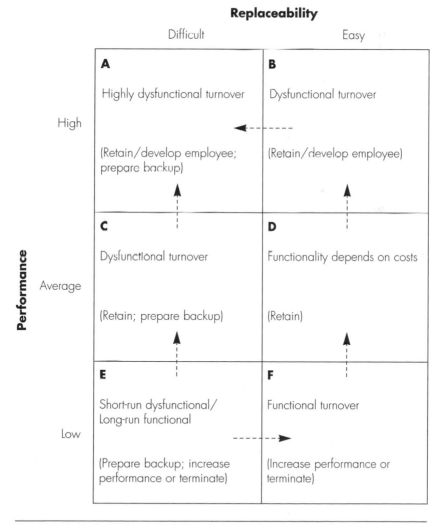

Source: Martin, D. C., and Bartol, K. M. Managing turnover strategically. Adapted from the November 1985 issue of *Personnel Administrator,* copyright 1985, the American Society for Personnel Administration, 606 N. Washington Street, Alexandria, VA 22314.

functional for the organization (loss of unproductive employees) or dysfunctional (loss of valued employees). Fortunately, cumulative evidence of
the relationship between performance and turnover across 24 studies and
7,717 employees indicates that good performers are significantly less likely to leave an organization than are poor performers (McEvoy & Cascio
1987). The loss of employees in cells A, B, or C in Exhibit 2.5 represents
dysfunctional turnover. The organization highly values those in cell A because they are high performers who are difficult to replace. Two types of
employees tend to be particularly difficult to replace: those whose specific
knowledge about some aspect of the organization or its environment is difficult to acquire and crucial to effective performance, and those whose
skills are in relatively short supply. An example of a valuable type of cell-
A employee would be an effective line manager of a U.S. firm operating in
a foreign country—someone familiar with local customs, language, and
traditions, as well as the industry and the organization.

Employees in cell D are average performers who can be replaced easily. Whether turnover among the members of this group is functional or
dysfunctional depends on the net costs of turnover. If the costs of replacement and training are low (for example, for data-entry clerks) and
the leaver is replaced by a better performer (DP is negative), then
turnover is functional for the organization. If the opposite conditions are
found (for example, in the case of a geologist for an oil company), then
the turnover is dysfunctional for the organization. Over the long run, it is
functional to replace low performers in any organization, whether or not
they are easy to replace. Cells E and F of Exhibit 2–5 show individuals
in this category.

What are the implications of the model in Exhibit 2–5, and how can it
be used to improve the strategic management of turnover? The model
suggests that simple tabulation of turnover rates could mask serious underlying problems. Perhaps few employees leave, but the majority of
those who do leave fall in cell A. Merely inspecting the rates of turnover
could lead the organization's analysts to conclude—falsely—that they
don't have a turnover problem. The crucial issue in analyzing turnover,
therefore, is not how many employees are leaving, but the performance
and replaceability of those who are leaving versus those who are staying
(Martin & Bartol 1985).

The first step in implementing the model in Exhibit 2–5 is to classify
each position in the organization according to ease of replaceability.
This straightforward exercise should be done jointly by HR managers
and line managers from various units of the organization. The next step

is to complete the performance-replaceability strategy matrix by using the performance appraisals of position incumbents, which can be collected from employee records. The result is an assessment of the performance and replaceability of each employee in the organization. Having done that, the organization is in an excellent position to monitor and manage turnover relative to its overall strategic plan (Martin & Bartol 1985). It could use this information to monitor turnover in terms of who is leaving which positions and to obtain unit and overall organizational patterns. Using the model also facilitates the planning of appropriate HR programs (for example, career development, training, succession planning, and recruiting).

Each of the cells in Exhibit 2–5 calls for a different strategy, although the strategies are related and can be part of an overall approach to HRM. The basic strategies are shown in parentheses within each category. The arrows indicate the generally desirable movements of employees across cells.

The performance-replaceability strategy matrix is only as useful as it is current, and in most organizations things don't stay current for very long. The replaceability ratings of various positions might change as a result of new directions in strategic plans. At the same time, individual performance levels might improve as a result of feedback and constructive management of performance problems. In short, an organization must reevaluate the performance-replaceability strategy matrix periodically in order to remain responsive to organizational needs. The most practical approach for most organizations is to review replaceability and performance in conjunction with the annual performance appraisal cycle. To be meaningful, such a review must consider shifts in strategic plans and related implications for staffing. The reevaluation process then becomes the mechanism through which turnover patterns continually are monitored and HR programs are modified to meet the emerging needs of an organization's strategic plan (Martin & Bartol 1985).

Unfortunately, evidence indicates that few corporations have bothered to apply this approach. In a poll of 6,000 executives at 77 major corporations, McKinsey & Co. found that few keep precise data on a wide swath of midlevel managers, and that just 40 percent of HR executives keep tabs on the high performers. Said a McKinsey director: "Companies are aware that they're losing good people, but they don't know who is leaving, or why, or even where they're going" (Branch 1998, p. 248). Application of the performance-replaceability strategy matrix could be the first step in an effort to change that.

DEALING WITH EMPLOYEE TURNOVER

Now that we know how to cost turnover, and assuming management decides the costs are intolerable, how can we best deal with the problem? Although a complete treatment of solutions is beyond the scope of this chapter, we can distinguish voluntary turnover among newcomers from voluntary turnover among employees who have been with the organization for some time (at least a year).

One reason newcomers leave is that their inflated expectations about a job or organization often are not met after they begin working. Much of this turnover is unnecessary and therefore controllable. Over the last 15 years a number of studies have shown that when the expectations of job applicants are lowered to match organizational reality, job acceptance rates may be lower and job performance is unaffected, but job satisfaction and job survival are higher for those who receive a realistic job preview (RJP). Wanous (1980) suggests three reasons why RJPs work so well. The first is a vaccination effect: job candidates are given a small dose of organizational reality during the recruitment stage to protect against the negative aspects of real organizational life. The second is a self-selection, matching effect: because people strive to be satisfied, they tend to choose organizations that they believe will lead to personal satisfaction. The better the information that the job candidates possess, the more effective their choices can be. A final reason for the success of RJPs is a personal-commitment effect: when individuals believe that they made a decision without coercion or strong inducements from others, they tend to be much more committed to the decision.

Research has demonstrated the effectiveness of RJPs in a variety of organizational settings (for example, manufacturing and service jobs) and when different RJP techniques are used (for example, plant tours versus video presentations or written descriptions of the work) (Breaugh 1992; Premack & Wanous 1985). Longitudinal research shows that RJPs should be balanced in their orientation. That is, they should enhance overly pessimistic expectations and reduce overly optimistic ones. Doing so helps bolster the applicant's perceptions of the organization as caring, trustworthy, and honest (Meglino et al. 1988). A final recommendation is to develop RJPs even when there is no turnover problem (proactively rather than reactively). RJPs should employ an audiovisual medium, and, where possible, show actual job incumbents (Wanous 1989).

Nevertheless, RJPs are not appropriate recruitment strategies for all types of jobs. They are most appropriate when few applicants are actually hired, when they are used with entry-level positions (because those coming from outside to inside an organization are more likely to have inflated expectations than are those who make changes internally), and when unemployment is low (because job candidates are more likely to have alternative jobs from which to choose).

A quantitative cumulation of research results from 15 experiments that used RJPs (total sample size = 5,250) indicated that RJPs improve retention rates, on average, by approximately 9 percent (McEvoy & Cascio 1985). Such improvement can result in substantial savings to an organization. Suppose, for example, that turnover costs an average of $25,000 per departing employee. For every 100 employees that an organization has in a job category, therefore, it can expect to save $225,000 (9 × $25,000) through the application of RJPs prior to hiring. This money can then be deployed into areas that will enhance retention even further, such as family-friendly benefits (Pfeffer 1998; Schellhardt 1998; Symonds 1998).

Psychological and Performance Tests

One way to reduce turnover is to screen out potential leavers during the selection process. Psychological tests, although far from perfectly accurate, are capable of identifying future employees who will leave their jobs. In one study of public-safety officers, for example, optimally weighted test scores identified the greatest number of officers who were terminated within five years after hire (68 to 75 percent), but also resulted in false predictions of termination for 28 to 36 percent of the hired officers (Inwald 1988). Clearly the relative social and economic costs of erroneous acceptances and erroneous rejections should be considered by decision makers prior to implementing any such testing program.

Job performance or work sample tests have been used to instill realistic attitudes in prospective employees. Performance tests usually refer to standardized measures of behavior used to assess the ability to *do* rather than the ability to *know*. Performance tests may be classified either as *motor*, involving physical manipulation of things (for example, tests for jobs like carpenter, mechanic, mason), or as *verbal*, involving problems that are primarily language-oriented or people-oriented (for example, tests for jobs like maintenance supervisor, programmer/analyst, library assistant) (Asher & Sciarrino 1974).

To demonstrate the impact of performance testing on turnover, Cascio and Phillips (1979) examined the results of a broad spectrum of performance tests (11 motor and 10 verbal) used by a city government over two years. The tests were matched as closely as possible to actual job requirements in tasks, tools, equipment, work setting, and proportion of time spent on various activities. For example, in the test for sewer-pumping station operator (a promotional examination for laborers that requires no previous experience), all testing, proctoring, and rating was done underground at the sewer-pumping station. During an initial one-hour instruction period, a sewer mechanic explained and demonstrated, as if he were the applicants' supervisor, procedures for the general maintenance of sewer pipes and equipment—how to clean filters, grease fittings, read a pressure chart, and so on. Several applicants left immediately after the demonstration. During a second hour each applicant was required to repeat the demonstration (applicants were also free to ask questions) as if he or she were on the job. Applicants were then rated on the degree to which they understood instructions, followed the prescribed procedures, asked questions when they were unsure of something, and followed safety practices (used protective masks and other equipment). Follow-up interviews revealed that those who qualified for and accepted the job had a good idea of what they were getting into and felt that for them the job represented a step up the career ladder.

To examine the impact of performance testing on turnover, data on turnover were gathered for one year prior to the introduction of performance testing and for a period (from 9 to 26 months) after performance tests were introduced. Turnover rates for the 21 jobs during the year prior to performance testing varied from 0 to 300 percent, with an overall average of 40 percent. The turnover rate for those same jobs after the introduction of performance tests was less than 3 percent. Using the formulas presented earlier for calculating actual turnover costs (separation, replacement, and training costs), the 37 percent reduction in turnover translated into savings of $336,199 for the city (over $840,000 in 1998 dollars) during the 9- to 26-month period following the introduction of performance tests.

Instituting a Supportive Culture and Building Employee Commitment

For most of the 1990s, downsizing set the tone for the modern employment contract. Employees were told, "This isn't personal, it's business."

However, in the late 1990s, after several years of tight labor markets and increased workforce mobility, workers in many industries were saying, "You're right. It's not personal. It's business. And I have an offer somewhere else" (Branch 1998, p. 248). In response, organizations are trying to institute supportive cultures and to build employee commitment.

Don't confuse this new concept of commitment with the old concept of loyalty to a firm or to a brand. Insofar as commitment exists, it's to a boss, a team, a project. Thus any retention strategy has to be driven by individual managers. Substantive strategies have development programs at their core—career development, professional development, and work–life balance. The new approach requires a mutual commitment between employer and employee. "The company is responsible for providing an environment in which people can achieve their full potential, and employees are responsible for developing their skills," says Raymond V. Gilmartin, CEO of Merck & Co. "That's the key to our ability to attract and retain talent, and it defines the new employment relationship as I see it today" (Bernstein 1998, p. 68).

To bolster this new relationship, companies are helping workers to develop skills to advance their careers, making it easier to change jobs within the company, redeploying workers from downsized units to expanding ones, and persuading temporary workers to stay onboard, among other things. Here are some specific company examples.

International Paper Company rolled out a program for its 13,000 white-collar workers in which managers must sit down with employees every year to discuss their career desires, separate from the annual performance review. Procter & Gamble Company (P&G) learned just how important this is when it undertook a study to survey 50 women who had left the firm and that it most regretted losing. Only two of the women had dropped out of the workforce. The others went to very high-profile, high-stress jobs—and were working more hours than when they worked at P&G. Half of the women were stunned to learn that P&G considered them a "regretted loss." No one ever told them they were important.

The problem was rooted in P&G's insular company culture. P&G was so intent on keeping its business practices under wraps that employees were told never to discuss P&G business in public and to clean and lock their desks when they stepped out of the office. Communication with workers about their own jobs, where they stood, and where they might advance suffered as a result of this culture. P&G responded by creating an "Advancement of Women" task force. That group, in turn, instituted a number of programs, such as "Mentor Up," which turned the mentoring

concept on its head by having junior women "mentor" senior men on issues affecting women. The company also repackaged a variety of family-
friendly benefits and programs that were already offered, but that many
employees didn't know about, such as a five-year flexible work schedule
for employees with preschool-age children. One video, "Choices,"
shows senior P&G women talking about their jobs and family life, including how they delegate work and keep house. P&G's effort has begun
to pay off. Turnover among women is on a par with that of men, and
women's job satisfaction is up 25 percent in the last four years. More
tellingly, 31 percent of general managers are now women, compared
with 5 percent in 1992 (Parker-Pope 1998).

Like P&G, other firms are trying to make their cultures more employee-
friendly. Booz, Allen, & Hamilton, Inc., emphasizes programs to balance work and family life, and to create more flexible workdays. Merck
& Co. set up a leadership training program to teach managers to balance
getting results with how people are treated on the job. Managers' bonuses are now linked to their leadership ability as well as to the performance they deliver. Those qualities are assessed in "360-degree" performance reviews in which subordinates, peers, and bosses assess the
managers anonymously (Bernstein 1998).

Other firms are trying to make it easier to change jobs within the company, or redeploying workers from downsized units to expanding ones.
Marriott International, Inc., is expanding a new program to lump its
14,500 managers into four broad salary bands. Instead of assigning
every job a grade level with a narrow salary range, managers now have
wide latitude to get more pay or experience without a formal grade increase. The bands allow managers to seek broader opportunities across
Marriott's 10 hotel chains.

At Raytheon, the defense-electronics giant, as the defense side of the
business sagged, the commercial side, which makes everything from air-
craft parts to power plants, boomed. So while laying off 2,700 engineers
from the defense side, it is trying to redeploy them on the commercial
side of the business.

Some employers are even trying to enhance the commitment of temporary workers. Most large companies routinely use temporary-help
agencies to fill jobs that they do not want to make permanent. Now companies have to be creative to avoid losing their "temps." Xerox works
hard to make its temps feel like company employees, calling them "spe-
cial-assignment representatives." It also pays a $300 bonus to tempo-
rary workers who rejoin Xerox. Company lawyers had advised Xerox

that temporary workers employed for more than 18 months might be considered permanent Xerox employees, so to avoid a legal problem the temporary agency agreed to find other temp jobs for the Xerox staff every 18 months. Once operators went elsewhere, some didn't come back. Hence the $300 bonus, plus a bigger title, better desk, and a sweatshirt that says, "I'm back." Says a Xerox manager, "You can't just treat temps as temps anymore, or you'll lose them. We tell people we want them to work here for years" (Bernstein 1998, p. 72).

Vulnerability Maps

In an effort to prevent turnover before it happens, and to recognize key points in employees' tenures when they are at greatest risk of leaving, some firms are using "vulnerability maps." The maps show a specific job function and the points when the occupant's satisfaction level is likely to ebb (see Exhibit 2–6, page 52). Before the employee reaches these points, managers can offer incentives calculated to carry them over the hump.

The focus, however, cannot be exclusively on the individual worth retaining. To keep high-potential people, they have to get the bosses they deserve. Sun Trust Banks found that "C-level" managers not only have a minimal impact on the bottom line, they also rarely know how to develop, coach, and motivate "A-level" players. Consequently they may cause good performers to leave. To neutralize the effects of "C-level" managers, Sun Trust puts them into nonmanagerial, commission-based jobs where poor performance is appropriately compensated and fully exposed (Branch 1998).

Clearly a number of alternative strategies for reducing turnover in organizations exist, but the first step, as noted earlier, is to calculate the *cost* of turnover. Only then can managers make rational decisions based on the expected costs and benefits of each of the options available.

EXERCISES

1. Ups and Downs, Inc., a 4,000-employee organization, has a serious turnover problem, and management has decided to estimate its annual cost to the company. Following the formulas presented in Exhibits 2–2, 2–3, and 2–4, an HR specialist collected the following information. Exit interviews take about 45 minutes (plus 15 minutes preparation); the interviewer, an HR specialist, is paid an average of $19 per

EXHIBIT 2-6   *Employees' Breaking Points*

The Hanigan Consulting Group tries to identify certain junctures in employees' tenures at which they are at greatest risk of quitting. Armed with their start dates and a map like the one below, managers can take preventive steps.

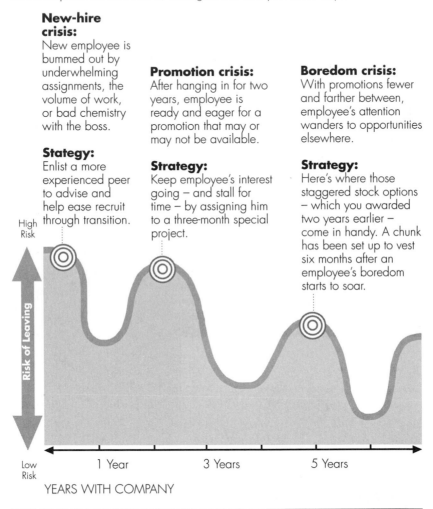

New-hire crisis:
New employee is bummed out by underwhelming assignments, the volume of work, or bad chemistry with the boss.

Stategy:
Enlist a more experienced peer to advise and help ease recruit through transition.

Promotion crisis:
After hanging in for two years, employee is ready and eager for a promotion that may or may not be available.

Strategy:
Keep employee's interest going – and stall for time – by assigning him to a three-month special project.

Boredom crisis:
With promotions fewer and farther between, employee's attention wanders to opportunities elsewhere.

Strategy:
Here's where those staggered stock options – which you awarded two years earlier – come in handy. A chunk has been set up to vest six months after an employee's boredom starts to soar.

High Risk

Risk of Leaving

Low Risk

1 Year   3 Years   5 Years

YEARS WITH COMPANY

Source: S. Branch. (1998, Nov. 9). You hired 'em. But can you keep 'em? *Fortune*, p. 248. Used with permission.

hour plus an additional 40 percent in benefits; and over the last year Ups and Downs, Inc., experienced a 27 percent turnover rate. Three groups of employees were primarily responsible for this: blue collar workers (40 percent), who make an average of $21.60 per hour plus benefits; clerical employees (36 percent), who make an average of $15.50 per hour plus benefits; and managers and professionals (24 percent), who make an average of $33.30 per hour plus benefits. The HR department takes about 90 minutes per terminating employee to perform the administrative functions related to terminations, and on top of that, each terminating employee gets two weeks' severance pay. All of that turnover also contributes to increased unemployment tax (old rate = 5.0 percent; new rate = 5.4 percent), and because the average taxable wage per employee is $19.90, that is likely to be a considerable (avoidable) penalty for having a high turnover problem.

It also costs money to replace those terminating workers. All pre-employment physical examinations are done by Biometrics, Inc., an outside organization that charges $150 per physical. Advertising and employment agency fees run an additional $450 per termination, on the average, and HR specialists spend an average of four more hours communicating job availability every time another employee quits. Pre-employment administrative functions take another two and a half hours per terminating employee, and this excludes pre-employment interview time (one hour, on average). Over the past year Ups and Downs's records also show that for every candidate hired, three others had to be interviewed. Testing costs per applicant are $10 for materials and another $10 for scoring. Travel expenses average $75 per applicant, and one in every ten new hires is reimbursed an average of $45,000 in moving expenses. For those management jobs being filled, a 90-minute staff meeting is also required, with a department representative (average pay of $27.75 per hour plus benefits) present. In the last year, 17 such meetings were held. Finally, post-employment acquisition and dissemination of information takes 75 minutes, on the average, for each new employee.

And, of course, all these replacements have to be trained. Informational literature alone costs $15 per package, the formal training program (run 12 times last year) takes four eight-hour days, and trainers make an average of $34 per hour plus benefits. New employees made an average of $16.50 per hour plus benefits, and about 65 percent of all training costs can be attributed to replacements for those who left. Finally, on-the-job training lasted three 8-hour days per new employee, with two new employees assigned to each experienced employee (average pay = $24.25 per hour plus benefits). During training each experienced employee's productivity dropped by 50 percent. Net *DP* was +$160,000. What did employee turnover cost Ups and Downs,

Inc., last year? How much did it cost per employee who left? (Use the worksheet provided for all computations.)

2. Management has decided that the cost of employee turnover at Ups and Downs, Inc., is intolerable. As an outside consultant, you have been retained to do two things. One, prepare a presentation to management that will help the managers better understand why employees leave. Two, recommend two *detailed* programs for reducing the turnover problems at Ups and Downs, Inc. (To do this, make whatever assumptions seem reasonable.)

WORKSHEET

Separation Costs

Exit interview cost of interviewer's time = _____

cost of terminating employees' time = _____

Administrative functions related to terminations = _____

Separation pay = _____

Unemployment tax = _____

Total separation costs = _____

Replacement Costs

Communicating job availability = _____

Pre-employment administrative functions = _____

Testing = _____

Staff meeting = _____

Travel/moving expenses = _____

*Post-employment acquisition and dissemination
  of information* = _____

Contracted medical examinations = _____

Total replacement costs = _____

Training Costs

Informational literature = _____

Instruction in a formal training program – _____

Instruction by employee assignment = _____

Total training costs = _____

Net differential in performance = _____

Total turnover costs   _____

Total cost per terminating employee   _____

REFERENCES

Alderman, L. (1996). Walk out the door with all the money you deserve. *Money* (August), 66–68.

Asher, J. J., Sciarrino, J. A. (1974). Realistic work sample tests: A review. *Personnel Psychology 27*, 519–533.

Auerbach, J. (1996). Executive relocations—and hassles—increase. *The Wall Street Journal* (April 5), B8.

Becker, G. S. (1964). *Human Capital.* New York: National Bureau of Economic Research.

Bernstein, A. (1998). We want you to stay. Really. *Time* (June 22), 67–72.

Branch, S. (1998). You hired 'em. But can you keep 'em? *Fortune* (Nov. 9), 247–250.

Breaugh, J. A. (1992). *Recruitment: Science and Practice.* Boston: PWS-Kent.

Cascio, W. F. (1998). *Applied Psychology in Human Resource Management* (5th ed.). Englewood Cliffs, NJ: Prentice Hall.

Cascio, W. F., Phillips, N. F. (1979). Performance testing: A rose among thorns? *Personnel Psychology 32*, 751–766.

Dalton, D. R., Todor, W. D., Krackardt, D. M. (1982). Turnover overstated: The functional taxonomy. *Academy of Management Review 7*, 117–123.

Harris, M. M., Heft, L. L. (1993). Preemployment urinalysis drug testing: A critical review of psychometric and legal issues and effects on applicants. *Human Resource Management Review 3*(4), 271–291.

Hirschey, M., Pappas, J. L. (1998). *Fundamentals of Managerial Economics* (6th ed.). New York: Harcourt Brace.

Inwald, R. E. (1988). Five-year follow-up study of departmental terminations as predicted by 16 pre-employment psychological indicators. *Journal of Applied Psychology 73*, 703–710.

Johnson, A. A. (1995). The business case for work-family programs. *Journal of Accountancy 180*(2), 53–57.

Lazear, E. P. (1998). *Personnel Economics for Managers*. New York: John Wiley & Sons.

Macy, B. A., Mirvis, P. H. (1976). Measuring the quality of worklife and organizational effectiveness in behavioral-economic terms. *Administrative Science Quarterly 21*, 212–226.

Martin, D. C., Bartol, K. M. (1985). Managing turnover strategically. *Personnel Administrator 30*(11), 63–73.

McEvoy, G. M., Cascio, W. F. (1985). Strategies for reducing employee turnover: A meta-analysis. *Journal of Applied Psychology 70*, 342–353.

McEvoy, G. M., Cascio, W. F. (1987). Do good or poor performers leave? A meta-analysis of the relationship between performance and turnover. *Academy of Management Journal 30*, 744–762.

Meglino, B. M., DeNisi, A. S., Youngblood, S. A., Williams, K. J. (1988). Effects of realistic job previews: A comparison using an enhancement and a reduction preview. *Journal of Applied Psychology 73*, 259–266.

Milkovich, G. T., Newman, J. M. (1999). *Compensation* (6th ed.). Burr Ridge, IL: Irwin/McGraw-Hill.

Parker-Pope, T. (1998). Inside P&G, a pitch to keep women employees. *The Wall Street Journal* (Sept. 9), B1, B6.

Pfeffer, J. (1998). *SAS Institute: A Different Approach to Incentives and People Management Practices in the Software Industry.* Palo Alto, CA: Graduate School of Business, Stanford University.

Premack, S. L., Wanous, J. P. (1985). A meta-analysis of realistic job preview experiments. *Journal of Applied Psychology 70*, 706–719.

Schellhardt, T. D. (1998). An idyllic workplace under a tycoon's thumb. *The Wall Street Journal* (Nov. 23), B1, B4.

Smith, H. L., Watkins, W. E. (1978). Managing manpower turnover costs. *Personnel Administrator 23*(4), 46–50.

Solomon, J. (1988). Companies try measuring cost savings from new types of corporate benefits. *The Wall Street Journal* (Dec. 29), B1.

Symonds, W. C. (1998). Where paternalism equals good business. *Business Week* (July 20), 16E4–16E6.

Take my job, please! (1996). *Business Week* (July 8), 6.

U.S. employers creating new ways to keep talented workers. (1998). *Manpower Argus 361* (Oct), 8.

Wanous, J. P. (1980). *Organizational Entry: Recruitment, Selection, and Socialization of Newcomers.* Reading, MA: Addison-Wesley.

Wanous, J. P. (1989). Installing a realistic job preview: Ten tough choices. *Personnel Psychology 42*, 117–134.

Wessel, D. (1989). Evidence is skimpy that drug testing works, but employers embrace practice. *The Wall Street Journal* (Sept. 7), B1.

Work week. (1996). *The Wall Street Journal* (Aug. 13), A1.

ENDNOTE

1. weighted average pay rate per terminated employee

$$= \frac{\sum_{i=1}^{m} \text{pay rate}_i \times \text{no. employees terminated at pay rate}}{}$$

$$= \frac{(14.65 \times 75) + (16.55 \times 87) + (18.50 \times 65) + (20.30 \times 37) + (24.75 \times 14) + (29.35 \times 10)}{288}$$

$$= \$17.82/\text{hour}$$

The Hidden Costs of Absenteeism and Sick Leave

In the United States, unscheduled employee absenteeism reached a seven-year high in 1998. Would it surprise you to learn that the leading causes of absenteeism were family-related issues? Personal illness, the reason you might have expected to be the main justification for calling in sick, was actually true in only about one in five cases (Van-DerWall 1998). The five most common causes of absence cited by employees are shown in Exhibit 3–1.

What does unscheduled absenteeism cost? Considering only the direct costs of sick leave, not the indirect costs such as other workers' overtime or temporary help, the average cost in 1998 was $757 per employee on the payroll, according to the survey cited above. For every 100 employees, the average tab *per year* comes to $75,700. Figures like that get management's attention. Responding to the need for many of its employees to meet family obligations, Prudential Insurance Co. of America, based in Newark, New Jersey, established a back-up childcare center (one that parents can use on a drop-in basis as necessary). The savings? More than $80,000 annually in reduced absenteeism. First Chicago (now part of Bank One Corp.) reports that employees who do not take advantage of its back-up childcare program miss an average of seven extra workdays per year (VanDerWall 1998).

Absenteeism is any failure to report for or remain at work as scheduled, regardless of the reason. The use of the words "as scheduled" is significant for they automatically exclude vacation, personal leave, jury duty leave, and the like. A great deal of confusion can be avoided simply by

EXHIBIT 3-1   *Why Are Workers Absent?*

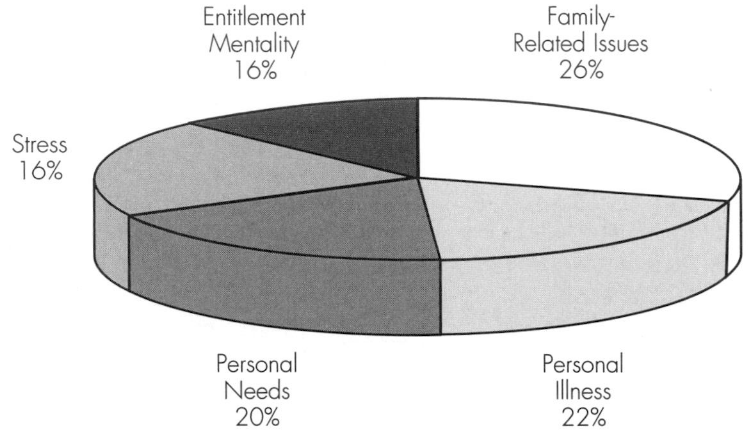

Entitlement Mentality 16%

Family-Related Issues 26%

Stress 16%

Personal Needs 20%

Personal Illness 22%

Source of data: S. VanDerWall. (1998). Survey finds unscheduled absenteeism hitting seven-year high. *HR News* (Nov.), 14. Used with permission of *HR News* published by the Society for Human Resource Management, Alexandria, VA.

recognizing that if an employee is not on the job as scheduled he or she is absent, no matter what the cause. The employee is not available to perform his or her job, and that job is probably being done less efficiently by another employee or is not being done at all.

> Another point of primary importance is the fact that absenteeism is to be judged on the record, and the record only. While this may seem elementary, it is essential. There is a tendency to view some absences as "excusable" and others as "inexcusable." Judgments concerning the nature of illness causing the absence also tend to make some absences seem "better" or "worse" than others, and the length of service of the employee makes certain absences seem excusable. Actually, the only absence which is really inexcusable is the absence due to malingering, but, unfortunately, it is difficult or nearly impossible to provide evidence to substantiate malingering, and mere suspicions can be erroneous. Regardless, excused time is by no means a right. Absence is absence regardless of reason—even for medically verified illness. Failure to recognize this simple fact will result in an attempt to make judgments that simply cannot be made. ("Establishing an Absence Control Policy" 1980, p. 3)

Although the definition of absenteeism might leave little room for interpretation, the concept itself is undergoing a profound change, largely as a result of the knowledge work that characterizes more and more jobs in our economy. Knowledge work has more of a professional flavor, where professionals are measured not by the tasks they perform but by the results they achieve. As an example, consider the job of a computer programmer. The programmer is judged not by the number of lines of code in a program, but rather by whether the program runs efficiently and whether it does reliably what it is supposed to do. It doesn't matter when the programmer works (9 a.m. to 5 p.m. or from midnight to dawn) or where the programmer works (at the office or at home). Results are the only barometer of performance.

In those types of work environments, if results are the only thing that matters, then the concept of absenteeism has no meaning. If workers never "report" for work at a central location, and if they vary their work hours to fit personal schedules, and are accountable only in terms of results, then the concept of absenteeism ceases to be relevant. It remains relevant only where workers are scheduled to report to a central location, such as a factory or an office.

At the outset, let us be clear about what this chapter does and does not include. The primary focus in this chapter is on the economic consequences of absenteeism, and on methods for managing absenteeism and sick-leave abuse—in work settings where those concepts remain relevant and meaningful. The chapter does not examine the causes of absenteeism, such as characteristics of jobs (Rentsch & Steel 1998), gender, age, depression, smoking, heavy drinking, drug abuse, or lack of exercise (Harrison & Martocchio 1998; Johns 1997). Nor does it focus on the noneconomic consequences of absenteeism, such as the effects on the individual absentee, co-workers, managers, the organization, the union, or the family.

ESTIMATING ABSENTEEISM COSTS

The following procedure will estimate the costs of absenteeism for a one-year period, although the procedure can be used just as easily to estimate those costs over shorter or longer periods as necessary.[1] Much of the information required should not be too time-consuming to gather if an organization regularly computes labor-cost data and traditional absence statistics. For example, the absenteeism rate is generally computed in one of two ways:

$$\text{Absenteeism rate} = \Sigma \, [\text{absence days} \div \text{average workforce size}] \times \text{working days, } or$$

$$\text{Absenteeism rate} = \Sigma \,[\text{hours missed} \div \text{average workforce size}]$$
$$\times \text{working hours}$$

Although some estimates will involve discussions with both staff and management representatives, the time spent should be well worth the effort. The overall approach is shown in Exhibit 3–2. To illustrate that approach, we will provide examples to accompany each step. The examples use the hypothetical firm Presto Electric, a medium-sized manufacturer of electrical components employing 3,000 people; the numbers are as realistic as possible in order to illustrate the magnitude of the problems and costs related to employee absenteeism.

Step 1

Determine the organization's total employee-hours lost to absenteeism for the period for all employees—blue-collar, clerical, and management and professional. Include both whole-day and part-day absences, and time lost for all reasons except such organizationally sanctioned time off as vacations, holidays, or official "bad weather" days. For example, absences for the following reasons should be included: illness, accidents, funerals, emergencies, or doctor's appointments (whether excused or unexcused).

As a basis for comparisons, Exhibit 3–3 illustrates monthly job absence rates as reported by the Bureau of National Affairs. While the time-series data shown in Exhibit 3–3 clearly reflect a seasonal component (highest rates in January and February, lowest rates in June, July, and August), average monthly rates by year do not indicate a long-term trend, at least for the years shown.

In our example, assume that Presto Electric's employee records show 102,900 total employee-hours lost to absenteeism for all reasons except vacations and holidays during the past year. That figure represents an absence rate of 1.75 percent of scheduled work time, about average for manufacturing firms (see Exhibit 3–3). Begin by distinguishing hours *scheduled* from hours *paid*. Most firms pay for 2,080 hours per year per employee (40 hours per week × 52 weeks). However, employees generally receive paid vacations and holidays as well, time for which they are not scheduled to be at work. If we assume two weeks of vacation time per employee (40 hours × 2), plus 5 holidays (40 hours), annual hours of scheduled work time per employee are 2,080 − 80 − 40 = 1,960.

Total scheduled work time for Presto's 3,000 employees is 3,000 × 1,960 = 5,880,000. Given a 1.75 percent rate of annual absenteeism, total scheduled work hours lost to employee absenteeism are 102,900.

EXHIBIT 3-2 *Total Estimated Cost of Employee Absenteeism*

1. Compute total employee hours lost to absenteeism for the period.

2. Compute weighted average wage or salary/hour/absent employee.

3. Compute cost of employee benefits/hour/employee.

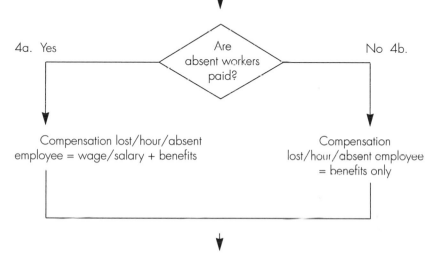

4a. Yes   Are absent workers paid?   No 4b.

Compensation lost/hour/absent employee = wage/salary + benefits

Compensation lost/hour/absent employee = benefits only

5. Compute total compensation lost to absent employees (1. × 4a. or 4b. as applicable).

6. Estimate total supervisory hours lost to employee absenteeism.

7. Compare average hourly supervisory salary + benefits.

8. Estimate total supervisory salaries lost to managing absenteeism problems (6. × 7.)

9. Estimate all other costs incidental to absenteeism.

10. Estimate total costs of absenteeism (Σ 5., 8., 9.).

11. Estimate total cost of absenteeism/employee (10. ÷ total no. of employees).

EXHIBIT 3-3   *Typical Monthly Job Absence Rates (Median Percent of Scheduled Workdays)*

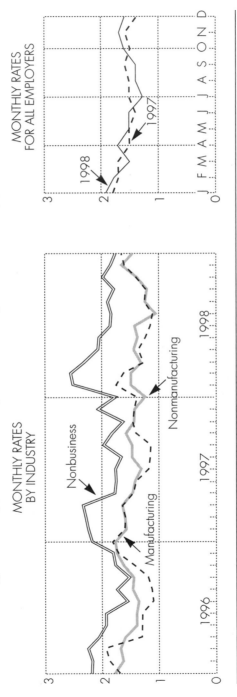

Source: BNA's job absence and turnover report—4th quarter 1998. Reprinted with permission from *Bulletin to Management* (BNA Policy and Practice Series), Vol. 50, No. 10, Part II (March 11, 1999). Copyright 1999 by The Bureau of National Affairs, Inc. (800-372-1033) <http://www.bna.com>

Step 2

Compute the weighted average hourly wage/salary level for the various occupational groups that claimed absenteeism during the period. If absent workers are not paid, skip this step and go directly to step 3.

For Presto Electric, assume that about 60 percent of all absentees are blue-collar, 30 percent are clerical, and 10 percent are management and professional. For purposes of illustration we also will assume that all employees are paid for sick days taken under the organization's employee benefits program. The average hourly wage rate per absentee is estimated by applying the appropriate percentages to the average hourly wage rate for each major occupational group. Thus:

Occupational Group	Approximate Percent of Total Absenteeism	Average Hourly Wage ($)	Weighted Average Hourly Wage ($)
Blue-collar	0.60	18.85	11.31
Clerical	0.30	15.20	4.56
Management and professional	0.10	29.50	2.95
			18.82 total

Step 3

Estimate the cost of employee benefits per hour per employee. The cost of employee benefits (profit sharing, pensions, health and life insurance, paid vacations and holidays, and so on) currently accounts for about 40 percent of total compensation (Cascio 1998). One procedure for computing the cost of employee benefits per hour per employee is to divide the total cost of benefits per employee per week by the number of hours worked per week.

First, compute Presto's weekly cost of benefits per employee. Assume that the average annual salary per employee is $18.82 per hour (which happens to correspond to the result we observed in step 2, though this need not be the case) × 2,080 (hours paid for per year), or $39,145.60. Let us further assume:

average annual salary × 40 percent = average cost of benefits per employee per year
$$\$39,145.60 \times 0.40 = \$15,658.24$$

average cost of benefits per employee = average weekly cost of per year ÷ 52 weeks per year   benefits per employee
$$\$15,658.24 \div 52 = \$301.12$$

average weekly cost of benefits = cost of benefits per hour
per employee ÷ hours worked per week   per employee
$$\$301.12 \div 40 = \$7.53$$

Step 4

Compute the total compensation lost per hour per absent employee. This figure is determined simply by adding the weighted average hourly wage/salary per employee (item 2 in Exhibit 3–2) to the cost of employee benefits per hour per employee (item 3 in Exhibit 3–2). Thus:

$$\$18.82 + \$7.53 = \$26.35$$

If absent workers are not paid, of couse, item 4 in Exhibit 3–2 is the same as item 3.

Step 5

Compute the total compensation lost to absent employees. Total compensation lost, aggregated over all employee-hours lost, is determined simply by multiplying item 1 in Exhibit 3–2 by item 4.a or 4.b, whichever is applicable. In our example:

$$102,900 \times \$26.35 = \$2,711,415.00$$

Step 6

Estimate the total number of supervisory hours lost to employee absenteeism for the period. Unfortunately, because existing records seldom provide the information necessary to compute this figure it will be more difficult to estimate than are wages and benefits. As a first step, estimate the average number of supervisory hours spent per day dealing with all the problems stemming from employee absenteeism—matters such as production problems, instructing replacement employees, checking on the performance of replacements, and counseling and disciplining absentees.

Such an estimate can be accurate only if the staff member making it talks to the first-line supervisors and higher-level managers who deal directly with employee absence problems. Interview a representative sample of supervisors using a semi-structured interview format to help them refine their estimates. In addition to the problems and tasks mentioned above, probe the effects of typically high-absence days (Mondays, Fridays, days before and after holidays, days after payday). No published data or industry-wide averages are available to determine whether those estimates are reasonable. It is true of estimates in general, however, that the more experience companies accumulate in making the estimates, the more accurate the estimates become (Wikstrom 1971).

After you have estimated the average number of supervisory hours spent per day dealing with employee absenteeism problems, compute the total number of supervisory hours lost to the organization by multiplying three figures:

1. Estimated average number of hours lost per supervisor per day
2. Total number of supervisors who deal with problems of absenteeism
3. Number of working days for the period (including all shifts and week-end work)

In our example, assume the following to be Presto Electric's data in those three areas:

> Estimated number of supervisory hours lost per day: 0.5 hours
> Total number of supervisors who deal with absence problems: 100
> Total number of working days for the year: 245

The total number of supervisory hours lost to employee absenteeism is therefore:

$$0.5 \times 100 \times 245 = 12{,}250$$

Step 7

Compute the average hourly wage rate for supervisors, including benefits. Be sure to include only the salaries of supervisors who normally deal with problems of employee absenteeism. Typically, first-line supervisors in the production and clerical areas bear the brunt of absenteeism problems. Estimate Presto Electric's cost for this figure as follows:

Average hourly supervisory salary:	$22.75
Cost of benefits per hour (40% of hourly salary):	+ 9.10
Total compensation per hour per supervisor:	$31.85

Step 8

Compute total supervisory salaries lost to problems of managing absenteeism by multiplying total supervisory hours lost on employee absenteeism (step 6) times average hourly supervisory wage (step 7). Thus:

$$12{,}250 \times 31.85 = \$390{,}162.50$$

Step 9

Estimate all other costs incidental to absenteeism that were not included in the previous steps. This last item is a catchall of costs, unique to each organization, that clearly relate to absenteeism but that fall outside the boundaries of all the other costs we have considered so far. Such costs might include the following items:

> temporary help
> labor pools for absent workers
> overtime premiums
> machine downtime
> quality problems
> production losses
> inefficient materials usage

As in step 6, these estimates will be difficult because many of the components are not reported routinely in accounting or human resource information systems. Initially, therefore, determination of the cost elements to be included in this category, plus estimates of their magnitude, should be based on discussions with a number of supervisors and managers. Over time, as the organization accumulates experience in costing absenteeism, it can make a more precise identification and computation of the costs to be included in this miscellaneous category. At Presto Electric, assume that overtime premiums, production losses, and inefficient materials usage as a result of absenteeism caused an estimated financial loss of $350,000 for the year.

Step 10

Compute the annual total estimated cost of employee absenteeism. Add the individual costs pertaining to wages and salaries, benefits, supervisory salaries, and other costs incidental to absenteeism (Σ items 5, 8, and 9). Considering the specific costs that we assumed for Presto, Exhibit 3–4 demonstrates that this cost is over $3.4 million per year.

Step 11

Compute the total estimated cost of absenteeism per employee per year. In some cases this figure (derived by dividing the total estimated cost by the total number of employees) may be more meaningful than the total cost estimate because it is easier to grasp. In the case of our hypothetical

EXHIBIT 3-4 *Total Estimated Cost of Employee Absenteeism*

Item	Presto Electric
1. Total employee-hours lost to absenteeism for the period	102,900
2. Weighted average wage/salary per hour per absent employee	$18.82
3. Cost of employee benefits per hour per absent employee	$7.53
4. Total compensation lost per hour per absent employee	
a. if absent workers are paid (wage/salary plus benefits)	$26.35
b. if absent workers are not paid (benefits only)	
5. Total compensation lost to absent employees (total employee-hours lost × 4.a or 4.b, whichever applies)	$2,711,415.00
6. Total supervisory hours lost on employee absenteeism	12,250
7. Average hourly supervisory wage, including benefits	$31.85
8. Total supervisory salaries lost to managing problems of absenteeism (hours lost × average hourly supervisory wage—item 6 × item 7)	$390,162.50
9. All other costs incidental to absenteeism not included in the above items	$350,000.00
10. Total estimated cost of absenteeism (Σ items 5, 8, and 9)	$3,451,577.50
11. Total estimated cost of absenteeism per employee (total estimated costs ÷ total number of employees)	$1,150.53

firm, Presto Electric, this figure was $1,150.53 per year for each of the 3,000 employees on the payroll.

INTERPRETING ABSENTEEISM COSTS

To interpret absenteeism costs meaningfully, evaluate them against some predetermined cost standard or financial measure of performance, such as an industry-wide average. That is basically the same rationale that organizations use when conducting pay surveys to determine if their salaries and benefits are competitive. Unfortunately, absenteeism-cost data are not published regularly, as pay surveys are. Very little data are available to help determine whether the level of dollars and cents lost to employee absenteeism is a significant problem. The costs of absenteeism to individual organizations occasionally do appear in the literature, but these estimates are typically case studies of individual firms rather than survey data from specific industries.

Is the effort to analyze the absenteeism costs of the individual organization worthwhile? The answer is yes for at least two compelling reasons. First, such an analysis calls management's attention to the severity of the problem. Translating behavior into economic terms enables managers to grasp the burdens employee absenteeism imposes, particularly in organizations suffering from severe absence problems. A six- or seven-figure cost is often the spark needed for management to make a concerted effort to combat the problem. Second, an analysis of the problem creates a baseline for evaluating the effectiveness of absence-control programs. Comparing the quarterly, semiannual, and annual costs of absenteeism across various departments and supervisory work units provides a measure of the success—or lack of success—of attempts to reduce the problem. Organizations with computerized absence-reporting systems should find this additional information relatively easy and inexpensive to generate.

A common question at this point is "Are these dollars real?" Because supervisors are drawing their salaries anyway, what difference does it make if they have to manage absenteeism problems? The last question may be valid, but what is the best possible return to the organization for that pay?

We'll compare Firm A and Firm B, identical with regard to all resources and costs—all supervisors earn the same salary, work the same hours, manage the same-size staff, and produce the same kind of product. But absenteeism in Firm A is very low, and in Firm B it is very high. The salary officers' records show the same pay to supervisors, but the accountants show higher profits in Firm A than in Firm B. Why? Because the supervisors in Firm A spend less time managing absenteeism problems. They are more productive because they devote their energies to planning, scheduling, and troubleshooting. Instead of working a 10- to 12-hour day (which the supervisors in Firm B consider "normal"), they wrap things up after only 8 hours. In short, reducing the hours that supervisors must spend managing absenteeism problems has two advantages: it allows supervisors to maximize their productivity, and it reduces the stress associated with repeated 10- to 12-hour days, which in turn enhances the quality of the supervisors' work lives.

The material thus far describes the idea of *opportunity costs*—the difference between the maximum return that could be earned (Firm A) and that which actually was earned (Firm B). Supervisors in Firm B did put in their time to earn their pay, but those in Firm A made better use of their time while on the job. So the answer to the question "Are these dollars real?" is yes, but in all probability they are underestimates because they reflect only the payroll costs of supervisors' time and not the productive dollar value of that time.

MANAGING ABSENTEEISM AND SICK-LEAVE ABUSE

No Work, No Pay at Honda USA

Over a two-year period, Honda's absenteeism rate averaged just 2 percent in an industry that has been plagued by chronic absenteeism problems. For example, General Motors reported that absenteeism had run as high as 40 percent at one of its West Coast plants, and that it had to hire additional employees to keep production lines moving. How did Honda do it? According to the company, the low rate of employee absenteeism is due to the "Honda System." At the heart of the system is a simple dictum: no work, no pay. Absences shorter than seven days are not compensated, but absences longer than seven days are reimbursable through insurance.

On the other hand, if employees do report on time, and do not punch out early, they earn progressively larger and larger bonuses. The minimum bonus is $24 for four weeks of perfect attendance, but it graduates upward based on seniority. A worker with a year of perfect attendance moves into another category, and the bonus continues to build. Absenteeism control is only one part of Honda's broader management system, but one indicator of the program's success is the inability of the United Auto Workers to organize Honda employees, despite repeated attempts to do so (Allan 1983).

Controlling Absenteeism Through Positive Incentives

The Honda System focuses on a mix of reward and punishment. There is another approach that focuses exclusively on rewards; it provides incentives for employees to come to work, rather than punishments for not coming to work. This "positive incentive absence-control program" was evaluated over a five-year period: one year before and one year after a three-year incentive program (Schlotzhauer & Rosse 1985).

A 3,000-employee nonprofit hospital provided the setting for a study of this absence-control program. The experimental group comprised 164 employees who received the positive-incentive program, and the control group contained 136 employees who did not receive the program. According to the terms of the hospital's sick-leave program, employees could take up to 96 hours—12 days per year—with pay. Under the positive-incentive program, employees could convert up to 24 hours of unused sick leave into additional pay or vacation. To determine the amount of incentive, the number of hours absent was subtracted from 24. For example, 24 minus 8 hours absent equals 16 hours of additional pay or vacation. The hospital informed eligible employees both verbally and in writing.

During the year prior to the installation of the positive-incentive program, absence levels for the experimental and control groups did not differ significantly. During the three years in which the program was operating, the experimental group consistently was absent less frequently, and this difference persisted during the year following the termination of the incentives. The following variables were *not* related to absence: age, marital status, education, job grade, tenure, or number of hours absent two or three years previously. Two variables *were* related to absence, although not as strongly as the incentive program itself: gender (women were absent more than men) and number of hours absent during the previous year.

Had the incentive program been expanded to include all 3,000 hospital employees, net savings were estimated to have been $42,000 per year. This is an underestimate, however, because indirect costs were not included. Indirect costs include such things as:

> overtime pay
> increased supervisory time for managing absenteeism problems
> costs of temporary labor
> intentional overstaffing to compensate for anticipated absences

Cautions: A positive-incentive program may have no effect on employees who view sick leave as an earned "right" that should be used whether one is sick or not. Moreover, encouraging attendance when a person has a legitimate reason for being absent—for example, hospital employees with contagious illnesses—may be dysfunctional.

In and of itself, absence may simply represent one of many possible symptoms of job dissatisfaction. Attendance incentives may result in "symptom substitution," whereby declining absence is accompanied by increased tardiness and idling, decreased productivity, and even turnover. If this is the case, an organization needs to consider more comprehensive interventions that are based, for example, on the results of an attitude survey.

Despite the potential limitations, the Schlotzhauer and Rosse study warranted the following conclusions:

- Absenteeism declined an average of 11.5 hours per employee (32 percent) during the incentive period.
- Net dollar values to the organization (direct costs only) were based on wage costs of $11.67 per hour ($8.98 in direct wages plus 30 percent more in benefits).
- Savings were $22,010 per year (11.5 hours × average hourly wage [$11.67] × 164 employees). This is roughly $34,500 in 1998 dollars.
- Direct costs to the hospital included 2,194 bonus hours at an average hourly wage of $8.98 per hour = $19,702. This is about $30,800 in 1998 dollars.
- Net savings were, therefore, $2,308 per year, for an 11.7 percent return on investment ($2,308 ÷ $19,702).

No-Fault Absenteeism

An alternative approach to controlling employee absenteeism relies on the "no-fault" concept (Kuzmits 1984). The no-fault system eliminates fault as a basis for determining whether absenteeism or tardiness is to be excused. Under the no-fault policy, an employee is either at work or is absent, and each type of absence carries a predetermined penalty, with the exception of a few clearly defined, nonchargeable offenses.

The no-fault system defines absences in terms of *occurrences*. An occurrence is an absence of any length—a one-day absence and a three-day absence are treated as two occurrences. Management's costliest and most troublesome absenteeism problem is the chronic offender: the employee who incurs many single-day absences. Under the no-fault approach, the chronic offender quickly accumulates multiple occurrences and is subject to disciplinary action. On the other hand, an employee who is absent three or four consecutive days is probably ill. Thus, the no-fault approach places heavy penalties on the chronic absentee and light penalties on the employee who is, in all likelihood, absent because of sickness.

All absences, regardless of the reasons, are chargeable for purposes of disciplinary action. An employee either is at work or is not, and the burden of responsibility for good attendance is placed squarely on the shoulders of each employee. Note, however, that there is a reward system built into this policy. Employees can remove one occurrence through each calendar month of perfect attendance. The policy thus includes positive inducements for good attendance, as well as negative sanctions for abusing sick leave. The policy was written primarily to alter the behavioral patterns of chronic absentees and to provide a fair, concise disciplinary procedure for frequently absent employees who are unable or unwilling to change their behavior.

Does no-fault absenteeism work? A comparison of one year's experience under a traditional sick-leave policy that included provisions both for excused and unexcused absences with one year's experience under a no-fault policy provided some interesting evidence. The study was conducted with 289 blue-collar, unionized employees of a cabinet manufacturer in Louisville, Kentucky. Results indicated significant improvements under the no-fault policy in all forms of attendance (absence occurrences, tardiness, partial absences, and no-calls). In addition, disciplinary decisions were simplified considerably, and employees knew at all times where they stood within the system. Finally, absence-related union grievances dropped from 15 in the year prior to the no-fault system to 4 during the first year with the no-fault system (Kuzmits 1984).

A no-fault policy clearly has several advantages:

- It applies to all employees regardless of circumstances.
- Supervisors cannot judge the legitimacy of absences, so that bias does not determine whether an absence should be excused or unexcused.
- Disciplinary decisions are clear because they are related directly to the number of occurrences, or points, that an employee accumulates.

Arbitrators tend to support the no-fault system because of its objective standards, uniform administration, progressive disciplinary procedures, automatic exceptions, and opportunities to cleanse the record through perfect attendance. On the other hand, a no-fault policy is not without its disadvantages, and these must be considered carefully:

- Because the system leaves no room for supervisory discretion, individual circumstances cannot be considered when charging an employee with an absence or occurrence or when making a disciplinary decision.
- An occurrence is defined as an absence of *any length* so some employees may "game" the system by recognizing, for example, that a three-day absence entails the same penalty as a one-day absence.

- Employees may continue to game the system by rationalizing, "I've got 12 occurrences a year; I'm going to use them." Those employees feel that sick leave is a right ("Use it or lose it") rather than a privilege.
- Unions may resist a no-fault policy if they perceive it as part of a "give-back" bargaining strategy.[2]
- Short-term illnesses, even if medically verified, result in chargeable absences. Although arbitrators generally have upheld this aspect of the no-fault policy, unionized employees who traditionally have enjoyed such paid leave will probably oppose it.

Like any other HRM program, a no-fault absenteeism policy should be considered in light of the particular problems faced by management. No-fault seems to work best in controlling high incidences of one-day absences, partial absences, and tardiness; in distinguishing excused from unexcused absences; and in clarifying the disciplinary system and the organization's absenteeism policy. Finally, it virtually eliminates employee perceptions of supervisory inequity in the interpretation of absenteeism policy and the imposition of discipline for excessive absenteeism.

Paid Time Off

The consolidated annual leave approach to controlling absenteeism and the abuse of sick leave allows employees to manage their own sick and vacation time and to take a day off without having to offer an explanation. Sick days, vacation time, and holidays are consolidated into one bank to be drawn out at the employee's discretion. If the employee uses up all of this time before the end of the year and needs a day off, that time is unpaid. On the other hand, employees can convert unused time to vacation or can accrue time and be paid for a portion of it.

Employers (primarily banks and hospitals) that have instituted this kind of policy feel that it is a win–win situation for employees and managers. It eliminates the need for lying by employees (that is, abuse of sick leave), and it takes managers out of the role of enforcers. Employees typically view sick-leave days as a right—that is, as something to be used or forfeited. Paid-time-off policies provide an incentive to employees not to take unnecessary time off because excessive absence is still cause for dismissal. Only about 25 percent of companies use such programs, although the programs are generally regarded as some of the most effective ways to prevent unplanned absences. As one observer noted, "I think the main issue becomes the design of PTO [paid-time-off] programs. A lot of companies have a fear of increasing the amount of time people get off work. It is not a case of 'free reign' of sick days. Companies have to really look at how they design the program" (VanDerWall 1998, p. 14).

Summary Comments on Absence-Control Policies

A comprehensive review of research findings in this area revealed that absence-control systems can neutralize some forms of absence behavior and can catalyze others (Harrison & Martocchio 1998). Although the positive-incentive program described earlier was effective in reducing absenteeism over a three-year period, Dalton and Mesch (1991) showed that absence-control policies actually could encourage absence. In the firm they studied, employees had to accumulate 90 days of unused sick leave before they could have paid sick leave (for one- to two-day absences). The policy suppressed absences only until employees reached the paid threshold, at which time they took sick leave ferociously.

Other studies have shown that punishments, or stricter enforcement of penalties for one type of absence, tend to instigate other forms of missing work (Miners et al. 1995). This is not to suggest, however, that absence-control policies should be lenient. Unionized settings, where sick-leave policies are typically more generous, are clearly prone to higher absenteeism (Drago & Wooden 1992). Such policies convey a relaxed norm about absenteeism, and research evidence clearly indicates that those norms can promote absence-taking (Harrison & Martocchio 1998).

A Systems Approach

Some employers are beginning to adopt a broader approach to controlling behavioral risks, such as absenteeism, as well as workplace violence, accidents, theft, and substance abuse (Yandrick 1997). That approach includes strict standards, supplemented by helping services and a supportive environment. The overall approach begins with the assumption that the carrot-and-stick method to controlling behavioral risks is too simplistic in the current era of employee participation and empowerment. The key is to train employees to assume personal responsibility for behavioral problems, but training is just one part of a four-pronged approach. That approach includes the following:

- Delegation of authority in a work environment where resources are readily available—for example, assigning to work teams the power to make decisions about their daily operations.
- Training for managers, work teams, and employees that focuses on helping to define and understand the boundaries of intolerable, unacceptable, marginal, and acceptable behavior.
- Supportive programs and services—such as EAPs, wellness programs, and conflict-management programs—that provide workers with tools to resolve their own problems.
- Policies that proscribe unacceptable behaviors, such as failure or refusal to carry out job assignments or legitimate requests from management, falsification of records, unauthorized taking of funds or property, fighting, or other serious misconduct.

Where employers were once faced with the question of how to control behavioral problems, they are now starting to ask what resources can be provided to help workers deal more effectively with their problems and what changes can be made in the work environment to prevent problems from occurring. Does that approach work? A recent study at Xerox showed that work alternatives such as flexible scheduling not only improve morale, but can also reduce absenteeism by as much as 30 percent (Yandrick 1997).

EXERCISES

1. Consolidated Industries, an 1,800-employee firm, is faced with a serious and growing absenteeism problem. Last year total employee-hours lost to absenteeism came to 119,808. Of the total employees absent, 65 percent were blue collar (average wage $19.10 per hour), 25 percent were clerical (average wage $15.60 per hour), and the remainder were management and professional (average salary $29.07 per hour). On the average, the firm spends 38 percent more of each employees' salary on benefits and, as company policy, pays workers even if they are absent.
    The 45 supervisors (average salary $22.21 per hour) involved in employee absenteeism problems estimate they lose 25 minutes per day for each of the 245 days per work year just dealing with the extra problems imposed by those who fail to show up for work. Finally, the company estimates it loses $229,500 in additional overtime premiums, in extra

help that must be hired, and in lost productivity from the more highly skilled absentees. As HR director for Consolidated Industries your job is to estimate the cost of employee absenteeism so that management can better understand the dimensions of the problem. (Use the worksheet provided below to record your answers.)

2. Inter-Capital, Ltd., is a 500-employee firm faced with a 3.7 percent annual absenteeism rate over the 1,960 hours that each employee is scheduled to work. About 15 percent of absentees are blue-collar (average wage $18.90 per hour), 55 percent are clerical employees (average wage $15.20 per hour), and the remainder are management and professional workers (average salary $32.50 per hour). About 40 percent more of each employee's salary is spent on benefits, but employees are not paid if they are absent from work. In the last six months, supervisors (average salary $23.95 per hour) estimate that managing absenteeism problems costs them about an hour a day for each of the 245 days per work year. It is a serious problem that must be dealt with because about 20 supervisors are directly involved with absenteeism. On top of that, the firm spends approximately $186,000 more on costs incidental to absenteeism. Temporary help and lost productivity can really cut into profits. Just how much is absenteeism costing Inter-Capital per year per employee? (Use the worksheet provided below to record your answers.)

3. As a management consultant, you have been retained to develop two alternative programs for reducing employee absenteeism at Consolidated Industries (question 1). Write a proposal that addresses the issue in specific terms. Exactly what should the firm do? (To do this, make whatever assumptions seem reasonable.)

WORKSHEET: TOTAL ESTIMATED COST OF EMPLOYEE ABSENTEEISM

Item	Consolidated Industries	Inter-Capital, Ltd.
1. Total employee-hours lost to absenteeism for the period	_____	_____
2. Weighted average wage/salary per hour per absent employee	_____	_____

3. Cost of employee benefits per hour per employee   _____   _____
4. Total compensation lost per hour per employee   _____   _____
   a. if absent workers are paid (wage/salary plus benefits)   _____   _____
   b. if absent workers are not paid (benefits only)   _____   _____
5. Total compensation lost to absent employees (total employee-hours lost × 4.a or 4.b, whichever applies)   _____   _____
6. Total supervisory hours lost on employee absenteeism   _____   _____
7. Average hourly supervisory wage, including benefits   _____   _____
8. Total supervisory salaries lost to managing problems of absenteeism (hours lost × average hourly supervisory wage—item 6 × item 7)   _____   _____
9. All other costs incidental to absenteeism not included in the above items   _____   _____
10. Total estimated cost of absenteeism— summation of items 5, 8, and 9   _____   _____
11. Total estimated cost of absenteeism per employee (total estimated costs ÷ total number of employees)   _____   _____

REFERENCES

Allan, W. (1983). No work, no pay slices Honda absenteeism. *Rocky Mountain News* (May 7), 2A.

Cascio, W. F. (1998). *Managing Human Resources: Productivity, Quality of Work Life, Profits* (5th ed.). Burr Ridge, IL: Irwin/McGraw-Hill.

Dalton, D. R., Mesch, D. J. (1991). On the extent and reduction of avoidable absenteeism: An assessment of absence policy provisions. *Journal of Applied Psychology 76*, 810–817.

Drago, R., Wooden, M. (1992). The determinants of labor absence: Economic factors and workgroup norms across countries. *Industrial and Labor Relations Review 45*, 764–778.

Establishing an absence control policy. (1980). *City and County Government 14*(Oct.), 1–4.

Harrison, D. A., Martocchio, J. J. (1998). Time for absenteeism: A 20-year review of origins, offshoots, and outcomes. *Journal of Management 24*(3), 305–350.

Johns, G. (1997). Contemporary research on absence from work: Correlates, causes, and consequences. In C. L. Cooper and L. T. Robertson (eds.), *International Review of Industrial and Organizational Psychology* (Vol. 12, pp. 115–173). New York: John Wiley & Sons.

Kuzmits, F. E. (1984). Is your organization ready for no-fault absenteeism? *Personnel Administrator 29*(12), 119–127.

Miners, I. A., Moore, M. L., Champoux, J. E., Martocchio, J. J. (1995). Time-serial substitution effects of absence control on employee time use. *Human Relations 48*(3), 307–326.

Rentsch, J. R., Steel, R. P. (1998). Testing the durability of job characteristics as predictors of absenteeism over a six-year period. *Personnel Psychology 51*, 165–190.

Schlotzhauer, D. L., Rosse, J. G. (1985). A five-year study of a positive incentive absence control program. *Personnel Psychology 38*, 575–585.

VanDerWall, S. (1998). Survey finds unscheduled absenteeism hitting seven-year high. *HR News* (Nov.), 14.

Wikstrom, W. S. (1971). *Manpower Planning: Evolving Systems*. Report No. 521. New York: Conference Board.

Yandrick, R. M. (1997). Help employees reach for the stars. *HRMagazine 42*(1), 97–100.

ENDNOTES

1. The method that follows is based on that described in F. E. Kuzmits (1979), "How Much Is Absenteeism Costing Your Organization?" *Personnel Administrator 24*(June), 29–33.
2. Such a collective bargaining strategy by unions involves concessions of gains previously won on wages and benefits. It is a fairly common

practice in situations where unions work with management to help their companies survive in the face of adverse business conditions. Subsequently, however, unions have found that such give-backs are hard to win back for their members.

The High Cost of Mismanaging Human Resources

Mismanaging people can be expensive. Failure to treat employees with respect, with dignity, and with procedures that are seen as fair by all concerned parties can lead to a host of negative outcomes. Consider direct cash payments and negative publicity, as examples. Texaco, the big producer of oil and gas, refiner, and marketer of petroleum products, learned this lesson in a painful and expensive way.

In 1994, six African-American officials in the company's finance department filed a lawsuit alleging that white men in Texaco's "good-old-boy" network secured coveted promotions and the biggest raises and treated African-Americans dismissively. Initially, Texaco believed it stood a chance of winning the case in court, but its opinion changed when audiotape transcripts of managers' belittling African-American employees' grievances became public. Texaco settled the lawsuit for $176.1 million, the largest sum ever paid in the United States to resolve such a case. That represented about 68 cents per share of Texaco stock in 1996 ("Texaco to Pay" 1996).

Although the size of the monetary payout was enormous, the impact on the way Texaco does business at every level was even larger, for the firm opened itself up to an exceptional level of outside scrutiny. As part of the settlement agreement, the company established a seven-member "equality and tolerance task force" with extraordinary powers. The task force is authorized to help shape HR policies and practices, and its recommendations are mandatory, unless Texaco can convince the federal judge supervising the settlement that to do so would be unsound business or technically unrealistic. The seven members of the task force include three members designated by Texaco, and three by the plaintiffs in the suit. The seventh member is jointly named by both sides, and serves as chairman. The overall objective of the task force is to ensure greater racial diversity within the 27,000-employee company. Said one energy-industry analyst: "It's unprecedented that external forces ... play such a strong role" ("Texaco to Pay" 1996, p. A3).

As another example, consider the results of a six-month *Business Week* investigation of Astra USA, Inc., the American arm of Swedish pharmaceutical company Astra. The investigation revealed a bizarre case of abuse of power, where a 15-year pattern of sexual harassment emanated from the president's office and worked its way down through the ranks of the organization. According to the federal Equal Employment Opportunity Commission (EEOC), Astra USA's president routinely replaced mothers and older female employees with attractive, young, single women who were pressured into having sex with company executives, including the president. The president himself was fired in 1996, accused by Astra of spending company cash on home repairs, vacations, and prostitutes. Astra then sued him for $15 million to recover costs related to the EEOC investigation (Miller 1998).

The results? Terrible publicity for the company, payments in the millions of dollars to the victims, and a 21-month prison term without parole for the president of the U.S. subsidiary (for failing to report more than $1 million in income on his federal tax returns). The firm agreed to pay almost $10 million to 79 women and one man who said he was punished for speaking out ("Lars Bildman" 1998; "Sex, Lies" 1997). Indirect costs included lowered productivity among surviving employees, poor morale, increased voluntary turnover, and difficulty in attracting new employees to work for the company. Who needs that?

The cases described above are not isolated instances. In 1993, Shoney's paid $105 million in another race-based case. Lucky Stores and State Farm Insurance settled sex discrimination suits for $107 million and $157 million, respectively (Seligman 1999). Every year, thousands of complaints of unlawful discrimination are filed with local, state, and federal enforcement agencies. In 1997 alone, the EEOC received more than 80,000 such complaints, and the number of employment lawsuits is increasing by more than 20 percent annually (Sharf & Jones, in press).

Civil rights complaints by job applicants or employees may allege unfair discrimination on the basis of age, race, ethnic group, gender, religion, or disability. What happens after a complaint is filed? As an example, consider that once it receives a complaint of discrimination, the EEOC, a main enforcement agency for civil rights complaints, follows a three-step process: investigation, voluntary reconciliation, and (if that doesn't work) litigation. In response to work-related complaints, companies do their own internal investigations, and when sued, they prepare for litigation.

Everyone knows that litigation is an expensive process, but investigation is expensive, too. Recall that Astra sued its former president for $15 million to recover costs related to a very extensive EEOC investigation. In this chapter we will identify each of the intermediate steps involved in investigating and litigating a typical civil rights complaint. Then we will attach realistic time and cost estimates to each step in the investigation–litigation process.

It has often been said that litigation is a luxury that few can afford. In this chapter we will see just how expensive that luxury really is. As a framework for analysis and discussion, consider Exhibit 4–1, a detailed breakout of the steps involved in investigating and litigating a typical civil rights complaint.

COSTS OF INVESTIGATION AND LITIGATION IN SINGLE-PLAINTIFF CASES AND COMPLEX CLASS ACTION CASES

To provide a realistic estimate of the costs involved, we will examine such costs at each step shown in Exhibit 4–1. Because there may be considerable variability in the costs incurred at each step, largely as a function of the complexity of any case at hand, we will provide two estimates of costs at each step—those associated with a single-plaintiff case, and those associated with a complex class-action case.

With respect to the size of a class-action case, consider that under the federal rules governing class actions, one of the requirements for class certification is called "numerosity." That is, the number of similarly situated plaintiffs must be so large as to make individual trials on the merits of each case impractical. Generally speaking, a class smaller than about 20–30 people would not satisfy the numerosity requirement, and thus would not qualify for certification. Although any boundaries on relative class size are admittedly arbitrary, a class considered "small" generally comprises roughly 30 to 100 people. A "medium-sized" class may include from about 100 to several thousand individuals, and a

EXHIBIT 4-1   *General Civil Rights Complaint Process Example*

Step 1—Complaint filed: analysis and investigation
a. Establish a contract with outside counsel
b. Interview and investigate (two hours per witness; background research —eight hours)
c. Background research of the applicable law—three hours
d. Find relevant documents (time to locate, copy, and organize—roughly eight hours per 1,000 pages)
e. Enlargement of time to answer in response to plaintiff's original complaint (beyond the 20 days allowed by federal rules)
f. Responsive pleadings—either provide answers to plaintiff's original complaint (three to four hours), or file a motion to dismiss (the case)— eight hours for preparation of motion plus four additional hours for a reply to plaintiff's opposition to the motion to dismiss
g. File answer to complaint with court and serve opposing party/counsel (one hour at courthouse filing room plus travel time)

Step 2—Conduct discovery conference with opposing counsel; work out pretrial order with the judge.
This step includes a review of rules of civil procedure, discussions with opposing counsel to attempt a mutual agreement without having to see the judge, and preparing agreements or preparing for a hearing in front of the judge or magistrate (who may deal with discovery issues in complex cases) —eight hours

Step 3—Written discovery
a. Prepare interrogatories—three hours
b. Prepare request for production of documents—three hours
c. Prepare request for admissions of fact—three hours
d. Answer interrogatories and request from opposing party for admissions of fact (you have 30 days to respond from the date you were served with the interrogatories and request for admissions)—four hours to write; excludes investigation time
e. Answer request from opposing party for production of documents (you have 30 days to respond from the date you were served with the request)—two hours
f. Resolve discovery disputes with plaintiff over failure to answer discovery (may include filing with the court a motion to compel complete answers to interrogatories or production of documents)—four hours

Step 4—Depositions
a. Preparation and taking of depositions—20 hours each. A single-plaintiff case typically includes depositions of the plaintiff plus key employees

(continued)

EXHIBIT 4-1 *Continued*

such as co-workers, the HR manager, the accused individual, and his or her immediate supervisor

b. Review and summarize depositions—five hours each
c. Court reporter and transcription service—$2.50 per page multiplied by six hours per day, roughly $800 per day per deposition

Step 5—Pretrial dispositive motions

a. Motion for summary judgment—Either side can move for summary judgment. Such a motion can be filed with respect to a specific issue ("partial summary judgment") or to the entire case. The motion includes a statement of the undisputed facts in the case (if the parties agree) or the facts as the moving party presents them (time estimate: 16 hours to write the motion plus 8 additional hours for a reply to plaintiff's opposition, assuming you are the moving party)
b. Legal Research—20 hours per issue in the preparation of each motion (for example, review case law on similar issues and previous rulings by judges in the same jurisdiction to determine the nature of their decisions)

Step 6—In cases involving class action, plaintiff files a motion for class certification and defendant responds

a. Opposing certification may involve contracting and working with expert(s), and conducting certification-related discovery—assume that each expert charges an average of $200 per hour for his or her services
b. Research and write a brief in opposition to class certification—25 hours minimum

Step 7—Prepare jury instructions—eight hours

Step 8—Prepare pretrial brief and trial book—60 hours

Step 9—Witness preparation—eight hours each
Preparation of key or primary witness—20 hours each

Step 10—Preparation of exhibits—10 hours

Step 11—The trial itself—for a complex class action, two to three weeks; attorney time charged at 14–16 hours per day, seven days per week. In a case involving an individual plaintiff, allow two days for the trial.

Step 12—Settlement negotiations/settlement—four to eight business days

Additional related costs—court reporter—$2.50 per page multiplied by six hours per day, roughly $800 per day; 15-day trial = $12,000 in transcription costs

All of these costs are incurred *prior* to the jury's verdict; they do not include any costs associated with appeals; and they assume that your side wins.

"large-sized" class may include many more than that. In a product-liability case, involving an allegation of defective brakes on an automobile, for example, the class could include hundreds of thousands of potential plaintiffs. Likewise a lawsuit involving shareholders of a large corporation could include hundreds of thousands of potential plaintiffs.

Step 1a

For the single-plaintiff case, let us say it is a lawsuit over alleged sexual harassment. The contract for outside counsel will include pay at $120 per hour for a junior associate (who will do legal research and draft briefs) and $250 an hour for a partner (who will oversee the work of the associate and argue on behalf of the company at trial).

For purposes of our class-action example, let us consider a class of 75 people suing over alleged age discrimination in layoffs. The company in question receives a complaint from the plaintiff's lawyer and, after a brief analysis and investigation, contracts with outside counsel to handle the case. The outside counsel's firm is a moderate-sized midwestern law firm that charges $120 an hour for junior associate lawyers, $150 an hour for senior associate lawyers, and $250 an hour for partners. Established law firms in major cities typically charge more for their services, but the rates presented here are intended to be both representative and conservative. For the class-action lawsuit, assume that the contract is for two associates (average billing rate: $135 per hour), plus a partner.

Step 1b

For the single-plaintiff case, assume that the associate interviews six witnesses (two hours each), and conducts eight hours of background research. The total cost is 20 hours multiplied by $120 per hour, or $2,400.

For the class-action lawsuit, assume that the associates interview 20 witnesses (two hours each) and conduct 12 hours of background research. The total cost is 40 hours + 12 hours = 52 hours multiplied by $135 per hour, or $7,020.

Step 1c

For the single-plaintiff case, background research of the applicable law takes three hours, at a (3 × $120) cost of $360. For the class action, background research of the applicable law takes five hours, at a (5 × $135) cost of $675.

Step 1d

Locating, copying, and organizing relevant documents takes approximately 4 hours (at $120 per hour) for the single-plaintiff case, and approximately 12 hours (at $135 per hour) for the class action. Those costs are, therefore, $400 and $1,620, respectively.

Step 1e

For the single-plaintiff case, the firm's outside counsel is able to answer the plaintiff's complaint within the 20 days allowed by federal rules. For the class action, however, outside counsel requests an additional 30 days to respond to the plaintiff's complaint. Time to prepare and file the request: 1.5 hours, at a (1.5 × $135) cost of $202.50.

Step 1f

For the single plaintiff case, the firm's outside counsel files a motion to dismiss (the case), which requires eight hours for preparation of motion (six hours for the associate and two hours for the partner) for a ($720 + $500) cost of $1,220. Plaintiff's counsel then files a motion in opposition to the motion to dismiss, and defendant firm's counsel spends four additional hours working on a reply. The cost of the reply is three associate hours plus one partner hour, or $610. The total cost for this phase of Step 1f is $1,830.

As in the single-plaintiff case, the firm's outside counsel for the class action also files a motion to dismiss (the case), which requires eight hours for preparation of motion (six hours for the associates and two hours for the partner)—for a ($810 + $500) cost of $1,310. Plaintiff's counsel then files a motion in opposition to the motion to dismiss, and defendant firm's counsel spends four additional hours working on a reply. The cost of the reply is three associate hours plus one partner hour, or $655. The total cost for this phase of Step 1f is $1,965.

The judges assigned to each case deny each of the motions to dismiss. It then becomes necessary to provide answers to the plaintiff's original complaint. For the single-plaintiff case, outside counsel requires four hours for this (three hours by the associate and one hour by the partner), at a cost of $610 [(3 × $120) + $250]. For the class action, it takes eight hours to complete the responsive pleadings (six hours by the associates and two hours by the partner), at a ($810 + $500) total cost of $1,310.

Step 1g—Filing the Complaint

To file an answer to the plaintiff's original complaint with the court and to deliver answers to the opposing counsel, an associate spends 0.5 hours in transit plus one hour at the courthouse filing room, for a total of 1.5 hours. For the single-plaintiff case, this cost is $180 ($120 × 1.5). For the class-action case, the cost is $202.50 ($135 × 1.5).

Step 2—Conferring on Discovery and Working Out the Pretrial Order with the Judge

Assume that in both the single-plaintiff case and class-action suits, the opposing parties are able to arrive at a mutual agreement without having to see the judge. They, therefore, prepare agreements to submit to the court. For the single-plaintiff case, outside counsel spends a total of eight hours on this process—five hours by the associate and three hours by the partner, for a total cost of $1,350 ($600 + $750). For the class action, counsel spends a total of 10 hours on the process—7 hours by the associates and 3 hours by the partner, for a total cost of $1,695 ($945 + $750).

Steps 3a, b, and c—Written Discovery

For the single-plaintiff case as well as for the class action, outside counsel spends a total of nine hours preparing interrogatories (three hours), requests for production of documents (three hours), admissions of fact (three hours). All of this work is done by the associates at a ($120 × 9) cost of $1,080 for the single-plaintiff case, and ($135 × 9) $1,215 for the class-action lawsuit.

Step 3d

Answering interrogatories and responding to the request from the opposing party for admissions of fact take four hours of writing time by the associate plus one hour of review by the partner. Additional time is required to conduct an investigation in order to generate answers. All investigation is done by associates. For the single-plaintiff case, assume that counsel must answer a total of 20 interrogatories. On average, each requires 1.5 hours to investigate, for a total of 30 hours. The total cost of investigation and writing for this phase of the case is [(4 × $120) + $250 + (30 × $120)], or $4,330.

For the class action, assume that counsel must answer a total of 50 interrogatories. On average, each requires 1.5 hours to investigate, for a total of 75 hours. Writing time adds another 10 hours of associates' time, plus 2 hours of review by the partner. The total cost of investigation and writing for this phase of the case is $[(10 \times \$135) + (2 \times \$250) + (75 \times \$135)]$, or $11,975.

Step 3e

To answer the request from the opposing party for production of documents takes two hours of writing time by the associate plus one hour of the partner's time. To copy, organize, and actually produce the documents requires an additional three hours of the associate's time. For the single-plaintiff case, the cost is $[(5 \times \$120) + \$250]$, or $850. For the class action, because the request for production of documents is more extensive, it takes three hours of writing time by the associates plus one hour of the partner's time. To copy, organize, and actually produce the documents requires an additional five hours of the associates' time. For the class action, the cost is $[(8 \times \$135) + \$250]$, or $1,330.

Step 3f

Discovery disputes with the counsel for the single plaintiff consume four hours of the associate's time, at a cost of $(4 \times \$120)$, or $480. Assume, however, that for the class action, resolution of discovery disputes with the counsel for the class occurs only after filing with the court a motion to compel complete answers to interrogatories. All of this takes eight hours of the associates' time and two hours of the partner's time, for a total cost of $[(8 \times \$135) + (2 \times \$250)]$, or $1,580.

Step 4a—Depositions

For the single-plaintiff case, assume that the following people are deposed: the plaintiff, two co-workers, the HR manager, the individual accused of sexual harassment, and his or her immediate supervisor. To prepare and take each deposition requires a total of 20 hours of the associate's time. The total cost is $(6 \times 20 \times \$120)$, or $14,400.

For the class-action case, however, assume that a total of 14 named plaintiffs are deposed, the HR manager, 10 supervisors, and the plaintiff's expert witness. To prepare and take each deposition requires a total of 20 hours of the associates' time. However, the partner deposes the plaintiff's expert, and bills 20 hours' time for doing so. The cost is $(26 \times 20 \times \$135)$, or $70,200, for the associate, and $(20 \times \$250)$, or $5,000 for the partner, yielding a total cost of $75,200.

Step 4b

Because it takes an average of five hours each to review and summarize depositions, the cost for the single-plaintiff case is (6 × 5 × $120), or $3,600. For the class action, however, the total cost is [(26 × 5 × $135) + (5 × $250)], or $18,800.

Step 4c

The final cost associated with depositions is the cost of the court reporter and transcription service. Assume that, on average, each deposition requires one full day to complete (some will take less time, but others will take longer). For the single-plaintiff case, the cost for this service (roughly $800 per day per deposition) is (6 × $800), or $4,800. For the class-action case, however, the cost is (27 × $800), or $21,600.

Step 5a—Pretrial Dispositive Motions

For the single-plaintiff case, the plaintiff files a motion for summary judgment. Counsel for the defendant firm then writes a response in opposition to the motion. Total time includes six hours for the associate and two hours for the partner, at a cost of [(6 × $120) + (2 × $250)], or $1,220. Subsequently, the motion is denied by the judge assigned to hear the case. The case is going to trial.

For the class action, the defendant firm files a motion for summary judgment (12 hours of associates' time plus 4 hours of the partner's time). The plaintiff prepares a response in opposition to the motion, and the defendant firm then spends eight additional hours to prepare a reply to the plaintiff's opposition (six hours for the associates and two hours for the partner). The total cost is [(18 × $135) + (6 × $250)], or $3,930. Subsequently, the motion is denied by the judge assigned to hear the case. This case, also, is going to trial.

Step 5b

For the single-plaintiff case, assume that there are only two major issues that require legal research. All research is done by the associate, at 20 hours per issue. The total cost of the legal research is (40 × $120), or $4,800. For the class action, however, assume that there are four major issues that require legal research. All research is done by the associates, at 20 hours per issue. The total cost of the legal research for this phase of the case is (80 × $135), or $10,800.

Step 6a—Certifying a Class

To oppose the plaintiff's motion in the class action, the defendant firm's counsel contracts with three outside experts—an economist, an industrial/organizational psychologist, and a statistician. Each expert is hired to do two things: work with counsel to provide information in opposition to class certification, and conduct studies related to class certification. Providing information in opposition to class certification may involve writing an affidavit or expert report. Assume that each expert spends 25 hours preparing his or her affidavit or expert report. The total cost for three experts is (3 × 25 × $200), or $15,000.

Experts also conduct studies related to class certification. Assume that each expert spends another 60 hours researching and preparing a report on his or her study. The total cost for the three reports is (3 × 60 × $200), or $36,000.

Step 6b

Outside counsel spends 35 hours researching and writing a brief in opposition to class certification. Of these 35 hours, the associates spend 30 hours (30 × $135) and the partner spends 5 hours (5 × $250), for a total cost of $5,300 ($4,050 + $1,250).

Step 7—Preparation of Jury Instructions

For the single-plaintiff case, as well as for the class action, counsel spends eight hours (six by the associates and two by the partner) preparing instructions for the jury who will decide the outcome of the trial. For the single-plaintiff case, the cost is $1,220; for the class action, the cost is $1,310.

Step 8—Preparation of a Pretrial Brief and Trial Book

Because we are moving into the trial phase of the case, the partner will take a more active role in all remaining phases. To prepare a pretrial brief and trial book in the single-plaintiff case, counsel will spend 60 hours—30 by the associate and 30 by the partner—for a total cost of [(30 × $120) + (30 × $250)], or $11,100. For the class-action case, counsel will spend 80 hours preparing a pretrial brief and trial book—40 by the associates and 40 by the partner—for a total cost of [(40 × $135) + (40 × $250)], or $15,400.

Step 9—Witness Preparation

Assume that for the single-plaintiff case, the firm's counsel plans to call six witnesses, of whom three are key witnesses. To prepare these witnesses to testify, counsel spends eight hours with each of the non-key witnesses and 20 hours with each of the key witnesses. Half of this time is spent by the associate and half by the partner. For the non-key witnesses the cost is [(12 × $120) + (12 × $250)], or $4,440; for the key witnesses it is [(30 × $120) + (30 × $250)], or $11,100. The total cost of witness preparation for the single-plaintiff case is $15,540.

For the class-action case, the firm's counsel plans to call 16 witnesses, of whom 8 are key witnesses. To prepare these witnesses to testify, counsel spends 8 hours with each of the non-key witnesses and 20 hours with each of the key witnesses. Half of that time is spent by the associate and half by the partner. For the non-key witnesses the cost is [(32 × $135) + (32 × $250)], or $12,320; for the key witnesses it is [(80 × $135) + (80 × $250)], or $30,800. The total cost of witness preparation for the class-action case is $43,120.

Step 10—Preparation of Exhibits

For the single-plaintiff case, the associate spends 10 hours preparing exhibits to be introduced at trial. The cost (10 × $120) is $1,200. For the class action, the associates spend 20 hours preparing exhibits. The cost (20 × $135) is $2,700.

Step 11—Trial

For the single-plaintiff case, the trial takes two full days (eight hours per day), and both the associate and the partner are present in the courtroom. The two attorneys spend an additional 14 hours on trial-related work outside of the courtroom. The total cost of the attorneys' time is [(30 × $120) + (30 × $250)], or $11,100.

For the class-action case, the trial takes 15 days (eight hours per day). Both associates and the partner are present in the courtroom, and each bills his or her time at 14 hours per day for 19 days (two weekends included). The cost of the attorney's time is [(14 × 19 × $135 × 2) + (14 × 19 × $250)], or $138,320. In addition, each of the three experts is paid for his or her time during trial. Assume that each expert incurs 12 hours' time, for a (3 × 12 × $200) total cost of $7,200.

Step 12—Settlement Negotiations

For the single-plaintiff case, assume that the associate and the partner each spend a total of four 8-hour days trying to work out the terms of a settlement. That cost is [(4 × 8 × $120) + (4 × 8 × $250)], or $11,840. Ultimately, the settlement negotiations prove futile. Both sides await the jury's verdict.

For the class-action case, assume that the two associates and the partner each spend a total of six 8-hour days trying to work out the terms of a settlement. That cost is [(6 × 8 × $135 × 2) + (6 × 8 × $250)], or $24,960. Ultimately, these settlement negotiations also prove futile. Both sides await the jury's verdict.

Additional Related Costs

For the single-plaintiff case, the cost of a court reporter is two days at $800 per day, or $1,600. For the class action, the cost of a court reporter is 15 days at $800 per day, or $12,000.

Just how much do investigation and litigation cost? Let us tally the costs for each type of case. Results are shown in Exhibit 4–2. After examining those numbers, you can understand why investigation and litigation are so expensive, especially in class actions. And those costs are incurred *before* the jury reaches a verdict. If proceedings get that far, you had better hope that you win because when the plaintiff wins, juries tend to award large sums. Consider this: the average jury award over the seven-year period from 1988 to 1995 was about $250,000 for a claim of race or sex discrimination, $300,000 for age discrimination, $400,000 for sexual harassment, and $500,000 for breach of contract or tort claims under common law (for example, challenges to layoff decisions or to nonpromotion decisions) (Copus 1996). Not only are those costs high, but firms that lose discrimination suits also pay a penalty in the marketplace with respect to the price of their stock, as we will discuss below.

ECONOMIC GAINS AND LOSSES ASSOCIATED WITH THE EFFECTIVE AND INEFFECTIVE MANAGEMENT OF DIVERSITY

Only human and organizational resources, not physical resources, can provide a firm with a sustained competitive advantage (Pfeffer 1994; Lado, Boyd, & Wright 1992). In the past, executives in all firms found

EXHIBIT 4-2   *Sample Cost of Investigation–Litigation*

Step	Single Plaintiff ($)	Class Action ($)
1b	2,400.00	7,020.00
1c	360.00	675.00
1d	480.00	1,620.00
1e	—	202.50
1f	1,830.00	1,965.00
	610.00	1,310.00
1g	180.00	202.50
2	1,350.00	1,695.00
3a,b,c	1,080.00	1,215.00
3d	4,330.00	11,975.00
3e	850.00	1,330.00
3f	480.00	1,580.00
4a	14,400.00	75,200.00
4b	3,600.00	18,800.00
4c	4,800.00	21,600.00
5a	1,220.00	3,930.00
5b	4,800.00	10,800.00
6a	—	51,000.00
6b	—	5,300.00
7	1,220.00	1,310.00
8	11,100.00	15,400.00
9	15,540.00	43,120.00
10	1,200.00	2,700.00
11	11,100.00	145,520.00
12	11,840.00	24,960.00
Additional costs	1,600.00	12,000.00
Totals	96,370.00	462,430.00

similar human resources to manage, for the average worker was a white man with a wife and children at home (Jamieson & O'Mara 1991). More recently, the American workforce has become increasingly diverse. To appreciate this, consider the following facts:

- More than half the U.S. workforce now consists of racial (that is, non-white) and ethnic (that is, groups of people classified according to common traits and customs) minorities, immigrants, and women (Judy & D'Amico 1997).
- White, native-born males, although still numerically dominant in the workforce, are themselves a statistical minority (Kaufman 1996).

- Women will fill almost two-thirds of the new jobs created between 1990 and 2000, and by 2005, projections indicate that 6 in 10 new workers will be female ("Affirmative Action" 1995).
- The so-called mainstream is now almost as diverse as the society at large. Today more than 20 million Americans were born in another country ("The New Face of America" 1993).
- White males will make up only 15 percent of the increase in the workforce over the next decade, and about 40 percent of the workforce will be over 45 years of age— a dramatic jump from 31 percent today (Judy & D'Amico 1997; Labich 1996).

Those demographic facts do not indicate that a diverse workforce is something a company ought to have, but what all companies do have or soon will have. In view of such workforce changes, it seems reasonable to ask whether there are economic gains associated with the effective management of diversity, and whether there are economic losses associated with unlawful discrimination.

On the surface, it appears that the answer to both questions is yes for the following reasons. Firms with high-quality programs for managing diversity may have lower absenteeism, turnover, and job dissatisfaction in their workforces, and thus lower operating costs (Schwartz 1989). In addition, firms with such programs may enhance their reputations with potential customers. Just as women and minority-group members may prefer to work for companies that value diversity, they may likewise choose to purchase goods and services from those firms (Cox & Blake 1991). In the aggregate, such firms may be more creative, may have better problem-solving capabilities, and may find strong community and institutional support because of their cultivated diverse workforces. Thus they may be more capable of distinguishing themselves from their competitors. Changes in their stock prices should be significant and positive.

Conversely, firms with discriminatory employment practices will find fewer people to recruit among because the pool of white men is decreasing (Judy & D'Amico 1997). Because of public disclosure of the names of firms that discriminate unlawfully, few if any talented women or minority-group members will apply for jobs in those companies (Cox & Blake 1991). Likewise, the cost structure of firms with discriminatory employment practices will probably be higher, not only because they tend to have high absenteeism, turnover, and job dissatisfaction, but also because the probability is high that they will face costly legal actions. Moreover, their customer bases may shrink because most buyers are women and minority-group members (Cox & Blake 1991). Finally, such firms are less likely to find community and institutional support, as the members of the institutions interacting with them and of the broader community are increasingly women and minorities. As a result, such firms may not only be less efficient, but also less likely to be able to distinguish themselves from their competitors. Changes in their stock prices should be significant and negative.

Event-Study Methodology

To examine the impacts of exemplary diversity programs and damage awards for discriminations suits, Wright, Ferris, Hiller, and Kroll (1995) used event-study methodology that is common in financial economics research. The essence of this approach is to determine if there is a significant change in the price of a firm's stock on the days immediately surrounding the announcement of an event of interest. In their study, the events of interest were the U.S. Department of Labor's Exemplary Voluntary Efforts Award (to recognize firms with high-quality diversity programs), from 1986 to 1992, and announcements found in *The Wall Street Journal Index* and the Dow Jones News Retrieval Service, of major settlements by firms found to be guilty of unlawful discrimination in employment. Exact dates were available for each of these events. Wright et al. scanned the *Index* and the Dow Jones News Retrieval Service for 90 days before and after each event. To prevent bias in the empirical findings as a result of other economically relevant events that investors might respond to, Wright et al. dropped firms reporting other events from their sample. The final sample consisted of 34 award-winning firms representing a variety of businesses and 35 firms that had been found guilty of discriminatory practices.

Analysis and Results

Application of the event-study method focuses on the pattern of daily stock rates occurring over a period surrounding an event, in this case, 10 days before and 10 days after the announcement of the event. Generally, the impact on shareholder wealth is focused on the actual event-day itself because investors are quick to respond to events that contain information relevant to a firm's future financial performance. Examining the surrounding period allows a researcher to determine if there is evidence of information leakage prior to the event or a lingering effect in the postevent period (Wright et al. 1995).

The actual daily rates of return on a firm's stock are adjusted for expected rates of return, which are estimated through the use of an empirical model called the capital asset pricing model (CAPM) (Brown & Warner 1985). The assumption underlying the CAPM is that high rates of expected return compensate investors for bearing high risk. The model makes an important distinction between systematic and unsystematic risk. Only systematic risk, which is market-wide and therefore not able to be diversified, is rewarded in the capital markets. A firm's measure of its systematic risk is its beta coefficient. Unsystematic risk is not rewarded because its effects can be dispersed through the construction of a portfolio of securities.

Wright et al. (1995) estimated a stock's expected return on a given day as follows:

$$\text{Expected return} = \text{risk-free return} + \text{beta} \times (\text{market return} - \text{risk-free return})$$

where expected return = the expected daily rate of return for the stock; risk-free return = the return on an asset with no risk, such as a U.S. government bond; beta = a measure of a firm's systematic risk; and market return = the expected return on the market portfolio for that day.

The expected return incorporates the impact of market-wide or macro-economic factors such as the gross national product, unemployment, and interest rates. The expected return is subtracted from the actual return to obtain what is known as the excess return (the outcome of interest in the study). The excess rate of return controls for systematic influences on the level of stock returns that could distort the estimate of the rate of return attributable to firm-specific performance.

For each day in the period of analysis, known as the event window, Wright et al. (1995) calculated a firm-specific excess return. They then averaged the excess returns of the firms in each sample to obtain mean daily excess returns and reported results both on a daily basis and on a cumulative basis.

Results For Award-Winning Firms

Exhibit 4–3 shows the results of the event study for the winners of U.S. Department of Labor awards. Column 3 of the exhibit shows the results of statistical tests ("*t*"). Those results indicate that in the period preceding the announcement of the awards, the excess returns are not statistically significant. The variations in these excess returns are random fluctuations, driven by chance rather than by economic factors. There

EXHIBIT 4–3   *Results of Event-Study Analysis for Award Winners*

Day	Daily Percentage Residual Rates of Return	t	Cumulative Daily Percentage Residual Rates of Return	t
-10	0.012	1.069	0.012	1.069
-9	0.025	1.053	0.037	1.408
-8	0.033	0.401	0.070	0.810
-7	-0.012	-0.084	0.058	-0.347
-6	0.016	1.346	0.074	0.442
-5	0.003	0.834	0.077	0.460
-4	0.010	1.013	0.087	0.518
-3	0.025	0.819	0.112	0.657
-2	0.073	1.101	0.185	1.011
-1	0.014	1.342	0.199	1.086
0	0.467	1.892*	0.666	1.866*
1	0.502	2.207†	1.168	2.101†
2	0.022	1.083	1.190	1.643
3	-0.054	-1.389	1.136	1.555
4	0.013	1.109	1.149	1.372
5	-0.020	-1.434	1.129	1.561
6	0.031	1.011	1.160	0.842
7	-0.012	-0.989	1.148	0.933
8	0.045	0.763	1.193	0.671
9	-0.024	-1.024	1.169	0.771
10	0.013	0.827	1.182	1.543

* $p < 0.10$.
† $p < 0.05$.

Source: Wright, P., Ferris, S. P., Hiller, J. S., Kroll, M. (1995). Competitiveness through management of diversity: Effects on stock price valuation. *Academy of Management Journal 38*, 282. Used with permission.

appears to have been no leakage of the names of the Department's selectees, and the market was unable to anticipate the likely winners.

For the announcement day itself (day 0), however, there is a mean excess return of 0.467 percent (see Exhibit 4–3, column 2). The *t*-statistic indicates that the likelihood of obtaining a residual value of this size purely by chance is less than 10 percent. A more significant effect is present on the day following the announcements (day +1). This increase probably occurred because the Department of Labor often announces the award winners late in the afternoon. As a result, investors are unable to capitalize completely on the information on the day of the announcement. As the *t*-statistic for day +1 in Exhibit 4–3 indicates, the likelihood of obtaining an excess return of 0.502 percent on that day is less than 5 percent. For the remaining nine days following an announcement, the excess rates of return again vary insignificantly.

The results for the cumulative excess returns further confirm the daily residual returns. Taken together, these results indicate that announcements of awards for the exemplary management of diversity are associated with significant and positive excess returns, which represent the capitalization of positive information concerning improved business prospects (Wright et al. 1995).

Results for Firms Agreeing to Damage Settlements for Unlawful Discrimination

Exhibit 4–4 shows the results of the event study for the discriminatory firms. Column 3 of the exhibit (labeled "t") indicates that in the period preceding the announcement of a damage settlement, the excess returns vary without statistical significance. On the day of an announcement (day 0), however, there is a significant, negative, excess return of –0.372 percent (see column 2). The t-statistic indicates that the probability of obtaining a residual of this size by chance alone is less than 5 percent. Actually, the full effect of the settlement announcements is not fully realized on the day of the announcement. However, on the day following an announcement (day +1) there is another significant loss (–0.098 percent). This effect may be the result of late reporting of some of the settlement announcements.

For the remaining days, the daily excess rates of return again vary randomly, and the results for the cumulative excess returns further confirm the results. Taken together, those results suggest that announcements of discrimination settlements are associated with significant and negative stock price changes, which represent the capitalization of negative economic implications associated with discriminatory corporate practices (Wright et al. 1995).

In the aggregate, what do these results tell us? They tell us that firms in every industry should take special measures to ensure that bias (by age, race, gender, ethnicity, disability, or any other characteristic) does not influence employment-related decisions. Such bias not only is morally and ethically wrong, but the results of this study suggest that it does not make economic sense. The cost of mismanaging human resources is very high. Conversely, America's workforce diversity can be a source of competitive advantage for firms that capitalize on it. It can be an advantage relative to domestic firms that discriminate unlawfully,

EXHIBIT 4-4   *Results of Event-Study Analysis for Discriminatory Firms*

Day	Daily Percentage Residual Rates of Return	t	Cumulative Daily Percentage Residual Rates of Return	t
-10	0.024	0.989	0.024	0.989
-9	0.008	0.575	0.032	1.143
-8	-0.012	-1.143	0.020	0.669
-7	-0.017	-0.765	0.003	0.805
-6	0.037	1.243	0.040	1.020
-5	0.019	1.549	0.059	1.162
-4	0.038	1.178	0.097	1.468
-3	0.053	0.997	0.150	1.089
-2	-0.002	-1.249	0.148	1.086
-1	0.001	0.874	0.149	1.107
0	-0.372	-2.122†	-0.223	-2.462†
1	-0.098	-1.874*	-0.321	-2.214*
2	0.010	1.666	-0.311	-1.466
3	0.024	1.539	-0.287	-1.321
4	-0.017	-1.272	-0.304	-0.927
5	0.063	0.843	-0.241	-0.781
6	0.047	0.849	-0.194	-1.274
7	0.033	0.771	-0.161	-1.341
8	0.029	1.217	-0.132	-0.986
9	-0.076	-1.098	-0.208	-0.979
10	0.034	1.293	0.174	-1.124

* $p < 0.10$.
† $p < 0.05$.

Source: Wright, P., Ferris, S. P., Hiller, J. S., Kroll, M. (1995). Competitiveness through management of diversity: Effects on stock price valuation. *Academy of Management Journal 38,* 283. Used with permission.

and also relative to foreign firms for whom the concept makes little sense in the context of their own cultures (Fernandez 1993).

EXERCISES

1. Your securities brokerage firm has just received a complaint alleging unfair discrimination on the basis of gender in promotion actions. The plaintiff's lawyer is seeking to certify a class of 65 women who, over a five-year period, did not receive promotions for which he claims they were qualified. Use Exhibit 4–1 to assess the cost of litigating the

complaint, assuming the following information to be accurate. Your firm decides to contract with outside counsel to handle the case. The firm in question is a moderate-sized law firm that charges $125 an hour for junior associate lawyers, $175 an hour for senior associate lawyers, and $250 an hour for partners. Two associates (average billing rate: $150 per hour) and a partner will handle your case.

The associates plan to interview 25 witnesses (2 hours each) and conduct 14 hours of background research. Researching the background of the applicable law takes seven hours. Locating, copying, and organizing relevant documents takes approximately 15 hours (at $150 per hour). Outside counsel requests an additional 30 days to respond to the plaintiff's complaint. The associates take 1.5 hours to prepare and file the request at an average cost of $150 per hour. Your firm's outside counsel files a motion to dismiss (the case) that requires eight hours to prepare (six hours for the associates and two hours for the partner). Plaintiff's counsel then files a motion in opposition to the motion to dismiss, and your counsel spends five additional hours working on a reply (3.5 associate hours at an average billing rate of $150 plus 1.5 partner hours).

The judge assigned to the case denies the motion to dismiss, so it becomes necessary to provide answers to the plaintiff's original complaint. Your firm's outside counsel requires seven hours to complete the responsive pleadings (five hours by the associates at an average billing rate of $150, and two hours by the partner). In order to file with the court an answer to the plaintiff's original complaint and to deliver answers to the opposing counsel, the junior associate spends 0.5 hours in transit plus one hour at the courthouse filing room.

With respect to the rules that will guide discovery, the opposing parties are able to arrive at an agreement without seeing the judge, so they prepare agreements to submit to the court. Outside counsel spends a total of 11 hours on the process—7.5 hours by the associates and 3.5 hours by the partner. Counsel also spends a total of 10 hours preparing interrogatories (four hours), requests for production of documents (three hours), and admissions of fact (three hours). All of that work is done by the associates. To answer interrogatories and to respond to the request from the opposing party for admissions of fact takes four hours of writing time by the associate plus one hour of review by the partner. Additional time is required to conduct an investigation in order to generate answers. All investigation is done by associates. Counsel also must answer a total of 48 interrogatories. On average, each requires 1.5 hours to investigate, for a total of 72 hours. To answer the request from the opposing party for production of documents takes four hours of writing time by the associates plus 1.5 hours of the partner's time. To copy, organize, and actually produce the documents requires an additional 6.5 hours of the associates' time. In addition, resolution of discovery disputes with opposing counsel takes three hours of the senior associate's time, and 1.5 hours of the partner's time.

Twelve named plaintiffs are deposed, along with the HR manager, 10 supervisors, and the plaintiff's expert witness. To prepare and take each deposition requires a total of 18 hours of the associates' time. However, the partner deposes the plaintiff's expert and bills 21 hours' time for doing so. It takes an additional five hours each to review and summarize depositions. Reviews and summaries are done by the individuals who take the depositions. Court reporting and transcription services cost $800 per day per deposition, and each deposition requires one full day to complete.

Your counsel files a motion for summary judgment (10 hours of associates' time plus 3 hours of the partner's time). The plaintiff prepares a response in opposition to the motion, and your counsel then spends eight additional hours preparing a reply to the plaintiff's opposition (six hours for the associates and two hours for the partner). Subsequently, your motion is denied by the judge assigned to hear the case. This case is also going to trial.

There are three major issues that require legal research. All research is done by the associates, at 23 hours per issue. After receiving the plaintiff's motion for class certification, your counsel contracts with three outside experts, each of whom will address one of the three major legal issues in the case, at a cost of $225 per hour per expert. Each expert spends 25 hours preparing an affidavit or expert report, and another 60 hours researching and preparing a report on his or her study. Your counsel then spends 30 hours researching and writing a brief in opposition to class certification. Of those 30 hours, the associates spend 25 and the partner spends 5 hours.

Your counsel spends an additional seven hours (five by the associates and two by the partner) preparing instructions for the jury who will decide the outcome of the trial and another 75 hours preparing a pretrial brief and trial book (40 hours by the associates and 35 by the partner). They plan to call 15 witnesses, of whom 7 are key witnesses. To prepare those witnesses to testify, counsel spends 8 hours with each of the non-key witnesses and 20 hours with each of the others, half of which time is spent by the associates and half by the partner. The two associates also spend 17 hours preparing exhibits. The trial itself takes 12 days (eight hours per day). Both associates and the partner are present in the courtroom, and each bills his or her time at 14 hours per day for 16 days (two weekends included). In addition, each of the three experts incurs 12 hours' time during trial, for which he or she is paid. The court reporter's services cost $800 per day for each day of the trial.

As a final matter, the two associates and the partner each spend a total of five 8-hour days trying to work out the terms of a settlement. Ultimately, those negotiations prove futile, and both sides await the jury's verdict. What is the total cost of the litigation process?

2. How have demographic changes altered the composition of the American workforce? Why is it in an organization's best interest to manage a diverse workforce effectively?

REFERENCES

Affirmative action on the edge. (1995). *U.S. News & World Report* (Feb. 13), 33–47.

Brown, S. J., Warner, J. B. (1985). Using daily stock returns: The case of event studies. *Journal of Financial Economics 14*, 3–31.

Copus, D. (1996). *Employment Law 101 Deskbook*. Larkspur, CA: National Employment Law Institute.

Cox, T. H., Blake, S. (1991). Managing cultural diversity: Implications for organizational competitiveness. *Academy of Management Executive 5*(3), 45–56.

Fernandez, J. P. (1993). *The Diversity Advantage: How American Business Can Outperform European and Japanese Companies in the Global Marketplace*. New York: Lexington Books.

Jamieson, D., O'Mara, J. (1991). *Managing Workforce 2000: Gaining the Diversity Advantage*. San Francisco: Jossey-Bass.

Judy, R. W., D'Amico, C. (1997). *Workforce 2020: Work and Workers in the Twenty-first Century*. Indianapolis, IN: Hudson Institute.

Kaufman, J. (1996). Mood swing: White men shake off that losing feeling on affirmative action. *The Wall Street Journal* (Sept. 5), A1, A4.

Labich, K. (1996). Making diversity pay. *Fortune* (Sept. 9), 177–180.

Lado, A. A., Boyd, N. G., Wright, P. (1992). A competency-based model of sustained competitive advantage: Toward a conceptual integration. *Journal of Management 18,* 77–91.

Lars Bildman: Go directly to jail. (1998). *Business Week* (Feb. 9), 48.

Miller, L. (1998). Workers' sex suit settled: Harassment claim nets $9.85 million. *The Wall Street Journal* (Feb. 6), A3.

Pfeffer, J. (1994). *Competitive Advantage Through People.* Boston: Harvard Business School Press.

Schwartz, F. (1989). Management women and the new facts of life. *Harvard Business Review 67*(1), 65–76.

Seligman, D. (1999). What's your job-bias liability? *Forbes 163*(Feb. 8), 90–91.

Sex, lies, and home improvements? (1997). *Business Week* (Mar. 31), 40.

Sharf, J. C., Jones, D. P. (in press). Employment risk management. In J. Kehoe, (ed.), *Managing Selection in Today's Organizations.* San Francisco: Jossey-Bass.

Texaco to pay $176.1 million in bias suit. (1996). *The Wall Street Journal* (Nov. 18), A3, A4.

The new face of America: How immigrants are shaping the world's first multicultural society. (1993). *Time* (Fall), special issue, 3.

Wright, P., Ferris, S. P., Hiller, J. S., Kroll, M. (1995). Competitiveness through management of diversity: Effects on stock price valuation. *Academy of Management Journal 38,* 272–287.

PART   II
Costing EAPs and Worksite Health-Promotion Programs, Attitudes, and Work–Life Programs

Costing the Effects of Employee Assistance and Worksite Health-Promotion Programs

"The corporate culture has historically told employees to leave their personal problems at home. But for most employees, that's no longer possible, because nobody is at home to solve those problems" (Lancaster 1990, p. B1). Consider the following sobering facts (Bahls 1998):

- Substance abuse and mental illness cost U.S. companies over $100 billion per year in lost time, accidents, health care, and workers' compensation costs.
- Substance abusers are absent three times more often and use 16 times as many health-care benefits as nonabusers.
- Sixty-five percent of all accidents on the job are directly related to drugs or alcohol.
- Substance abusers are six times more likely than are their co-workers to file a workers' compensation claim.
- Nearly four million American women suffer domestic abuse each year, and one in four American women between the ages of 18 and 65 has experienced some form of domestic abuse. The abuse exists at every level of society, and the effects spill over into the workplace. Victims of domestic abuse miss 175,000 days of paid work annually. Domestic abuse costs employers $3 billion to $5 billion a year in absenteeism, reduced productivity, and increased health-care expenditures (Woodward 1998).

Statistics like those lead to one inescapable conclusion: the personal problems of troubled employees have a devastating economic impact on employers. To deal with those problems, more and more employers have adopted programs that focus either on rehabilitation (employee assistance programs, or EAPs) or on prevention (worksite health-promotion, or WHP, programs). In this chapter, the objective is not to describe the structure, content, or operational features of such programs, but rather to present methods for estimating their economic impact at the level of the individual company. The first part of the chapter will focus on EAPs and the second part will focus on WHP programs.

EAPs—PREVALENCE, ATTRIBUTES, COSTS, AND GENERAL BENEFITS

An EAP is a system that provides confidential, professional care to employees whose job performance is or may become adversely affected by a variety of personal problems. Supervisors are taught to look for symptoms of declining work performance such as the following, and then to refer employees to the EAP for professional help: predictable absenteeism patterns (for example, Mondays, Fridays, or days before or after holidays), unexcused or frequent absences, tardiness and early departures, arguments with fellow employees, causing injuries to other employees through negligence, poor judgments and bad decisions, unusual on-the-job accidents, increased spoilage or breaking of equipment through negligence, involvement with the law, or deteriorating personal appearance (Filipowicz 1987).

Prevalence of the Programs

Two major forces, legal and economic, have combined to fuel the development of EAPs. In the legal arena, civil rights legislation, the Americans with Disabilities Act, federal rehabilitation laws, and erosion of the at-will doctrine severely constrain an employer's ability to fire employees (Segal 1997). Employers are becoming more economically aware of the considerable "sunk" costs invested in employees in the form of recruitment, selection, and training. They are also well aware of the substantial costs of replacing employees who leave (see chapter 2). For those reasons, employers are finding that rehabilitation of troubled employees is more cost effective than simply firing them. About a third of all worksites with more than 50 employees have access to an EAP, and among large firms the figure rises to more than 80 percent (Seppa 1997).

Critical Attributes for a Successful EAP

Critical attributes for a successful EAP include the following (Seppa 1997; Dickman & Emener 1987): top-management backing, labor support, confidentiality of EAP data, easy access, supervisor training, union steward training (if employees are so represented), insurance involvement, breadth of service components (to handle a wide variety of problems), professional leadership of the EAP, and follow-up/evaluation to measure the effectiveness of the program.

Costs and General Benefits

EAPs cost employers only $20 to $30 per employee annually (Seppa 1997) but can save many times that amount by reducing insurance claims and absenteeism. Consider results from four different evaluations (Blum & Roman 1995):

- The public school system of Orange County, Florida, found that medical-claim costs dropped by two-thirds over five years for those employees who used the EAP. The same EAP clients—who had taken 10 percent more sick leave than the average worker the year before the EAP was instituted—were taking 26 percent less than average by the sixth year of EAP use.
- At NCR Corp., the company offered financial incentives to employees to use its EAP before seeking mental health care or substance abuse treatment elsewhere. After a year, 80 percent of the cases were resolved without using health-care benefits.
- McDonnell-Douglas Corp. estimated that it saved $4 for every $1 spent on its EAP. Workers treated for alcohol or drug dependency subsequently missed 44 percent fewer days of work than they had before entering the EAP. Turnover among those employees also dropped from 40 percent to 8 percent after the EAP had been in place for four years. Those treated for psychiatric conditions within the EAP missed 34 percent fewer days than those who sought treatment on their own.
- In a one-year pilot study, Campbell Soup Co. found a 28 percent reduction in mental health-care costs in plants where its EAP was implemented, with costs falling from $261 to $188 per worker. On the

basis of those results, Campbell expanded its EAP to cover 50,000 workers and their dependents at more than 40 locations.

An evaluation of one company's EAP by an outside agency (Professional Employee Advisement Program) found that employees use the EAP for the following reasons: drug and alcohol problems (38 percent), domestic problems (20 percent), problems with one's children (24 percent), and job stress (18 percent) (Leib 1986). It is important to emphasize that program costs, benefits, and reasons for using an EAP are likely to vary across situations. However, a comprehensive review published by the U.S. Department of Health and Human Services found no published evidence that EAPs are harmful to corporate economies or to individual employees (Blum & Roman 1995).

DIFFICULTIES IN EVALUATING EAPs

Actual results may not be quite as rosy as have been reported in the literature or in the media. Evaluation may be *ex-ante* (estimates computed before implementation of an EAP) or *ex-post* (measurement of the costs and benefits of actual program operations and impacts after the fact). Evaluation may be expressed in qualitative terms or in quantitative terms.

If evaluation is expressed in quantitative terms—as many operating executives demand—there are three major problems. One problem is how to establish all program costs and benefits. To establish its costs, an EAP must incorporate an information system that can track factors such as insurance use, absenteeism, performance analysis, accidents, and attendance data. A second problem is how to express and translate the costs and benefits into monetary values. Benefits derived from an EAP may be very difficult to translate into economic terms. Third, unless proper experimental controls are exercised, cause–effect relations between EAP involvement and one or more dependent variables may be difficult or impossible to identify.

In the following sections, therefore, we will examine detailed methods for expressing the returns of EAPs in economic terms for the following dependent variables: productivity, turnover, unemployment costs, outpatient versus inpatient treatment for substance abuse, absenteeism, supervisors' time, accidents, training and replacement costs, and the use of insurance benefits.

EXPRESSING AN EAP'S ECONOMIC RETURNS

Productivity

The productivity losses associated with troubled employees can be staggering. One method for determining the productivity cost (ex-ante) attributable to employees who abuse alcohol was developed by Parker et al. (1987). They recommended that the following formula be computed separately for each age–gender cohort. Costs for all age–gender cohorts should then be summed.

Equation 1

      No. of workers in age–gender cohort in workforce
  ×   Proportion of workers in age–gender cohort with alcohol abuse problems
  ×   Annual earnings
  ×   Productivity decrease attributable to alcohol
  =   Cost of alcohol-related reduced productivity

Two key inputs to this formula that might be difficult to acquire are the proportion of workers in each age–gender cohort with alcohol abuse problems, and the productivity decrease attributable to alcohol. Over all cohorts, however, national figures suggest that 5 to 10 percent of a typical workforce suffers from alcohol abuse ("Substance Abuse" 1988), and that the figure may be as high as 10 to 15 percent among construction workers ("Labor Letter" 1988). In well-controlled studies, productivity losses attributable to alcohol abuse have ranged from 14 to 21 percent (Parker et al. 1987). However, Masi (1984) suggested that personal problems, in toto, affect 18 percent of the workforce, resulting in an estimated productivity loss of 25 percent. It is important to note that the latter figure is an *estimate*, not a precise number derived on the basis of controlled research. It is used in the calculations shown below simply for illustrative purposes. Keep this in mind in analyzing the example and in applying the formula to actual work situations.

For one age–gender cohort in any given workforce, inputs to equation 1 might be:

      100 workers in age–gender cohort in workforce
  ×   10 percent with alcohol abuse problems
  ×   Annual earnings of $35,000 per worker in cohort
  ×   20 percent productivity decrease attributable to alcohol
  =   Cost of alcohol-related reduced productivity of $70,000

At a more general level, through its Project Concern the City of Phoenix developed the following formula to determine the costs due to troubled employees, as well as (ex-ante) the amount of money that could be saved in terms of improved productivity through an EAP (Wagner 1987):

Equation 2
1. To determine the average annual wage of employees, divide average total number of employees into annual payroll for employees.
2. To obtain the payroll for troubled employees, multiply average annual wage by 18 percent of the total number of employees (average percentage of troubled employees identified by Masi 1984).
3. To determine the present loss due to troubled employees, multiply the result of step 2 by 25 percent (average productivity loss estimated by Masi 1984).
4. To identify the potential amount saved per year by an EAP, multiply the result of step 3 by 50 percent (actual success rate reported by Project Concern).

To illustrate, let us assume that a firm employs 100 workers, at an annual payroll cost of $3.5 million, or $35,000 per worker (step 1). To calculate the payroll for troubled employees, let us assume that 18 percent or 18 workers are troubled × $35,000 annual earnings/worker = $630,000 (step 2). To determine the present cost of reduced productivity for those troubled workers, multiply $630,000 × 25 percent = $157,500. Finally, to determine the potential amount of money that could be saved per year through an EAP, multiply $157,500 × 50 percent = $78,750.

Note that potential savings reflect only the cost of labor, and labor is only one component of productivity. Such savings are therefore conservative, for they do not reflect the contribution of improved use of capital and equipment that can be realized by a fully productive employee.

Turnover

Turnover savings realized through the implementation of an EAP may be termed "opportunity savings" because they reflect costs that were not actually incurred. An example of such ex-post evaluation was provided by St. Benedict's Hospital in Ogden, Utah (Featherston & Bednarek 1987). Over the two-year period of the study, the hospital's turnover rate averaged 31 percent. Using that rate, out of 67 employees who were involved with the EAP, 67 × 0.31 = about 21 who should have quit. Because only 6 actually did quit, 15 expected turnovers were avoided through EAP counseling. Replacement costs for nursing and non-nursing employees averaged $1,900 (roughly $2,775 in 1998 dollars). Hence the opportunity savings or costs avoided amounted to $2,775 × 15 = $41,625 (excluding the cost of the EAP program itself).

Unemployment Compensation

The St. Benedict's Hospital study reported that employees who quit drew unemployment compensation for an average of six weeks. Let us assume that such compensation equaled 60 percent of full-time pay. If the hospital's average hourly wage rate was $12 per hour in 1998, then the savings in unemployment compensation would be $12 × 15 people × 40 hours/week × 6 weeks × 0.60 = $25,920. Obviously, that figure could be considerably larger if the hourly rate, the number of employees saved, or the duration of the unemployment compensation were to increase.

Outpatient Versus Inpatient Treatment for Substance Abuse

There is a large difference in costs between outpatient and inpatient treatment for substance abuse. For example, outpatient costs range from $5 to $100 per counseling session, and generally last from six weeks to 18 months. The cost of a typical month-long residential program ranges from $9,000 to $12,000 or more (Bahls 1998).

After examining literature for the two types of treatment programs showing that the relative levels of effectiveness do not differ, United Technologies chose to adopt an outpatient treatment program (Bensinger & Pilkington 1985). Over a one-year period, that program resulted in 50 percent less time off the job for treatment, 50 percent fewer days of sick pay (relative to what would have been incurred with an inpatient program), and no out-of-pocket expenses for treated employees.

United Technologies treats approximately 225 employees for substance abuse each year, at a cost differential of between $2,300 and $8,800 per treated employee per year, relative to the cost of an inpatient residential program. Those savings, therefore, total between $500,000 and $2 million in direct treatment costs annually.

Absenteeism

Klarreich, Digiuseppe, and Dimattia (1987) studied the impact of a form of psychotherapy known as rational-emotive therapy (RET) applied in the context of an in-house EAP. Their three-year (ex-post) study investigated the impact of RET in a large oil company. The population served by the EAP consisted of about 2,500 white-collar, nonunion employees in a major metropolitan area. During the study, the program served 600 employees, 96 percent of whom had problems other than alcohol or drugs. The problems were personal-emotional (54 percent), job-related behavior (22 percent), marital or family (20 percent), and alcohol or drugs (4 percent). The average number of sessions per client over the three-year period was 4.1.

Absenteeism data were available for two of the three years of the study. During that time, 431 employees used the EAP, and 364 completed RET counseling. Absenteeism data were complete and available for 295 of those employees. Attrition resulted from the fact that data had to be available for one year prior to involvement with the EAP and one year after it.

One year prior to their EAP involvement, the 295 employees were absent a total of 3,033 days. One year after their involvement, the same 295 employees were absent only a total of 878 days, a reduction of 74 percent. According to the company's accounting department, one day of absence costs an average of $144.50 (roughly $211 in 1998 dollars). When that value is multiplied by the number of days of absenteeism saved (2,155), the result is $311,398 for the days saved ($454,705 in 1998 dollars). That estimate is conservative because complete data were not available for the 364 employees who completed treatment. The figure is overstated, however, to the extent that the costs of the therapy sessions themselves were not taken into account.

Supervisors' Time

In the same study, Klarreich et al. (1987) reasoned that if the EAP were not available, supervisors would be forced to deal with employee problems. The minimum time in hours that supervisors did not have to deal with problems is equal to the total number of hours spent in counseling sessions for the employees in the study (1,880 hours). Thus, the supervisors had at least 1,880 hours to carry out their duties more effectively. The average cost of one hour of supervisory time was $23.80 ($34.75 in 1998 dollars). Therefore, $23.80 × 1,880 = $44,744 ($65,324 in 1998 dollars), which the authors reported as "the net benefit in dollars." The term "net" implies that the cost of the program itself was subtracted from the total benefits. Because that cost was not reported, we really do not know what, if any, savings there might have been in supervisory time.

Accidents

As we noted earlier, troubled employees are involved in more on-the-job accidents than employees who are not troubled. An EAP might be able to save a company money if the number of accidents could be reduced. In fact, statistics bear this out, as illustrated in a three-and-one-half year study of the effects of the EAP at AT&T.

The ex-post study followed each of 110 employees for 22 months before and 22 months after their involvement with the company's EAP program (Gaeta, Lynn, & Grey 1982). To be conservative, estimates were not used. In areas where savings formulas could be developed, cost figures for actual company expenditures were used. In estimating benefits, however, the study did not include the cost of creating the EAP or of training supervisors and other staff employees.

To be considered in the study, accidents must have involved lost work time. The cost per accident (in 1998 dollars) of $6,755 is the actual company cost for expenses, including administrative costs, medical expenses, replacement costs, and disability expenses under law. Costs associated with lost productivity and lost time were not included in that figure. As the following data show, the reduction in the cost of accidents for EAP clients during the 22 months following their involvement in the program was $141,855.

	No. of Accidents	Cost per Accident ($)	Total Cost ($)
Before EAP	26	6,755	175,630
After EAP	5	6,755	33,775
Difference ($)			141,855

Training and Replacement Costs

Motorola's employee assistance program in Austin, Texas, has developed some methodologies that have served as measures of costs and benefits (Starr & Byram 1985). The net savings in training and replacement costs (in 1998 dollars) are shown below. The actual numbers of employees are not shown because Motorola treats that information as confidential.

Let us assume that 10 percent of 2,500 employees (250) can be expected to quit each year. Potential turnover costs may be stated as follows:

	No. of People	Individual Cost ($)	Total Cost ($)
Production	150	1,173	175,950
Office/technical	50	2,346	117,300
Exempt	50	39,100	1,955,000
Total potential cost			2,248,250

Actual number of employees who terminate or quit after EAP involvement:

	No. of People	Individual Cost ($)	Total Cost ($)
Production	24	1,173	28,152
Office/technical	4	2,346	9,384
Exempt	3	39,100	117,300
Total actual cost			154,836

To obtain the total actual cost:

Annual budget ($)	273,700
Terminations/quit ($)	154,836
Hospitalization ($)	148,575
Total actual cost ($)	577,111

To compute the return-on-investment (ROI):

Potential cost ($)	2,248,250
Minus actual cost ($)	–577,111
Total ($)	1,671,139
ROI ($)	1,671,139 ÷ 577,111
	= 2.90, or approximately 3:1

Compiling those data year after year is particularly useful because the data can be compared and trends can be identified.

Use of Insurance Benefits

Another measure that is frequently used to evaluate EAPs is the use of insurance benefits. This type of measure may be most informative when computed after an EAP has been in operation for a number of years. The use of insurance as a measure of EAP involvement may actually increase at first because of referrals for counseling, but referrals are likely to stabilize over time. The method described here for computing benefit/ cost ratios was developed originally by Foote et al. (1978). It can be used in any organization that uses an information system (in conjunction with its EAP) capable of tracking such data. Costs shown refer to average annual health insurance costs incurred by a single EAP client. To be useful, therefore, such costs must be aggregated over all EAP users.

Medical Costs

A. Before intervention (\$)	4,500
B. After intervention (C + D) (\$)	1,500
C. Costs incurred due to intervention (\$)	1,000
D. Other medical costs (\$)	500
Cost savings (A–B) (\$)	3,000

Then we obtain the benefit/cost ratio:

Benefit/Cost Ratio

Cost savings (\$)	3,000
Costs of the intervention (\$)	1,000
ROI (\$)	3,000/1,000 = 3, or \$3.00 saved for every \$1 spent on the program

There is no one model of EAP evaluation that is universally appropriate, and as we have seen, companies tend to emphasize one or more of the outcome measures discussed above. What can we conclude? Judicious choice of the outcomes of interest, careful measurement of costs and benefits in economic terms, and the use of one or more control groups will permit stronger inferences regarding the practical impact of EAPs.

COSTING THE EFFECTS OF WORKSITE HEALTH-PROMOTION PROGRAMS

The *theory* of WHP is simple: it is cheaper to keep an employee healthy and on the job than it is to pay the costs of ill health, rehabilitation, and replacement. Convinced that if employees were healthier they would take fewer sick days, four out of every five companies in the United States with 50 or more workers have some type of WHP program designed to prevent illness (U.S. Department of Health and Human Services 1992).

It is important to note that the concept of health includes more than just the absence of illness. Wellness represents the balance of physical, emotional, social, spiritual, and intellectual health (O'Donnell 1989). Although there is no generally accepted agreement about what constitutes WHP, there is agreement that a worksite intervention should include at least two elements (Terborg 1998):

1. Periodic or continual delivery of educational or behavior-change materials and activities that are designed to maintain/improve employee fitness, health, and well-being; and
2. Changes in organizational practices and policies that are conducive to health promotion.

Most WHP interventions focus on educational and skill-building materials and activities. Fewer target organizational practices and policies. Still fewer emphasize both educational/skill-building activities *and* organizational policies. WHP programs vary along a number of dimensions, including facilities, budget, eligibility, scope, employee involvement, and target outcomes (Terborg 1998).

Why Establish a WHP Program?

Worksite interventions have the potential to: reach people with health risks who might not otherwise participate; provide long-term social and environmental support for the adoption and maintenance of healthy behaviors; reduce company and employee health-care expenditures by providing convenient and free or low-cost preventive and early-detection interventions; improve labor–management relations; improve productivity; reduce absenteeism due to illness or injury; and reduce voluntary turnover (Terborg 1998). Although the potential for benefits is high, as we shall see, there is considerable variability in results across worksites with health-promotion programs.

Companies that adopt WHP programs do not do so only for the anticipated financial return on their investments. They do so because their employees want them, because senior managers have a strong personal commitment to healthy lifestyles, because managers believe that WHP projects a favorable corporate image and is an important benefit that improves recruitment and retention, and because they think it will reduce health-care costs and improve morale and productivity (Wolfe, Slack, & Rose-Hearn 1993; Terborg 1988).

Although companies adopt WHP programs for a variety of reasons, Howard (1987) has noted that in a free-enterprise economy the bottom line is the great persuader. For American business, health-care costs threaten to reduce profits just as surely as do competitors from Europe and the Far East. In the opinion of many, WHP programs may be the best weapon to hold the line.

Levels and Types of WHP Programs

Most authorities in the field of WHP stress the importance of defining a strategy when such a program is introduced. Generally, such a strategy includes the following features (Howard 1987):

- Identify individual risk factors among employees, using screening and assessment tools.
- Educate employees about risk factors and their relationship to disease.
- Motivate employees to reduce the risk factors.
- Encourage employees to make a personal commitment to risk reduction.
- Offer specific programs to control major risk factors such as smoking, substance abuse, excess weight, and high blood pressure.
- Follow up and support employees in their efforts to change.

WHP programs can be implemented at three functional levels (Gebhardt & Crump 1990). Level I programs attempt to make employees aware of the consequences of unhealthy habits. Such programs may include health fairs, screening sessions, newsletters, or educational classes.

Level II programs target lifestyle modification by providing specific programs. For example, the WHP program at the Adolph Coors Company offers traditional classes in exercise, weight loss, smoking cessation, stress management, and diet and nutrition. It also includes such nontraditional offerings as specially designed aerobics classes for older employees; pre- and postnatal exercise, dietary, and nutritional programs; classes in anger management and parenting skills; breast cancer and skin cancer self-examination procedures for employees and spouses; dental education; and rehabilitation for employees with cardiac and orthopedic problems (Andrews 1989). The goal of Level II programs is to provide employees with a knowledge base to help alter negative health habits.

Level III programs attempt to create an environment at work that will assist employees in sustaining their healthy lifestyles and behaviors. Some common changes include eliminating cigarette machines; providing healthy food and beverages in vending machines, the company cafeteria, and at meetings; labeling foods with nutritional information; building covered areas for storage of employee bicycles to encourage bicycling to work instead of driving; and prohibiting staff expense reimbursements for alcoholic beverages (Terborg 1988; Sciacca 1987).

Problem: Low Participation by Employees "at Risk"

Before any company jumps on the WHP bandwagon, it should be aware of a major problem: employee participation. While there are many WHP programs available, evidence indicates that only a small percentage of employees participate in them. Jeffery et al. (1993) found that recruitment of employees to worksite smoking cessation programs ranged from 0 percent to 88 percent, and that drop-out rates from worksite weight-loss programs ranged from 0.5 percent to 80 percent. Another review (Gebhardt & Crump 1990) found that participation in worksite fitness programs usually ranged from 15 to 30 percent for white-collar workers, with an occasional high participation rate of 50 percent. However, the same white-collar workers, prior to their participation, weighed less and were less likely to smoke than were nonparticipants. That finding suggests that many "at risk" employees are not participating in the programs. Participation among blue-collar workers in workplace-fitness programs (3 to 5 percent) is even less.

The key to attracting workers is emphasis on facts such as: good health can help reduce lost time from work as a result of accidents, participation will not affect employment status, and participation will not be considered a substitute for worksite safety initiatives (Metcalfe 1987). The challenge is to recruit and retain high-risk individuals— those who are most likely to get sick and to cost the most in medical claims. The trick is to get enough high-risk employees into the WHP program to generate a "critical mass," a point at which cost savings begin to accrue. Unfortunately, no one knows what number the critical mass needs to be (Aberth 1986).

Incentives for Participation

To boost low participation rates in WHP programs, some companies offer inducements to employees. For example, at Johnson & Johnson employees get $500 discounts on their insurance premiums if they agree to have their blood pressure, cholesterol, and body fat checked and to fill out detailed health-risk questionnaires. Workers found to be at high risk for health problems receive letters urging them to join a diet and exercise program. Those who refuse lose the $500 discount. Roughly 96 percent of the company's 35,000 U.S. employees completed the health assessments in the year after the program was begun, compared with only 40 percent before the discount was offered. To keep employees' health information confidential, the company stores the data from the employees' questionnaires in a separate computer that is not linked to any others in the corporate system (Jeffrey 1996). Although a strong financial argument can be made for using health benefits as an incentive for health promotion at the worksite, evaluative data are limited, and ethical challenges continually arise (Kaman 1995). Now that we know how WHP programs work, it seems reasonable to ask, "What do they cost?"

Cost of WHP Programs

The cost of offering a WHP program includes direct costs, such as fees paid to vendors, and indirect costs, such as lost employee time during participation. Direct costs vary considerably depending on the method of delivery. Programs that enlist the services of organizations such as the American Heart Association, the American Cancer Society, or the Red Cross may be much less expensive than those delivered by a private, for-profit company.

Other direct costs include the construction or modification of facilities, promotional materials, and, perhaps, incentive payments to employees for their participation. However, costs will be lower if employees must pay a fee to participate, or if they must participate in WHP activities on their own time (Fletcher 1987).

Erfurt, Foote, and Heirich (1992) estimated that a comprehensive WHP program that includes direct and indirect costs will cost between $70 to $130 per employee annually (roughly $85 to $155 in 1998 dollars), depending on local salary levels and overhead costs, on how frequently follow-up is conducted, and on how many employees participate. Costs will also vary, however, depending on the size of an organization and on the extent of the facilities and programs offered.

In a Health Research Institute survey (Kittrell 1988), responding companies employed a total of 3.66 million people in the United States. They reported an average cost per start-up of a WHP program as $99.10 per eligible employee for internal costs, plus $18.37 per eligible employee for outside costs (roughly $139 and $26, respectively, in 1998 dollars).

Kimberly-Clark's Neenah, Wisconsin, plant falls toward the high end in WHP expenditures. It incorporates levels I, II, and III of WHP activities. For example, it has a $2.5 million fitness facility, offers a variety of health-related and first-aid classes, and offers occupational health nursing services. The program is open to spouses and retirees and costs about $400 per year for each of the 5,500 eligible employees, or about $2 million annually (Fletcher 1987).

This magnitude of expenditures leads naturally to our next question, "What are firms getting in return?" Before we can answer that question, however, we need to consider some of the difficult problems associated with the evaluation of WHP programs.

DIFFICULTIES IN EVALUATING WHP PROGRAMS

The savings that accrue from participation in a WHP program are variable. The basic difficulty in estimating these savings lies in choosing which health-related costs are actually reduced. To deal with this problem, some firms have established WHP programs with specific objectives. Sunbeam Corporation's WHP program focuses specifically on reducing the rising costs associated with premature births. Pennzoil targets early cancer detection and treatment. The American Cancer Society estimates that the costs associated with treating just one individual's late-detected cancer can be $60,000 or more. Pennzoil invested more than $100,000 in its program, and detected pre-cancerous conditions in 150 employees, malignancies in 14. However, Pennzoil recovered more than its initial investment cost by detecting just two cancerous conditions in the early stage (Andrews 1989). Programs like these with specific objectives make evaluation more straightforward. This is not true, however, for the great majority of firms that have implemented WHP programs.

Although companies that market their WHP programs provide statistics to support their claims of savings in health-care costs, calculating how much any employer can expect to save is difficult because program sponsors use different methods to measure and report cost–benefit data. As the director of the Health Research Institute noted, "The offerings of programs are light years ahead of the measurement of the programs" (Fletcher 1987, p. 26).

When a program's effects are measured and *for how long* they are measured are crucial considerations. For example, DuPont de Nemours found that the greatest drop in absenteeism resulting from illness occurred in the first two or three years, and then it leveled off. Other effects, which might not appear for three years or longer, are so-called *lagged effects.* The greatest savings should accrue over time because of the chronic nature of many illnesses that WHP programs seek to prevent. However, employers should actually expect to see an *increase* in health-care claims after initial health assessments are done, as employees remedy newly identified problems (Fletcher 1987).

A major problem is that many companies use no control groups when evaluating their programs. Without a control group of nonparticipating employees, there is no way to tell how much of the improved health results from the WHP program and how much arises from popular trends (for example, the general fitness craze), changes in state or local health policies and regulations, and changes in medical insurance (Terborg 1998; Aberth 1986).

Other potential methodological problems, as we have seen, include biases resulting from self-selection and exclusion from evaluation of employees who drop out of a program. The resulting evaluations have little internal or external validity because they report results only for employees who voluntarily participate in and complete the program (Fielding 1996). Unit-of-analysis problems can make matters even worse. Thus, if data are evaluated across worksites at the level of the individual employee, the effect of a WHP program tends to be overstated because the design ignores within-worksite variation. In practice, substantial differences have been found across different worksites receiving the same intervention (Glasgow et al., 1995; Jeffery et al. 1993). Conversely, if the unit of analysis is the plant or worksite, then a very large number of sites per intervention is necessary to achieve adequate statistical power to detect effects, if they exist.

Another limiting factor is the availability of data. Often firms commit to health promotion without any corresponding commitment to data collection (Smith 1987). Without data, evaluation is impossible. Typically, however, the evaluation of a WHP program relies on some form of cost-effectiveness or cost–benefit analysis.

Cost-Effectiveness Analysis

Cost-effectiveness (C/E) analysis identifies the cost of producing a unit of effect within a given program. To illustrate, let us use an example presented by Smith, Haight, and Everly (1986). Suppose a worksite hypertension-control program incurs an annual cost of $20,000 for a 100-employee population. The average reduction in diastolic blood pressure per treated individual is 8 millimeters of mercury (mm/Hg). The C/E ratio is:

$$\$20,000/100 \div 8 \text{ mm/Hg} = \$25 \text{ per mm/Hg reduction}$$

C/E analysis permits comparisons of alternative interventions designed to achieve the same goal. For example, the \$25 cost per mm/Hg reduction achieved by the above program could be compared with alternative programs not offered at the worksite. As another example, consider the results of a three-year study of the cost-effectiveness of three types of WHP programs for reducing cardiovascular disease risk factors (hypertension, obesity, cigarette smoking, and lack of regular physical exercise) at three manufacturing plants, compared with a fourth site that provided health education classes only (Erfurt et al. 1992). The plants were similar in size and in the demographic characteristics of their employees. Plants were allocated randomly to one of four WHP models. Site A provided health education only. Site B provided a fitness facility; site C provided health education plus follow-up that included a menu of different intervention strategies; and site D provided health education, follow-up, and social organization of health promotion within the plant.

Over the three-year period studied, the annual, direct cost per employee was \$17.68 for site A, \$39.28 for site B, \$30.96 for site C, and \$38.57 for site D. The reduction in risks ranged from 32 percent at site B to 45 percent at site D for high-level reduction or relapse prevention, and from 36 percent (site B) to 51 percent (site D) for moderate reduction. Those differences were statistically significant.

At site B the greater amount of money spent on the fitness facility produced less risk reduction (–3 percent) than did the comparison program (site A). The additional cost per employee per year (beyond those incurred at site A) for each percent of risks reduced or relapses prevented was –\$7.20 at site B (fitness facility), \$1.48 for site C (health education plus follow-up), and \$2.09 at site D (health education, follow-up, and social organization of health promotion at the plant). At sites C and D, the percent of effectiveness in reducing risks/preventing relapse was about 1.3 percent to 1.5 percent per dollar spent per employee per year, and the total cost for each percent of risk reduced or relapse prevented was less than \$1 per employee per year (\$0.66 and \$0.76, at sites C and D, respectively).

Unfortunately, C/E analysis fails to address from a financial perspective whether the program ever should have been offered. Cost–benefit analysis overcomes that latter problem.

Cost–Benefit Analysis

Cost–benefit (C/B) analysis is similar to C/E analysis in that both focus on goals, costs, and benefits. The difference is that C/B analysis expresses benefits in monetary terms. One of the most popular forms of C/B analysis is return-on-investment analysis. Although traditionally associated with investments in hard assets, ROI analysis also can be used to evaluate returns on investments in WHP activities by relating program profits to invested capital. It does so in terms of a ratio in which the numerator expresses some measure of profit related to the project, and the denominator represents the firm's investment in the program (Smith et al. 1986).

Suppose a WHP program costs a firm $450,000 during its first year of operation. The measured savings from reduced absenteeism is $25,000, from reduced employer health-care payments (assuming a self-funded plan) is $40,000, and from reduced employee turnover is $35,000. The ROI before interest and taxes would be calculated as follows:

Benefit Type	Benefit Amount ($)
Reduced absenteeism	25,000
Reduced health-care payments	40,000
Reduced employee turnover	35,000
Total expected benefits	100,000

ROI = Total expected benefit/program investment
ROI = $100,000/$450,000 = 22 percent

The advantage of ROI is that it blends in one number all the major ingredients of profitability, and the ROI statistic can be compared with other investment opportunities inside or outside of a company. It is also simple and widely accepted.

However, as Terborg (1998, 1988) has noted, although the logic and techniques of C/E and C/B analysis (including ROI) appear straightforward, there are several unresolved issues. There is much subjectivity in the choice of variables to include in these models, in estimating the dollar value of indirect costs and indirect benefits, in estimating the timing and duration of program effects, and in discounting the dollar value of costs and benefits that occur in future time periods. Because of this subjectivity, it is important to conduct sensitivity analyses (to examine the impact of variations in assumptions on C/E and C/B ratios) and breakeven analysis (see chapter 10) to identify the minimum levels of dependent variables (such as early cancer detection or savings in absenteeism) that will allow recovery of investments in the WHP program.

A summary of the WHP program-evaluation issues discussed thus far is presented in Exhibit 5–1.

DATA NEEDED TO EVALUATE A WHP PROGRAM

A sound experimental design is one that allows cause-and-effect relationships to emerge and be evaluated (Exhibit 5–2). Gebhardt and Crump (1990) have outlined an evaluation strategy that includes a mix of features rarely all gathered in actual evaluations. They are, however, an ideal toward which companies should aim. Their strategy begins with a determination of the demographics of an organization (age, gender, race, ethnicity), expected participation rates, and start-up and maintenance costs required to reach an organization's goals (such as reducing the incidence and costs of undetected cancerous conditions). The next step is to develop a testing and tracking system that will quantify the outcomes of the WHP program for both participants and nonparticipants. Pre- and post-comparisons can be made for both groups in terms

EXHIBIT 5–1   *Difficulties in Evaluating WHP Programs*

1. Managers have difficulty identifying the health-related costs that actually decreased.
2. Program sponsors use different methods to measure and report costs and benefits.
3. Program effects may vary depending on when they are measured (immediate versus lagged effects).
4. Program effects may vary depending on how long they are measured.
5. Few studies use control groups.
6. Potential biases exist as results of self-selection and exclusion of dropouts.
7. Analysis at the level of the individual employee ignores within-site variation; analysis at the level of the worksite may produce low statistical power to detect effects.
8. Data on effectiveness are limited in the choice of variables, estimation of the economic value of indirect costs and benefits, estimation of the timing and duration of program effects, and estimation of the present values of future benefits.

EXHIBIT 5-2   *How to Evaluate a WHP Program*

1. Classify employees according to demographic characteristics.
2. Determine expected participation rates.
3. Estimate program start-up and maintenance costs.
4. Develop a testing and tracking system to quantify outcomes for participants and nonparticipants.
5. Measure pre- and post-program changes on outcomes of interest.
6. Analyze quantitative variables separately by demographic group and by participation or nonparticipation in the program.
7. Conduct cost–benefit analyses of present and future benefits; determine the present values of all such benefits.

of behavioral changes, health-care costs, fitness levels, absenteeism, turnover, injury rate and severity, productivity, and job satisfaction. Quantifiable variables (such as health-care costs, absenteeism) should be analyzed separately by demographic or socioeconomic cohort, and for both participants and nonparticipants. Finally, C/B analyses should include present and future benefits, expressed in current dollar values.

Although a growing number of studies report favorable C/E or C/B results, it is difficult to evaluate and compare the studies because no widely accepted approach currently exists for estimating costs and benefits (Kaman 1995). Different authors use different assumptions in their estimates of WHP intervention costs and dollar benefits, and small changes in assumptions can have large effects on the interpretation of results. Even though computer simulations of WHP interventions suggest that such programs may be beneficial (Terborg 1995), economic benefits primarily come from avoiding the opportunity costs of lost productivity rather than from real dollar decreases in health-care costs. Keep those ideas in mind as we examine published results from several firms that have attempted to assess the outcomes of their WHP programs.

COMPANY-LEVEL EVALUATIONS OF WHP PROGRAMS

The benefits of WHP programs may be expressed in terms of a number of possible outcomes, three of which we will examine here: health-care costs, absenteeism, and turnover.

Health-Care Costs

A study by the Pacific Mutual Life Insurance Company found that illness resulting from poor nutrition costs employers $30 million annually. People with cardiovascular disease related to high blood pressure cost industry 27 million work days and $4 to $5 billion per year. Back problems cause a loss of 91 million work days per year and more than $9 billion in lost productivity, disability payments, and lawsuits (Renner 1987). Another study found that nonexercising employees use 60 percent more sick-time hours than do their counterparts who jog, swim, bike, or engage in other forms of regular exercise each week (Gettings & Maddox 1988).

Demonstrating a cause-and-effect relationship between WHP program expenditures and health-care costs avoided is far from an exact science. Nevertheless, longitudinal research now shows that employees' unhealthy behaviors lead to significantly higher health-care costs over time. Thus, a four-year study of 15,000 workers at Control Data Corporation revealed that employees with the worst lifestyle habits had the highest medical bills. For example, people whose weekly exercise was equivalent to climbing fewer than 5 flights of stairs or walking less than one-half mile spent 114 percent more on health-care claims than did those who climbed at least 15 flights of stairs or walked 1.5 miles a week. Less surprisingly, people who smoked an average of one or more packs of cigarettes a day had 118 percent higher medical expenses than did nonsmokers. Health-care costs for obese people were 11 percent higher than were those for thin people. And workers who routinely failed to use seatbelts spent 54 percent more days in the hospital than did those who usually buckled up (James 1987).

As we noted earlier, some companies have established very specific objectives for their WHP programs. As an example, consider the mammography screening program used by Adolph Coors Company. By calculating exactly how many examinations showed breast cancer in the early stages, Coors can accurately calculate the costs avoided, assuming that without mammography the problem would have gone undetected and the cancer would have matured. Coors spent $232,500 to perform 2,500 screenings, and avoided $828,000 in health-care costs. This yielded the company a savings of $595,500, or an ROI of greater than 3.5:1 (Johnson 1988).

Descriptions of two other studies are drawn from the excellent literature review provided by Gebhardt and Crump (1990). Prudential Insurance

Company instituted a voluntary fitness program for sedentary, white-collar workers engaged in clerical, underwriting, claims, and management jobs. The study, conducted over a five-year period, included people employed for at least one year prior to entry into the program, and one year after entry into the program. Results showed that the average sick days for the exercisers dropped 20.1 percent when compared with their previous year's sick days (each person was compared to his or her own baseline) prior to entry into the program. This represented a 31.7 percent savings in salary costs and a 45.7 percent savings in major medical costs for each participant in the exercise program. The savings in major medical costs occurred during a year when health costs for the nation rose 13.9 percent. The program cost $244 (in 1998 dollars) per participant and saved $717 per participant, for a net savings of $473, or a savings in company health-care costs of $1.94 for every $1 used to operate the program.

Blue Cross and Blue Shield of Indiana studied the impact of its on-site health-promotion program (Level I and Level II) for 667 participants and 1,744 nonparticipants over a 4.75-year period. Analysis of those two groups six months prior to initiation of the program indicated that health-care payments were similar for both groups. After the first six months, costs for participants actually increased, as participants sought medical care for newly discovered health conditions. However, the benefit payments (hospital inpatient and outpatient, major medical, and medical–surgical) across the 4.75 years of the study were 24 percent lower for participants. In 1998 dollars, the health-care cost savings per employee ($315) exceeded the total program cost per employee ($217) by a ratio of 1.45:1. When the start-up costs were amortized over the 4.75-year period, the ROI increased to 2.51:1 ($315/$125).

Absenteeism and Turnover

Cost savings from WHP programs can also be derived from the reduction of costly behaviors such as absenteeism and turnover. Absenteeism has been shown to drop 20 percent to 55 percent for programs ranging in length from one to five years (Gebhardt & Crump 1990).

For example, Cox, Shephard, and Corey (1981) studied white-collar employees at two similar insurance companies. In Company A, 435 employees enrolled voluntarily in a 30-minute exercise program that met three times per week at an on-site facility. Absenteeism for this group was compared with that of the 846 employees in the same company who did not participate, and with that of the 577 employees in Company B, which served as the control group. Prior to the implementation of the fitness program, members of all three groups had similar absenteeism rates. One year later, absenteeism dropped by 22 percent among the exercisers in Company A. This represented an average reduction of 1.3 days per employee. If the same result could be observed for all 1,281 employees in Company A, Cox et al. estimated a net savings to the company (in 1998 dollars) of $150,000 per year.

Cox et al. (1981) also investigated relative rates of turnover among exercisers and non-exercisers in Company A for one year prior to the initiation of the program and 10 months after initiation of the program. Turnover rates in the two groups were not significantly different prior to the inception of the program. Although the program period of 10 months was short, the exercisers had significantly less turnover (1.5 percent) than did the non-exercisers (15 percent). Because tenure with the company was similar for the members of both groups (roughly 8 to 11 years), turnover was not attributed to differences in past employment history. (However, it may be that better performers were in the exercising group, and better performers are less likely to leave; McEvoy & Cascio 1987). The savings—calculated from training costs of $11,217, difference in turnover rate (13.5 percent), and program participation rate (20 percent) prorated over 10 months—were $364 per company employee per year, resulting in an annual company savings of $466,700 (in 1998 dollars). Despite those encouraging results, a thorough review of the literature on WHP concluded:

> To our knowledge, no WHP intervention has established that reductions in health-care costs, health-care utilization or absenteeism, and increases in productivity, are causally dependent, either directly or indirectly, on improvements in health-risk status brought about by WHP interventions. Until such research is forthcoming, a conservative interpretation of the economic benefits of WHPs is recommended. (Terborg 1998, p. 214)

FUTURE OF EMPLOYEE ASSISTANCE AND WHP PROGRAMS

Based on the research reviewed in this chapter, it is clear that EAPs and WHP programs can yield significant payoffs to organizations that adopt them. However, it also is clear that the programs do not work under all circumstances and that the problems associated with assessing relative costs and benefits may be complex. At the very least, we need more well-controlled, longitudinal studies to investigate program costs and benefits and the extent to which behavior changes are maintained over time. Second, as Gebhardt and Crump (1990) have noted, the type and structure of programs should be evaluated for their success and impact on different populations of workers (older–younger, male–female, blue collar–white collar, racial or ethnic group), especially in light of the changes in the workforce that are expected in the early part of the next century. We need to understand the factors that affect employee participation or nonparticipation, as well as the factors that promote long-term changes in behavior. If we then build these factors into EAP and WHP programs, and if we are successful in attracting troubled or at-risk employees into the programs, then the programs will flourish, even in an era of limited resources in organizations.

EXERCISES

1. What is the difference between ex-ante and ex-post evaluation? Describe the major problems associated with the evaluation of EAPs.
2. Sobriety, Inc., a marketer of substance-abuse programs, is concerned about the cost of alcohol abuse among its own employees. Based on the following data, what is the productivity cost associated with employees who abuse alcohol? Among all cohorts, the productivity decrease attributable to alcohol abuse is 20 percent.

Gender–Age Cohort	No. of Individuals	Percentage with Alcohol Abuse Problems	Average Annual Earnings of Cohort ($)
Males, 25 and under	43	7	24,000
Males, 26–44	59	10	39,000
Males, 45 and over	38	5	48,000
Females, 25 and under	41	5	25,000
Females, 26–44	64	10	39,000
Females, 45 and over	34	7	47,000

3. The following data show termination, replacement, and training costs for the 4,000 employees of Hulakon, Inc., for one year. In any given year, 12 percent of the employees can be expected to quit.

Employee Group	No. of Employees	Individual Cost of Replacement and Training ($)
Production	250	2,500
Clerical	175	3,000
Management	55	18,000

As a result of involvement in the company's EAP, the following numbers of employees actually quit.

Employee Group	No. of Employees
Production	75
Clerical	40
Management	12

Hospitalization costs made up $189,000, or 56 percent of the total amount annually budgeted for the EAP. What is Hulakon's ROI for its EAP for this one year?

4. Your firm is considering establishing an EAP but it is unsure of which provider to select. Top management has asked you to assess the strengths and weaknesses of possible providers. Make a list of questions to ask each one.

5. Top management has asked you to summarize results from available studies regarding the relationship between employee lifestyle behaviors and health-care costs. Present your results in a report.

6. Based on the company-level evaluations of worksite health-promotion programs presented in this chapter, what specific outcomes of such programs might you investigate? Why did you choose those outcomes? What might be the advantages and disadvantages of using cost-effectiveness or cost–benefit analysis to assess those outcomes?

REFERENCES

Aberth, J. (1986). Worksite WHP programs: An evaluation. *Management Review 75*(Oct.), 51–53.

Andrews, C. (1989). *The Coors Wellness Program.* Unpublished manuscript. Executive MBA Program, University of Colorado, Denver.

Bahls, J. E. (1998). Drugs in the workplace. *HRMagazine 43*, 81–87.

Bensinger, A., Pilkington, C. F. (1985). Treating chemically dependent employees in a non-hospital setting. *Personnel Administrator 30*, 45–52.

Blum, T., Roman, P. (1995). *Cost-effectiveness and preventive implications of employee assistance programs.* Washington, D.C.: U.S. Dept. of Health and Human Services.

Cox, M. H., Shephard, R. J., Corey, P. (1981). Influence of an employee fitness programme upon fitness, productivity, and absenteeism. *Ergonomics 24*, 795–806.

Dickman, F., Emener, W. G. (1987). *Employee Assistance Programs: Basic Concepts, Attributes, and an Evaluation.* Personnel Administrator Reprint Collection Series, Employee Assistance Programs, pp. 39–44. Alexandria, VA: Society for Human Resource Management.

Erfurt, J. C., Foote, A., Heirich, M. A. (1992). The cost-effectiveness of worksite wellness programs for hypertension control, weight loss, smoking cessation, and exercise. *Personnel Psychology 45*, 5–27.

Featherston, H. J., Bednarek, R. J. (1987). *A Positive Demonstration of Concern for Employees.* Personnel Administrator Reprint Collection Series, Employee Assistance Programs, pp. 36–38. Alexandria, VA: Society for Human Resource Management.

Fielding, J. E. (1996). Getting smarter and maybe wiser. *American Journal of Health Promotion 11*, 109–111.

Filipowicz, C. (1987). *The Troubled Employee: Whose Responsibility?* Personnel Administrator Reprint Collection Series, Employee Assistance Programs (pp. 5–10). Alexandria, VA: Society for Human Resource Management.

Fletcher, M. (1987). WHP plan savings are difficult to measure. *Business Insurance* (Feb. 16), 26, 28.

Foote, A., Erfurt, J., Strauchy, P., Gazzardo, T. (1978). *Cost-Effectiveness of Occupational Employee Assistance Program: Test of an Evaluation Method.* Ann Arbor, MI: Institute of Labor and Industrial Relations.

Gaeta, E., Lynn, R., Grey, L. (1982). AT&T looks at program evaluation. *EAP Digest* (May-June), 22–31.

Gebhardt, D. L., Crump, C. E. (1990). Employee fitness and WHP programs in the workplace. *American Psychologist 45*, 262–272.

Gettings, L., Maddox, E. N. (1988). When health means wealth. *Training and Development Journal* (April), 81–85.

Glasgow, R. E., Terborg, J. R., Hollis, J. F., Severson, H. H., Boles, S. M. (1995). Take heart: Results from the initial phase of a worksite wellness program. *American Journal of Public Health 85*, 209–216.

Howard, J. S. (1987). Employee WHP: It's good business. *D&B Reports* (May-June), 34–37.

James, F. B. (1987). Study lays groundwork for tying health costs to workers' behavior. *The Wall Street Journal* (Apr. 14), 37.

Jeffery, R. W., Forster, S. H., French, S. H., Kelder, R. W., Lando, H. A., McGovern, P. G., Jacobs, D. R., Baxter, J. E. (1993). The healthy worker project: A worksite intervention for weight control and smoking cessation. *American Journal of Public Health 83*, 395–501.

Jeffrey, N. A. (1996). "Wellness plans" try to target the not-so-well. *The Wall Street Journal* (June 21), B1, B6.

Johnson, S. (1988). Breast screening's bottom line—lives saved. *Administrative Radiology* (June), 4.

Kaman, R. (ed.). (1995). *Worksite Health Promotion Economics: Consensus and Analysis.* Champaign, IL: Human Kinetics.

Kittrell, A. (1988). Wellness plans can save money: Survey. *Business Insurance* (Mar. 28), 9–11.

Klarreich, S. H., Digiuseppe, R., Dimattia, D. J. (1987). Cost effectiveness of an employee assistance program with rational–emotive therapy. *Professional Psychology: Research and Practice 18*, 140–144.

Labor letter. (1988). *The Wall Street Journal* (Dec. 6), A1.

Lancaster, H. (1990) Managing your career. *The Wall Street Journal* (Jan. 9), B1.

Leib, J. (1986). Companies wrestle with substance abuse. *Denver Post* (Sept. 1), 1E, 6E.

Masi, D. (1984). *Designing Employee Assistance Programs.* New York: American Management Association.

McEvoy, G. M., Cascio, W. F. (1987). Do good or poor performers leave? A meta-analysis of the relationship between performance and turnover. *Academy of Management Journal 30*, 744–762.

Metcalfe, L. L. (1987). The plant worker—singing the health and fitness blues. *Fitness in Business 1*(6), 230, 233–234.

O'Donnell, M. P. (1989). Definition of health promotion. Part III: Expanding the definition. *American Journal of Health Promotion 3*, 5.

Parker, D. L., Shultz, J. M., Gertz, L., Berkelman, R., Remington, P. L. (1987). The social and economic costs of alcohol abuse in Minnesota, 1983. *American Journal of Public Health 77*, 982–986.

Renner, J. F. (1987). WHP programs: An investment in cost containment *EAP Digest* (Mar.-Apr.), 49–53.

Sciacca, J. P. (1987). The worksite is the best place for health promotion. *Personnel Journal* (Nov.), 42–49.

Segal, J. A. (1997). Looking for trouble? *HRMagazine* (July), 76–83.

Seppa, N. (1997). EAPs offer quality care and cost-effectiveness. *Monitor* (Mar.), 32, 33.

Smith, K. J. (1987). A framework for appraising corporate WHP investments. *Internal Auditor* (Dec.), 28–33.

Smith, K. J., Haight, G. T., Everly, G. S. Jr. (1986). Evaluating corporate WHP investments. *Internal Auditor* (Feb.), 28–34.

Starr, A., Byram, G. (1985). Cost/benefit analysis for employee assistance programs. *Personnel Administrator 30*(8), 55–60.

Substance abuse cost at work: $100 billion. (1988). *Denver Post* (Dec. 12), 1A.

Terborg, J. R. (1988). The organization as a context for health promotion. In S. Oskamp and S. Spacapan (eds.), *The Social Psychology of Health* (pp. 129–174). Newbury Park, CA: Sage.

Terborg, J. R. (1995). Computer simulation: A promising technique for the evaluation of health promotion programs at the worksite. In R. L. Kaman (ed.), *Worksite Health Promotion Economics: Consensus and Analysis* (pp. 193–211). Champaign, IL: Human Kinetics.

Terborg, J. R. (1998). Health psychology in the United States: A critique and selected review. *Applied Psychology: An International Review 47*(2), 199–217.

U.S. Department of Health and Human Services. (1992). 1992 national survey of worksite health promotion activities: Summary. *American Journal of Health Promotion 6*, 452–464.

Wagner, W. G. (1987). *Assisting Employees with Personal Problems.* Personnel Administrator Reprint Collection Series, Employee Assistance Programs (pp. 45–49). Alexandria, VA: Society for Human Resource Management.

Wolfe, R., Slack, T., Rose-Hearn, T. (1993). Factors influencing the adoption and maintenance of Canadian facility-based worksite health-promotion programs. *American Journal of Health Promotion* 7(4), 189–198.

Woodward, N. H. (1998). Domestic abuse policies in the workplace. *HRMagazine* (May), 117–123.

C H A P T E R 6

The Financial Impact of Employee Attitudes

Anumber of studies in behavioral science have examined the relationship between job attitudes and characteristics of individuals (for example, age, gender, work–family conflict), characteristics of work environments (for example, perceived discrimination, just and flexible policies, supervisor/co-worker support), and outcomes (for example, absenteeism, turnover, job performance, customer satisfaction) (for reviews, see Lease 1998; Eagly & Chaiken 1993). Attitudes are internal states that are focused on particular aspects of or objects in the environment. They include three elements: *cognition,* the knowledge a person has about the focal object of the attitude; the *emotion* an individual feels toward the focal object; and an *action* tendency, a readiness to respond in a predetermined manner to the focal object.

Job satisfaction may be viewed as a multidimensional attitude; it is made up of attitudes toward pay, promotions, co-workers, supervision, the work itself, and so on. Likewise, organizational commitment is a bond or linking of a person to the organization that makes it difficult to leave (Mathieu & Zajac 1990). Management is interested in employees' job satisfaction and commitment principally because of the relationship between attitudes and behavior. Other things being equal, it is assumed that employees who are dissatisfied with their jobs and who are not committed strongly to their employers will tend to be absent or late for work, to quit more often, and to place less emphasis on customer satisfaction than do those whose attitudes are positive. Poor job attitudes therefore lead to lowered productivity and organizational performance. Evidence indicates that those assumptions are true and that management's concern is well placed (Ryan, Schmit, & Johnson 1996; Cohen 1993; Ostroff

1992). To explain the connection between attitudes and behavior, we must look at the precursors of attitudes: each individual's beliefs (Ajzen & Fishbein 1980). Attitudes are a function of beliefs.

LINKING ATTITUDES TO BEHAVIOR

Generally speaking, a person who believes that a particular behavior (for example, service helpfulness) will lead mostly to positive outcomes (for example, increased sales commissions) will hold a favorable attitude toward that behavior. A person who believes that the behavior will lead mostly to negative outcomes (for example, more effort, but no increase in sales commissions) will hold an unfavorable attitude. According to that approach, any behavior can be predicted from a person's attitude toward it, provided that the measure of attitude corresponds to that measure of behavior (that is, they are evaluated in similar terms). A revision to the original theory takes into account "perceived behavior control"—situational or behavioral obstacles to performance (Ajzen 1991). That is known as the theory of planned behavior and it holds that attitudes influence behavior through a process of deliberate decision making, but that the impact of attitudes is limited in four respects (see Exhibit 6–1).

First, behavior is influenced less by general attitudes (for example, people with "friendly" dispositions) than by attitudes toward a specific behavior (such as service helpfulness in the context of one's job). Second, behavior is influenced not only by attitudes, but also by *subjective norms*—beliefs about what others think we should do (for example, one's boss or co-workers). Third, attitudes give rise to behavior only when we perceive the behavior to be within our *control*. To the extent that a person lacks confidence in his or her ability to behave in a certain way (for example, to be friendly and helpful to customers), he or she is unlikely to form an intention to behave that way. Fourth, although attitudes (along with subjective norms and perceived control) contribute to an *intention* to behave in a particular way, people often do not or cannot follow through on that intention (Brehm & Kassin 1996). Reviews of research on the theory of planned action support its power to explain the links between attitudes and behavior in a variety of situations (Baron & Byrne 1997; Lord 1997).

From a costing perspective, the important questions are: what is the financial impact of the behavioral outcomes associated with job attitudes, and can we measure the costs associated with different levels of

EXHIBIT 6-1   *How the Theory of Planned Behavior Links Attitudes and Behavior*

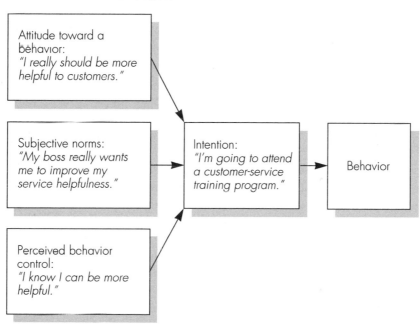

job satisfaction and commitment? Behavioral scientists need to be able to speak in dollars-and-cents terms when they argue the merits of HR development programs designed to change attitudes or improve job satisfaction. As discussed in chapters 2 and 3, methods for attaching costs to absenteeism and turnover are fairly well developed. Measures of employee attitudes are even more finely developed (Lord 1997; Feldman & Lynch 1988). This chapter will show how the two types of measures, financial and attitudinal, can be synthesized to produce an estimate in dollars of the costs and benefits of human resource development programs designed to improve employee attitudes.

MEASURING THE COSTS OF HR DEVELOPMENT PROGRAMS

Although the costs of HR development programs will be considered in much greater detail in chapter 11, for the present we'll distinguish three broad classes of costs: fixed, variable, and opportunity costs (see page 7). Fixed costs include salaries, wages, and benefits associated with employees' lost time and the resulting unabsorbed overhead costs (see chapters 2 and 3). Variable costs include, for example, consultants' fees and expenses associated with their activities. Those costs vary depending on the type of program and the intensity and duration of the development activities. They should be reported in deflated dollar terms. To do this, divide the costs for any year by the Consumer Price Index (CPI)/ 100 for that year. For example, assume that the 1994 CPI is 100; the 1998 CPI is 112; 1994 costs are $10,000; and 1998 costs are $13,000. The *apparent* increase in costs is $3,000 or 30 percent. However, the *real* increase in costs is $13,000/1.12 = $11,607.14, which is only 16.07 percent ($1,607.14 ÷ $10,000). The worksite also incurs variable costs in the form of lost worker productivity and overtime. Finally, opportunity costs reflect the profit contribution of the employees' lost time. There may be an additional opportunity cost, that of "opportunities foregone" (Rothenberg 1975), which might have been realized had the resources allocated to the program been directed toward other organizational ends.

On the other side of the ledger we can distinguish fixed, variable, and opportunity savings resulting from successful development programs. Fixed savings might be realized if some of the service demands placed on the HR, industrial relations, safety, and quality-control departments were reduced. Variable savings might include improved marginal productivity through increased product quality and quantity, limited overtime, reduced consumption of supplies and materials, and less unscheduled maintenance. Wages and other expenses arising from absenteeism, accidents, and grievances (including the expense of maintaining a replacement workforce) might also decrease. Finally, opportunity savings might be realized if the work time that supervisors spent in replacing absent employees or turnovers could be put to more productive use. Behavioral-economic measurement provides the methods for documenting these cost savings, and two early studies proposed methods for undertaking such calculations. We'll examine the limitations of those methods in order to illustrate the complexity of the problem and then present two subsequent approaches that circumvent many of the shortcomings of the first two methods.

EARLY ATTEMPTS TO ESTIMATE THE FINANCIAL IMPACT OF ATTITUDES

Human Asset Valuation

Myers and Flowers (1974) presented a simple framework for measuring human assets. They viewed job performance as the end product of a five-part flow process: knowledge, skills, health, availability, and attitudes add up to job performance. The individual's knowledge enables him or her to summon skills, and the individual's health enables him or her to apply them. The individual must be available when needed and must have the desire to apply his or her talents and energy toward productive effort. The five dimensions are not additive, so that if any one of them is lacking, the others are rendered ineffective. Before deciding to improve one dimension, therefore, consideration must be given to the levels of the others. Thus, it may not be cost effective to improve the job knowledge of an employee who has a poor attitude. The first priority may well be to improve attitudes before improving job knowledge.

According to Myers and Flowers, job attitudes are a symptom of the other four human assets as these are interpreted by each individual's value system. Therefore, a quantitative, reliable measure of attitudes is probably the best single measure of how well an individual uses all five assets. Attitude survey results, however, should not be lumped together indiscriminately. Each attitude score should be weighted by the individual's job-grade level and company tenure: the higher the job-grade level and the longer the tenure with the firm, the greater the weight attached to that person's score. Myers and Flowers attempted to quantify attitudes by multiplying salary dollars times weighted attitude scores to measure the potential dollar value increases that would be associated with improved employee attitudes (for example, see Exhibit 6–2).

This approach is a traditional one to human asset valuation; it assigns a value to individuals rather than to their behavior. Employees' salaries are equated with their value to the organization, and it is assumed that attitudinal improvements make employees more valuable to the organization. As Mirvis and Lawler (1977) have noted, that approach suffers from three shortcomings. First, it doesn't state the effects of improved attitudes on job behavior. We don't know whether attitudinal improvement implies higher employee productivity, lower absenteeism, reduced turnover, or some combination of these. Second, the approach ignores whether the actual savings associated with any behavioral changes will

EXHIBIT 6-2   *Human Asset Valuation Approach to Dollarizing Attitudes*

Unit: Digital Assembly

Employee	Annual Salary ($)	Job Grade	Tenure (years)	Attitude Weight	Attitude Score	Weighted Attitude Score
1. Tom Hill	30,000	18	15	6	1.05	6.30
2. Cindy Fleming	19,000	12	6	3	1.12	3.36
3. Ben Williams	43,000	23	22	9	1.25	11.25
4. Judy Francis	21,000	12	6	3	1.26	3.78
5. Amy Fox	34,000	19	15	7	1.16	8.12
	147,000			28		32.81

$$\text{attitude index} = \frac{(\Sigma \text{ weighted attitude score})}{(\Sigma \text{ attitude weights})} = \frac{32.81}{28} = 1.17$$

dollarized attitudes = attitude index × annual payroll = $1.17 \times \$147,000$
$$= \$171,990$$

gain = $117,990 - \$147,000 = \$24,990$

gain per person = $4,998

equal their estimated value improvement (that is, validation of predicted savings). Finally, Myers and Flowers present no data on the relationship between the attitudes they measure and the behaviors of employees. At best, this framework provides a way for organizations to judge the impact of organizational investment on employee morale. It provides no clues to the direct financial impact of job satisfaction and commitment.

THE UNIT-COST APPROACH

The unit-cost approach to assigning dollar values to attitudes was developed by Likert (1973) and Likert and Bowers (1973). Rather than trying to assign a value to the overall worth of an employee to an organization, the method attempts to determine the short-term costs of employee behavior by correlating standardized attitude scores with unit cost. It then predicts changes in unit cost from anticipated changes in attitudes and argues that the cost change represents the economic impact of the attitudes.

That approach also has problems, as Mirvis and Lawler (1977) have noted. The first problem stems from the choice of unit cost as a performance criterion. Cost per unit includes fixed costs (those incurred regardless of the number of units or level of service produced) and variable costs (those directly related to the level of activity). *Only variable costs can be affected immediately by such employee behaviors as increased productivity and reduced absenteeism and turnover.* Furthermore, both cost components are influenced by inflationary trends. Including fixed costs and inflationary trends in the criterion measure builds in a significant amount of variance that has nothing to do with changes in attitudes.

A second problem with this approach is that it ignores the processes that intervene between changes in attitude and changes in unit cost. That is, previous research suggests that improvements in job satisfaction and commitment should reduce levels of absenteeism and turnover, which in turn should result in lower unit cost. Simply relating attitudes to unit costs and bypassing the intervening processes ignores this sequential effect. The resulting relationship and financial consequences might well be over- or understated.

A third problem with the unit-cost approach is its assumption of a constant attitude–behavior relationship over time. In fact, improvement in attitude scores could be accompanied by stronger or weaker predictive relationships to behavior. Predicted savings based on a constant relationship would understate the resulting benefits if the relationship was stronger than had been assumed, and it would overstate the benefits if the relationship was weaker than had been assumed.

A final problem with this approach is that it relies on analysis at the work-group level, but much of the behavior change would occur at the individual level. Unless organizations are extremely large, and there is theoretical and empirical support for aggregating attitudes measured at the individual level into the work-group level, relationships derived at the group level may be unreliable indicators of individual-level change (Ryan et al. 1996).

In view of the shortcomings of the human asset valuation and unit-cost approaches, I do not recommend that they be used. An awareness of their shortcomings is instructive, however, especially as a yardstick for measuring progress in methods proposed subsequently. One of these approaches, behavior costing, was developed by Mirvis and Lawler (1977).

THE BEHAVIOR-COSTING APPROACH

Behavior costing is based on the assumption that attitudinal measures are indicators of subsequent employee behaviors. Those behaviors can be assessed using cost-accounting procedures, and they have economic implications for organizations. Only short-term, direct costs associated with the behaviors are used. This approach clearly builds on Likert and Bowers' unit-cost approach.

The conceptual framework underlying behavior costing stems from expectancy theory, which emphasizes that employees' behavior at work is the result of choices about whether to appear at the workplace ("participation-membership" [March & Simon 1958]) and of choices about how to behave at work ("work strategies" [Lawler 1973]). The framework assumes that employees will be more likely to come to work than be absent or quit if they are satisfied with their jobs, and that they are likely to give more effort and to choose more effective job performance strategies if they expect to be rewarded, either intrinsically or extrinsically, for their efforts (Vroom 1964).

Those ideas suggest that attitudinal indexes of employee satisfaction and job involvement should be the best predictors of participation-membership because they reflect perceptions of the rewards associated with being at work (Lawler 1973). Employee intrinsic motivation should be the best predictor of job performance because it reflects some of the performance outcomes contingent on doing a good job: competence, achievement, and self-realization.

Methodology Used to Test the Theory

Those theoretical ideas were tested empirically on a sample of 160 tellers from 20 branches of a Midwestern banking organization. The tellers (average age, 30) were predominantly female (94 percent). They served as cashiers, handling customer deposits, withdrawals, and other transactions.

Attitude measures were taken from the Michigan Assessment of Organizations (Survey Research Center 1975), and reflected intrinsic satisfaction (six items), organizational involvement (two items), and intrinsic motivation (three items). For example:

- *Intrinsic satisfaction:* Please indicate how satisfied you are with the following aspects of your job: (1) the chances you have to do the things you do best; (2) the chances you have to learn new things; (3) the opportunity you have to develop your skills and abilities.
- *Organizational involvement:* Is what happens in this branch really important to you?

- *Intrinsic motivation:* When you do your job well, do you feel you've done something worthwhile? Do you get a feeling of personal satisfaction from doing your job well?

Measures of participation-membership behavior and work performance were collected monthly after administration of the attitude questionnaire. Using standardized definitions and measures of behavioral outcomes (Macy & Mirvis 1976), the following data were collected:

- *Short-term absence or illness:* unauthorized absences of fewer than three consecutive days, including short-term illness and absence for personal reasons.
- *Voluntary turnover:* voluntary employee departure from the bank, excluding terminations, maternity leaves or turnovers, and transfers.
- *Teller balancing shortages:* the number of shortages in tellers' balances (overpayments to customers).

Results of the Study

Over a three-month period there was no statistical measure of relationship (correlation, r) between the outcome measures of absenteeism and turnover, and there were few significant correlations between the outcome measures of absenteeism and shortages (median $r = -0.06$) or turnover and shortages (median $r = 0.15$). The absenteeism measure reflected some stability across months 1, 2, and 3 ($r_{12} = 0.61$, $r_{23} = 0.71$, $r_{13} = 0.52$). However, no one who was absent the first month was absent the next two months. In contrast, the number of teller balancing shortages was more stable ($r_{12} = 0.82$, $r_{23} = 0.71$, $r_{13} = 0.59$).

Each behavior has a cost to the organization. The major cost elements associated with turnover and absenteeism were outlined in chapters 2 and 3. With respect to teller shortages, the direct cost was estimated to be $24.02 per shortage.[1] That figure includes the cash outlay minus recoveries, and is reported in constant dollar terms. Each incident of absenteeism was estimated to cost $193.56, of which $67.25 (salary) was a variable cost (because the supervisor either must find a suitable replacement or must extend the existing staff). The total cost of each turnover incident was estimated at $7,361.96, of which $858.05 (direct hiring costs) was variable.

The distinction between variable and total costs is important, for a reduction in absenteeism and turnover will result in variable cost savings only. A reduction in fixed costs or realization of opportunity savings depends on subsequent reallocation of fixed costs or staff workloads. Thus, fixed costs and opportunity savings were not included in the financial estimates.

Exhibit 6–3 shows the relationship between teller attitudes and the outcome measures of absenteeism, turnover, and balancing shortages three months later. Correlations between attitudes and turnover are generally low to moderate, and negative. This is consistent with results found in other research (Cohen 1993; Mathieu & Zajac 1990). Notice also the significant negative correlation between tellers' intrinsic motivation and shortages three months later. Finally, the high negative correlation between satisfaction and absenteeism is probably an artifact. July is a primary vacation month for the tellers and some took additional, unauthorized days off. The findings suggest that the most dissatisfied employees took this extra time off. Further, individual absences varied over time, and the correlations between attitude measures and absenteeism fluctuated over the three-month reporting period. Thus the cost savings attributable to reduced absenteeism may be particular to the measurement period.

We are now in a position to relate the attitudinal measures to financial results and to estimate the potential benefits resulting from improvements in employee attitudes. The statistical approach for doing this was developed by Likert (1973). As an example, we'll relate tellers' intrinsic motivation scores ($M = 6.11$, $SD = 0.96$) and the average number of balancing shortages per month ($M = 3.07$, $SD = 1.74$).[2] To estimate the

EXHIBIT 6–3   *Relationship Between Attitudes and Behavior*
(Lagged Three Months)

Attitudes (measured in April)	Behaviors (measured in July)		
	Absenteeism	Turnover	Shortages
Intrinsic satisfaction	−0.81[a]	−0.20[b]	0.10
Job involvement	0.08	−0.29[a]	−0.12
Intrinsic motivation	−0.26[a]	−0.16[b]	−0.23[a]

[a] $p < 0.01$.
[b] $p < 0.05$.

Source: Mirvis, P. H., and Lawler, E. E. III. (1977). Measuring the financial impact of employee attitudes. *Journal of Applied Psychology* 62, 4. Copyright © 1977 by the American Psychological Association. Reprinted with permission.

potential savings from a 0.5 SD improvement in motivation, the steps are as follows:

1. present cost level = average number of balancing shortages
$$\times \text{ cost per incident}$$
$$= 3.07 \times \$24.02$$
$$= \$73.74 \text{ per employee per month}$$
2. planned attitudinal improvement = 0.5 SD
3. estimated behavioral improvement = (planned attitudinal
$$\text{improvement in } SD \text{ units)}$$
$$\times (SD \text{ of balancing shortages})$$
$$\times (r_{mot., shortages})$$
$$= 0.5 \times 1.74 \times -0.23$$
$$= -0.20$$
4. new behavioral rate = present average number of shortages +
$$\text{estimated behavioral improvement}$$
$$= 3.07 + (-0.20)$$
$$= 2.87 \text{ per employee per month}$$
5. new cost level = new behavioral rate $\times$ cost per incident
$$= 2.87 \times \$24.02$$
$$= \$68.94 \text{ per employee per month}$$

A similar procedure was used to estimate the cost levels associated with the other attitudes that were measured. For most measures, more positive attitudes were associated with lower costs. The cost figures are conservative for they reflect only the variable costs per teller for one month. For the bank tellers as a whole ($N = 160$) over a one-year period, an improvement in teller satisfaction of 0.5 SD was estimated to result in direct savings (in 1998 dollars) of $51,562. Potential total savings were estimated to be $365,349.

Advantages of the Behavior-Costing Approach

Behavior costing has three important advantages. First, it is a practical method for relating attitudes to costs that can be used in a variety of organizations. Moreover, it has the potential to increase significantly the impact and usefulness of attitudinal data. By focusing attention on employee satisfaction and motivation, results of the behavior-costing approach could stimulate changes designed specifically to improve satisfaction and motivation. As we shall see later in this chapter, this is exactly what Sears, Roebuck, & Co. did 20 years later.

A second advantage of this approach is that it relates attitudes to future costs. Thus, organizations could use it as a way of diagnosing future costs and as a basis for initiating programs designed to reduce those costs. That makes it possible for managers to estimate the cost savings and potential benefits associated with improved morale and group functioning.

A third advantage of the behavior-costing approach is that it yields the financial measure most related to employee attitudes. Traditionally, HRA has valued employee service at gross book value (the original investment expense), net book value (the original investment minus depreciation), and economic value (the anticipated financial return of the investment). In contrast, behavior costing shifts the emphasis from assigning a value to employees to assessing the economic consequences of their behavior (Mirvis & Lawler 1977).

Problems with the Behavior-Costing Approach

Despite its advantages, the behavior-costing approach also creates a number of difficulties. One important issue concerns validation of the predicted cost savings, which can be done only by observing what happens when attitude changes actually occur. To test the validity of the cost figures presented earlier, Mirvis and Lawler collected data one year later from the same tellers. At that time the tellers' personal motivation had increased to 6.25 or 0.145 *SDs*. Actual shortages had decreased to $63.38 (in 1998 dollars) per month, somewhat below the anticipated level, but in the predicted direction. Such evidence suggests that the changes in attitude caused the changes in behavior, but because behavior costing is based on correlational analyses, other causal explanations are possible.

Two additional problems in predicting behavioral rate changes and costs from attitudinal data stem from the nature of the attitude–behavior relationship. The first problem has to do with the appropriateness of the time lag. Mirvis and Lawler used a three-month lag, but they also examined one- and two-month lags. They found relationships between attitudes and behavior in all cases, but the relationships were strongest in the three-month lag. Findings in the organizational literature suggest that a variety of time lags produce significant effects (Meyer & Raich 1983). At this time, therefore, the safest course is probably to collect time-series data on attitudes and behavior at multiple measurement points and then choose the interval that yields the most stable and representative relationships.

A related problem is that the size and form of the relationship between these variables can change over time. In the Mirvis and Lawler study, for example, secondary analyses revealed that monthly time-series relationships between a single-item measure of intrinsic satisfaction and teller shortages ranged from −0.67 to −0.06 over a four-month period. Unless that relationship is stable, predicted financial changes will not be accurate. In addition, the behavior-costing model assumes a linear attitude–behavior relationship, but the actual relationship may be curvilinear. Correlational methods are available to deal with curvilinear relations (for example, eta, the correlation ratio), but the point is that both the size and the form of attitude–behavior relationships must be monitored over time with periodic corrections in the predicted savings based on the new relationships.

Special care must be taken not to over- or understate potential cost savings. Motivation and job satisfaction are likely to be improved by a combination of factors, such as job enrichment programs, participative management styles, or better employee selection procedures. Because the components of job attitudes (satisfaction, job involvement, intrinsic motivation, and so on) are rarely independent, separately estimating the cost savings associated with each would overstate the resulting benefits. That fact suggests that monthly behavior measures should be related to the *set* of relevant attitude measures, which would probably result in more accurate estimates of the attitude–behavior relationships and the eventual financial benefits.

Behavior Costing at Sears:
The Employee–Customer–Profit Chain

A fundamental component of the transition from big losses to big profits at Sears, Roebuck & Company was the development of a new business model. The model altered the logic and culture of the business. Indeed, the process of altering the logic is what changed the culture (Rucci, Kirn, & Quinn 1998). In retailing, there is a chain of cause and effect running from employee behavior to customer behavior to profits. Employee behavior depends largely on attitude. What is different about the Sears model is that instead of trying to relate employee attitudes directly to financial outcomes, the model treats customer behavior as a critical intervening variable.

Another important point is that the challenge of realizing the full benefit of the model includes three important components: creating and refining the employee–customer–profit model and the measurement system that supports it; creating management alignment around the use of the model to run the company; and deploying the model so as to build business literacy and trust among employees. This implies that any retailer could copy the Sears measures, even the modeling techniques, and still fail to realize much benefit from the model, because the mechanics of the system are not in themselves enough to make it work. Although a discussion of the latter two challenges above is beyond the scope of this chapter, keep them in mind as you examine the measurement model.

From Concept to Measurement: The Three "Compellings"

Careful analysis of the output of company task forces and customer focus groups led Sears managers to think in terms of a business model that would link employees, customers, and investors. The managers became convinced that for Sears to succeed financially, it had to be a compelling place *both* to work and to shop (that is, work × shop, not work + shop). The right merchandise at the right prices would not enable the company to succeed financially if its employees were poorly motivated. These ideas formed the three "compellings": Sears should be a compelling place to work, to shop, and to invest. The formula *work × shop = invest* brought together the leading, not lagging, indicators. As Rucci et al. (1998) noted: ". . . financial results are a rearview mirror; they tell you how you did in the last quarter, and not how you will do in the next . . . few if any companies have ever come up with dependable predictive metrics, and that's what we were after" (p. 88).

The next step was to convert the three compellings into a set of measures and a measurement model. The objective was to devise a kind of balanced scorecard for the company—the Sears Total Performance Indicators, or TPI—that would show pathways of actual causation all the way from employee attitudes to profits. The nonfinancial measures (for example, measures of employee attitudes) had to be every bit as rigorous and auditable as the financial ones.

Possibilities

Information about causation would be invaluable, if Sears could develop it. Suppose, for example, Sears wanted to spend money on training to increase its sales associates' knowledge of the products they sell. Would customers notice? Would the investment lead to increased customer retention, better word of mouth, higher revenues, greater market share? If so, how long would it take? Alternatively, suppose the firm wanted to measure the effects of an improvement in management skills. That measure is critically important because 70 percent of its employees work part-time, and part-time employees have a high turnover rate. The model and the TPI could tell *how* important those management skills actually were, measured in terms of employee attitudes and customer satisfaction. A chain of causation would help answer those questions and guide Sears' managers in running the company.

Metrics, Data, and a Causal Model

Over two quarters, Sears' managers collected survey data from employees and customers and financial data from 800 of its stores. A team of consulting statisticians then factor-analyzed the data into meaningful clusters and used causal pathway modeling to assess cause–effect relationships. On the basis of the initial results, Sears adjusted the model and continued to collect data for a new iteration at the end of the next quarter.

How did Sears benefit from the model? The company could see how employee attitudes drove not only customer service, but also employee turnover and the likelihood that employees would recommend Sears and its merchandise to friends, family, and customers. It discovered that an employee's ability to see the connection between his or her work and the company's strategic objectives was a driver of positive behavior. It also found that asking customers whether Sears is a "fun place to shop" revealed more than a long list of more specific questions would reveal. It began to see exactly how a change in training or business literacy affected revenues.

Although Sears used a 70-item questionnaire to assess employees' attitudes, it found that a mere 10 of those questions captured the predictive relationship among employee attitudes, behavior toward the customer, and customer satisfaction. Items such as the following predicted an employee's attitude about his or her job:

- I like the kind of work I do.
- I am proud to say I work at Sears.
- How does the way you are treated by those who supervise you influence your *overall attitude* about your job?

Items such as the following predicted an employee's attitude about the company:

- I feel good about the future of the company.
- I understand our business strategy.
- Do you see a connection between the work you do and the company's strategic objectives?

In summary, Sears produced a model, revised it three times, and created a TPI for the company as a whole. The company conducts interviews and collects data continually, assembles its information quarterly, and recalculates the impacts on its model annually to stay abreast of the changing economy, demographics, and competitive circumstances. The revised model (see Exhibit 6–4) helps Sears' managers run the company. For example, consider the quality of management as a driver of employee attitudes. The model shows that a 5-point improvement in employee attitudes will drive a 1.3-point improvement in customer satisfaction in the next quarter, which in turn will drive a 0.5 percent improvement in revenue growth. If Sears knew nothing about a local store except that employee attitudes had improved by 5 points on its survey instrument, it could predict with confidence that if revenue growth in the district as a whole were 5 percent, revenue growth at this particular store would be 5.5 percent. Every year, an outside accounting firm audits those numbers as closely as it audits the company's financial measures.

Impact on Managers' Behavior

In a revolutionary step, Sears now bases all long-term executive incentives on the TPI. Such incentives rest on nonfinancial as well as on financial performance—one-third on employee measures, one-third on customer measures, and one-third on traditional investor measures. The use of nonfinancial measures for performance assessment has also cascaded down to lower levels. A significant portion of the pay of field managers is at risk, depending on targeted improvements in customer satisfaction. At some locations, even hourly associates are being given the opportunity to earn valuable incentive pay that is almost always based on improved customer satisfaction.

Impact on the Firm

Independent surveys show that national retail customer satisfaction has fallen for several consecutive years, but in calendar year 1997 employee satisfaction on Sears' TPI rose 4 percent, and customer satisfaction rose by almost 4 percent. The 4 percent improvement translated into more than $200 million in additional revenues for that year. That increased

EXHIBIT 6–4 *Revised Model: The Employee–Customer–Profit Chain*

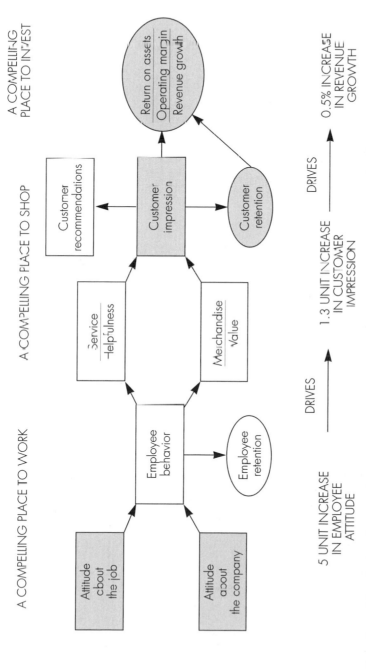

A COMPELLING PLACE TO WORK   A COMPELLING PLACE TO SHOP   A COMPELLING PLACE TO INVEST

Attitude about the job

Attitude about the company

Employee behavior

Employee retention

Service / Helpfulness

Merchandise / Value

Customer recommendations

Customer impression

Customer retention

Return on assets / Operating margin / Revenue growth

5 UNIT INCREASE IN EMPLOYEE ATTITUDE   DRIVES   1.3 UNIT INCREASE IN CUSTOMER IMPRESSION   DRIVES   0.5% INCREASE IN REVENUE GROWTH

This is the model used today. The rectangles represent survey information, the ovals represent hard data. The shaded measurements are those collected and distributed in the form of the Sears Total Performance Indicators.

Source: A. J. Rucci, S. P. Kim, R. T. Quinn. (1998), The employee–customer–profit chain at Sears. *Harvard Business Review* (Jan.-Feb.), p. 91. Used with permission.

EXHIBIT 6-5 *Assumptions, Advantages, and Disadvantages of Attitude-Cost Models*

Model	Assumptions	Advantages	Disadvantages
Human Asset Valuation	Salary = value to organization; therefore attitudinal improvement enhances value to the organization	a. Simple framework for measuring human assets b. Atitude Index may serve as a standard metric	a. Effects of improved attitudes on job behavior are unknown b. No validation of predicted savings
Unit Cost	Changes in unit costs can be predicted from anticipated changes in attitudes. Therefore cost change = economic impact of attitudes	a. Reduces errors associated with equating to zero changes in the value of human organization from Time 1 to Time 2 b. Offers statistical method for relating attitudinal measures to financial results	a. Inclusion of fixed costs + inflationary trends in cost per unit yields irrelevant variance b. Ignores intervening processes between changes in attitudes and changes in unit cost c. Assumes constant attitude–behavior relationship over time d. Analysis is at workgroup level, not at individual level
Behavior Costing	Attitudinal measures are indicators of subsequent employee behaviors—participation-membership and job performance	a. Relates attitudes to future costs b. Yields the financial measure most closely related to employee attitudes c. Analysis is at individual, not at workgroup level	a. Difficult to validate cost savings because analyses are based on correlational data b. "Best" time lag for determining attitude–behavior relationships is unknown c. Instability in attitude–behavior relationships yields inaccurate financial changes

| Employee–Customer–Profit Chain | Employee attitudes influence employee behavior, which affects customer satisfaction, which drives financial results | a. Identifies cause–effect relations
b. Is predictive in nature
c. Enables answers to "What if . . ." questions
d. Guides management actions | a. Data collection and annual updates may be time-consuming and expensive
b. Managers must align their actions with the model
c. Managers must deploy the model to employees at every level |

Sears' market capitalization (price per share multiplied by the number of shares outstanding) by nearly one-quarter of a billion dollars. Even more impressive, according to Rucci et al. (1998), is what the model reveals: "It is our managers and employees who, at the moment of truth in front of the customer, have achieved this prodigious feat of value creation" (p. 97).

A FINAL WORD ON ATTITUDE VALUATION

It is clear that the time has arrived for behavioral scientists to speak the language of business. The methods described in this chapter provide a useful start in that direction, but the nonfinancial impact of changes in employee attitudes and motivation (for example, individual growth and well-being, organizational adaptability, and goodwill) cannot, and perhaps should not, be assigned an economic value. Management decisions made solely to optimize financial gains will miss completely the effects of organizational development or attitude-change programs on nonfinancial results.

Nonetheless, although a number of problems are associated with relating attitudes to costs (see Exhibit 6–5), and refinements may be needed in the methods described here, the potential of cost–benefit comparisons of attitude–behavior relationships is enormous. The possible payoffs in improved HR and financial planning amply justify expending the necessary effort and resources to develop further methods for estimating the financial impact of employee attitudes.

EXERCISES

1. You are given the following data relative to the five-member troubleshooting team of the Behrens Corporation:

Employee	Annual Salary ($)	Job Grade	Tenure (years)	Attitude Weight	Attitude Score
1. D. Hobbs	34,000	32	10	8	1.15
2. P. Smith	18,000	24	6	5	1.04
3. T. Studley	30,000	37	14	10	1.28
4. B. Woo	28,000	30	10	7	1.20
5. W. Finkel	21,500	23	5	4	0.78

a. Use a human asset valuation approach to dollarize these attitudes, to compute the overall gain (or loss), and to compute the gain (or loss) per person.

b. What are two advantages and two drawbacks to this approach?

2. As a special project, top management wants to use behavior-costing methodology as one input to its HR planning model. Over a three-month period, you have found the correlation between job satisfaction and absenteeism to be −0.34 for a sample of clerical employees. Chronic absenteeism is a serious problem in this firm, and clerical employees average 2.2 days per month absent from work $(SD = 1.43)$. Each such incident costs $208.26, of which $102.04 is a variable cost. If management were to institute a job enrichment program that would improve attitudes among the clerical employees by 0.45 SD, what might be the potential savings per employee per month?

3. You have read about the employee–customer–profit chain at Sears, and how it serves as a business model for the company. As a senior manager, how would you respond to the following questions:

a. What implications might such a model have for recruitment, selection, orientation, training, performance management, and incentive compensation?

b. What practical issues have to be considered in deploying the model throughout the company?

REFERENCES

Ajzen, I. (1991). The theory of planned behavior. *Organizational Behavior and Human Decision Processes 50*, 179–211.

Ajzen, I., Fishbein, M. (1980). *Understanding Attitudes and Predicting Social Behavior.* Englewood Cliffs, NJ: Prentice Hall.

Baron, R. A., Byrne, D. (1997). *Social Psychology* (8th ed.). Boston: Allyn & Bacon.

Brehm, S. S., Kassin, S. M. (1996). *Social Psychology* (3rd ed.). Boston: Houghton-Mifflin.

Cohen, A. (1993). Organizational commitment and turnover: A meta-analysis. *Academy of Management Journal 36*, 1140–1157.

Eagly, A. H., Chaiken, S. (1993). *The Psychology of Attitudes.* New York: Harcourt, Brace, Jovanovich.

Feldman, J. M., Lynch, J. G. Jr. (1988). Self-generated validity and other effects of measurement on belief, attitude, intention, and behavior. *Journal of Applied Psychology 73*, 421–435.

Lawler, E. E. III. (1973). *Motivation in Work Organizations.* Monterey, CA: Brooks/Cole.

Lease, S. H. (1998). Annual review, 1993–1997: Work attitudes and outcomes. *Journal of Vocational Behavior 53*, 154–183.

Likert, R. (1973). Human resource accounting: Building and assessing productive organizations. *Personnel 50*, 8–24.

Likert, R., Bowers, D. G. (1973). Improving the accuracy of P/L reports by estimating the change in dollar value of the human organization. *Michigan Business Review 25*, 15–24.

Lord, C. G. (1997). *Social Psychology.* Fort Worth, TX: Harcourt Brace College Publishers.

Macy, B. A., Mirvis, P. H. (1976). Measuring the quality of work life and organizational effectiveness in behavioral-economic terms. *Administrative Science Quarterly 21*, 212–226.

March, J. O., Simon, H. A. (1958). *Organizations.* New York: John Wiley & Sons.

Mathieu, J. E., Zajac, D. M. (1990). A review and meta-analysis of the antecedents, correlates, and consequences or organizational commitment. *Psychological Bulletin 108*(2), 171–194.

Meyer, H. H., Raich, M. S. (1983). An objective evaluation of a behavior modeling training program. *Personnel Psychology 36*, 755–761.

Mirvis, P. H., Lawler, E. E. III. (1977). Measuring the financial impact of employee attitudes. *Journal of Applied Psychology 62*, 1–8.

Myers, M. S., Flowers, V. S. (1974). A framework for measuring human assets. *California Management Review 16*(4), 5–16.

Ostroff, C. (1992). The relationship between satisfaction, attitudes, and performance: An organizational-level analysis. *Journal of Applied Psychology 77*, 963–974.

Rothenberg, J. (1975). Cost–benefit analysis: A methodological exposition. In M. Guttentag and E. Struening (eds.), *Handbook of Evaluation Research* (Vol. 2, pp. 75–106). Beverly Hills, CA: Sage.

Rucci, A. J., Kirn, S. P., Quinn, R. T. (1998). The employee–customer–profit chain at Sears. *Harvard Business Review 76*, 82–97.

Ryan, A. M., Schmit, M. J., Johnson, R. (1996). Attitudes and effectiveness: Examining relations at an organizational level. *Personnel Psychology 49*, 853–883.

Survey Research Center, (1975) *Michigan Organizational Assessment Package.* Ann Arbor, MI: Institute for Social Research.

Vroom, V. H. (1964). *Work and Motivation.* New York: John Wiley & Sons.

ENDNOTES

1. All costs are expressed in terms of 1998 dollars, assuming an average annual inflation rate of 6 percent between 1977 and 1990, and 4 percent from 1990 to 1998.
2. M = mean; SD = standard deviation, a measure of the variability or dispersion of scores about their mean.

C H A P T E R 7

The Strategic and Financial Effects of Work–Life Programs

C onsider the following facts about the American workforce (Bond, Galinsky, & Swanberg 1998).

- Eighty-five percent of employees have some day-to-day family responsibility, and virtually identical proportions of men and women report work–family conflicts.
- Among wage and salaried workers, 46 percent are parents with children under 18 years of age who live with them at least half of the time.
- Among married employees, 78 percent have spouses or partners who are also employed.

For workers who are parents, consider the following facts about childcare issues (Johnson 1999).

- Nearly one in five American workers (19 percent) has at least one child under six years of age living at home.
- More than one-third of employees in the United States must have childcare arrangements in place in order to come to work.
- Among employed parents, 29 percent experienced some kind of childcare breakdown in the three months preceding the survey, and 33 percent regularly spend time on the job worrying about childcare.
- Childcare breakdowns are associated with absenteeism, tardiness, impaired concentration, and lowered marital and parental satisfaction.

Children are not the only cause of concern; eldercare issues are also prevalent—and increasing (Johnson 1999).

- One-quarter of U.S. workers had eldercare responsibilities during the year preceding the survey.
- Of those workers, one-third lost time at work because of eldercare responsibilities.
- Older workers are more likely to have eldercare responsibilities (37 percent of workers over 50 years of age), but many younger workers do, too (18 percent of workers under 30 years of age).
- The impact of eldercare responsibilities is gender-blind; men and women are affected equally.

Finally, at a general level, family and personal concerns are sources of stress in all workplaces.

- In professional-service firms, well over half of the employees can be expected to experience some kind of work–family stress in a three-month period.
- Staff members with work–family conflict are three times more likely to consider quitting (43 percent versus 14 percent) (Johnson 1999).
- Staff members who believe that work is causing problems in their personal lives are much more likely to make mistakes at work (30 percent) than are those who have few job-related personal problems (19 percent) (Johnson 1995).
- Employees with supportive workplaces report greater job satisfaction and more commitment to helping their companies succeed (Johnson 1999).

And speaking of commitment, whether you work in a retail store or a research laboratory, wouldn't it be great if employees at every level were fully engaged and willing to "go the extra mile" to help the organization as a whole prosper and to help their peers and team members accomplish their objectives? Wouldn't it be great if :

- your call-center operator went out of his or her way to satisfy your customer?
- you kept that creative 20-something engineer from moving to a start-up competitor?
- your plant employees took more ownership in fixing production problems and reducing cycle time? (Rodgers 1998)

Those few examples illustrate the difference people can make in an organization and the importance of employee commitment. Building or increasing that commitment in an era of high-stress work environments, downsizing, and restructuring is one of the most difficult challenges organizations face today. Although the challenge is great, so also is the payoff from a loyal, committed workforce in terms of enhanced customer satisfaction, increased revenues and profits, and improvements in shareholder value. To illustrate the power of employee commitment, consider the following evidence (Rodgers 1998).

- Highly committed employees work harder and generate higher sales than do employees with weak commitment (Bashaw & Grant 1994), they are more effective in controlling operational costs (DeCotiis & Summers 1987), and they receive higher overall performance ratings from supervisors (Moorman, Niehoff, & Organ 1993).
- Employee loyalty is related to customer loyalty, which, in turn, is related to company growth and profits (Heskett, Sasser, & Schelsinger 1997).
- As we saw in chapter 6, Sears, Roebuck, & Co. found that employee attitudes drive both customer satisfaction and changes in revenue. Using causal-modeling methods, Sears found that a 5 percent improvement in employee attitudes drives a 1.3 percent improvement in customer satisfaction, which drives a 0.5 percent increase in store revenue (Rucci, Kirn, & Quinn 1998).
- Employee retention is a key driver of customer retention, which, in turn, is a key driver of company growth and profits. A study at MBNA's credit card business showed that a 5 percent increase in customer retention translates into a 125 percent increase in per-customer profits (Reichheld 1996). In another study, a 7 percent decrease in employee turnover led to increases of more than $27,000 in sales per employee and increases in profits per employee of almost $4,000 (Huselid & Becker 1995).

Although such outcomes are desirable, in many organizations they represent only wishful thinking because for many employees there is a spillover effect from issues at work to their personal lives off the job. Research has shown that more than one-third of employees frequently experience negative spillover from the job to their personal lives (Johnson 1999; Bond et al. 1998). Summarizing four previous studies, Friedman (1991) sought to determine what suffers most, work or family. On average, almost a third of men and 45 percent of women said that work interferes with family. Only 12 percent of men and 26 percent of women said that family interferes with work.

That spillover is reflected in high stress, bad moods, poor coping, and insufficient quality and amount of time for family and friends. When employees are worried about personal issues outside of work they become distracted, and their job commitment wanes, along with their productivity. Ultimately, both absenteeism and turnover (voluntary or involuntary) increase. As we have noted, family/personal issues are widespread sources of stress in every workplace, and conflicts between work and personal life affect productivity and general well-being.

In response to competitive pressures, tight labor markets, changing workforce demographics, and a growing body of evidence that documents the bottom-line benefits to employers of acknowledging and supporting the personal lives of their employees, more firms are instituting work–life programs.

WORK–LIFE PROGRAMS: WHAT ARE THEY?

Although originally termed "work–family" programs, in this book we use the term "work–life" programs to reflect a broader perspective on the issue. "Work–life" recognizes that employees at every level in an organization, whether parents or nonparents, face personal or family issues that can affect their performance on the job. *A work–life program includes any employer-sponsored benefit or working condition that helps an employee to balance work and nonwork demands.* At a general level, such programs span the following five broad areas (Bardoel, Tharenou, & Moss 1998):

1. Child- and dependent-care benefits (for example, on-site or near-site child- or eldercare programs, summer and weekend programs for dependents)
2. Flexible working conditions (for example, flextime, job sharing, teleworking, part-time work, compressed work weeks)
3. Leave options (for example, maternity, paternity, and adoption leaves; sabbaticals; phased re-entry or retirement schemes)
4. Information services and HR policies (for example, cafeteria benefits, life-skill educational programs such as parenting skills, health issues, financial management, and retirement, exercise facilities, professional and personal counseling)

5. Organizational cultural issues (for example, an organizational culture that is supportive with respect to the nonwork issues of employees; co-workers and supervisors who are sensitive to family issues)

STRATEGIC IMPLICATIONS OF WORK–LIFE PROGRAMS

Several studies have investigated the relationship between a host of HR practices and company performance (Delaney & Huselid 1996; Youndt, Snell, Dean, & Lepak 1996; MacDuffie 1995; Arthur 1994), but they have not included work–life programs in their taxonomies of HR practices. Such policies may be considered progressive and innovative, but they are rarely considered to be strategic, let alone "best practices" (Perry-Smith & Blum 1998). This may be changing, as work–life programs begin to be viewed as strategic responses to competitive environments and as sources of competitive advantage for firms (Konrad & Mangel 1998).

At least two related arguments support the view that work–life initiatives are a strategic response to the competitive environment (Konrad & Mangel 1998). First, such initiatives are important mechanisms for protecting a firm's investments in human capital. They can help to attract, retain, and motivate employees to work to their full potential. Second, work–life initiatives are fully compatible with empowerment-oriented strategic-control frameworks that enable HR polices and practices to fit together. In the following sections, we will develop each of these arguments further.

Protecting Investments in Human Capital

In the field of strategic management, the resource-based view of the firm holds that sustainable competitive advantage derives from systems or "unique bundles" of resources that competitors cannot copy (Coff 1997; Barney 1991). Human resources are particularly attractive, especially to the extent that their scarcity, specialization, and tacit knowledge make them difficult to imitate (Coff 1997). Thus, although an innovative design for an automobile may be easy for competitors to identify and copy, it is often difficult or impossible to identify and copy the precise features of a strong and effective corporate culture (Collis & Montgomery 1995). Let us consider some other barriers to imitation.

A single work–life program, such as a dependent-care program, may be relatively easy to imitate, but a full *system* of work–life programs, which may include different configurations of the five broad areas described earlier, is difficult or impossible to imitate precisely.

Adopting a single work–life program actually may engender negative feelings or resentment and perceptions of unfairness (Kossek & Nichol 1992; Grover 1991), but a system of work–life programs may reflect an overall philosophy about the importance of employee well-being or a strategy about managing people. However, such systems of work–life policies continue to be rare among U.S. firms. Some individual work–life policies are more common than others, but comprehensive arrays are exceptions within many industries (Osterman 1995; Perry-Smith & Blum 1998).

Another reason why copying systems of work–life programs is difficult is that the process of adoption is complex. Noneconomic barriers, such as management's belief systems and attitudes about managing employees, may hinder the adoption of progressive practices, even those that may have economic benefits (Pfeffer 1997). For many organizations, an enormous amount of change would be necessary to go from providing no work–life benefits to offering a comprehensive system. In some cases, management would have to relinquish some control (for example, with respect to flexible scheduling or teleworking), and to trust employees a lot more than they do. That may be difficult, especially in highly structured work environments with clearly defined roles for managers and nonmanagers. As Perry-Smith and Blum (1998) have noted, "Resistance can occur because of the unique feature of these systems that can take the employee outside the organization or bring the family inside" (p. 8). In summary, because it is difficult to copy entire systems of work–life programs, and because the process of adoption is complex, such programs may be sources of competitive advantage. However, there are also some important caveats that need to be recognized.

Threats to Competitive Advantage Based on Human Resources

Perhaps the biggest threat to creating sustainable competitive advantage through human resources is voluntary turnover. Companies can own tangible assets, such as patents, copyrights, and equipment, but they cannot own their own employees (Coff 1997). Other employee-withdrawal behaviors, such as reduced effort while at work, lateness, and absenteeism, also diminish the value of human resources to an employer

(Konrad & Mangel 1998). As illustrated in Exhibit 3–1, the primary reason for unscheduled absenteeism in 1998 was family-related issues (26 percent). The number three reason was personal needs (20 percent). Taken together, these causes account for almost half of all absentee incidents. It is precisely those underlying reasons for employee withdrawal that work–life programs are designed to address. For firms that are trying to build valuable human assets that are difficult to copy or to lure away, such programs may be powerful tools.

Another threat is voluntary turnover. Conflicts between job demands and the demands of nonwork life may lead some employees to reduce such tensions by leaving the workforce altogether, by moving to positions in other organizations that generate less work–life stress, or by putting less time and effort into their current jobs (Brett 1997). Work–life initiatives that incorporate flexibility in work scheduling, together with "family-friendly" features, can play an important role in protecting a firm's investment in its human capital.

WORK–LIFE PROGRAMS AND ORGANIZATIONAL CONTROL SYSTEMS

As Arthur (1994) noted, control and commitment represent two distinct approaches to shaping employee behaviors and attitudes at work. The goal of control-oriented HR systems is to reduce direct labor costs, or to improve efficiency, by enforcing employee compliance with rules and procedures and by basing employee rewards on some measurable output criteria. In traditional bureaucratic organizations, the primary motivation to act in the best interests of the firm is the opportunity to advance up the corporate career ladder. The potential for promotion is a powerful motivator for employees to exert effort on behalf of the firm, to stay with the firm over time, and to invest in firm-specific skills (Capelli 1997).

However, many U.S. organizations have had to modify their traditional bureaucratic structures as a result of downsizing, restructuring, and reengineering. They have become flatter, with fewer layers of management, and so have lost the motivating potential of the career ladder, and replaced it with performance-based rewards (Capelli 1997; Useem 1996). Such rewards may motivate employees to perform in the short term but they may not be effective in inducing employees to stay with the same firm over a long period of time. Employees who are motivated by short-term, performance-based rewards have little incentive to stay with the same organization if competitors wish to bid them away (Konrad & Mangel 1998).

In contrast to control-oriented HR systems, commitment-oriented HR systems shape desired employee behaviors and attitudes by forging psychological links between organizational and employee goals (Arthur 1994). Such systems focus on developing committed employees who can be trusted to use their discretion to carry out their assigned tasks in ways that are consistent with organizational goals (Organ 1988). Those systems are characterized by higher levels of employee involvement in managerial decisions, formal participation programs, and training in group problem solving and by higher percentages of skilled employees and average wage rates (Arthur 1992).

Organizations with commitment-oriented HR systems in place are more likely to implement work–life programs to the extent that employees in these systems have discretion in how they perform their jobs and to the extent that communication, teamwork, and feedback are important to effective performance. In support of this argument, Osterman (1995) found that the importance of employee commitment to the firm, the extent of employee discretion in performing job functions, and the use of total quality management techniques were strong predictors of the development of work–life programs in organizations. Certainly it is easier to implement flexible work schedules and various leave programs in organizations that give employees more discretion in how they perform their jobs. The very same programs are likely to fit less well with the traditional and highly structured managerial approaches that characterize bureaucratic firms.

WORK–LIFE PROGRAMS AND PROFESSIONAL EMPLOYEES

Viewing work–life programs as a strategy for protecting investments in human capital and as a good fit with commitment-oriented HR systems is particularly appropriate with professional employees. Those workers are critical resources for organizations because of their expense, their relative scarcity, and the transferability of their skills (Konrad & Mangel 1998). Furthermore, professionals tend to be highly autonomous, posing problems of organizational control.

Attracting and retaining professionals is difficult because their skills are general and valued by other employers. Investing in work–life programs may be an effective strategy for attracting and retaining such talented employees. As Konrad and Mangel (1998) noted, more American workers are delaying having their first child until they have achieved some measure of financial and career security. Given the relatively long years of education and training required of professionals, these people in particular are likely to delay starting their families. For that reason, work–family tensions tend to rise for many professionals as they reach their 30s and 40s. If organizations fail to provide assistance in handling that tension, they risk losing these valuable employees. From a competitive standpoint, because work–life programs are more highly developed in some organizations than in others, those with extensive work–life benefits may be better able to retain top-performing professionals despite efforts by competitors to bid them away.

A theoretical perspective that helps to explain why work–life programs are effective in attracting, retaining, and motivating employees is known as "symbolic action" (Pfeffer 1981). The basic idea is that organizational actions provide signals to employees that allow them to draw conclusions about the values and philosophies of the organization. When these values are employee-centered, employees are likely to respond in a reciprocal manner with favorable beliefs and attitudes toward the organization and with higher performance. If employees believe that the employer is investing in their well-being, they tend to reciprocate by contributing extra effort beyond their formal job requirements, by developing a concern for the overall success of the organization beyond their individual advancement, and by embracing the goals of the organization (Pfeffer 1994). The result is a culture of committed employees, exactly the kind that most firms find especially desirable.

WHO ADOPTS WORK–LIFE PROGRAMS?

We noted earlier that companies differ in their responsiveness to work–life issues. A recent, large-scale empirical study (Bardoel et al. 1998) sought to identify characteristics of organizations that are associated with the adoption of work–life programs. Five such characteristics were investigated: organizational size measured on a 10-point scale from 1 (fewer than 25 employees) to 10 (more than 8,000 employees), the percentage of women in the organization, the percentage of employees under age 35 in the organization, public- versus private-sector ownership, and the organization's track record in HRM (good versus poor).

Only two of the five characteristics were associated with the adoption of work–life programs: organization size and HRM track record. Larger organizations were better able to provide a broad base of work–life benefits than were smaller organizations. Larger organizations tended to adopt more policies related to individual support (for example, personal counseling, relocation assistance), leave, life–career strategies, and child- and dependent-care benefits than were smaller organizations. That finding is consistent with Glass and Fujimoto's (1995) explanation that organizational size is related to professional HRM that produces more rapid diffusion of innovative HR programs, such as work–life programs. Similarly, organizations rated as having good track records in HRM tended to implement more flexible work options, individual growth, and life–career policies—all of which is consistent with the symbolic action theory discussed earlier. However, the percentage of women in the organization, the percentage of employees under age 35, and public- versus private-sector ownership were unrelated to the provision of work–life benefits.

THE BUSINESS CASE FOR WORK–LIFE PROGRAMS

Now that we understand what work–life programs are, their strategic implications, and who tends to adopt them, let us consider some business reasons for adopting them. We will look at some of the outcomes associated with such programs, and at examples of company studies that have assessed the effect of programs on those outcomes. First, however, we need a conceptual model to guide our discussion.

Conceptual Model

This model, termed the "Bright Horizons Investment Index," was developed by Cascio, Friedman, and Ochsman (Friedman 1999), to show the linkages among work–life initiatives, employee behaviors, customer satisfaction, operating performance, and financial performance. It builds on the Sears model described in chapter 6 (Rucci et al. 1998), and the body of research that shows key factors related to the success of work–life programs.

The model (Exhibit 7–1) begins by showing how work–life initiatives drive employee behaviors (turnover, absenteeism, motivation, affiliation). The mere presence of a work–life initiative, however, is no guarantee of success. As shown in the upper-left corner of the model, one must

EXHIBIT 7-1 *Bright Horizon's "Investment Index"*

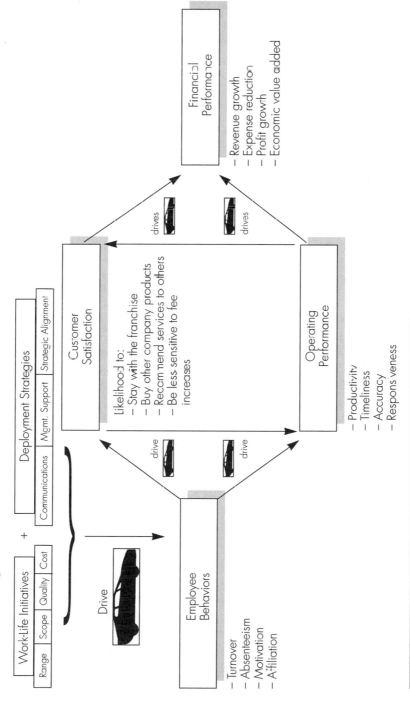

Source: Bright Horizons Family Solutions, 1998. Used by permission.

also consider the range, scope, quality, and cost of work–life initiatives, along with the overall quality and care with which they are deployed. Key factors to consider are the extent and quality of communications about the programs, the extent of management and supervisory support for the programs, and the careful alignment of the programs chosen with the strategic objectives of the organization. If done well, work–life initiatives should reduce employee withdrawal behaviors, increase retention, and increase employees' motivation to perform well.

As illustrated in chapter 6, employee attitudes and behaviors clearly affect customer satisfaction and the likelihood that the customer will do four things: stay with the franchise (that is, be loyal), buy other company products, recommend the company to others, and be less sensitive to fee increases. At the same time, positive employee attitudes and behaviors affect productivity on the job as well as the timeliness and accuracy of performance. Note the arrows showing how customer satisfaction affects operating performance (for example, customer loyalty and willingness to buy other products clearly affect employee productivity) and how operating performance affects customer satisfaction (for example, productivity, timeliness, and accuracy affect the customer's decision to be loyal to the organization and to recommend it to others). Finally, customer satisfaction and operating performance both drive financial performance, specifically, growth in revenues and profits, reductions in expenses, and added economic value.

Although work–life initiatives are only one determinant of employee behaviors, along with factors such as pay, working conditions, and the work itself, research indicates that they can have substantial effects on employee decisions to stay with the organization and to produce high-quality work. Employee behaviors, in turn, are by no means the sole determinant of customer satisfaction and operating performance, for a fuller explanation must also consider factors such as the quality of goods and services and the impact of technology on productivity, timeliness, and accuracy. Finally, financial performance is also complexly determined, and any explanation must consider factors such as competitive conditions within the industry and the general economy, along with specific management actions to control costs and to grow the business (for example, the effects of marketing strategies and new products from research and development). The point is that work–life initiatives can have a modest impact on strategic outcomes of interest to an organization, and Exhibit 7–1 shows a mechanism through which work–life initiatives might have effects.

Work–Life Programs and Employee Behaviors

Childcare

Several studies have examined the impact of work–life programs on absenteeism, turnover, and employee commitment. A 1996 study at Allied Signal compared the number of days missed by parents 12 months prior to the opening of a company-sponsored childcare center versus 12 months after its introduction. Days missed dropped from 259 to 30 (Bright Horizons Family Solutions 1997). In a cost–benefit analysis of its programs for care of sick children, Honeywell found it saved $45,000 beyond the cost of the programs in the first nine months of operation. Small employers can save money, too: a 38-person accounting firm in California found that providing seasonal on-site childcare netted the firm an additional $25,000 annual income through increased staff availability (Johnson 1995).

A study at a major aerospace firm reported the following savings in the first year of operation of a childcare center (Bright Horizons Family Solutions 1997).

- Reduced absences arising from childcare breakdowns: 5.28 days saved per employee, or $243,302
- Reduced tardiness resulting from childcare problems: 8.37 times late or left early per employee (multiplied by two hours), or $96,422
- Reduced work time spent looking for childcare: seven hours per employee, or $12,900

The total estimated net savings for this very large employer was $352,624.

Finally, investigators in a study of ROI of back-up childcare (that is, childcare used in emergencies or when regular childcare is unavailable) at Chase Manhattan Bank reported the following findings. Childcare breakdowns were the cause of 6,900 days of potentially missed work by parents. Because back-up childcare was available, these lost days were not incurred. When multiplied by the average daily salary of the employees in question, gross savings were $1,523,175. The annual cost of the back-up childcare center was $720,000, for a net savings of $803,175, and an ROI of better than 110 percent (Bright Horizons Family Solutions 1997).

Eldercare

At the national level, a Metropolitan Life Insurance Company study of employer costs for eldercare provided by full-time employees found that the aggregate cost to U.S. employers was almost $400 million per year.

That result was based on the number of full-time caregivers by gender, the median weekly wage in the United States by gender, and a finding that 10.5 percent of employed caregivers were absent a minimum of six days per year to perform such caregiving responsibilities as taking an older relative to the doctor or for other health-care visits, visiting elders, arranging for services, and so forth ("The MetLife Study" 1997).[1]

The same study also examined U.S. employers' aggregate cost of partial absenteeism—arriving late for work, leaving early, or extending lunch breaks—that was prompted by eldercare responsibilities. Among caregivers employed full time, 59 percent reported that they had to adjust their schedules in those ways. Scharlach (1994) reported that 22 percent of caregivers were unable to make up time missed by working late, coming in on weekends, or taking work home. Experts on caregiving estimate that, on average, caregivers lose a minimum of 1 hour per week or 50 hours per year that cannot be made up. Based on the number of full-time caregivers by gender, the median weekly wage in the United States by gender, the number experiencing partial absenteeism (59 percent), and the number unable to make up 50 hours per year (22 percent), the total cost to employers was estimated to exceed $488 million.

Some caregivers find that their eldercare responsibilities are so great that they have to quit their jobs. In the MetLife study, over 17 percent of caregivers fell into that category. Based on the average length of time that such employees were providing eldercare before leaving their jobs—four years—the researchers estimated that slightly more than 4 percent will leave their jobs in a given year. The cost of turnover was estimated very conservatively at 75 percent of annual salary costs for those employees who quit. Multiplying that figure by the number of caregivers by gender who quit in a given year (4.2 percent), times the median weekly wage of U.S. employees by gender, produces an estimated total cost to employers of approximately $5 billion annually.

Johnson & Johnson found that policies on time and leave were very significant in employees' decisions to stay with the firm, *even if they personally had not made use of the policies' provisions.* That finding is not atypical, and it is consistent with other published research (for example, Grover & Crooker 1995). People are more committed to organizations that offer work–life programs, regardless of the extent to which they personally benefit from them. In one group of employers with work–life programs, 78 percent reported that the programs helped their companies retain valuable employees. At NationsBank, two-thirds of employees on flexible schedules said they would have left had those policies not been in place (Johnson 1995).

Stress

In a study of organizations with and without work–life programs, Northwestern Mutual Life found that employees in companies without supportive policies were twice as likely to report burnout and stress (Johnson 1995). Employer-sponsored work–life programs do not erase the difficulties of balancing responsibilities, but they do provide resources for employees to manage and solve their own problems.

Open communication policies and supportive work environments combine to reduce work–life stress. Thus a recent survey found that the top five retention practices as rated by employees were, in descending order, salary increases, health care, open communications policy and base salary (tied for third place), 401(k) plan, and flexible work schedules (Society for Human Resource Management 1997). It is not only the policies but also the environment in which they are implemented that make the biggest difference for employees. The evaluation of Johnson & Johnson's work–life programs found that although employees appreciated and made use of the company's array of progressive policies, the factors most often associated with workers' ability to balance work and nonwork roles were a supportive supervisor and workplace culture (Families and Work Institute 1993).

Even the most progressive work–life policies are useless, or can be counter-productive, if the company culture does not support them. When supervisors or co-workers do not support employees' taking parental leave or using flextime, the policies themselves will fail to promote the kind of commitment and organizational attachment that employers hope to have. Companies considering work–life policies should take steps to promote a corporate culture that values, or at least accepts, the necessity and potential long-term benefits of the policies (Grover & Crooker 1995). The bottom line is that the success of work–life policies really rests with the first-line supervisor (Kossek & Nichol 1992).

Work–Life Programs, Customer Satisfaction, and Financial Performance

First Tennessee Bank also demonstrated the existence of an employee–customer–profit chain. It was able to define a direct link from addressing work–life issues to employee satisfaction, to employee retention, to customer retention, to profits. Employee retention was significantly higher (93 percent versus 81 percent) among those who made use of work–life programs. Managers who were rated as "supportive" enjoyed a 50 percent higher retention rate than did those not rated as supportive. Finally, employee satisfaction and retention led to a 7 percent increase in customer retention, which led to a $106 million profit gain in two years (Johnson 1999).

At the national level, Perry-Smith and Blum (1998) used data from the National Organizations Survey (telephone interviews of a national sample of U.S. work establishments) to collect information about HR policies and practices at 545 establishments. The probability that a firm was included in the sample is proportional to its number of employees. Fifty percent of the firms in the study employed fewer than 50 workers, and only 27 percent of the firms employed more than 250 people. The major finding from the study was that a *system* of work–life policies (not merely the existence of individual policies) is positively associated with firm-level performance. Specifically, organizations with a greater range of family-friendly policies have higher levels of perceived organizational performance relative to other firms doing the same kind of work, higher market performance relative to other firms, and greater profit/sales growth over the previous 12-month period.

Another study examined the HR practices and productivity per employee of 195 large, publicly traded firms with average numbers of employees exceeding 7,500 (Konrad & Mangel 1998). The authors matched the HR practices of each firm, as determined from a large, national survey, with publicly available information on productivity. Doing so overcame a common problem in many studies, namely, that data on predictors and criteria come from the same source (for example, respondents). That is known as "common method variance." The productivity measure used, sales per employee, does not equate directly with profitability or long-term performance, but it is one important indicator of organizational performance, and one that is tied closely to workforce efficiency.

Results indicated that larger firms with supportive cultures and higher percentages of female and professional employees were most likely to adopt a wide range of work–life initiatives. Higher levels of productivity were associated with organizations that employed higher percentages of professionals and adopted work–life programs. Thus, work–life programs complement HR policies designed to build and maintain an effective workforce, and their impact extends beyond protecting key employees from competitors. Such programs also complement commitment-oriented control strategies, and contribute to the overall efficiency of the work-force.

"Family-friendly" rankings have become popular in a number of business publications. *Working Mother* magazine, for example, ranks companies based on pay; opportunities for women to advance; childcare; flexibility; other family-friendly benefits, such as maternity leaves; and on work–life supports, such as management training on work–life issues. Employers and prospective employees are placing more emphasis on those rankings as indicators of "employers of choice." To test the hypothesis that the presence of work–life policies is related to performance in the marketplace, D'Andrea (1999) grouped the public companies that made the *Working Mother* list of the "best companies for women to work for" into a stock portfolio and compared their price performance to that of the Standard & Poor's (S&P) 500 stocks (the 500 largest firms traded on the New York Stock Exchange). As shown in Exhibit 7–2, those companies,

EXHIBIT 7-2   *Financial Performance of Companies in the* Working Mother *Index Compared with the S&P 500*

The *Working Mother* Index reflects the stock price performance (equal-weighted) of the 61 *Working Mother* companies that have publicly traded shares.

Source: C. D'Andrea (1999). *Wall Street and Work Life.* Port Washington, NY: Bright Horizons Family Solutions. Used by permission.

on average, outperformed the S&P 500 Index between 1996 and 1998, a time period of extraordinary returns for the S&P 500 Index.

Cautions in Making the Business Case for Work–Life Initiatives

Johnson (1995) recommended three important cautions when making the business case for work–life programs. First, recognize that no one set of facts and figures will make the case for all firms. It depends on the priority of the organization in question—is it primarily attraction and public image, retention of talent, or the costs versus benefits of alternative programs?

Second, do not rely on isolated facts to make the case. Considered by itself, any single study or fact is only one piece of the total picture. Develop a dynamic understanding of the importance of the relationship between work and personal life by focusing on an organization's overall culture and values, not only on programs or statistics. Often a combination of quantitative information and employees' experiences in their own words (qualitative information that brings statistics to life) is most effective.

Third, don't place work–life initiatives under an unreasonable burden of proof. Decision makers may well be skeptical even after all the facts and costs have been presented to them. More deeply rooted attitudes and beliefs may underlie that skepticism—such as a belief that addressing personal concerns may erode service to clients or customers, or that people will take unfair advantage of the benefits, or that work–life issues are "just women's issues." Constructing a credible business case means addressing attitudes and values as well as assembling research (Johnson 1995).

WHY THE GAP BETWEEN RESEARCH AND PRACTICE?

Evidence indicates, unfortunately, that companies are not adopting changes such as flexible work schedules, telework, and on-site childcare that might help workers balance work and life. Fewer than 10 percent of companies mandate training on work–life issues, and almost two-thirds of HR officers polled in a recent survey said it is either somewhat or very true that their companies do not make a genuine effort to inform employees of the work–life programs that are available to them (Armour 1999). Why is progress so slow? Experts cite the following reasons:

- Employers do not believe that work–life programs have a bottom-line impact.
- Some programs get lost in mergers and acquisitions.
- Employees are reluctant to demand more in an age of frequent job layoffs.
- Programs are seen as perks for working mothers that are not available to all employees.
- Managers are not receptive to employee requests. (Armour 1999)

Higher-level managers often fail to communicate to line supervisors the business rationale for these flexible arrangements. Doing so is a key element of a strategic approach to work–life programs, as we shall see in the next section.

IMPLEMENTING A STRATEGIC APPROACH TO WORK–LIFE PROGRAMS

In a national study of the changing workforce, Bond et al. (1998) found that the quality of jobs and supportiveness of co-workers and supervisors are the most powerful predictors of job satisfaction, commitment, loyalty to the employer, job performance, and retention. The researchers defined job quality as autonomy on the job, learning opportunities, meaningfulness of work, opportunities for advancement, and job security. They defined workplace support as flexibility in work arrangements, supervisor support, supportive workplace culture, positive co-worker relations, the absence of discrimination, respect in the workplace, and equal opportunity for workers of all backgrounds.

As Bond et al. (1998) noted, "The implications for employers are potentially far-reaching. While offering competitive pay and benefits is undoubtedly necessary to achieving business goals, it is insufficient on its own. If employers want to maximize satisfaction, commitment, performance, and retention, they must provide high-quality jobs—whatever the employee's occupation, and supportive workplaces—whatever the industry" (p. 12). Doing so may be difficult because it requires real organizational change.

Key first steps in that process include the following (Johnson 1999):

- Before adopting specific work–life policies, assess the demographics and needs of the workforce—currently and in the future.

- Study how work gets done and the impact of work on the business and on its people. Then create an infrastructure to support flexible work arrangements.
- At the organization level, link work–life efforts to key HR and business initiatives. In other words, make the business case for work–life programs and policies.
- Brief senior managers and initiate regular communications to first-line supervisors about the business impact of such policies.

Systems of work–life programs and a coordinated approach to developing the kind of organizational culture that will support those systems help an organization to create competitive advantages through people.

EXERCISES

1. Your boss has asked you to prepare a report on the strategic implications of work–life programs. Develop an outline of the major points you will make in the report.
2. Explain why commitment-oriented HR systems are likely to be more effective than control-oriented HR systems in attracting, retaining, and motivating professional employees.
3. In the Bright Horizons Investment Index, Exhibit 7–1, how do employee attitudes and behaviors affect customer satisfaction? What factors determine whether work–life programs will affect employee attitudes and behaviors? How is customer satisfaction related to a firm's financial performance?
4. A number of firms have reported positive outcomes from implementing work–life programs, and one might assume that the same outcomes will generalize to other firms. What cautions would you recommend for making the business case for such programs?
5. Your company has decided to implement a variety of work–life programs as primary vehicles for attracting and retaining a diverse group of employees. Your task is to brief senior management about key steps to follow in implementing the programs. Prepare an outline of your presentation.

I am deeply grateful to Dr. Dana E. Friedman, senior vice president, Bright Horizons Family Solutions, for her help in collecting source materials and critically reviewing earlier drafts of this chapter.

REFERENCES

Armour, S. (1999). Family-friendly work policies get cold shoulder. *USA Today* (Apr. 30), B1.

Arthur, J. B. (1992). The link between business strategy and industrial relations systems in American steel minimills. *Industrial and Labor Relations Review 45*, 488–506.

Arthur, J. B. (1994). Effects of human resource systems on manufacturing performance and turnover. *Academy of Management Journal 37*(3), 670–687.

Bardoel, E. A., Tharenou, P., Moss, S. A. (1998). Organizational predictors of work–family practices. *Asia Pacific Journal of Human Resources 36*(3), 31–49.

Barney, J. B. (1991). Firm resources and sustained competitive advantage. *Journal of Management 17*, 99–120.

Bashaw, E. R., Grant, S. E. (1994). Exploring the distinctive nature of work commitments: Their relationships with personal characteristics, job performance, and propensity to leave. *Journal of Personal Selling and Sales Management 14*, 41–56.

Bond, J. T., Galinsky, E., Swanberg, J. E. (1998). *The 1997 National Study of the Changing Workforce.* New York: Families and Work Institute.

Brett, J. M. (1997). Family, sex, and career advancement. In S. Parasuraman and J. H. Greenhaus (eds.), *Integrating Work and Family: Challenges and Choices for a Changing World* (pp. 143–153). Westport, CT: Quorum.

Bright Horizons Family Solutions. (1997). *An ROI Study of Back-up Childcare at Chase Manhattan Bank.* Port Washington, NY: Author.

Bright Horizons Family Solutions. (1997). *The Financial Impact of On-site Childcare.* Port Washington, NY: Author.

Capelli, P. (1997). Rethinking the nature of work: A look at the research evidence. *Compensation and Benefits Review 29*(4), 50–59.

Coff, R. W. (1997). Human assets and management dilemmas: Coping with hazards on the road to resource-based theory. *Academy of Management Review 22*, 374–403.

Collis, D. J., Montgomery, C. (1995). Competing on resources: Strategy in the 1990s. *Harvard Business Review 73*(4), 119–128.

D'Andrea, C. (1999). *Wall Street and Work Life.* Port Washington, NY: Bright Horizons Family Solutions.

DeCotiis, T. A., Summers, T. P. (1987). A path analysis model of the antecedents and consequences of organizational commitment. *Human Relations 40,* 445–470.

Delaney, J. T., Huselid, M. A. (1996). The impact of human resource management practices on perceptions of organizational performance. *Academy of Management Journal 39*(4), 949–969.

Families and Work Institute. (1993). *An Evaluation of Johnson & Johnson's Work–Life Programs.* New York: Author.

Friedman, D. E. (1991). *Linking Work–Family Issues to the Bottom Line.* New York: The Conference Board.

Friedman, D. E. (1999). *A Study of the Return on Work–Life Investment.* Paper presented at the 1999 Work and Family Conference. New York: The Conference Board.

Glass, J., Fujimoto, T. (1995). Employer characteristics and the provision of family-responsive policies. *Work and Occupations 22*(4), 380–411.

Grover, S. L. (1991). Predicting the perceived fairness of parental leave policies. *Journal of Applied Psychology 76*(2), 247–255.

Grover, S. L., Crooker, K. J. (1995). Who appreciates family-responsive human resource policies: The impact of family-friendly policies on the organizational attachment of parents and non-parents. *Personnel Psychology 48,* 271–288.

Heskett, J. L., Sasser, W. E., Schelsinger, L. A. (1997). *The Service–Profit Chain: How Leading Companies Link Profit and Growth to Loyalty, Satisfaction, and Value.* New York: Free Press.

Huselid, M. A., Becker, B. I. (1995). *The Strategic Impact of Human Resources: Building High-Performance Work Systems.* New York: Coopers & Lybrand.

Johnson, A. A. (1995). The business case for work–family programs. *Journal of Accountancy 180*(2), 53–57.

Johnson, A. A. (1999). *Strategic Meal Planning: Work/Life Initiatives for Building Strong Organizations.* Paper presented at the conference on Integrated Health, Disability, and Work/Life Initiatives, February 1999, New York.

Konrad, A. M., Mangel, R. (1998). *The Performance Effect of Work–Family Programs.* Paper presented at the annual convention of the Academy of Management, August, San Diego.

Kossek, E. E., Nichol, V. (1992). The effects of on-site child care on employee attitudes and performance. *Personnel Psychology 45,* 485–509.

MacDuffie, J. P. (1995). Human resource bundles and manufacturing performance: Organizational logic and flexible production systems in the world auto industry. *Industrial and Labor Relations Review 48*(2), 197–221.

Moorman, R. H., Niehoff, B. P., Organ, D. W. (1993). Treating employees fairly and organizational citizenship behavior: Sorting the effects of job satisfaction, organizational commitment, and procedural justice. *Employee Responsibilities and Rights Journal 6,* 209–225.

Organ, D. W. (1988). *Organizational Citizenship Behavior: The Good Soldier Syndrome.* Lexington, MA: Lexington Books.

Osterman, P. (1995). Work–family programs and the employment relationship. *Administrative Science Quarterly 40,* 681–700.

Perry-Smith, J. E., Blum, T. C. (1998). *Work–Family Human Resource Systems and Perceived Organizational Performance.* Paper presented at the annual convention of the Academy of Management, August 1998, San Diego.

Pfeffer, J. (1981). Management as symbolic action: The creation and maintenance of organizational paradigms. In L. L. Cummings and B. M. Staw (eds.), *Research in Organizational Behavior* (Vol. 3, pp. 1–52). Greenwich, CT: JAI Press.

Pfeffer, J. (1994). *Competitive Advantage Through People: Unleashing the Power of the Workforce.* Boston: Harvard Business School Press.

Pfeffer, J. (1997). *New Directions in Organization Theory.* New York: Oxford University Press.

Reichheld, F. F. (1996). *The Loyalty Effect: The Hidden Force Behind Growth, Profits, and Lasting Value.* Boston: Harvard Business School Press.

Rodgers, C. S. (1998). *The Drivers of Employee Commitment.* Boston: Work/Family Directions.

Rucci, A. J., Kirn, S. P., Quinn, R. T. (1998). The employee–customer–profit chain at Sears. *Harvard Business Review 76*(1), 82–97.

Scharlach, A. E. (1994). Caregiving and employment: Competing or complementary roles? *The Gerontologist 34,* 378–385.

Society for Human Resource Management. (1997). *What Keeps Employees from Quitting?* Alexandria, VA: Author.

The MetLife Study of Employer Costs for Working Caregivers. (1997). Westport, CT: Metropolitan Life Insurance.

Useem, M. (1996). Corporate restructuring and the restructured world of senior management. In P. Osterman (ed.), *Broken Ladders: Managerial Careers in the New Economy* (pp. 23–54). New York: Oxford University Press.

Youndt, M. A., Snell, S. A., Dean, J. W., Lepak, D. P. (1996). Human resource management, manufacturing strategy, and firm performance. *Academy of Management Journal 39*(4), 836–866.

ENDNOTE

1. To ensure that absenteeism was not overstated, the percent of employees providing personal eldercare who were absent six or more days was reduced by the percent of employees with no caregiving responsibilities who were also absent six or more days. For example, if 15 percent of those providing personal care were absent six or more days, and 5 percent of those with no caregiving responsibilities were also absent six or more days, the personal caregiver prevalence rate was reduced from 15 percent to 10 percent.

HR Programs:
A Return-on-Investment
Perspective

CHAPTER 8

Utility: The Concept and Its Measurement

In the past, HR programs often have been selected and implemented because they were fashionable (especially human relations programs) or commercially appealing, or because of the entertainment value they offered the target audience. In an era of downsizing, deregulation, and fierce global competition, however, HR costs continue to be examined closely by operating executives and HR executives may be under increased pressure to justify new or continuing programs. Such justification requires a consideration of the relative utilities to the organization of alternative strategies for reaching targeted objectives.

Utility analysis is the determination of institutional gain or loss (outcomes) anticipated from various courses of action. When faced with a choice among strategies, management should choose the strategy that maximizes the expected utility for the organization across all possible outcomes (Brealey & Myers 1999). To make the choice, management must be able to estimate the utilities associated with various outcomes. Estimating utilities traditionally has been the Achilles heel of decision theory (Cronbach & Gleser 1965), but is a less acute problem in business settings. Although difficult to calculate, institutional gains and losses may be estimated by relatively objective behavioral or cost-accounting procedures, that is, in terms of dollars.

The objective of this chapter is to introduce the concept of utility analysis, to describe four different models of utility analysis, and to describe situations in which each is most appropriate. Chapters 9, 10, and

11 will build on those ideas to show how HR programs can be evaluated from a return-on-investment perspective.

OVERVIEW

Utility analysis (or decision theory) is a tool particularly well suited to applications in business settings because it insists that costs and expected consequences of decisions always be taken into account. It stimulates the decision maker to formulate clearly what he or she is after, as well as to anticipate the consequences of alternative courses of action. Decision makers must state clearly their overall objectives and attempt to anticipate the consequences of each alternative before they make a decision.

It should serve as some comfort to know that all HR decisions can be characterized identically. In the first place there is an individual about whom a decision is required. On the basis of certain information about the individual (for example, performance appraisals, assessment center ratings, a disciplinary report), decision makers may elect to pursue various alternative courses of action. What follows is a simple example.

After conducting an extensive screening process, an organization has narrowed its list of candidates for vice president of finance to three candidates. Each candidate has particular strengths that are attractive to the company. Candidate A works for a large Eastern conglomerate, candidate B is employed by an elite firm in the Midwest, and candidate C works for a small, innovative company on the West Coast. The candidates' financial requirements are all relatively similar so the HR cost to the company is an inconsequential measure of the comparative value of each candidate. The task for the organization, then, is to construct a payoff model and to determine payoff measures for each candidate. The organization must process the list of choices (candidates) according to well-defined criteria and then select the alternative that best satisfies its objectives. The payoffs assigned to each possible outcome must, therefore, be assessed in value units consistent with those objectives—and those value units may not always be measurable in dollars. Assume that the organization selects technical knowledge, human relations skills, and administrative skills as valid measures of value payoff to associate with each candidate. On the basis of assessment results, the organization assigns a rating from zero to 10 to measure the contribution of each component of payoff for each candidate. Those ratings are shown in Exhibit 8–1.

EXHIBIT 8-1   *Payoff Table for Selection Problem*

	Candidate A	Candidate B	Candidate C
Technical knowledge	6	4	10
Human relations skills	6	9	5
Administrative skills	7	6	4

To combine the components of payoff, the organization must determine their relative importance to payoff. Suppose the organization views technical knowledge as the most important component to this position, twice as important as either human relations or administrative skills. Thus, it assigns a weight of 2 to the scaled values for technical skills, and it assigns a weight of 1 to human relations skills and to administrative skills. The following payoff measures may then be obtained:

$$\text{payoff, candidate A} = 6(2) + 6(1) + 7(1) = 25$$
$$\text{payoff, candidate B} = 4(2) + 9(1) + 6(1) = 23$$
$$\text{payoff, candidate C} = 10(2) + 5(1) + 4(1) = 29$$

On the basis of those results, candidate C should be selected.

To summarize thus far, in any given situation some strategies are better than others. Strategies are better or worse when evaluated against possible outcomes or consequences of decisions (payoffs). The first and most difficult step is to assign values to possible outcomes. Once this is accomplished, particular decisions or general strategies can be compared, as Cronbach and Gleser (1965) noted:

> The unique feature of decision theory or utility theory is that it specifies evaluations by means of a payoff matrix or by conversion of the criterion to utility units. The values are thus plainly revealed and open to criticism. This is an asset rather than a defect of this system, as compared with systems where value judgments are imbedded and often pass unrecognized. (p. 121)

Utility theory provides a framework for making decisions by forcing the decision maker to define goals clearly, to enumerate the expected consequences or possible outcomes of his or her decision, and to attach differing utilities or values to each. Such an approach has merit because resulting decisions are likely to rest on a foundation of sound reasoning and conscious forethought.

UTILITY MODELS

In the context of HR selection, three of the best-known utility models are those of Taylor and Russell (1939); Naylor and Shine (1965); and Brogden (1946, 1949) and Cronbach and Gleser (1965). A fourth model has been proposed by Raju, Burke, and Normand (1990). The utility of a selection device is the degree to which its use improves the quality of the individuals selected beyond what would have occurred had that device not been used (Blum & Naylor 1968). Quality, in turn, may be defined in terms of the proportion of individuals in the selected group who are considered successful, the average standard score on some job performance criterion for the selected group, or the dollar payoff to the organization resulting from the use of a particular selection procedure. In the remainder of this chapter we will consider each of those utility models and its associated measure of quality.

The Taylor-Russell Model

Taylor and Russell (1939) developed perhaps the most well-known utility model and pointed out that the overall utility of a selection device is a function of three parameters: the validity coefficient (r) (the correlation between a predictor of job performance and a criterion measure of actual job performance), the selection ratio (SR) (the proportion of applicants selected), and the base rate (BR) (the proportion of applicants who would be successful without the selection procedure). This model demonstrates convincingly that even selection procedures with relatively low validities can increase substantially the percentage successful among those selected when the selection ratio is low. Let us consider the concepts of selection ratio and base rate in greater detail.

Whenever a quota exists on the total number of applicants that may be accepted, the selection ratio is a major concern. As the SR approaches 1.0 (all applicants must be selected), it becomes high or unfavorable from the organization's perspective. Conversely, as the SR approaches zero, it becomes low or favorable; the organization can afford to be selective. The wide-ranging effect that the SR may exert on a predictor with a given validity is illustrated in Exhibit 8–2. In each case, X_c represents a cutoff score on the predictor. As can be seen in Exhibit 8–2, even predictors with very low validities can be useful if the SR is low and if an organization needs to choose only the cream of the crop. Conversely, given high selection ratios, a predictor must possess very high validity in order to increase the percentage successful among those selected.

EXHIBIT 8-2   *Effect of Varying Selection Ratios on a Predictor with a Given Validity*

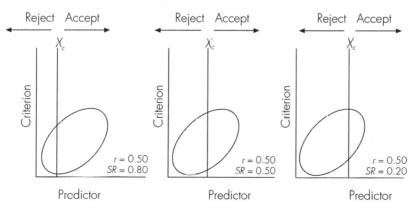

Note: The oval is the shape of a scatterplot corresponding to $r = 0.50$; r = validity coefficient; SR = selection ratio; X_c = cutoff score.

It might appear that, given a particular validity, decreasing the SR (becoming more selective) always should be advocated, but the optimal strategy is not so simple (Sands 1973). When the HR manager must achieve a certain quota of satisfactory individuals, lowering the SR forces the manager to expand the recruiting and selection effort. In practice, that strategy may be costly to implement.

Utility, according to Taylor and Russell (1939), is also affected by the base rate. To be of any use in selection, a measure must demonstrate incremental validity by improving on the BR. That is, the selection measure must result in more correct decisions than could be made without using it. As Exhibit 8–3 demonstrates, the higher the BR, the more difficult it is for a selection measure to improve upon it.

In each case, X_c represents the minimum level of job performance (criterion cutoff score) necessary for success. That value should not be altered arbitrarily. Rather it should be based on the selection situation (the level of minimally acceptable criterion performance for the job in question) and the applicant population (the proportion of the population that would exceed that level if hired; Boudreau 1991). Exhibit 8–3 illustrates that with a BR of 0.80, it would be difficult for any selection measure to improve on the base rate. In fact, when the BR is 0.80 and half of the applicants are selected, a validity of 0.45 is required in order to produce an improvement of even 10 percent over base rate prediction. This is also true at very low BRs (as would be the case, for example, in the

EXHIBIT 8-3   *Effect of Varying Base Rates on a Predictor with a
Given Validity*

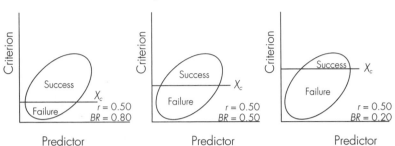

Note: The oval is the shape of a scatterplot corresponding to $r = 0.50$; BR = base rate; r = validity coefficient; X_c = minimum level of job performance.

psychiatric screening of job applicants). Given a BR of 0.20, an SR of 0.50, and a validity of 0.45, the percentage successful among those selected is 0.30—once again representing only a 10 percent improvement in correct decisions. Selection measures are most useful, however, when BRs are about 0.50 (Taylor & Russell 1939). As the BR departs radically from that value in either direction, the benefit of an additional predictor becomes questionable, especially in view of the costs involved in gathering the additional information. The lesson is obvious: Applications of selection measures to situations with markedly different SRs or BRs can result in quite different predictive outcomes and cost–benefit ratios. If it is not possible to demonstrate significant incremental validity by adding a predictor, then the predictor should not be used because it cannot improve on the BR classification of people.

Taylor and Russell (1939) published a series of tables illustrating the interaction of the validity coefficient, the SR, and the BR on the success ratio (the proportion of selected applicants who subsequently are judged successful). The success ratio, then, serves as an operational measure of the value or utility of a selection device when used in conjunction with methods presently used to select applicants.

Exhibit 8–4 presents the Taylor-Russell approach graphically. In this figure, the criterion cutoff (set as described earlier) separates the present employee group into satisfactory and unsatisfactory workers. The predictor cutoff (set by the SR) defines the relative proportion of workers who would be hired at a given level of selectivity. Areas A and C represent correct decisions—that is, if the selection measure were used to select applicants, those in area A would be hired and become satisfactory

EXHIBIT 8-4 *Effect of Predictor and Criterion Cutoffs on a Bivariate Distribution of Scores*

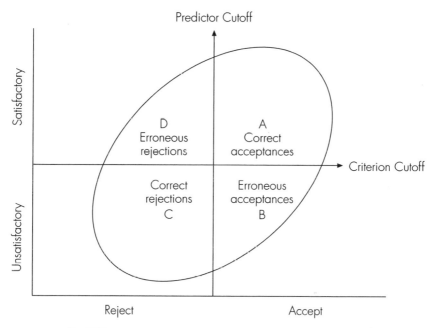

Note: The oval is the shape of the scatterplot that shows the overall relationship between predictor and criterion scores.

employees, and those in area *C* would be rejected correctly because they scored below the predictor cutoff and would have performed unsatisfactorily on the job. Areas *B* and *D* represent erroneous decisions—those in area *B* would be hired because they scored above the predictor cutoff, but they would perform unsatisfactorily on the job, and those in area *D* would be rejected because they scored below the predictor cutoff, but they would have been successful if hired.

The following ratios were used by Taylor and Russell in developing their tables:

Equation 1

$$\text{base rate} = \frac{A + D}{A + B + C + D}$$

Equation 2

$$\text{selection ratio} = \frac{A + B}{A + B + C + D}$$

Equation 3

$$\text{success ratio} = \frac{A}{A + B}$$

By specifying the validity coefficient, the *BR,* and the *SR,* and making use of Pearson's Tables for Finding the Volumes of the Normal Bivariate Surface (1931), Taylor and Russell developed their tables (see Appendix A). The usefulness of a selection measure thus can be assessed in terms of the success ratio that will be obtained if the selection measure is used. The gain in utility to be expected from using the instrument (the expected increase in the percentage of successful workers) then can be derived by subtracting the *BR* from the success ratio (equation 3 minus equation 1). For example, given an *SR* of 0.10, a validity of 0.30, and a *BR* of 0.50, the success ratio jumps to 0.71—a 21 percent gain in utility over the *BR* (to verify that figure, see Appendix A).

The validity coefficient referred to by Taylor and Russell is based on present employees who have already been screened using methods other than the new selection procedure. The *SR* then is applied to this population. It is assumed that the new procedure will simply be added to a group of selection procedures used previously, and that the incremental gain in validity from the use of the new procedure is what is most relevant.

The Taylor-Russell approach also makes three other assumptions. First, it assumes fixed-treatment selection (that is, individuals are chosen for one specified treatment or course of action that cannot be modified). For example, if a person is selected for treatment A, a training program for slow learners, then transfer to treatment B, fast-track instruction, is impossible regardless of how well the person does in treatment A. Second, the Taylor-Russell model does not take into account the percentage of rejected individuals who would have been successful if hired (erroneous rejections). Finally, the model classifies accepted individuals into successful and unsuccessful groups. All individuals within a group are regarded as making equal contributions. Because of those assumptions, Taylor and Russell find different shapes for the validity–utility relationship at different *SR*s and nonlinear relationships at high validities and high *BR*s. However, the Taylor-Russell model is not used to choose optimal *SR*s (or cutoff scores), but rather only to evaluate those already selected.

Perhaps the major shortcoming of this utility model is that it allows the usefulness of a predictor to be reflected only in terms of the success ratio. Job performance is described as a dichotomous classification—

successful and unsuccessful—and as the tables in Appendix A demonstrate, when validity is fixed the success ratio increases as the *SR* decreases. (Turn to Appendix A, choose any particular validity value, and note what happens to the success ratio as the *SR* changes from 0.95 to 0.05.) Under those circumstances the success ratio tells us that more people are successful, but not *how much more* successful. In practice, situations may arise in which one would not expect the average level of job performance to change as a function of higher selection standards. For many jobs, however, one would expect to see improvements in the average level of job performance as a result of increased selectivity as long as the relationship between performance on the predictor and performance on the job can be described best by a straight line (that is, as long as the relationship is linear). If the predictor–criterion relationship is not linear, then the Taylor-Russell tables are inappropriate because they are based on the assumptions of bivariate normal,[1] linear, homoscedastic[2] relationships between predictor and criterion. In short, when it is reasonable to assume that the use of higher cutoff scores will lead to higher levels of average job performance by those selected, the Taylor-Russell tables will underestimate the actual amount of gain to be expected.

The Naylor-Shine Model

In contrast to the Taylor-Russell utility model, the Naylor-Shine (1965) approach assumes a linear relationship between validity and utility—a relationship that holds at all *SR*s. That is, given any arbitrarily defined cutoff on a selection measure, the higher the validity, the greater the increase in average criterion score for the selected group over that observed for the total group (average criterion score of selectees minus average criterion score of total group). Thus, the Naylor Shine index of utility (originally derived by Kelley [1923]) is defined in terms of the increase in average criterion score to be expected from the use of a selection measure with a given validity and *SR*. Like Taylor and Russell, Naylor and Shine assume that the relationship between predictor and criterion is bivariate normal, linear, and homoscedastic and that the validity coefficient used is based on the concurrent validity model.[3] Such a model is used in order to assess the gain in validity from the use of the new selection procedure *over and above* that which is presently available using current information. Unlike Taylor and Russell, however, Naylor and Shine do not require that employees be dichotomized into satisfactory and unsatisfactory groups by specifying an arbitrary cutoff on the criterion (job performance) dimension that represents minimally acceptable performance. Thus, the Naylor-Shine utility model requires less information than does the Taylor-Russell model. The basic equation underlying the Naylor-Shine model is

Equation 4

$$\bar{Z}_{yi} = r_{xy} \frac{\lambda_i}{\phi_i}$$

where $\bar{Z}_{yi}$ is the mean criterion score (in standard-score units)[4] of all cases above the predictor cutoff; r_{xy} is the validity coefficient; λ_i is the ordinate of the normal distribution at the predictor cutoff, Z_{xi} (expressed in standard-score units); and ϕ_i is the selection ratio. Equation 4 applies whether r_{xy} is a zero-order correlation coefficient or a multiple regression coefficient.[5]

Using equation 4 as a basic building block, Naylor and Shine present a series of tables (see Appendix B) that specify, for each *SR*, the standard (predictor) score corresponding to that *SR*, the ordinate of the normal curve at that point, and the quotient λ_i/ϕ_i. The tables can be used to answer several important HR questions: (1) Given a specified *SR*, what will be the average performance level of those selected? (2) Given a desired *SR*, what will $\bar{Z}_{yi}$ be? (3) Given a desired improvement in the average criterion score of those selected, what *SR* and/or predictor cutoff value (in standard-score units) should be used? Let us work through some examples, using the tables in Appendix B.

In each of the following examples assume that r_{xy}, the validity of our predictor, is positive and equal to 0.40.

1. Given the selection ratio $\phi_i = 0.50$, what will be the average performance level of those selected?
   Solution: Enter the table at $\phi_i = 0.50$ and read $\lambda_i/\phi_i = 0.80$.

   $$\bar{Z}_{yi} = r_{xy}\lambda_i/\phi_i = (0.40)(0.80) = 0.32$$

   Thus, the average criterion score of those selected, using a *SR* of 0.50, is 0.32 *Z*-units (roughly one-third of a standard deviation) better than the unselected sample.

2. Given the desired cutoff score $Z_{xi} = -0.96$, what will $\bar{Z}_{yi}$ be?
   Solution: Enter the table at $Z_{xi} = -0.96$ and read $\lambda_i/\phi_i = 0.30$.

   $$\bar{Z}_{yi} = r_{xy}\lambda_i/\phi_i = (0.40)(0.30) = 0.12$$

Thus, using this cutoff score on our predictor results in an improvement of 0.12 Z-units in the average criterion score of those selected.

3. Given the desired improvement in the average criterion score of those selected $\bar{Z}_{yi} = 0.50$, what SR and/or predictor cutoff value should be used?

Solution: Because $\bar{Z}_{yi} = r_{xy}\lambda_i/\phi_i$ then

$$\lambda_i/\phi_i = \bar{Z}_{yi}/r_{xy} = 0.50/0.40 = 1.25$$

Enter the table at $\lambda_i/\phi_i = 1.25$ and read $\phi_i = 0.2578$ and $Z_{xi} = 0.65$. Thus, to achieve an average improvement of 0.50 (one-half) standard deviation in job performance, an SR of 0.26 is necessary, and to achieve that particular ratio, one should employ a cutoff score on the predictor of 0.65 in Z-score (standard deviation) units.

In each of the following examples assume that r_{xy}, the validity of our predictor, is negative and equal to -0.40. The general rule for this case is to reverse the sign of r_{xy} and Z_{xi} everywhere in the calculations.

1. Given the SR $\phi_i = 0.50$, what will be the average performance level of those selected?

Solution: Enter the table at $\phi_i = 0.50$ and read $\lambda_i/\phi_i = 0.80$. Taking the sign reversal on r_{xy} into account,

$$\bar{Z}_{yi} = (-r_{xy})\lambda_i/\phi_i = -(-0.40)(0.80) = 0.32$$

Thus, the average criterion score of those selected, using an SR of 0.50, is 0.32 Z-units better than the unselected sample.

2. Given the desired cutoff score $Z_{xi} = -0.96$, what will $\bar{Z}_{yi}$ be?

Solution: When r_{xy} is negative, ϕ_i is in the *left* tail of the score distribution instead of the right tail, where it is when r_{xy} is positive. Thus, a cutoff score of -0.96 for the negative case is equivalent to a cutoff score of 0.96 with r_{xy} positive. We therefore reverse the sign of Z_{xi}, enter the table at $Z_{xi} = 0.96$, and read $\lambda_i/\phi_i = 1.49$. Taking the sign reversal on r_{xy} into account, we have

$$\bar{Z}_{yi} = (-r_{xy})\lambda_i/\phi_i = -(-0.40)(1.49) = 0.596$$

Thus, using a cutoff score of $Z_{xi} = -0.96$ on our predictor produces an improvement of approximately 0.60 Z-units in the average criterion score of those selected.

3. Given the desired improvement in the average criterion score of those
selected $\bar{Z}_{yi} = 0.50$, what *SR* and/or predictor cutoff value should be
used?

Solution: Reversing the sign on r_{xy} gives

$$\bar{Z}_{yi} = (-r_{xy})\frac{\lambda_i}{\phi_i}$$

or

$$\frac{\lambda_i}{\phi_i} = \frac{\bar{Z}_{yi}}{(-r_{xy})}$$

Therefore,

$$\frac{\lambda_i}{\phi_i} = \frac{0.50}{-(-0.40)} = 1.25$$

Enter the table at $\lambda_i/\phi_i = 1.25$ and read $\phi_i = 0.2578$ and $Z_{xi} = -0.65$
(note that the sign on Z_{xi} has been reversed). Thus, to achieve the desired improvement in average criterion performance, an *SR* of 0.26 is
necessary, and to achieve that particular ratio, one should employ a
cutoff score on the predictor of –0.65 in *Z*-score units.

The Naylor-Shine utility index appears more generally applicable
than the Taylor-Russell index because in many if not most cases, given
valid selection procedures, an organization could expect an increase in
average criterion performance as it becomes more selective in deciding
whom to accept. However, "average criterion performance" is expressed
in terms of standard (*Z*) scores, which are more difficult to interpret than
are outcomes more closely related to the specific nature of a business,
such as dollar volume of sales, units produced or sold, or costs reduced.
Moreover, as Boudreau (1988) has noted, with a standardized criterion
scale one must ask questions such as, "Is it worth spending $10,000 to
select 50 people per year, in order to obtain a criterion level 0.50 *SD*s
greater than what we would obtain without the predictor?" Some HR
managers may not even be familiar with the concept of a standard deviation, and would find it difficult to attach a dollar value to a 0.50 *SD* increase in criterion performance.

Finally, neither the Taylor-Russell nor the Naylor-Shine model formally integrates the concept of cost of selection, or dollars gained or
lost, into the utility index. Both simply imply that larger differences in
the percentage of successful employees (Taylor-Russell) or larger increases in average criterion score (Naylor-Shine) will yield larger benefits to the employer in terms of dollars saved. The Brogden-Cronbach-
Gleser model addressed those issues specifically.

The Brogden-Cronbach-Gleser Model

Brogden (1946) showed that when the predictor and criterion are continuous (that is, they can assume an infinite number of values theoretically) and identical (not necessarily normal, but identical) in distribution form, the regression of the criterion on the predictor is linear, and the *SR* is held constant, then the validity coefficient itself is a direct index of selective efficiency. If criterion performance is expressed in standard-score units, then over all individuals r_{xy} represents the ratio of the average criterion score made by people selected on the basis of their predictor scores $(\Sigma \bar{Z}_y)$ to the average score made by selecting the same number of persons on the basis of their criterion scores $(\Sigma \bar{Z}_{y'})$. That is,

Equation 5

$$r_{xy} = \frac{\Sigma \bar{Z}_y}{\Sigma \bar{Z}_{y'}}$$

As an illustration, suppose a firm wants to hire 20 people for a certain job and must choose the best 20 from among 85 applicants. Ideally, the firm would hire all 85 for a period of time, collect job performance (criterion) data, and retain the best 20, those obtaining the highest criterion scores. The average criterion score of the 20 so selected obviously would be the highest obtainable by any possible combination of 20 of the 85 original workers. Because such a procedure is usually out of the question, we administer a selection measure and select the 20 highest scorers. Equation 5 indicates that the validity coefficient may be interpreted as the ratio of the average criterion performance of the 20 people selected on the basis of their predictor scores to the average performance of the 20 who would have been selected had the criterion itself been used as the basis for selection. Thus, if people could be selected on the basis of their actual behavior on the job (or by means of a perfect selection device), and that would save an organization $100,000 per year over random selection, then a selection device with a validity of 0.50 could be expected to save $50,000 per year. Utility is therefore a direct linear function of validity, given the assumptions noted above.

Although equation 5 does not include formally the cost of selection, and it was not developed as an estimate of utility, in a later publication (1949) Brogden used the principles of linear regression to demonstrate the relationships of cost of selection, validity, and *SR* to utility. The derivation is straightforward.

Let r_{xy} equal the correlation between a predictor (x) and job performance measured in dollars (y). The basic linear model is

$$y = \beta Z_x + \mu_y + e$$

where y = job performance measured in dollars, β = the linear-regression weight on the predictor for forecasting job performance, Z_x = performance on the predictor in standard-score form in the applicant group, μ_y = mean job performance in dollars of randomly selected employees, and e = error of prediction

For those selected (s), the equation that gives the average job performance in this group is

$$E(y_s) = E(\beta Z_{xs}) + E(\mu_y) + E(e)$$

where E = expected value. Because the expected value of e is zero, and β and μ are constants, the equation reduces to

$$\overline{Y}_s = \beta \overline{Z}_{xs} + \mu_y$$

Remember that $\beta = r_{xy}(SD_y/SD_x)$, where SD_y is the standard deviation of dollar-valued job performance among randomly selected employees. Because $SD_x = 1.00$, $\beta = r_{xy}SD_y$. We therefore obtain

$$\overline{Y}_s = r_{xy}SD_y\overline{Z}_{xs} + \mu_y$$

That equation tells us the *absolute* dollar value of average job performance in the selected group. What we really want, however, is an equation that gives the *increase* in the dollar value of average performance which results from using the predictor. To get that equation, suppose that the new predictor was not used. Then $\overline{Y}_s = \mu_y$, for mean job performance in the selected group would be the same as mean performance in a group selected randomly from the applicant pool. Thus, the increase resulting from use of a valid predictor is $r_{xy}SD_y\overline{Z}_{xs}$. The equation we want is produced by transposing μ_y to give

$$\overline{Y}_s - \mu_y = r_{xy}SD_y\overline{Z}_{xs}$$

The right side of the above equation represents the difference between mean productivity in the group selected using the new predictor and mean productivity in a group selected without using the new predictor, that is, a group selected randomly. The equation thus provides the mean gain in productivity per selectee (marginal utility) resulting from the use of the new predictor; that is

Equation 6

$$\Delta \bar{U}/\text{selectee} = r_{xy}SD_y\bar{Z}_{xs}$$

where $\bar{U}$ is utility and $\Delta \bar{U}$ is marginal utility.

Equation 6 states that the average productivity gain in dollars per person hired is the product of the validity coefficient, the *SD* of job performance in dollars, and the average standard score on the predictor of those hired. The value $r_{xy}\bar{Z}_{xs}$ is the mean standard score on the dollar criterion of those selected, $\bar{Z}_y$.

Assuming predictor scores are distributed normally and the predictor–criterion relationship is linear, then $\bar{Z}_{xs}$ for the selected group may be computed by the formula λ/ϕ, where λ is the height of the normal curve at the point of cut, and ϕ is the percentage in the selected group (the selection ratio). $\bar{Z}_{ys}$ (the average standard criterion score for the selected group) is then obtained as the product $r\lambda/\phi$. That is the same formula (equation 4) used by Naylor and Shine to derive the values in their tables.

The total utility of the new predictor depends on the number of applicants hired. The total utility (total productivity) gain is simply the mean gain per selectee times the number of people selected, N_s. That is, the total productivity gain is

Equation 7

$$\Delta U = N_s r_{xy}SD_y\lambda/\phi$$

Suppose the average marginal utility per new person hired is $5,000. If 10 people were hired, the actual utility would be $50,000. If 100 people were hired, then the utility would be $500,000. Obviously, the total dollar value of the new predictor is greater for large employers than for small employers, but that fact can be misleading. On a percentage basis it is *average* gain in utility that counts, and that is what counts to each individual employer.

The cost of selection is another factor that must be considered in estimating the savings expected from a selection program. Because the expected saving per individual selected is $r_{xy}SD_y\lambda/\phi$, the saving with allowance for the cost of testing can be determined by subtracting c/ϕ from the above value, where c is the cost of testing a single individual. The cost of testing is divided by the *SR* (ϕ) so that c/ϕ represents the total cost of the testing required to fill one vacancy. For example, if the per-applicant cost of testing is \$25, and one of every four applicants is selected ($SR = 0.25$), then the cost to fill one vacancy is $\$25/0.25 = \$100$. The expected saving per selectee, corrected for the cost of testing, is

Equation 8

$$\Delta U = r_{xy}SD_y\lambda/\phi - c/\phi$$

and the total gain is

Equation 9

$$\Delta U = N_s r_{xy}SD_y\lambda/\phi - N_s c/\phi$$

The effect of the cost of testing can be evaluated, as Brogden (1949) has shown, by computing the ratio, per-applicant cost of testing/(validity $\times SD_y$). This value represents the ratio of the cost of testing to the expected gain in the dollar value of production with an increase in applicant test score of one SD unit. Thus, if the cost of evaluating an applicant for an executive position is \$300, the validity of the selection procedure is 0.35, and the criterion SD is \$15,000, then the ratio is approximately 0.06. If that ratio can be held below 0.05, then Taylor and Russell's conclusions are substantially correct. In practice, that will almost always be the case because the benefits of improved selection will accrue for more than one time period (in fact, over the entire tenure of the group selected). Thus, SD_y will be large, relative to the one-time cost of testing, and testing costs are unlikely to reduce utility significantly except at very low selection ratios.

Cronbach and Gleser (1965) elaborated and refined Brogden's (1949) derivations with respect to utility in fixed-treatment selection and thoroughly explored the application of utility theory to selection with adaptive treatment, two-stage and multistage selection, placement decisions, and classification decisions. With respect to utility in fixed-treatment selection, Cronbach and Gleser adopt Taylor and Russell's interpretation of the validity coefficient for utility calculations, that is, concurrent validity. The validity coefficient based on present employees presupposes a population that has been screened using information other than the new selection measure. It is to that population that the selection ratio will be applied.

Cronbach and Gleser argue, as did Taylor and Russell and Naylor and Shine, that selection procedures should be judged on the basis of their contribution over and above the best strategy available that makes use of prior information. Thus, any new procedure must demonstrate incremental utility before it is put to use. Suppose, however, that an organization wishes to replace its old selection procedures with new ones. Under such circumstances, as Boudreau (1991) has noted, the appropriate population for deriving a validity coefficient, SD_y, and SR, should be the *unscreened* population. In short, selection procedures should be evaluated in light of the conditions under which they actually will be applied. With respect to fixed-treatment selection, Cronbach and Gleser (1965, p. 307) make the following assumptions.

1. Decisions are made regarding an indefinitely large population. This "a priori population" consists of all applicants after screening by any procedure that is presently in use and that will continue to be used.
2. Regarding any person, i, there are two possible alternative decisions: accept (t_a) and reject (t_b).
3. Each person has a test score, y_i, which has a mean of zero and an SD of one. (Test scores are assumed to be distributed normally.)
4. For every person there is a payoff e_{ita} that results when a person is accepted. This payoff has a linear regression on test score. The test will be scored so that r_{ye} is positive.
5. When a person is rejected, the payoff e_{itb} results. This payoff is unrelated to test score, and may be set equal to zero.
6. The average cost of testing a person on test y is c_y, where $c_y > 0$.
7. The strategy will be to accept high scorers in preference to others. A cutoff y' will be located on the y continuum so that any desired proportion $\phi(y')$ of the group falls above y'. Above that point the probability of acceptance is 1.00; below it, 0.00. Cochran (1951) shows that such a strategy is optimal for selection with a fixed quota of individuals.

The assumption of a normal distribution of test scores (assumption 3 above) implies that the expected payoffs from randomly selected applicants also are normally distributed. As both Brogden (1949) and Cronbach and Gleser (1965) have noted, that assumption may not always be met, nor would it be desirable that it always be met. Standards set by management often place a lower limit on production (which produces a positively skewed payoff distribution) and voluntary restrictions on output by a work group skew the curve negatively. In the extreme, complete standardization of tasks eliminates variability entirely among those who remain on the job. However, with highly skewed distributions, as long as linear regression is present, payoffs resulting from cutoff points on the tail of the distribution skew could be relatively greater than those obtained at the same percentile point of cut with a normally distributed variable. This implies a comparison of relative payoffs at different selection ratios.

When the assumptions noted earlier are met, however, Cronbach and Gleser demonstrate that the net gain in utility from testing N people in fixed-treatment selection is

Equation 10

$$\Delta U = NSD_e r_{ye} \lambda(y') - Nc_y$$

where c_y is the cost of testing one person; r_{ye} is the correlation of the selection procedure with the dollar-based criterion in the a priori population; SD_e is the standard deviation of this criterion; y' is the cutoff score on the selection procedure; and $\lambda(y')$ is the ordinate of the normal curve at that point. In that equation, $SD_e r_{ye}$ is the slope of the payoff function relating expected payoff to score. An increase in validity leads to an increase in slope, but as equation 10 demonstrates, slope also depends on the dispersion of criterion scores. For any one treatment, SD_e is constant and indicates both the magnitude and practical significance of individual differences in payoff. Thus a selection procedure with $r_{xy} = 0.25$ and $SD_e = \$10,000$ for one selection decision is just as useful as a procedure with $r_{xy} = 0.50$ and $SD_e = \$5,000$ for some other decision (holding other parameters constant). Even procedures with low validity can be useful when SD_e is large.

If equation 10 is expressed as the net gain in utility per person accepted in fixed-treatment selection, it is identical to Brogden's (1949) formula (equation 8). Therefore,

Equation 11

$$\Delta U = SD_e r_{ye} \frac{\lambda(y')}{\phi(y')} - \frac{c_y}{\phi(y')}$$

where all terms are as defined above. In short, both Brogden (1946, 1949) and Cronbach and Gleser (1965) arrived at the same conclusions regarding the effects of r, SD_e, the cost of selection, and the SR on utility in fixed-treatment selection. Utility properly is regarded as a linear function of validity and, if cost is zero, is proportional to validity. Contrary to the Taylor-Russell results, the linear relation holds at all SRs.

The Raju-Burke-Normand Model

Raju et al. (1990) proposed a different model of utility analysis, one based on the proposition that the relationship between *true* job performance (typically expressed as an overall weighted or unweighted rating, R_t) and the *true* dollar value of an employee's job performance (Y_t) is linear. This can be written as

Equation 12

$$Y_t = AR_t + B$$

where A is the slope of the regression line, and B is the y-intercept (the point where the regression line crosses the y-axis). Using that assumption, and the assumption that the regression of job performance ratings on the predictor scores (X) is linear, Raju et al. (1990) derived the following equation:

Equation 13

$$\Delta U = N(A\sigma_R)\rho_{XR}\overline{X} - C$$

where ΔU = increase in dollar value over random selection, N = number of selectees, A = multiplicative constant in equation 12 that represents the slope of the regression line when dollar-valued utility is regressed on performance ratings, σ_R = SD of observed rating scores (after the appropriate transformation, see below), ρ_{XR} = correlation between the selection device and performance ratings, $\overline{X}$ = mean standard score on the predictor of those selected (computed as in equation 6), and C = the total cost of selection.

In equation 13, Raju et al. (1990) suggested that the parameter A be set equal to average salary, and that average salary be used as a proxy for average productivity. However, as Judiesch, Schmidt, and Hunter (1993) noted, the use of average salary rather than average sales per employee leads to an underestimate of utility. To estimate the contribution of selection utility to pretax profits, A must be set equal to the average sales per employee less the average variable costs per employee (those that change with levels of productivity).

To determine the *SD* of observed rating scores, it is necessary to transform the performance rating scale into a standardized metric because the *SD* of the original raw performance ratings, σ_{RO}, can always be increased or decreased simply by changing values on the scale. The required transformation is as follows (Law & Myors 1999):

Equation 14

$$\sigma_R = \left(\frac{\dfrac{Y_h}{Y_a} - \dfrac{Y_l}{Y_a}}{R_h - R_l} \right) \sigma_{RO}$$

where Y_h, Y_l, and Y_a are the upper and lower limits and the average of the standardized performance scale, respectively, identified by raters; and R_h and R_l are the upper and lower limits, respectively, of the original performance scale.

The key feature of the Raju et al. (1990) model is that it eliminates the need to estimate the *SD* of dollar-valued job performance (σ_y). It therefore shifts the judgment process to a scale with which managers are more familiar, namely, performance appraisal ratings. Although making estimates on a performance-rating scale may be a less cognitively demanding task than trying to think in terms of dollar-valued performance (Law & Myors 1999), this has not eliminated the use of subjective judgments in utility analysis (Judiesch et al. 1993).

Let us now compare the Raju et al. (1990) utility equation (equation 13) with the linear-regression–based utility equation of Brogden and Cronbach and Gleser (equation 10), shown here with Raju et al.'s notation[6]:

Equation 15

$$\Delta U = (N\sigma_y)(\rho_{XY}\bar{X}) - C$$

Note that equation 13 differs from equation 15 in only two respects: $A(\sigma_R)$ appears in place of σ_y, and ρ_{XR} appears instead of ρ_{XY}. Brogden assumed that $\rho_{XR} = \rho_{XY}$; Raju et al. (1990) assumed that

$$\rho_{XR_t} = \rho_{XY_t}$$

That is, it is assumed that the correlation between the observed predictor score (X) and true job performance expressed as a rating (R_t), and the correlation between X and the true dollar value of an employee (Y_t) are equal. In summary, the Raju et al. approach and Brogden's approach are quite comparable mathematically, but their application requires estimates of different parameters. Note that it is A in Raju et al.'s approach, and σ_y in Brogden's approach, that translate the product of the validity coefficient and the average predictor score (expressed in standard-score units) into the appropriate utility estimates. Such estimates need not be defined only in terms of dollars. Rather, either A or σ_y can be expressed in terms of measured performance, percentage increase in performance, or dollars. The choice depends on the nature of the organization (manufacturing versus service), the degree to which performance can be measured objectively, and the context of the decision to be made (Bobko, Karren, & Kerkar 1987). Exhibit 8–5 summarizes the approaches discussed so far.

APPROPRIATE APPLICATIONS OF EACH MODEL

Only by understanding thoroughly the theory, assumptions, and data requirements of the various utility models can the models be used properly. Yet their proper (and more widespread) use is essential to satisfy the demand for accountability in HR programs.

The Taylor-Russell Model

The Taylor-Russell (1939) model is most appropriate under the following circumstances:

- Differences in ability beyond the minimum necessary to perform the job do not yield differences in benefit (for example, in various types of clerical or technician's jobs).
- Individuals are placed into two (or more) groups based on their scores on a test battery, interest inventory, or other procedure. All individuals remain within the organization, but they are treated differently. By assigning particular values to "hits" and "misses" for each possible assignment, cutoff scores can be adjusted to maximize expected utility.
- Differences in output are believed to occur but are presently not measurable (for example, in nursing care, teaching performance, or credit counseling).

In those instances, estimating utility according to the magnitude of the increase in the success ratio makes good sense. It makes even better sense, however, to attach cost estimates to expected payoffs. Thus, Sands (1973) developed the Cost of Attaining Personnel Requirements (CAPER) model on the basis of the Taylor-Russell approach. CAPER is a decision-oriented system intended to determine an optimal recruiting-selection strategy for minimizing the total cost of recruiting, selecting, inducting, and training a sufficient number of people to meet a quota of satisfactory employees. The two major advantages to such an approach are

EXHIBIT 8–5 *Summary of the Utility Indexes, Data Requirements, and Assumptions of Four Utility Models*

Model	Utility Index	Data Requirements	Distinctive Assumptions
Taylor-Russell (1939)	Increase in percentage successful in selected group	Validity, BR, SR	All selectees classified either as successful or unsuccessful. Equal criterion performance by all members of each group; cost of selection = $0.
Naylor-Shine (1965)	Increase in mean criterion score of selected group	Validity, SR	Validity linearly related to utility; cost of selection = $0
Brogden-Cronbach-Gleser (1965)	Increase in dollar payoff of selected group	Validity, SR, criterion SD in dollars	Validity linearly related to utility; cost of selection ≠ $0; criterion performance evaluated in dollars.
Raju-Burke-Normand (1990)	Increase in payoff in selected group in terms of percentage increase in performance or in terms of dollars	Validity, SR, average sales per employee, SD of transformed performance appraisal ratings	Linear relationship between true employee job performance (e.g., supervisory rating) and the economic value of that performance

Notes: All models assume a validity coefficient based on present employees (concurrent validity); *BR* = base rate; *SR* = selection ratio.
Source: Adapted from Cascio, W. F. (1980). Responding to the demand for accountability: a critical analysis of three utility models. *Organizational Behavior and Human Performance 25,* 42.

(1) results can be communicated and understood easily by operating managers (that is, they are given in numbers of people and dollar costs), and (2) broadening the perspective of HR selection from selection per se to all phases of the HR system (from initial recruiting through the completion of training) minimizes the likelihood of over- or under-optimization of one component of the system at the expense of all others. Nevertheless, CAPER, like the Taylor-Russell model, can be justified only under the conditions noted above. Its lack of general applicability is its major drawback.

The Naylor-Shine Model

The Naylor-Shine model (1965) is most appropriate when differences in job performance cannot be expressed in dollar terms, but the function relating payoff (performance under some treatment) to predictor score can be assumed to be linear. Consider the following examples.

1. In classification and placement decisions (for example, in the military or in large organizations) all selected individuals are assigned to available treatments (jobs, training programs) so that individual and institutional outcomes are maximized. In classification, for example, the decision maker has a number of available jobs on the one hand and a number of people on the other. The objective is to make the most effective matching of jobs and people (Ghiselli 1956). Thus the level of job performance must be forecast for each individual for each job, for example, by using least-squares estimates.[7] If the predicted performance scores for each job (units produced, dollar value of sales, and so on) are expressed in standard-score units, then the expected increase in average job performance as a function of variation in the SR can be assessed by means of the Naylor-Shine model.
2. In the prediction of labor turnover, expressed as a percentage, based on scores from a predictor that demonstrates some validity, if percentages are expressed as standard scores, then the expected decrease in the percentage of turnover can be assessed as a function of variation in the SR (the predictor cutoff score). If appropriate costing procedures are used to calculate actual turnover costs (see chapter 2), expected savings resulting from reduced turnover can be estimated.
3. In the selection of students based on predicted academic performance in college or graduate school, or in training programs where the cost-per-trainee is high (for example, pilot training), if academic

performance is expressed in standard-score units, institutions profitably might examine variations in expected levels of performance as a function of variations in predictor scores by means of the Naylor-Shine utility model.

The Brogden-Cronbach-Gleser Model

This continuous-variable utility model is the most versatile utility model available, and it has received considerable attention by researchers and practitioners alike. It is most appropriate in situations where relative levels of job performance (the criterion) can be expressed in dollars, and where linear regression of the criterion on the predictor can be assumed. In short, the model provides a direct estimate of the monetary value of a selection program by making use of the "dollar criterion" (Brogden & Taylor 1950). Consider the following examples.

1. Roche (1961) used cost-accounting procedures to estimate the payoff from a program designed to select radial drill operators in a manufacturing operation. Although the cost-accounting methods were relatively straightforward, many subjective estimates and arbitrary allocations entered into the estimated profit accruing to the firm as a result of the radial drill operator's work. Such elements as the cost of materials used in producing the company's products, the cost of direct labor hours consumed in the manufacture of a product, and the cost of capital investment, jigs, fixtures, power, perishable tools, and floor space all had to be expressed in dollars. The determination of the *SD* of job performance outcomes expressed in dollars is clearly a complex undertaking, as a later study of route salesmen for a soft-drink company also demonstrated (Greer & Cascio 1987). However, joint efforts by HR professionals and cost accountants may make such a problem more tractable. Chapter 9 is devoted exclusively to that topic.
2. In a service organization, Schmidt and Hoffman (1973) applied the Brogden-Cronbach-Gleser model to a weighted application blank developed to predict turnover among nurse's aides. Using cost-accounting methods, the dollar cost of turnover was estimated. When the actual dollar savings over a two-year period were compared to the estimated dollar savings at two *SR* values using the Brogden-Cronbach-Gleser model, the differences were no greater than 7 percent.
3. Two other studies investigated the usefulness of an assessment center in selection by means of the Brogden-Cronbach-Gleser utility model

(Cascio & Ramos 1986; Cascio & Silbey 1979). In the Casio and Ramos study, the payoff associated with first-level management assessment, given that 1,116 managers were selected and that their average tenure at first level was 4.4 years, was over $13 million (almost $20 million in 1998 dollars). That represents about $18,000 in improved job performance per manager over 4.4 years, or about $4,100 per year (in 1998 dollars).

The Raju-Burke-Normand Model

As we have seen, the Raju et al. (1990) approach is mathematically quite comparable to that of the Brogden-Cronbach-Gleser model. The major difference lies in the parameters that are estimated. The key assumption of the Raju et al. approach is that of a linear relationship between true employee job performance (for example, supervisory ratings) and the economic value of that performance. Instead of estimating the *SD* of job performance in dollars, as is done in the Brogden-Cronbach-Gleser model, it is necessary to estimate the parameter *A*, a multiplicative constant that represents the slope of the regression line when dollar-valued utility is regressed on performance ratings. This value may be estimated using either the average total compensation of employees or the average sales per employee. It is also necessary to estimate the parameter σ_R, the *SD* of transformed performance appraisal ratings.

Law and Myors (1999) applied the Raju et al. (1990) approach to two small samples of supervisors in two organizations—supervisors of entry-level computer programmers in a large financial institution, and supervisors from a nationwide fast-food chain. To provide a basis for comparison, they computed overall utility estimates using both the Raju et al. procedure and the Brogden-Cronbach-Gleser procedure. When the average total compensation of employees was used as a proxy for average productivity, overall utility estimates were lower in both samples than those computed using the Brogden-Cronbach-Gleser procedure. However, when the average sales per employee was used as a proxy for average productivity, overall utility estimates were much higher than those computed using the Brogden-Cronbach-Gleser procedure.

Those results led Law and Myors (1999) to question the usefulness of rating-based procedures. They concluded, "Unless there are improvements which control for possible estimation errors in rating-based methods, their future contribution to dollar-value utility estimation may be limited" (pp. 49–50).

In summary, as HR costs and the costs of HR programs continue to escalate, demands for accountability also are likely to rise. Utility-based decision systems can meet that challenge, but their proper application requires careful attention to the assumptions and data requirements of each model. "Garbage in–garbage out" is as true in this context as it is in the context of an information system.

EXERCISES

1. Use the Taylor-Russell tables (Appendix A) to solve the following problems.

Validity	SR	BR	Success Ratio
0.25	0.20	0.30	_____
0.55	0.70	0.80	_____
0.20	0.70	0.80	_____
0.10	0.50	0.50	_____
0.55	0.50	0.50	_____

2. Use the Naylor-Shine tables (Appendix B) to solve these problems.

r_{xy}	ϕ_i	Z_{xi}	$\bar{Z}_{yi}$
0.35	0.7019		_____
0.22		−0.30	_____
0.47	_____	_____	0.65
−0.47	_____	_____	0.65

3. Using the Brogden-Cronbach-Gleser continuous-variable utility model, what is the net gain over random selection (ΔU overall, and per selectee) given the following information?

- quota for selection: 20
- SR: 0.20
- SD_e (standard deviation of job performance expressed in dollars): $10,000
- r_{ye}: 0.25
- $\lambda(y')$: 0.28
- c_y: $25

Hint: To find N, the number recruited, divide the quota for selection by the SR.

4. Using the Raju-Burke-Normand utility model, find the net gain in utility (ΔU) over random selection overall and per selectee, given the following information:

- quota: 125
- *SR:* 0.50
- *A:* \$55,000
- σ_R: 0.34
- ρ_{XR}: 0.35
- $\lambda(y')$: 0.3765
- *c*, the cost of testing one candidate: \$400 (to determine the total cost of testing, see equations 8 and 9)

5. Given the following information on two selection procedures, and using the Brogden-Cronbach-Gleser model, what is the relative *difference* in payoff (overall and per selectee) between the two procedures? For both procedures, quota = 50, *SR* = 0.50, $\lambda(y')$ = 0.3989, and SD_e = \$15,000.

- r_{y1}: 0.20 c_1: \$100
- r_{y2}: 0.40 c_2: \$500

6. You are a management consultant whose task is to perform a utility analysis using the following information regarding secretaries at Inko, Inc. The validity of the Secretarial Aptitude Test (SAT) is 0.40, applicants must score 70 or better (Z_x of 0.5) to be hired, and only about half of those who apply actually are hired. Of those hired, about half are considered satisfactory by their bosses. How selective should Inko be in order to upgrade the average criterion score of those selected by $\overline{Z}_y$ = 0.5? What utility model did you use to solve the problem? Why?

REFERENCES

Blum, M. L., Naylor, J. C. (1968). *Industrial Psychology: Its Theoretical and Social Foundations* (rev. ed.). New York: Harper & Row.

Bobko, P., Karren, R., Kerkar, S. P. (1987). Systematic research needs for understanding supervisory-based estimates of SD_y in utility analysis. *Organizational Behavior and Human Decision Processes 40*, 69–95.

Boudreau, J. W. (1991). Utility analysis for decisions in human resource management. In M. D. Dunnette and L. M. Hough (eds.), *Handbook of Industrial and Organizational Psychology* (Vol. 2, 2nd ed., pp. 621–745). Palo Alto, CA: Consulting Psychologists Press.

Brealey, R., Myers, S. (1999). *Principles of Corporate Finance* (6th ed.). Burr Ridge, IL: Irwin/McGraw-Hill.

Brogden, H. E. (1946). On the interpretation of the correlation coefficient as a measure of predictive efficiency. *Journal of Educational Psychology 37*, 64–76.

Brogden, H. E. (1949). When testing pays off. *Personnel Psychology 2*, 171–185.

Brogden, H. E., Taylor, E. K. (1950). The dollar criterion—applying the cost accounting concept to criterion construction. *Personnel Psychology 3, 133–154*.

Cascio, W. F., Ramos, R. A. (1986). Development and application of a new method for assessing job performance in behavioral/economic terms. *Journal of Applied Psychology 71*, 20–28.

Cascio, W. F., Silbey, V. (1979). Utility of the assessment center as a selection device. *Journal of Applied Psychology 64*, 107–118.

Cochran, W. G. (1951). Improvement by means of selection. In J. Neyman (ed.), *Second Berkeley Symposium on Mathematical Statistics and Probability* (pp. 449–470). Berkeley: University of California Press.

Cronbach, L. J., Gleser, G. C. (1965). *Psychological Tests and Personnel Decisions* (2nd ed.). Urbana: University of Illinois Press.

Ghiselli, E. E. (1956). The placement of workers: Concepts and problems. *Personnel Psychology 9, 1–16*.

Greer, O. L., Cascio, W. F. (1987). Is cost accounting the answer? Comparison of two behaviorally based methods for estimating the standard deviation of job performance in dollars with a cost-accounting-based approach. *Journal of Applied Psychology 72*, 588–595.

Judiesch, M. K., Schmidt, F. L., Hunter, J. E. (1993). Has the problem of judgment in utility analysis been solved? *Journal of Applied Psychology 78*, 903–911.

Kelley, T. L. (1923). *Statistical Method.* New York: Macmillan.

Law, K. S., Myors, B. (1999). A modification of Raju, Burke, and Normand's (1990) new model for utility analysis. *Asia Pacific Journal of Human Resources 37*(1), 39–51.

Naylor, J. C., Shine, L. C. (1965). A table for determining the increase in mean criterion score obtained by using a selection device. *Journal of Industrial Psychology 3*, 33–42.

Pearson, K. (1931). *Tables for Statisticians and Biometricians: Vol. 2.* London: Biometric Laboratory, University College.

Raju, N. S., Burke, M. J., Normand J. (1990). A new approach for utility analysis. *Journal of Applied Psychology 75*, 3–12.

Roche, W. J. Jr. (1961). The Cronbach-Gleser utility function in fixed-treatment employee selection. *Dissertation Abstracts International 22*, 4413. (University Microfilms No. 62-1570). Portions reproduced in L. J. Cronbach and G. C. Gleser (eds.), *Psychological Tests and Personnel Decisions* (2nd ed., pp. 254–267). Urbana: University of Illinois Press.

Sands, W. A. (1973). A method for evaluating alternative recruiting-selection strategies: The CAPER model. *Journal of Applied Psychology 58*, 222–227.

Schmidt, F. L., Hoffman, B. (1973). An empirical comparison of three methods of assessing the utility of a selection device. *Journal of Industrial and Organizational Psychology 1*, 1–11.

Taylor, H. C., Russell, J. T. (1939). The relationship of validity coefficients to the practical effectiveness of tests in selection. *Journal of Applied Psychology 23*, 565–578.

ENDNOTES

1. *Bivariate normal* means that the two variables in question (in this case, predictor and criterion scores) are each normally distributed; that is, scores are dispersed in a bell-shaped fashion.
2. *Homoscedastic* means that the variability in criterion scores is the same at high predictor scores as it is at low predictor scores.
3. That means that the new selection procedure is administered to present employees who already have been screened using other methods. The correlation (validity coefficient) between scores on the new procedure and the employees' job performance scores is then computed.
4. To transform raw scores into standard scores, the following formula is used: $x - \bar{x}/SD$ where x is the raw score, $\bar{x}$ is the mean of the distribution of raw scores, and SD is the standard deviation of the distribution. Assuming the raw scores are distributed normally, about 99

percent of the standard scores will lie within the range −3 to +3. Standard scores (*Z*-scores) are expressed in standard-deviation units.

5. A zero-order correlation coefficient is based on two variables. A multiple-regression coefficient represents the correlation between a criterion and two or more predictors.

6. In this chapter, and in most articles on utility analysis, the *SD* of dollar-valued job performance has been symbolized as SD_y. However, Raju et al. (1990) used σ to symbolize the standard deviation, and ρ to symbolize the correlation (validity) coefficient.

7. In attempting to forecast job performance on the basis of a composite of predictor scores, it is necessary to develop a mathematical formula (regression equation). Although many such equations are possible, statisticians generally agree that the most accurate equation is that for which the sum of the squared deviations between actual and predicted job performance scores is a minimum—thus the term *least-squares*.

C H A P T E R 9

Estimating the Economic Value of Job Performance

As equation 6 in chapter 8 showed, the function of the parameter SD_y (the dollar value of a difference of one SD in criterion level) is to translate into economic terms the incremental gain that results from the use of a more valid selection procedure into economic terms. If the SD_y parameter was not included in the general utility equation, then the effect of a change in criterion performance could be expressed only in terms of standard Z-score units. However, when the product $r_{xy}\bar{Z}_{xs}$ is multiplied by the dollar value SD_y, the result is an expression of gain that decision makers understand and are familiar with—dollars.

Although most parameters of the general utility equation can be obtained from records such as the number of people tested, the cost of testing, and the selection ratio, SD_y cannot. Traditionally, as now, SD_y has been the most difficult parameter of the general utility equation to obtain (Raju, Burke, & Normand 1990; Cronbach & Gleser 1965, p. 121). In the past, it was assumed that SD_y could be estimated only by using complicated cost-accounting methods that are both expensive and time-consuming. In general, those procedures involve first costing out the dollar value of the job behaviors of each employee (Brogden & Taylor 1950) and then computing the SD of those values. Several newer approaches require only estimates from knowledgeable people. In this chapter, first we shall examine briefly the cost-accounting approach to estimating SD_y, and then examine in greater detail the newer estimation procedures.

COST-ACCOUNTING APPROACH

In the simplest terms, the objective of a business is to make money. Consequently, monetary gain is the appropriate measure of the degree to which on-the-job activity of the individual worker contributes to or detracts from that overall objective. Brogden and Taylor (1950) summarize this idea as follows:

> Only after we have succeeded in evaluating on-the-job performance in these terms can we be sure that our criterion measures conform to the objectives of the organization. . . . Unless criterion elements are of such a nature that they can be expressed in dollar units, their use as criterion measures cannot be justified and do [sic] not satisfy the requirement of logical face validity. (pp. 139–140)

In using cost accounting to develop a dollar criterion, a number of elements must be considered. Brogden and Taylor list the following as examples:

1. Average value of production or service units.
2. Quality of objects produced or services accomplished.
3. Overhead—including rent, light, heat, cost depreciation, or rental of machines and equipment.
4. Errors, accidents, spoilage, wastage, damage to machines or equipment due to unusual wear and tear, etc.
5. Such factors as appearance, friendliness, poise, and general social effectiveness in public relations. (Here, some approximate value would have to be assigned by an individual or individuals having the required responsibility and background.)
6. The cost of spent time of other personnel. This would include not only the time of the supervisory personnel but also that of other workers. (p. 146)

Roche (1961) attempted to apply these ideas to 291 beginning-level radial drill operators (RDO-1s) working in a large midwestern industrial plant that employs about 25,000 people. The company's job description for an RDO-1 is

> Sets up and operates a radial drill, performing drill, ream, line ream, tap (stud, pipe, and standard), countersink, chamfer, bore, counterbore, spotface, backface, and hollow mill operations. Involves various types of parts such as castings, forgings, bar stock, structural steel and welded fabrications. Grinds drills when necessary. (Cronbach & Gleser 1965, p. 257)

Work assignments to the RDO-1s are made by the planning department according to machine number, not according to specific operators. Consequently, the RDO-1s have no control over the types of parts on which they perform machining operations. Typically, any single operator will work on a variety of parts, and the mix differs from worker to worker.

It was assumed that the dollar profit that accrues to the company as a result of an individual's work provides the best estimate of his or her worth to the company. The following cost-accounting procedures were used to develop that dollar criterion. As described by Roche (1961), the method is one of "standard costing," which is an effective tool for volume-production accounting. It also permits the application of the "principle of exception," whereby attention is directed chiefly to variations from standard cost that indicate trends in volume output. Standard cost for the company's products is determined by identifying the costs of three basic factors: material used to produce products; direct labor hours used to alter the size, shape, quality, or consistency of material; and facility usage required to perform direct labor. Standard cost must remain stable or fixed for a specific period in order to attain its objective. Usually, all standards remain frozen for a period of five years, or until a general cost revision is officially authorized.

The company uses "lifo" (last in–first out) inventory accounting,[1] so that latest costs are used first to allocate costs in a manner closely related to price levels prevailing at the time of sale. The major cost elements in the accounting are

- material, unformed steel
- material, grey iron castings
- material, forgings, stampings, and so on
- material, purchased finished
- direct labor
- general burden
- machine burden

Prime product costs are built up from costs of piece-parts or units into costs for assemblies, then costs for groups, arrangements, and finally for the general arrangements or complete model. The total cost figure has four basic components: variable, fixed, office, and parts warehousing. Variable or out-of-pocket cost includes only those costs that fluctuate with production output: actual cost of material plus material-handling burden; direct labor cost plus an allocation to cover indirect labor, supplies, and so on; and facility usage, which generally reflects normal maintenance, power consumption, perishable tool usage, and facility supplies. Those variable costs are most useful in determining costs where facility usage is not affected. Fixed costs are used where facility usage is affected. Such costs are based on a given percentage of the production capacity of the plant. In determining them, allocations are made to cover portions of material-handling burden, plant labor and burden (such as overtime premiums, special indirect labor, and management salaries), and plant facility usage (such as building and machinery depreciation, repairs and maintenance, tool design). Office and parts-warehousing costs are figured as a percentage allocation.

The income from an RDO-1's work is determined readily because the parts manufactured are sold to dealers and a price for each part has been established. Subtracting the cost at standard production from the price yields a profit figure.

Measuring Each Worker's Productivity

A productivity measure called the *performance ratio* was developed to express the payoff for each individual worker. Because the length of time it takes a competent operator to complete a machining operation on a particular piece-part was established by standard time-study procedures, the number of piece-parts per hour that an operator should be able to process was known. A performance ratio for any period of work could then be computed by dividing actual production per hour by the standard hourly production for the piece-part on which an RDO-1 was then working. For example, if the standard production for a piece-part is 10 pieces per hour and an operator produces 7 pieces in an hour, his or her performance ratio for that one hour's work is 0.70. This index makes it possible to determine the operator's performance ratio over a month or more during which he or she has worked on a number of different piece-parts, each of which has a different production standard. Only rarely does an operator turn out more than standard production over an extended period of time. At the time of the study, operators had varying lengths of time of company service, ranging from a few months to more than 10 years. A rigid attempt to control the experience factor would have seriously reduced the size of the group. Management personnel stated that most people with no previous machine operator experience could reach their typical level of RDO-1 performance within a few weeks. Roche (1961) obtained performance ratios for each operator on a monthly basis for a six-month period. He considered the mean of these ratios to be the

EXHIBIT 9-1   *Monthly Performance Ratios for RDO-1s as a Group*

Month	Mean	SD
First	79.92	17.84
Second	81.21	17.88
Third	79.70	16.71
Fourth	83.16	16.87
Fifth	79.23	20.25
Sixth	80.69	17.72

Source: Roche, W. J. Jr. (1965). A dollar criterion in fixed-treatment employee selection. In L. J. Cronbach and G. C. Gleser (eds.), *Psychological Tests and Personnel Decisions* (p. 262). Urbana: University of Illinois Press.

operator's typical performance. Exhibit 9–1 shows the results. An analysis of variance indicated that the mean performance ratios over the six-month period did not differ significantly from each other. Roche therefore concluded that the group's performance was stable over the period of study, and he used the mean performance for each of the operators as the operator's typical performance.

Burden Adjustment

If an operator produces at less than standard, the actual burden per hour for this inefficiency is greater than the standard burden per hour determined for his or her operation. An operator producing at 80 percent of standard actually takes one and one-quarter hours to produce an hour's work. To account for that additional burden, Roche (1961) corrected each below-standard performance ratio. He assumed that the amount of burden in excess of the standard burden reduced an operator's contribution in a proportional amount, and he used the following formula for such corrections: $2 - 1/PR$, where PR is performance ratio. Thus, when a person is working at 80 percent of standard, the burden is 1.25 hours instead of 1.00 hour, and the corrected performance ratio is 0.75.

Determination of Payoff

The procedures for determining each operator's payoff (y) were these:

1. Computation of each operator's typical performance ratio. That figure was his or her mean performance ratio for the six-month period of the study.

2. Adjustment of the typical performance ratio for below-standard production (burden adjustment).
3. Computation of the average profit at standard production, attributable to the radical drill operation.
   a. Tabulation of the standard production rate for each type of piece-part machined by radial drill operators. The time-study division provided those data.
   b. Profit for each type of piece-part attributable to the radial drill operation.
   c. Profit per hour for each piece-part attributable to the radial drill operation at standard production. Roche determined these figures by multiplying the profit per piece by the standard production rate for the piece.
   d. Average hourly profit attributable to the radial drill operation at standard production. That was determined by weighting the profit per hour for each piece-part (step 3c) by the number of such parts in the work flow.
4. Determination of y, the profit for each RDO at his or her corrected performance ratio and the standard hourly profit.
5. Computation of SD_y—the standard deviation of the y values computed in step 4.

In actually computing the payoff values, Roche (1961) reported that the 291 RDOs worked on approximately 2,500 different piece-parts. Because determining the profit attributable to the radial drill operation for every piece-part would require an enormous amount of clerical labor, a random sample of 275 parts (about 10 percent of the total) was drawn and the necessary computations were performed for those parts. Averaged over the sample of parts, the profit per hour attributable to the radial drill operation was \$5.512; the SD was \$3.947.[2] That amount is not directly a part of company earnings. Out of this line in the balance sheet must come various costs of doing business, such as interest on loans and bonds and taxes.

The y value for each operator was the hourly profit at standard production attributable to the RDO-1 multiplied by his or her corrected performance ratio. The standard deviation of this distribution (SD_y) was \$0.585.[3]

Despite the complexity and apparent objectivity of the cost-accounting approach, Roche (1961) admitted that "many estimates and arbitrary allocations entered into the cost accounting" (Cronbach & Gleser

1965, p. 263). The development of an estimate of SD_y clearly required a prodigious effort in the Roche study. (The actual utility estimates will be described in chapter 10.) That is probably a major reason why further such studies were not undertaken for more than 15 years following publication of the Roche study. A subsequent attempt to use cost-accounting methodology to develop an objective estimate of SD_y for the job of route salesperson for a soft-drink bottling company resulted in the same conclusion made by Roche (Greer & Cascio 1987). The researchers' method involved estimating the "contribution margin" (revenue less variable costs) associated with selling cases of different sizes and types, multiplying that value by the number of cases each salesperson sold, and then multiplying that value by the percentage of sales attributable to the salesperson's effort on each route. This produced an estimate of each salesperson's contribution margin, and the SD of those values represented SD_y.

Cost-accounting systems focus on determining the costs and benefits of units of product, not units of performance. Hence, many estimates are needed, and the presumed objectivity and reliability of the cost-accounting data may become suspect. Paradoxically, therefore, if HR researchers can establish the validity of their methods, behavioral approaches may be more valid, reliable, and credible with practitioners than are cost-accounting approaches. Over the last 20 years, several new approaches for estimating the economic value of job performance have been developed. All require considerably less effort than the cost-accounting method, and comparative research has made possible some general conclusions about the relative merits of those methods. First we will consider the methods themselves; then we will consider the findings of comparative research.

THE 40 PERCENT RULE

When time or resources do not permit a more detailed estimation of SD_y, Schmidt and Hunter (1983) recommended that 40 percent of average salary be used. Furthermore, because wages and salaries average 57 percent of the value of goods and services in the U.S. economy, that SD_y figure is 22.8 percent (0.40×0.57) or roughly 20 percent of mean output. If we substitute 40 percent of salary for SD_y, then utility can be expressed in terms of dollars. (Subsequent research [Judiesch, Schmidt, & Mount 1992] indicates that this guideline is quite conservative.) If instead we substitute 20 percent for SD_y (a value known as SD_p), then utility may be expressed in terms of the *percentage increase* in output.

In a later study, Hunter, Schmidt, and Judiesch (1990) tested the hypothesis that SD_p increases as the complexity (that is, information-processing requirements) of jobs increases. Results of 68 studies that measured work output on the job, and 17 work-sample studies revealed that as jobs increase in complexity from routine clerical or blue-collar work to medium complexity (for example, first-line supervisors, skilled craftspeople, technicians) to high complexity (managerial/professional, complex technical jobs), SD_p increased from 15 percent to 25 percent to 46 percent, respectively. For life insurance sales jobs, SD_p is very large (97 percent), and it is about 39 percent for other sales jobs. Those results suggest that there are sizable differences in performance across individuals and that potentially large gains in productivity may be realized when valid personnel selection procedures are used to identify the best talent available.

The substitution of SD_p for SD_y is provocative because it suggests that in situations where job complexity can be estimated, SD_p also can be estimated, thereby removing a barrier to more widespread application of utility-analysis methods. On the other hand, Boudreau (1991) has noted that SD_p allows one to estimate only the percentage increase that is likely to result from HRM programs. Determining whether such increases offset dollar costs, or whether to invest resources in different jobs, requires assumptions or estimates of the dollar value of that percentage. Therefore, researchers have developed other behavior-based methods for estimating the variability of job performance in dollars. We will consider several of them in the sections that follow.

GLOBAL ESTIMATION OF THE DOLLAR VALUE OF JOB PERFORMANCE

It is fortunate that estimates of utility need not be accurate down to the last dollar. Utility estimates typically are used to make decisions about selection procedures, and for this purpose only errors large enough to lead to incorrect decisions are of any consequence. Further, when cost-accounting procedures are used, errors may be as frequent or more frequent and may become a more severe problem as one moves up the corporate ladder. What objective cost-accounting techniques, for example, can be used to assess the dollar value of an executive's impact on the morale of his or her subordinates? It is precisely the jobs with the largest SD_y values—that is, the jobs for which ΔU/selectee is potentially greatest—that are handled least well by cost-accounting methods. Rational estimates, to one degree or another, are virtually unavoidable at the higher job levels.

One procedure for obtaining rational estimates of SD_y has been developed by Schmidt, Hunter, McKenzie, and Muldrow (1979). Their method was used in a pilot study of 62 experienced supervisors of budget analysts to estimate SD_y for that occupation. Supervisors were used as judges because they have the best opportunities to observe actual performance and output differences among employees on a day-to-day basis. The method is based on the following reasoning: If job performance in dollar terms is normally distributed, then the difference between the value to the organization of the products and services produced by an employee at the 85th percentile in performance and that of an employee at the 50th percentile in performance is equal to SD_y. Budget-analyst supervisors were asked to estimate both of those values; the final estimate was the average difference across the 62 supervisors.

Such a global estimation procedure (in which a total figure is derived directly instead of summing individual cost elements) has at least two advantages. First, the mental standard to be used by the supervisor-judges is the estimated cost to the organization of having an outside consulting firm provide the same products or services. In many occupations, this is a relatively concrete standard. Second, the idiosyncratic tendencies, biases, and random errors of individual experts can be controlled by averaging across a large number of judges. Unless the group has an upward or downward bias as a whole, such an average should be fairly accurate. In the budget-analyst example, the standard error of the mean was $1,120. That means that the interval $9,480 to $13,175 should contain 90 percent of such estimates. Thus, to be extremely conservative one could employ the lower bound of that interval in calculations.

Methods similar to the global estimation procedure have been used successfully by the Decision Analysis Group of the Stanford Research Institute to scale otherwise unmeasurable, but critical, variables. Resulting measures have been used in the application of the principles of decision theory to high-level policy decision making in such areas as nuclear power plant construction, corporate-risk policies, investment and expansion programs, and hurricane seeding (Howard, Matheson, & North 1972; Matheson 1969; Howard 1966). All indications are that the response to the work of that group has been positive; the methods have been judged by high-level decision makers to improve socially and economically important decisions.

A Sample Study

What follows is a detailed explanation of how the global estimation procedure has been used to estimate SD_y. The application to be described was reported by Schmidt et al. (1979) using supervisors of computer programmers in 10 federal agencies. To test the hypothesis that dollar outcomes are normally distributed, the supervisors were asked to estimate values for the 15th percentile (low-performing programmers), the 50th percentile (average programmers), and the 85th percentile (superior programmers). The resulting data thus provide two estimates of SD_y. If the distribution is approximately normal, those two estimates will not differ substantially in value. The following excerpt from Schmidt et al. (1979, p. 621) presents their instructions to the supervisors.

> The dollar utility estimates we are asking you to make are critical in estimating the relative dollar value to the government of different selection methods. In answering these questions, you will have to make some very *difficult judgments.* We realize they are difficult and that they are judgments or estimates. You will have to ponder for some time before giving each estimate, and there is probably no way you can be absolutely certain your estimate is accurate when you do reach a decision. But keep in mind three things:
>
> (1) The alternative to estimates of this kind is application of cost-accounting procedures to the evaluation of job performance. Such applications are usually prohibitively expensive. And in the end, they produce only imperfect estimates, like this estimation procedure.
> (2) Your estimates will be averaged in with those of other supervisors of computer programmers. Thus errors produced by too high and too low estimates will tend to be averaged out, providing more accurate final estimates.
> (3) The decisions that must be made about selection methods do not require that all estimates be accurate down to the last dollar. Substantially accurate estimates will lead to the same decisions as perfectly accurate estimates.
>
> Based on your experience with agency programmers, we would like for you to estimate the yearly value to your agency of the products and services produced by the average GS 9-11 computer programmer. Consider the quality and quantity of output typical of the *average programmer* and the value of this output. In placing an overall dollar value on this output, it may help to

consider what the cost would be of having an outside firm provide these products and services.

Based on my experience, I estimate the value to my agency of the average GS 9-11 computer programmer at _____ dollars per year.

We would now like for you to consider the *"superior" programmer.* Let us define a superior performer as a programmer who is at the 85th percentile. That is, his or her performance is better than that of 85% of his or her fellow GS 9-11 programmers, and only 15% turn in better performances. Consider the quality and quantity of the output typical of the superior programmer. Then estimate the value of these products and services. In placing an overall dollar value on this output, it may again help to consider what the cost would be of having an outside firm provide these products and services.

Based on my experience, I estimate the value to my agency of a superior GS 9-11 computer programmer to be _____ dollars per year.

Finally, we would like you to consider the *"low-performing" computer programmer.* Let us define a low-performing programmer as one who is at the 15th percentile. That is, 85% of all GS 9-11 computer programmers turn in performances better than the low-performing programmer, and only 15% turn in worse performances. Consider the quality and quantity of the output typical of the low-performing programmer. Then estimate the value of these products and services. In placing an overall dollar value on this output, it may again help to consider what the cost would be of having an outside firm provide these products and services.

Based on my experience, I estimate the value to my agency of the low-performing GS 9-11 computer programmer at _____ dollars per year.

The wording of that questionnaire was developed carefully and pretested on a small sample of programmer supervisors and personnel psychologists. None of the programmer supervisors who returned questionnaires in the study reported any difficulty in understanding the questionnaire or in making the estimates. Participation in the study was completely voluntary. Of 147 questionnaires distributed, 105 were returned (all in usable form), for a return rate of 71.4 percent.

Results

In the Schmidt et al. (1979) study of programmers, the two estimates of SD_y were similar. The mean estimated difference in dollar value of yearly job performance between programmers at the 85th and 50th percentiles in job performance was $10,871 (standard error [$SE$] = $1,673).

The difference between the 50th and 15th percentiles was $9,955 ($SE =$ $1,035). The difference of $916 was roughly 8 percent of each of the estimates and was not statistically significant. Thus, the hypothesis that computer programmer productivity in dollars is normally distributed could not be rejected. The distribution was at least approximately normal. The average of those two estimates, $10,413, was the SD_y figure used in the utility calculations to be described in chapter 10. That figure must be considered an underestimate because it applies to incumbents rather than to the applicant pool.

Subsequent Developments

Judiesch, Schmidt, and Mount (1992) showed that the global estimation procedure produces downwardly biased estimates of utility. That appears to be so because most judges equate average value with average wages despite the fact that the value of the output as sold of the average employee is much larger than average wages. However, estimates of the coefficient of variation of job performance ($SD_y/\bar{Y}$ or SD_p) calculated from supervisory estimates of the three percentiles (50th, 85th, and 15th) were quite accurate. That finding led the authors (1996, 1992) to propose a modification to the original Schmidt et al. (1979) method. Their approach estimated SD_y as the product of estimates of the coefficient of variation ($SD_y/\bar{Y}$ or SD_p) and an objective estimate of the average value of employee output ($\bar{Y}$). In using that procedure, one first estimates $\bar{Y}$ and SD_p separately, and then multiplies those values to estimate SD_y.

SD_p can be estimated in two ways: (1) by using the average value found by Hunter et al. (1990) for jobs of similar complexity, or (2) by dividing supervisory estimates of SD_y by supervisory estimates of the value of performance of the 50th-percentile worker. Judiesch et al. (1996) tested the latter method's accuracy by calculating supervisory estimates of SD_p from 11 previous studies of SD_y estimation, and then comparing those estimates with objective SD_p values. Across the 11 studies, the mean of the supervisory estimates was 44.2 percent, which was very close to the actual output-based mean of 43.9 percent. The correlation between the two sets of values was 0.70. Those results indicate that supervisors can estimate quite accurately the magnitude of relative (percent) differences in employee performance.

With respect to calculating the average revenue value of employee output, Judiesch et al. (1996, 1992) begin with the assumption that the average revenue value of employee output ($\overline{Y}$) is equal to total sales revenue divided by the total number of employees. However, total sales revenue is based on contributions from many jobs within an organization. Assuming that the contribution of each job to the total revenue of the firm is proportional to its share of the firm's total annual payroll, then an approximate average revenue value for a particular job (A) can be calculated as:

Equation 1

> Job A Value = Total Revenue × (Job A Payroll ÷ Total Payroll)

and *Equation 2*

> $\overline{Y}$ = Job A Value ÷ Job A Number of Employees

SD_y then can be estimated as $\overline{Y}(SD_p)$, where SD_p is computed using one of the two methods described earlier. An additional advantage of estimating SD_y from estimates of SD_p is that it is not necessary that estimates of SD_y be obtained from dollar-value estimates.

Although the global estimation procedure is easy to use and provides fairly reliable estimates across supervisors, it has these three drawbacks:

1. The dollar-valued job performance outcomes often are not normally distributed (Lezotte, Raju, Burke, & Normand 1996; Rich & Boudreau 1987; Burke & Frederick 1984).
2. The original procedure lacks face validity (that is, it does not appear to measure what it purports to measure) because the components of each supervisor's estimates are unknown and unverifiable.
3. Subjects often find the task of estimating the dollar value of various percentiles in the distribution of job performance to be difficult. Moreover, the variation among each rater's SD_y estimates is usually as large or larger than the mean SD_y estimate. In fact, DeSimone, Alexander, and Cronshaw (1986) found both the level of agreement among raters and the stability over time of their SD_y estimates to be low.

To improve consensus among raters, two strategies have been used: (1) provide an anchor for the 50th percentile (Burke & Frederick 1986, 1984; Bobko, Karren, & Parkington 1983); (2) have groups of raters provide consensus judgments of different percentiles. Despite those problems, several studies have reported close correspondence between estimated and actual *SD*s when sales dollars (Bobko et al. 1983) or cost-accounting estimates (Greer & Cascio 1987) were used. However, when medical claims cost data were used, the original Schmidt et al. (1979) procedure overestimated the actual value of SD_y by 26 percent (Lezotte et al. 1996). An alternative procedure that makes no assumption regarding the underlying normality of the performance distribution, and that does identify the components of each supervisor's estimate, is described next.

THE CASCIO-RAMOS ESTIMATE OF PERFORMANCE IN DOLLARS

The Cascio-Ramos estimate of performance in dollars (CREPID) was developed under the auspices of the American Telephone and Telegraph Company, and was tested on 602 first-level managers in a Bell operating company (Cascio & Ramos 1986). The rationale underlying CREPID is as follows. Assuming an organization's compensation program reflects current market rates for jobs, then the economic value of each employee's labor is reflected best in his or her annual wage or salary. CREPID breaks down each employee's job into its principal activities, assigns a proportional amount of the annual salary to each principal activity, and then requires supervisors to rate each employee's job performance on each principal activity. The resulting ratings then are translated into estimates of dollar value for each principal activity. The sum of the dollar values assigned to each principal activity equals the economic value of each employee's job performance to the company. Let us explain each of these steps in greater detail.

1. *Identify principal activities.* To assign a dollar value to each employee's job performance, first we must identify what tasks each employee performs. In many job analysis systems, principal activities (or critical work behaviors) are identified expressly. In others they can be derived, under the assumption that to be considered "principal" an activity should take up at least 10 percent of total work time. As an illustration, consider Exhibit 9–2, a portion of a hypothetical job description for an accounting supervisor. As Exhibit 9–2 indicates, this job involves eight principal activities.
2. *Rate each principal activity in terms of time/frequency and importance.* It has long been recognized that rating job activities simply in terms of the time or frequency with which each is performed is an incomplete

EXHIBIT 9-2 *Portion of a Job Description for an Accounting Supervisor*

Function

Under general supervision of the Manager-Accounting (Accounts Analysis and Bills and Vouchers) supervises the Accounts Payable System of the Central Region.

Know How

This position is responsible, through subordinates, for the processing, payment, and journalization of suppliers' bills (all bills except those handled by intercompany settlement) and employees' expense vouchers through input to the accounts payable system. Bills and vouchers are received along with authorization forms from company employees initiating the expense. The following steps then take place:

- Receive summaries and log into accounts payable system by office, summary, and total dollars for control purposes.
- Edit for correctness, for example, proper authorization or coding.
- Enter bill and voucher information into accounts payable system for check issuance and subsequently into mechanized system for journalization.
- Return to employee originating them all erroneous bills and vouchers for correction and then correct the initial cumulative total in accounts payable system.
- Update the master file of suppliers contained in system.

Incumbent is directly responsible for the manual processing, payment, and journalization of special bills that cannot be processed via computer (for example, relocation expenses, tuition aid, employee refunds and commissions) and various special reports. Also responsible for the issuance of Forms 1099—U.S. Information Return-to-Suppliers and the Internal Revenue Service.

Incumbent must have a thorough knowledge of accounting principles, of the accounts payable data entry system, and of the bill payment process. Also needed is a familiarity with disbursement accounting practices and other guides and reference manuals. Incumbent must have analytical and investigative ability, communication skills, mathematical aptitude, and supervisory skills.

Subordinates are eleven Senior Clerks.

Principal Activities

1. Performs normal supervisory functions.
2. Receives questions on billing problems from suppliers. Investigates and furnishes answers, expedites late checks.
3. Adjudicates bills and vouchers for legitimacy of purpose or amount when clerks cannot make determination. Contacts originators at all levels of management when necessary.

(continued on next page)

EXHIBIT 9-2 *Continued*

4. Verifies and signs reports sent to Corporate Books and other departments.
5. Performs immediate action in the event of computer problems, notifies programmer if necessary.
6. Interprets procedural changes, trains subordinates or arranges for formal training.
7. Coordinates the review of bills and vouchers by internal and external auditors or state authorities.
8. Ensures implementation of proper security precautions.

Problem Solving

The incumbent's major problems involve questions from subordinates and other departments regarding correct chargeable account, if expenditure is reimbursable, etc.; investigating and answering suppliers' inquiries regarding late or improper payment of bills; maintaining work production with a consistently changing force; contending with computer breakdowns.

Accountability

Incumbent in this position is accountable for receiving, logging, totaling, editing, payment, and journalization of all company vouchers and bills (except those handled through intercompany settlements) for the Central Region. Incumbent is also accountable for acting as the information center where suppliers and other departments can call to have their questions answered regarding bill payments and voucher processing information. Subordinates' salaries approximately $XXX,000 annually.

$$\text{Bills processed} = \$XX,000 \text{ per month}$$
$$\text{Totaling} = \$XX.X \text{ million}$$

indication of the overall weight to be assigned to each activity. For example, a nurse may spend most of the work week performing the routine tasks of patient care. However, suppose the nurse must respond to one medical emergency per week that requires, on an average, one hour of his or her time. To be sure, the time/frequency of this activity is short, but its importance is critical. Ratings of time/frequency and importance should be expressed on a scale that has a zero point so that, in theory, complete absence of a property can be indicated. Sample rating scales for principal activities are shown in Exhibit 9–3.

Research results using job analysis ratings derived from CREPID have shown two things. First, only the time/frequency and importance

EXHIBIT 9-3   *CREPID Rating Scales for Principal Activities*

1. **Time/frequency:** Please rate each principal activity on the 0–7 scale below. Stepping back and looking at the whole job, say, over a one-year period, how would you allocate the principal activities in terms of the time/frequency with which each is done?

0	1	2	3	4	5	6	7
very rarely		sometimes		often		very often	

2. **Importance:** Please rate each principal activity on a 0–7 scale that reflects, in your opinion, how important that principal activity is to overall job performance. Use the scale below as a guide to help you rate the activities.

0	1	2	3	4	5	6	7
of no importance		moderately important		very important		of greatest importance	

of each principal activity need to be rated in order to derive and assign an overall weight to each principal activity (Cascio & Ramos 1986). Second, for rating time/frequency and importance, simple 0–7-point Likert-type rating scales provide results that are almost identical to those derived from more complicated scales (Weekley, Frank, O'Connor, & Peters 1985).

3. *Multiply the numerical ratings for time/frequency and importance for each principal activity.* Perform this step to develop an overall relative weight to assign to each principal activity. The ratings are multiplied together so that if a zero rating is assigned to any category, the relative weight of that principal activity is zero. Thus, if an activity never is done, or if it is totally unimportant, then the relative weight for that activity should be zero. The following table presents hypothetical ratings of the eight principal activities identified for the accounting supervisor's job shown in Exhibit 9–2.

Principal Activity	Time/ Frequency	×	Importance	=	Total	Relative Weight (%)
1	4.0		4		16.0	16.8
2	5.0		7		35.0	36.8
3	1.0		5		5.0	5.3

4	0.5	3	1.5	1.6
5	2.0	7	14.0	14.7
6	1.0	4	4.0	4.2
7	0.5	3	1.5	1.6
8	3.0	6	18.0	19.0
			95.0	100.0

After doing all of the multiplication, sum the total ratings assigned to each principal activity (95.0 in the preceding example). Then divide the total rating for each principal activity by the grand total to derive the relative weight for the activity (for example, $16 \div 95 = 0.168$ or 16.8 percent). Knowing each principal activity's relative weight allows us to allocate proportional shares of the employee's overall salary to each principal activity, as is done in step 4.

4. *Assign dollar values to each principal activity.* Take an average (or weighted average) annual rate of pay for all participants in the study (employees in a particular job class) and allocate it across principal activities according to the relative weights obtained in step 3.

To illustrate, suppose the annual salary of each accounting supervisor is $50,000.

Principal Activity	Relative Weight (%)	Dollar Value ($)
1	16.8	8,400
2	36.8	18,400
3	5.3	2,650
4	1.6	800
5	14.7	7,350
6	4.2	2,100
7	1.6	800
8	19.0	9,500
		50,000

5. *Rate performance on each principal activity on a 0–200 scale.* Now that we know what each employee does, the relative weight of each principal activity, and the dollar value of each principal activity, the next task is to determine *how well* the employee does each principal activity. The higher the rating on each principal activity, the greater the economic value of that activity to the organization. CREPID uses a modified magnitude-estimation scale (Stevens 1971) to obtain information on performance. To use this procedure, a value (let's say

EXHIBIT 9–4 *Performance Appraisal Form Used with CREPID*

In this last part of the exercise we would like you to rate the job performance of your subordinate, _____, relative to the princi-
pal activities identified previously. Use the rating scale below for each of
the principal activities listed in the job analysis to rate your subordinate.

0	50	100	150	200
	better than 25% of employees I've seen do this activity	better than 50%	better than 75%	better than 99%

In your opinion, based on the principal activities described in the job analysis and relative to others you have seen do these activities, how does the
job performance of _____ compare? (Use any number on
the 0–200 scale shown above.)

Principal Activity   Points Assigned

1 _____   _____

2 _____   _____

3 _____   _____

4 _____   _____

5 _____   _____

6 _____   _____

7 _____   _____

8 _____   _____

100) is assigned to a referent concept (for example, the average employee, one at the 50th percentile on job performance), and then all
comparisons are made relative to that value. Discussions with operating managers indicated that, given current selection procedures, it is
highly unlikely that even the very best employee is more than twice
as effective as the average employee. Thus, a continuous 0–200 scale
was used to rate each employee on each principal activity. The actual
form used is shown in Exhibit 9–4. Managers reported that they found
the format helpful and easy to use.

6. *Multiply the point rating (expressed as a decimal number) assigned to
   each principal activity by the activity's dollar value. To illustrate,*

suppose the following point totals are assigned to accounting supervisor C. P. Ayh:

Principal Activity	Points Assigned	×	Dollar Value of Activity ($)	=	Net Dollar Value ($)
1	1.35		8,400		11,340.00
2	1.00		18,400		18,400.00
3	1.25		2,650		3,312.50
4	2.00		800		1,600.00
5	1.00		7,350		7,350.00
6	0.50		2,100		1,050.00
7	0.75		800		600.00
8	1.50		9,500		14,250.00

7. *Compute the overall economic value of each employee's job performance by adding the results of step 6.* In our example, the overall economic value of Mr. Ayh's job performance is $57,902.50, or $7,902.50 more than he is being paid.

8. *Over all employees in the study, compute the mean and standard deviation of dollar-valued job performance.* When CREPID was tested on 602 first-level managers at a Bell operating company, the mean of dollar-valued job performance was only $988 (3.4 percent) more than the average actual salary of all employees in the study. However, the SD_y was over $10,000, which was more than three-and-one-half times larger than the SD of the actual distribution of salaries. Such high variability suggests that supervisors recognized significant differences in performance throughout the rating process. As we shall see in chapter 10, that is precisely the type of situation in which valid selection procedures have the greatest payoff—when individual differences in job performance are high, and therefore the cost of error is substantial.

It is important to point out that CREPID requires only two sets of ratings from a supervisor: (1) a rating of each principal activity in terms of time/frequency and importance (the job analysis phase), and (2) a rating of a specific subordinate's performance on each principal activity (the performance appraisal phase). Actually identifying principal activities (step 1), multiplying the numerical ratings assigned during the job analysis phase (step 3), assigning dollar values to each principal activity (step 4), and determining the overall economic value of job performance (steps

EXHIBIT 9-5 *Summary of the Cascio-Ramos Procedure for Determining the Economic Value of Management Performance*

Steps
1. Identify principal activities.
2. Rate each principal activity in terms of time/frequency and importance.
3. Multiply the numerical ratings for time/frequency and importance for each principal activity.
4. Assign dollar values to each principal activity. Take an average rate of pay of participants in the study and allocate it across principal activities according to the results obtained in step 3.
5. Rate each principal activity on a 0–200 scale.
6. Multiply (for each principal activity) its dollar value by the point rating assigned (expressed as a decimal number).
7. Compute the overall economic value of job performance by adding together results of step 6.
8. Over all employees in the study, compute the mean and standard deviation of dollar-valued job performance.

6, 7, and 8) are done by HR specialists who use a simple, computerized scoring program. A summary of the entire CREPID procedure is presented in Exhibit 9–5.

Subsequent Developments

The valuation base (average annual salary) used in the CREPID model has generated considerable discussion among researchers in this field (Judiesch et al. 1996, 1992; Lezotte et al. 1996). It is generally accepted now that the use of salary as the valuation base produces a more conservative estimate of overall utility than does the use either of "direct costs" (Lezotte et al. 1996), which comprise average salary, benefits, and overhead costs, or of the average sales revenue of the output of the average employee on a job (Judiesch et al. 1996, 1992). However, the use of a 0–200 performance range (performance of the very best performer not more than twice that of the average performer) has been replicated in two ways (Lezotte et al. 1996): (1) based on evaluations by subject matter experts, and (2) based on an empirical performance measure (claims processed per hour).

Edwards, Frederick, and Burke (1988) modified the basic CREPID procedure by substituting archival data for either performance ratings or job analysis ratings, or for both. They found that when they substituted either archival performance ratings or archival job analysis ratings, results were similar to those produced using the original procedure. However, SD_y was much smaller when archival data were used for both performance ratings *and* job analysis.

As Boudreau (1991) has noted, CREPID has the advantage of assigning each employee a specific value that can be analyzed explicitly for appropriateness and that may provide a more understandable or credible estimate for decision makers. However, as noted earlier, CREPID assumes that average wage equals the economic value of a worker's performance. That assumption is used in national income accounting to generate the GNP and labor-cost figures for jobs where output is not readily measurable (for example, government services). That is, the same value is assigned to both output and wages. Because, as Boudreau (1991) pointed out, that assumption does not hold in pay systems based on rank, tenure, or hourly pay rates, CREPID should not be used in those situations.

SYSTEM EFFECTIVENESS TECHNIQUE

The system effectiveness technique was developed by Eaton, Wing, and Mitchell (1985) specifically for use in situations where individual salary is only a small percentage of the value of performance to the organization or of the equipment operated (in the case of an army tank commander or a fighter pilot). The method evaluates changes in the performance levels of system units that lead to improved overall performance.

With this approach, Eaton et al. distinguish $SD\$$, the standard deviation of performance in dollars, from SD_y, the standard deviation of output units of performance (for example, number of hits per firing from an army tank commander). They have shown that

Equation 3

$$SD\$ = C_u(SD_y/Y1)$$

where C_u is the cost of the unit in the system—it includes equipment, support, and personnel, rather than salary alone. $Y1$ is the mean performance of units at the initial performance level.

Equation 3 indicates that $SD\$$ equals the cost per unit times the ratio of the SD_y of performance to the initial mean level of performance, $Y1$.

However, estimates from equation 3 are appropriate *only when the performance of the unit in the system is largely a function of the performance of the individual in the job under investigation.* Examples of performance scales that might fit this method are probability of hits per firing (army tank commandor), number of convictions per year (detective), or other frequency-type variables.

To assess *SD$* using the system effectiveness technique, Eaton et al. collected data on U.S. Army tank commanders. They obtained those data from technical reports of previous research and from an approximation of tank costs. Previous research indicated that meaningful values for the ratio $SD_y/Y1$ ranged from 0.2 to 0.5. Tank costs, consisting of purchase costs, maintenance, and personnel, were estimated to fall between $300,000 and $500,000 per year. For purposes of equation 3, C_u was estimated at $300,000 per year, and $SD_y/Y1$ was estimated at 0.2. This yielded

$$SD\$ = \$300,000 \times 0.2 = \$60,000$$

An alternative method, also developed by Eaton et al. for similar kinds of situations, is the superior equivalents technique. It is somewhat like the global estimation procedure, but with one important difference. Instead of using estimates of the dollar value of performance at the 85th percentile, the technique uses estimates of how many superior (85th-percentile) performers would be needed to produce the output of a fixed number of average (50th-percentile) performers. That estimate, combined with an estimate of the dollar value of average performance, provides an estimate of SD_y, and is the basis for the title "superior equivalents technique."

SUPERIOR EQUIVALENTS TECHNIQUE

The basic concept of this method is that of estimating the *SD* of performance in performance units and then converting that estimate to dollar units. Accordingly, the first step is to estimate the number (*N*85) of 85th-percentile employees required to equal the performance of some fixed number (*N*50) of average performers. Where the value of average performance (*V*50) is known, or can be estimated, SD_y may be estimated by using the ratio *N*50 ÷ *N*85 × *V*50 to obtain *V*85 and then subtracting *V*50. That reduces to

Equation 4

$$SD_y = V85 - V50$$

but, *Equation 5*

$$V85 = (V50 \times N50) \div N85$$

Hence, *Equation 6*

$$SD_y = V50 [(N50 \div N85) - 1]$$

Eaton et al. (1985) developed a questionnaire to obtain an estimate of the number of tanks with superior tank commanders (TCs) needed to equal the performance of a standard company of 17 tanks with average commanders. A fill-in-the-blanks format was used, as shown in the following excerpt.

> For the purpose of this questionnaire an "average" tank commander is an NCO or commissioned officer whose performance is better than about half his fellow TCs. A "superior" tank commander is one whose performance is better than 85% of his fellow tank commanders.
>
> The first question deals with relative value. For example, if a "superior" clerk types 10 letters a day and an "average" clerk types 5 letters a day then, all else being equal, 5 "superior" clerks have the same value in an office as 10 "average" clerks.
>
> In the same way, we want to know your estimate or opinion of the relative value of "average" vs. "superior" tank commanders in combat.
>
> 1. *I estimate that, all else being equal, _____ tanks with "superior" tank commanders would be about equal in combat to 17 tanks with "average" tank commanders.*

Questionnaire data were gathered from 100 tank commanders enrolled in advanced training at a U.S. Army post. $N50$ was set at 17 as a fixed number of tanks with average commanders, because a tank company has 17 tanks. Assuming that organizations pay average employees their approximate worth, the equivalent civilian salary for a tank commander was set at \$30,000 (in 1985 dollars).

Results

The median response given for the number of superior TCs judged equivalent to 17 average TCs was 9, and the mode was 10. The response

"9" was used as most representative of central tendency. Making use of equation 3, *V*85 was calculated as follows:

$$(\$30,000 \times 17) \div 9 = \$56,666$$

In terms of equation 1,

$$SD_y = \$30,000 \left[(17 \div 9) - 1\right] = \$26,666$$

That result is considerably less than the *SD*$ value ($60,000) that resulted from the system effectiveness technique. *SD*$_y$ also was estimated using the global estimation procedure. However, there was minimal agreement either within or between groups for estimates of superior performance, and the distributions were skewed positively. Distributions of average performance also were skewed positively. For those reasons, results of the global estimation procedure were not used in calculating overall utility. Such extreme response variability illustrates the difficulty of making these kinds of judgments when the cost of contracting work is unknown, equipment is expensive, or other financially intangible factors exist. Such is frequently the case for public employees, particularly when private-industry counterparts do not exist. Under these circumstances, the system effectiveness technique or the superior equivalents technique may apply.

Eaton et al. (1985) pointed out that one possible problem with both of those techniques is that the *quality* of performance in some situations may not translate easily into a unidimensional, quantitative scale. For example, a police department may decide that the conviction of one murderer is equivalent to the conviction of five burglars. Whether managers do, in fact, develop informal algorithms to compare the performance of different individuals, perhaps on different factors, is an empirical question. Certainly, the terms or dimensions that are most meaningful and useful will vary across jobs.

ESTIMATING ECONOMIC VALUE OF JOB PERFORMANCE IN THE RAJU ET AL. MODEL

As noted in chapter 8, Raju et al. (1990) defined economic value in terms of $A\sigma_R$, where A is the full labor-cost multiplier that includes salary, benefits, and overhead (Raju, Burke, Normand, & Lezotte 1993), and σ_R is the standard deviation of observed performance ratings, transformed to a 0–2 scale. In a study involving 133 medical claims examiners, Lezotte et al. (1996) compared this estimate of economic value to that produced by the original global estimation procedure (Schmidt et al. 1979), and to an empirically derived estimate of SD_y. The empirical estimate was derived by the following steps.

1. Compute the average cost per claim for one year ($4.67).
2. Determine the expected number of processing hours per examiner per year. Because examiners worked an average of 37 hours per week times 48 weeks per year, the expected number of processing hours per year was 1,776.
3. Calculate the mean and *SD* of performance (claims per hour) over all examiners. The values were 5.46 and 1.16, respectively.
4. Calculate the average number of expected claims processed per examiner per year (average claims per hour times hours per year). The value was 5.46 × 1,776, or 9,697.
5. Multiply the average cost per claim by the average number of claims processed per examiner per year. This value was $4.67 × 9,697, or $45,285. That figure represents the economic value of the average performing employee.
6. Multiply the *SD* of claims per hour (1.16) by the number of processing hours per year (1,776) and the cost per claim ($4.67). The value, $9,620, is the empirically derived SD_y.

Lezotte et al. (1996) defined A as total direct costs (salary, benefits, and overhead costs), which, for the medical claims examiners, was $33,150.

The estimate of σ_R was obtained by first calculating the *SD* of the supervisory performance ratings for the medical claims examiners. This value was 0.49, with a mean rating of 3.57 on a five-point scale. After verifying empirically and with subject matter experts that a 0–2 scale was appropriate, Lezotte et al. (1996) converted the five-point performance rating scale to a 0–2 scale using equation 14 in chapter 8. The transformed rating *SD* was 0.245, with a mean of 1.285. Thus A_R is 0.245 × $33,150, or $8,122. That value was about 15.5 percent below the empirically derived value of $9,620. However, the global estimation procedure yielded an SD_y estimate of $12,099, which was about 26 percent higher than the empirically derived value.

More recently, Law and Myors (1999) developed a modification to the rating scale transformation used by Raju et al. (1990). Their formula, which uses the ratio of the highest to the lowest rating on the transformed scale, rather than the ratio of the highest to the average rating, is

Equation 7

$$\sigma_R = \left(\frac{2 \left[1 - \dfrac{2}{\dfrac{Y_h}{Y_l} + 1} \right]}{R_h - R_l} \right) \sigma_{RO}$$

where σ_R is the transformed performance rating, Y_h and Y_l are the highest and lowest limits of the standardized performance scale, R_h and R_l are the highest and lowest limits of the original performance scale, and σ_{RO} is the *SD* of the original performance ratings. This transformation is appropriate when it is reasonable to assume that performance ratings are symmetrical and normally distributed. Law and Myors assume further that Y_l is non-zero, and they argue that in almost all cases it would be positive as well.[5] Applications of the modified Raju et al. (1990) procedure in two Australian samples indicated that the meaning of *A* is critical to interpreting the resulting utility estimate. Estimates using the Raju et al. (1990) model may be higher or lower than those generated by the original Schmidt et al. (1979) procedure depending on whether *A* is defined in terms of average salary, total direct costs, or dollar value of sales generated (Law & Myors 1999).

Having examined six different methods for estimating the economic value of job performance, at this point, the reader might naturally ask whether any one method is superior to the others. Our final section addresses that question.

COMPARATIVE RESEARCH

After reviewing 34 studies that included more than 100 estimates of SD_y, Boudreau (1991) concluded that differences among alternative methods for estimating SD_y are often less than 50 percent (and may be less than $5,000 in many cases). Small differences can become magnified, however, when multiplied by the number of people selected, the validity, and the selection ratio. Without any meaningful external criterion against which to compare SD_y estimates, one is left with little basis for choosing one method over another. In terms of the perceived usefulness of the utility information, Hazer and Highhouse (1997) found that different SD_y techniques did influence managers' reactions differently (the 40 percent rule was perceived as more credible than CREPID), but those differences accounted for less than 5 percent of the variance in the dependent measure.

Yet let us not lose sight of our overall objective—to improve HRM decision making. To be useful, utility analyses should reflect the context in which decisions are made (Cascio 1996, 1993; Russell, Colella, & Bobko 1993). For example, is the task to choose among alternative selection procedures? Or is it to decide whether to fund a selection program or to buy new equipment? All utility analyses are plagued by uncertainty and risk. By taking uncertainty into account through sensitivity or breakeven analysis, any one of the SD_y estimation methods may be (and often is) acceptable because none yields a result so discrepant as to change the decision in question. Chapter 10 examines the actual outcomes of utility analyses, and the role of economic factors, employee flows, and breakeven analysis in interpreting such results.

EXERCISES

1. Organize yourselves into four- to six-person teams and do either (a) or (b), depending on feasibility.

   a. Choose a production job at a fast-food restaurant and, using the standard costing approach described by Roche (1961), estimate the mean and *SD* of dollar-valued job performance.

   b. The Tiny Company manufactures components for word processors. Most of the work is done at the 2,000-employee Tiny plant in the Midwest. Your task is to estimate the mean and *SD* of dollar-valued job performance for Assembler-1s (about 200 employees). You are free to make any assumptions you like about the Tiny Assembler-1s, but be prepared to defend your assumptions. List and describe all of the factors (including how you would measure each one) that your team would consider in using standard costing to estimate SD_y.

2. Using the instructions provided for the Schmidt et al. (1979) global estimation procedure, attempt to estimate the mean, *SD*, standard error of the mean $SD/\sqrt{N}$, and 90 percent confidence interval for the mean value of a stockbroker working for a major brokerage firm in New York.[4] Make three estimates of the dollar value to the firm of a stockbroker: (1) at the 50th percentile in merit, (2) at the 85th percentile in

merit, and (3) at the 15th percentile in merit. For purposes of this exercise, accuracy of your estimates is less important than your understanding of the process and mechanics of the estimation procedure.
3. Jim Hill is manager of subscriber accounts for the Prosper Company. The results of a job analysis indicate that Jim's job includes four principal activities. A summary of Jim's superior's ratings of the activities and Jim's performance of each of them follows.

Principal Activity	Time/ Frequency	Importance	Performance Rating (points)
1	4.5	3	1.00
2	3.0	5	2.00
3	6.0	2	0.50
4	1.0	7	1.00

Assuming Jim is paid $42,000 per year, use CREPID to estimate the overall economic value of his job performance.
4. Assume that an average SWAT team member is paid $38,000 per year. Complete the following questionnaire, and then use the results to estimate SD_y by means of the superior equivalents technique.

For purposes of this questionnaire, a "superior" SWAT team member is one whose performance is better than approximately 85 percent of his fellow SWAT team members. Please complete the following item:

I estimate that, all else being equal, _____ "superior" SWAT team members would be about equal to 20 "average" SWAT team members.

5. You are given the following information regarding a group of customer service representatives for a large mail-order firm. The total direct costs (salary, benefits, and overhead) of each representative average $46,500 per year. Supervisors used a 0–7 scale to rate the performance of the customer service representatives, yielding a mean rating of 4.75, and an *SD* of 0.74. Assuming that the performance of the very best representative is not more than twice that of the average representative, convert the observed *SD* to a 1-to-3 scale using equation 7 in this chapter. Using that value in the context of the Raju et al. (1990) utility model, determine $A\sigma_R$, the economic value of each customer service representative's job performance.

REFERENCES

Bobko, P., Karren, R., Parkington, J. J. (1983). The estimation of standard deviations in utility analyses: An empirical test. *Journal of Applied Psychology 68*, 170–176.

Boudreau, J. W. (1991). Utility analysis for decisions in human resource management. In M. D. Dunnette and L. M. Hough (eds.), *Handbook of Industrial and Organizational Psychology* (Vol. 2, 2nd ed., pp. 621–745). Palo Alto, CA: Consulting Psychologists Press.

Brogden, H. E., Taylor, E. K. (1950). The dollar criterion—applying the cost accounting concept to criterion construction. *Personnel Psychology 3*, 133–154.

Burke, M. J., Frederick, J. T. (1984). Two modified procedures for estimating standard deviations in utility analyses. *Journal of Applied Psychology 69*, 482–489.

Burke, M. J., Frederick, J. T. (1986). A comparison of economic utility estimates for alternative rational SD_y estimation procedures. *Journal of Applied Psychology 71*, 334–339.

Cascio, W. F. (1993). Assessing the utility of selection decisions: Theoretical and practical considerations. In N. Schmitt and W. C. Borman (eds.), *Personnel Selection in Organizations* (pp. 310–335). San Francisco: Jossey-Bass.

Cascio, W. F. (1996). The role of utility analysis in the strategic management of organizations. *Journal of Human Resource Costing and Accounting 1*(2), 85–95.

Cascio, W. F., Ramos, R. A. (1986). Development and application of a new method for assessing job performance in behavioral/economic terms. *Journal of Applied Psychology 71*, 20–28.

Cronbach, L. J., Gleser, G. C. (eds.). (1965). *Psychological Tests and Personnel Decisions* (2nd ed.). Urbana: University of Illinois Press.

Desimone, R. L., Alexander, R. A., Cronshaw, S. F. (1986). Accuracy and reliability of SD_y estimates in utility analysis. *Journal of Occupational Psychology 59*, 93–102.

Eaton, N. K., Wing, H., Mitchell, K. J. (1985). Alternate methods of estimating the dollar value of performance. *Personnel Psychology 38*, 27–40.

Edwards, J. E., Frederick, J. T., Burke, M. J. (1988). Efficacy of modified CREPID SD_y's on the basis of archival organizational data. *Journal of Applied Psychology 73*, 529–535.

Greer, O. L., Cascio, W. F. (1987). Is cost accounting the answer? Comparison of two behaviorally based methods for estimating the standard deviation of job performance in dollars with a cost-accounting–based approach. *Journal of Applied Psychology 72*, 588–595.

Hazer, J. T., Highhouse, S. (1997). Factors influencing managers' reactions to utility analysis: Effects of SD_y method, information frame, and focal intervention. *Journal of Applied Psychology 82*, 104–112.

Horngren, C. T. (in press). *Cost Accounting: A Managerial Emphasis* (10th ed.). Englewood Cliffs, NJ: Prentice Hall.

Howard, R. A. (ed.). (1966). *Proceedings of the Fourth International Conference on Operations Research*. New York: John Wiley & Sons.

Howard, R. A., Matheson, J. E., North, D. W. (1972). The decision to seed hurricanes. *Science 176*, 1191–1202.

Hunter, J. E., Schmidt, F. L., Judiesch, M. K. (1990). Individual differences in output variability as a function of job complexity. *Journal of Applied Psychology 75*, 28–42.

Judiesch, M. K., Schmidt, F. L., Mount, M. K. (1992). Estimates of the dollar value of employee output in utility analyses: An empirical test of two theories. *Journal of Applied Psychology 77*, 234–250.

Judiesch, M. K., Schmidt, F. L., Mount, M. K. (1996). An improved method for estimating utility. *Journal of Human Resource Costing and Accounting 1*(2), 31–42.

Law, K. S., Myors, B. (1999). A modification of Raju, Burke, and Normand's (1990) new model for utility analysis. *Asia Pacific Journal of Human Resources 37*(1), 39–51.

Lezotte, D. V., Raju, N. S., Burke, M. J., Normand, J. (1996). An empirical comparison of two utility analysis models. *Journal of Human Resource Costing and Accounting 1*(2), 19–30.

Matheson, J. E. (1969). Decision analysis practice: Examples and insights. *Proceedings of the Fifth International Conference on Operations Research*. London: Tavistock.

Raju, N. S., Burke, M. J., Normand, J. (1990). A new approach for utility analysis. *Journal of Applied Psychology 75*, 3–12.

Raju, N. S., Burke, M. J., Normand, J., Lezotte, D. V. (1993). What would be if what is wasn't? Rejoinder to Judiesch, Schmidt, and Hunter (1993). *Journal of Applied Psychology 78*, 12–16.

Rich, J. R., Boudreau, J. W. (1987). The effects of variability and risk on selection utility analysis: An empirical simulation and comparison. *Personnel Psychology 40*, 55–84.

Roche, W. J. Jr. (1961). The Cronbach-Gleser utility function in fixed-treatment employee selection. *Dissertation Abstracts International 22, 4413. (University Microfilms No. 62-1570).* Portions reproduced in L. J. Cronbach and G. C. Gleser (eds.), *Psychological Tests and Personnel Decisions* (2nd ed.). Urbana: University of Illinois Press.

Roche, W. J. Jr. (1965). A dollar criterion in fixed-treatment employee selection. In L. J. Cronbach and G. C. Gleser (eds.), *Psychological Tests and Personnel Decisions* (2nd ed., pp. 254–267). Urbana: University of Illinois Press.

Russell, C. J., Colella, A., Bobko, P. (1993). Expanding the context of utility: The strategic impact of personnel selection. *Personnel Psychology 46*, 781–801.

Schmidt, F. L., Hunter, J. E. (1983). Individual differences in productivity: An empirical test of estimates derived from studies of selection procedure utility. *Journal of Applied Psychology 68*, 407–414.

Schmidt, F. L., Hunter, J. E., McKenzie, R. C., Muldrow, T. W. (1979). Impact of valid selection procedures on work-force productivity. *Journal of Applied Psychology 64*, 609–626.

Stevens, S. S. (1971). Issues in psychophysical measurement. *Psychological Review 78*, 426–450.

Weekley, J. A., Frank, B., O'Connor, E. J., Peters, L. H. (1985). A comparison of three methods of estimating the standard deviation of performance in dollars. *Journal of Applied Psychology 70*, 122–126.

ENDNOTES

1. Using lifo, the earliest-acquired stock is assumed still to be on hand; the last-acquired stock is assumed to have been used immediately. Lifo releases the most recent (or last) inventory costs as cost of goods used or sold. It attempts to match the most current cost of obtaining inventory against sales for a period (Horngren, in press).

2. Those figures are stated in 1961 dollars. Assuming a 6 percent inflation rate from 1961 to 1990, and a 3.5 percent inflation rate from
   1990 to 1998, the comparable figures in 1998 dollars are $39.33 and
   $28.17, respectively.
3. $4.17 in 1998 dollars.
4. A 90 percent confidence interval for the mean may be calculated by
   the following formula: $\overline{X} = 1.64\ SD/\sqrt{N}$. The interpretation of the result is: If we were to repeat the above procedure often, each time selecting a different sample from the same population, then, on the average, 90 out of every 100 intervals similarly obtained would contain
   the true value of the population mean.
5. A related assumption is that the ratio of the contribution of the average performer to that of the highest performer can approach, but not
   exceed, the limit of two.

C H A P T E R 1 0
Valid Selection Procedures Can Pay Off

Chapters 8 and 9 introduced the concept of utility analysis, described the assumptions and data requirements of alternative utility models, and presented methods for estimating the economic value of each employee's job performance. The objective in this chapter is to tie those ideas together to demonstrate how they can be and have been applied in work settings. The chapter will show how valid selection (or promotion) procedures can save organizations nationwide millions of dollars annually. The gains that can be realized have not yet been recognized because utility analysis has not been used widely. However, as the pressure increases on human resource executives to justify new or continuing HR programs in the face of budgetary constraints and escalating labor costs, one might expect that those programs that can be justified economically will be retained. As examples of reasonable savings from valid selection procedures, we will consider results from three studies previously mentioned: the Roche (1961) study of radial drill operators; the Schmidt, Hunter, McKenzie, and Muldrow (1979) study of computer programmers in 10 federal agencies; and the Hoffman and Thornton (1997) study of the assessment center in a large utility company. In addition, the chapter will include discussions of three new developments: the impact of variable costs, taxes, and discounting on utility estimates; the effect of employee flows on utility estimates; and the use of breakeven analysis as an aid in decision making.

UTILITY OF A SELECTION TEST FOR RADIAL DRILL OPERATORS

As noted in chapter 9, the average payoff of a radial drill operator (RDO-1) was calculated as the hourly profit at standard production ($5.51 in 1961 dollars; $39.33 in 1998 dollars) multiplied by his or her corrected performance ratio (the burden adjustment). The standard deviation of this distribution (SD_y) was $0.585 in 1961 dollars ($4.17 in 1998 dollars).

Calculation of Savings

Determination of the Validity of Test Performance (r_{ye})

Validities were determined by computing the Pearson product-moment correlations between payoff values and scores on the following predictors: the Personnel Test (Wonderlic, Form F), the Test of Mechanical Comprehension (Bennett, Form AA), the Cornell Word Form, and the Cornell Selectee Index. These tests made up the basic battery used by the company in selecting factory employees. Among the test-payoff correlations, only the correlation with the Test of Mechanical Comprehension was significant $(r = 0.313)$. Thus, utility was computed only for that variable.

Determination of the Ordinate Corresponding to the Selection Ratio Used, $\lambda(y')$

To determine the cutoff point at and above which selection is made, company records were checked for the 10 years preceding the study. During that time the company's average selection ratio for factory employees was 0.33. The ordinate, therefore, was set at the point corresponding to that selection ratio. (To verify that fact, consult a table of areas of the normal curve, find 0.33 under "area in the smaller portion," and read the ordinate corresponding to that area.) In other words, it was assumed that RDO-1s are taken at random from the highest third of the test-score distribution of applicants. Assuming a normal distribution, $\lambda(y')$ is therefore 0.366.

Determination of the Cost of Testing (c_y)

Only the actual cost of the tests used in the employment battery was considered in determining c_y because some of the pertinent cost elements were already included in the burden factor (for example, managers' salaries, office space rent, heat, light, and taxes). The cost of each test was taken from the most recent publisher's catalog. Because the element SD_y is expressed in dollars per hour, the cost of testing had to be expressed in comparable units. Cost of testing must be distributed over the period of time that an employee can be expected to work as an RDO-1. For purposes of the study, an employee was assumed to work in that classification for one year, or 2,080 hours. (That estimate is very conservative because company records indicate that most RDO-1 employees remain in that job for more than one year.) In determining c_y, the cost of those *not* selected also must be included in the cost of those selected. The cost of testing per employee selected, in dollars per hour, is derived by multiplying the cost of one battery of tests by three (three people are tested for each one hired), and dividing by 2,080 (hours per year). The total cost of the test battery per applicant in 1961 was $0.117 ($0.855 in 1998 dollars). Therefore, the cost of testing per employee selected is $(0.117 \times 3) \div 2,080$, or approximately $0.0002 per hour ($0.0012 in 1998 dollars).

Computation of ΔU

For the Test of Mechanical Comprehension (the only significant predictor), the gain in utility per person selected (ΔU) was computed by substituting into equation 11 from chapter 8:

$$\Delta U = SD_e r_{ye} \frac{\lambda(y')}{\phi(y')} - \frac{c_y}{\phi(y')}$$

where ΔU is the net gain in utility; SD_e is the standard deviation of the payoff; r_{ye} is the correlation of the predictor with the evaluated payoff; $\lambda(y')$ is the ordinate of the normal curve at the cutting score on the test; $\phi(y')$ is the area (upper tail) corresponding to the cutting score; and c_y is the cost of testing. The actual values included were

$$\Delta U = (\$0.585)(0.313)\frac{(0.336)}{(0.326)} - \frac{(\$0.0002)}{(0.326)} = \$0.205$$

Therefore, when the company selects an RDO on the basis of the test score rather than by a random process, the company can expect an average gain of 20 cents per hour ($1.46 per hour in 1998 dollars) for the duration of his or her employment—a potential per-hour gain in profit of 3.7 percent at standard production $(0.205 \div \$5.51)$. Hence, for each

RDO-1 who remains in that classification for three years (6,240 hours), the company would realize an average gain in profit of $9,110 (in 1998 dollars) by selecting RDO-1s on the basis of test scores rather than randomly. If only half of the 291 RDO-1s employed by the company remained RDO-1s for three years, the company still would save more than $1.3 million ($1,325,563).

Discussion

Roche's (1961) study is important for three reasons. First, it demonstrated that the economic value of job performance (the dollar criterion) can be developed and then applied in the Brogden-Cronbach-Gleser utility model. Second, the results demonstrated that a test of relatively low validity has appreciable practical value, as had been argued on theoretical grounds. In this case, selection with the aid of a test having a validity of 0.313 made possible an increase in pre-tax profits per hour of 3.7 percent on the operation in question. Benefits of such magnitude are important to management. Finally, and perhaps most importantly, Roche showed that the dollar criterion could be determined even where employees in a job classification are working on different tasks, where the tasks assigned to a particular employee vary from week to week, and where the tasks vary in profitability.

On the other hand, the study raised a number of questions about the accuracy of the cost-accounting procedures themselves. Consider the cost of testing. The analysis took into account only the cost of the actual tests. Factors classified by the cost accountants as overhead (for example, salaries of managers, cost of utilities, and rent), were included in the determination of payoff rather than in c_y. The employment division of the company offered the figure of $105 ($750 in 1998 dollars) as a conservative estimate of the cost of placing a factory employee on the job. That figure included the cost of recruiting and interviewing and the cost of a physical examination. It can be argued that a c_y that includes only the cost of tests is sufficient because most other employment procedure costs would be constant values if tests were not used. Those other costs need not be added to the determination of c_y. In fact, an organization will incur fixed utility costs, overhead costs, and so forth just to stay in business. Such costs are irrelevant to the determination of utility because costs or benefits that do not change as a result of a program have no role in defining the utility of that program. Ordinarily, HR programs do not affect fixed costs. Boudreau (1983a) pointed out that, although fixed costs lower the *average* profit obtained from all workers, the *variability* of fixed costs is zero. Hence, SD_y is the same whether it reflects fixed costs or not. That implies that Roche (1961) probably *underestimated* selection utility by allocating profit (revenue minus fixed *and* variable costs) to workers according to the speed of their production.

Secondly, Roche based his calculations on an assumed joint normal distribution of test and payoff, but as Cronbach (1965) later commented, using the *actual* joint distribution would have been preferable. If data are available for the total applicant population, complete information on skewness and curvature is taken into account. Roche's payoffs have a marked skew because few workers performed far above standard. If the available data come only from workers screened by a test or by on-the-job observations, extrapolation to the total applicant population is required; even so, comparing the actual mean payoff in the selected population with that estimated for the unselected population might be more useful. That estimate would depend on the regression line but would not entail an assumption of normality.

In summary, the dollar payoff resulting from an employee's work is clearly an elusive concept. As the costs of selection errors continue to grow, the economic implications of alternative selection procedures must be examined more closely. We cannot ignore the problem of cost–benefit analysis of HR programs. Rather we must deal directly with the issue, using the most current techniques that research makes available. In our next section, we will consider a more recent approach to analyzing the utility of a selection program.

UTILITY OF A SELECTION TEST FOR COMPUTER PROGRAMMERS

As we noted in chapter 9, Schmidt et al. (1979) studied computer programmers in the federal government to examine the productivity (economic utility) implications of a valid selection procedure (the Programmer Aptitude Test [PAT]). They used a global estimation procedure to estimate the standard deviation of job performance in dollars (SD_y). The average SD_y estimated was \$10,413 per year.[1] The PAT was selected for consideration because previous research had demonstrated that the validity of the total PAT score is high for predicting the performance of computer programmers (the estimated true validity is 0.76), and that the validity is essentially constant across situations (organizations). Thus it was possible to estimate payoffs from use of the PAT in the federal government, as well as in the economy as a whole. The estimated cost of the PAT per examinee was $10 ($25 in 1998 dollars).

The study focused on the selection of federal government computer programmers at the GS-5 through GS-9 levels, GS-5 being the lowest level in this occupational series. Beyond GS-9 it is unlikely that an aptitude test like the PAT would be used in selection: Applicants for higher-level programmer positions are required to have considerable expertise in programming and are selected on the bases of achievement and experience rather than directly on aptitude. Most programmers hired at the GS-9 level are promoted to GS-11 after one year. Similarly, all but a few of those hired at the GS-5 level advance to GS-7 in one year and to GS-9 the following year. Therefore, the SD_y estimates were obtained for the GS-9 through GS-11 levels. The average yearly selection rate of GS-5 through GS-9 programmers is 618, and their average tenure is 9.69 years. On the basis of 1970 U.S. Census data, by using the PAT an estimated 10,210 computer programmers could be hired each year in the U.S. economy. In view of the current rapid expansion of that occupation, the number is probably a substantial underestimate.

Because it was not possible to determine the prevailing selection ratio (*SR*) for computer programmers either in the general economy or in the federal government, utilities were calculated for *SR*s of 0.05 and in intervals of 0.10 from 0.10 to 0.80. The gains in utility or productivity are those that result when a valid procedure is introduced where previously no procedure or a totally invalid procedure has been used. That is gross utility, or the gain over random selection. The assumption that the true validity of the previous procedure is essentially zero may be valid in some cases, but in other situations the PAT would, if introduced, replace a procedure with lower but nonzero true validity. Hence, utilities were calculated assuming previous-procedure true validities of 0.20, 0.30, 0.40, and 0.50, as well as zero. Those are net utilities, or the net incremental gain in dollars of the procedure with a higher validity over that of the procedure with a lower validity.

To estimate the impact of the PAT on productivity, utilities that would result from one year's use of the PAT for selecting new programmers in the federal government and in the economy as a whole were computed for each of the combinations of *SR* and previous-procedure validity just given. When the previous procedure was assumed to have zero validity, its associated testing cost also was assumed to be zero; that is, it was assumed that no procedure was used and that otherwise prescreened

applicants were hired randomly. When the previous procedure was assumed to have a nonzero validity, its associated cost was assumed to be
the same as that of the PAT—$10 per applicant. As already mentioned,
average tenure for government programmers was found to be 9.69 years;
in the absence of other information, that figure also was assumed for the
private sector The average gain in utility per selectee per year was multiplied by 9.69 to give a total average gain in utility per selectee. Cost of
testing was charged only to the first year. The Brogden-Cronbach-Gleser
general utility equation then was modified to obtain the equation actually used in computing the utilities:

Equation 1

$$\Delta U = tN_s(r_1 - r_2)SD_y\lambda/\phi - N_s(c_1 - c_2)/\phi$$

where ΔU is the gain in productivity in dollars from using the new selection procedure for one year; t is the tenure in years of the average selectee (here 9.69); N_s is the number selected in a given year (that figure
was 618 for the federal government and 10,210 for the U.S. economy); r_1
is the validity of the new procedure, here the PAT ($r_1 = 0. 76$); r_2 is the
validity of the previous procedure (r_2 ranges from 0 to 0.50); c_1 is the
cost per applicant of the new procedure, here $10; and c_2 is the cost per
applicant of the previous procedure, here 0 or $10. The terms SD_y, ϕ,
and λ are as defined previously. The figure SD_y was the average of the
two estimates obtained by using the global estimation procedure. Note
that, although the equation gives the productivity gain that results from
substituting over one year the new (more valid) selection procedure for
the previous procedure, not all those gains are realized in the first year.
Rather, they are spread out over the tenure of the new employees.

Results

Exhibit 10–1 shows the estimated gains in productivity in millions of
dollars that would result from one year's use of the PAT to select computer programmers in the federal government for different combinations of
*SR*s and previous-procedure validities. As expected, those gains increase
as the *SR* decreases and as the validity of the previous procedure decreases. When the *SR* is 0.05 and the previous procedure has no validity,
using the PAT for one year produces an aggregate productivity gain of
$97.2 million ($243 million in 1998 dollars). At the other extreme, if *SR*
is 0.80 and the procedure the PAT replaces has a validity of 0.50, the estimated gain is only $5.6 million ($14 million in 1998 dollars).

EXHIBIT 10-1   *Estimated Productivity Increase from One Year's Use of the PAT to Select Federal Computer Programmers (in $Millions)*

Selection Ratio	True Validity of Previous Procedure				
	0.00	0.20	0.30	0.40	0.50
0.05	97.2	71.7	58.9	46.1	33.3
0.10	82.8	60.1	50.1	39.2	28.3
0.20	66.0	48.6	40.0	31.3	22.6
0.30	54.7	40.3	33.1	25.9	18.7
0.40	45.6	34.6	27.6	21.6	15.6
0.50	37.6	27.7	22.8	17.8	12.9
0.60	30.4	22.4	18.4	14.4	10.4
0.70	23.4	17.2	14.1	11.1	8.0
0.80	16.5	12.2	10.0	7.8	5.6

Note: PAT = programmer aptitude test.
Source: Schmidt, F. L., Hunter, J. E., McKenzie, R. C., Muldrow, T. W. (1979). Impact of valid selection procedures on work-force productivity. *Journal of Applied Psychology 64*, 622. Copyright © 1979 by the American Psychological Association. Reprinted with permission.

To illustrate how entries for Exhibit 10–1 were derived, assume that the $SR = 0.20$ and the previous procedure has a validity of 0.30. All other terms are as defined previously.

$$\Delta U = 9.69(618)(0.76 - 0.30)(10{,}413)(0.2789 \div 0.20) - 618(10 - 10) \div 0.20$$
$$\Delta U = 9.69(618)(0.46)(10{,}413)(1.3945) - 0$$
$$\Delta U = 40{,}000{,}412$$

To be sure, the figures in Exhibit 10–1 are larger than most of us would have expected; however, these figures are for total utility. The gain per selectee for any cell in the table can be obtained by dividing the cell entry by 618, the assumed yearly number of selectees. When that is done for our example (40,000,412 ÷ 618), the gain per selectee is $64,725.59 ($161,794 in 1998 dollars). That figure is still quite high, but remember that the gains shown in Exhibit 10–1 are produced by one year's use of the PAT. As we pointed out earlier, not all of those gains are realized during the first year; they are spread over the tenure of the new employees. Gains per year per selectee for any cell in Exhibit 10–1 can be obtained by dividing the cell entry first by 618 and then by 9.69, the average tenure of computer programmers. In our example, that produces a per-year gain of $6,679.63 per selectee or, to carry it even further, a $3.21 gain per hour annually per selectee (assuming 2,080 hours per work year). Comparable figures in 1998 dollars were $16,697 and $8.03, respectively. As might be expected, estimated productivity gains resulting from use of the PAT in the economy as a whole are even greater, exceeding $1 billion in several cells of Exhibit 10–1.

In addition to the assumptions of linearity of the predictor-criterion relationship and normality of dollar outcomes of job performance, the productivity gains in Exhibit 10–1 are based on two more assumptions. The first is that selection proceeds from top-scoring applicants down until the *SR* has been reached. That is, those analyses assume that selection procedures are used optimally. Because of the linearity of the relationship between test score and job performance, any other use of a valid test would result in lower mean productivity levels among selectees. For example, if a cutoff score were set at a point lower than that corresponding to the *SR* and if applicants scoring above that minimum score then were selected randomly (or selected using other nonvalid procedures or considerations), productivity gains would be considerably lower than those shown in Exhibit 10–1, although they would remain substantial.

Thus, Schmidt, Mack, and Hunter (1984) examined the impact of three modes of test use on the productivity of forest rangers: (1) top-down selection, (2) minimum required test scores equal to the mean, and (3) a minimum score set at one *SD* below the mean. Top-down selection produces an increase in productivity of about 13 percent (which translates into millions of dollars saved). Under mode 2, the dollar value of output gains was only 45 percent as large as the dollar value for top-down selection, and the percentage gain in output was only 5.9. Under mode 3, the dollar value of output gains was only 16 percent of the top-down figure, and the percentage increase in output was only 2.1. Conclusion: Employers who use mode 3 do so at substantial economic cost.

Both Hunter and Hunter (1984) and Hartigan and Wigdor (1989) found that hiring in a top-down fashion within both minority and nonminority groups produced about 90 percent of the gains that would be realized by strict top-down hiring. However, the Civil Rights Act of 1991 prohibited such "race norming." A third strategy, using a low cutting score, would decrease utility by 83 percent.

The second assumption is that all applicants who are offered jobs accept and are hired. That is probably not realistic because, in practice, lower-scoring candidates must be accepted in place of higher-scoring candidates who decline initial offers. Hence, the average ability of those actually selected almost always will be lower than the average ability of those who receive the initial offers.

The same effect may be observed in a tight labor market where the supply of available workers is low relative to the aggregate demand for them. Under those circumstances, unemployment is low, and, as Becker (1989) has shown, firms may be forced to lower their minimum hiring requirements in order to fill vacancies. Lower hiring requirements mean higher selection ratios.

In summary, rejection of job offers or a reduction in minimum hiring requirements produces identical effects: They increase *SR*s and thus lower the productivity gains from selection. For example, if an *SR* of 0.20 would yield the needed number of new employees given no rejections by applicants and if half of all job offers are rejected, the *SR* must be increased to 0.40 to yield the desired number of selectees. If the validity of the previous procedure were zero, Exhibit 10–1 shows that rejection by applicants would reduce productivity gains from $66.0 to $45.6 million, a reduction of 30.91 percent. If the validity of the previous procedure were not zero, job rejection by applicants would reduce both its utility and that of the new test. Because the utility function is multiplicative, however, the utility of the more valid procedure would be reduced by a greater amount. Therefore, the utility advantage of the more valid procedure over the less valid procedure would be reduced.

For example, Exhibit 10–1 shows that if the validity of the previous procedure were 0.30, the productivity advantage of the more valid test would be $40 million if the needed workers could be hired using a selection ratio of 0.20. But if half of the applicants rejected job offers, we would have to use an *SR* of 0.40, and the advantage of the more valid test would drop by almost 45 percent to $27.6 million. Murphy (1986) presented formulas for calculating the average ability of those actually selected when the proportion of initial offers accepted is less than 100 percent. He showed that under realistic circumstances, utility formulas currently used could overestimate gains by 30 to 80 percent. To some extent, the utility losses caused by job-offer rejection can be offset by additional recruiting efforts that increase the size of the applicant pool and, therefore, restore use of smaller *SR*s.

Thus far we have proceded on the assumption that a new, more valid selection procedure simply is substituted for an older, less valid one. Often, however, workforce productivity is optimized by combining an existing procedure and a new procedure to obtain validity higher than either procedure can provide individually. One should investigate that possibility whenever utility analysis is done.

Finally, Schmidt et al. (1979) cautioned that indivdual-job productivity gains from improved selection cannot be extrapolated directly to productivity gains in the composite of all jobs making up the national economy. To illustrate, if the potential gain economy-wide in the computer programmer occupation is $10.78 billion and if there is a total of N jobs in the economy (that is, programmers and all other jobs), the gain to be expected from using improved selection procedures in all N jobs will not be as great in general as N multiplied by $10.78 billion. The total talent pool is limited so gains resulting from selection in one job are offset partially by losses in other jobs. The size of the net gain for the economy depends on such factors as the number of jobs, the correlation between jobs of predicted success composites, and differences between jobs in SD_y. Nevertheless, potential net gains for the economy as a whole are large.

A later study examined similar productivity gains for most white-collar jobs in the federal government (Schmidt, Hunter, Outerbridge, & Trattner 1986). The researchers found that the job performance of test-selected employees averaged about one-half a standard deviation (roughly 17 percent) higher than that of non–test-selected employees. Results also indicated that use of valid measures of cognitive skills in place of less valid selection methods for selection of a one-year cohort in the federal government would lead to annual increases in output worth almost $600 million (almost $1 billion in 1998 dollars) for every year the new hires remained on the job. That gain corresponds to a 9.7 percent gain in output among new hires. If total output is to be held constant rather than increased, the use of more valid selection methods would allow a yearly decrease in the number of new hires of just over 20,000 (a 9 percent decrease), resulting in payroll cost savings of $272 million ($452 million in 1998 dollars) for every year the new employees remain on the job. Finally, the number of new hires in the bottom 10 percent of job performance would decrease from 10 percent to 3.86 percent.

Evidence presented in those studies leads to the inescapable conclusion that how people are selected makes an important, practical difference. The implications of valid selection procedures for workforce productivity are clearly much greater than most of us might have suspected.

Impact of Economic Considerations on Utility Estimates

Boudreau (1983a) pointed out that utility analyses computed according to equation 10 in chapter 8 or equation 1 in this chapter will misrepresent the benefits accrued by an organization as a result of increases in productivity under any or all of three conditions. First, where variable costs (for example, incentive- or commission-based pay, benefits, variable raw materials costs, variable production overhead) rise or fall with productivity, a portion (*V*) of the gain in product sales value will go to pay such costs (or will be reflected in additional cost savings). Second, for organizations that face tax liabilities, a portion (*TAX*) of the organization's profits (sales value less variable costs) must be allocated to pay taxes. Third, where costs and benefits accrue over time, the value of future costs and benefits must be discounted to reflect the opportunity costs of returns foregone. That is, future monetary values cannot be equated with present monetary values because benefits received in the present or costs delayed into the future would be invested to earn returns. Thus, $1.00 received today at a 10 percent annual return would be worth $1.21 in two years. Conversely, a future benefit worth $1.21 in two years has a "present value" of $1.00 ($1.21 ÷ 1.10^2). Boudreau (1983b) derived the following utility formula to take those three economic factors into account:

Equation 2

$$\Delta U = (N) \left\{ \sum_{t=1}^{T} [1/(1 + i)^t] \right\} (SD_{sv})(1 + V)$$
$$\times (1 - TAX)(r_{x,sv})(\overline{Z}_x) - C(1 - TAX)$$

where ΔU is the change in overall worth or utility after variable costs, taxes, and discounting; *N* is the number of employees selected; *t* is the time period in which an increase in productivity occurs; *T* is the total number of periods (for example, years) that benefits continue to accrue to an organization; *i* is the discount rate; SD_{sv} is the standard deviation of the sales value of productivity among the applicant or employee population (similar to SD_y in previous utility models); *V* is the proportion of sales value represented by variable costs; *TAX* is the organization's applicable tax rate; $r_{x,sv}$ is the validity coefficient between predictor (*x*) and sales value (similar to $r_{x,y}$ in previous utility models); and *C* is the total selection cost for all applicants.

Those economic considerations suggest large potential reductions in published utility estimates. For example, Schmidt et al. (1979) computed an SD_y value of $10,413 in their utility analysis of the PAT. That value does not account for variable costs or taxes. That computation may have been appropriate for the federal government jobs studied because the federal government is not taxed, but it would not be appropriate for private-sector organizations that face variable costs and taxes.

Assuming that the net effect of positively and negatively correlated variable costs is $V = -0.05$, and assuming a marginal tax rate (the tax rate applicable to changes in reported profits generated by a decision) of 45 percent, Boudreau (1983a) showed that the after-cost, after-tax, one-year SD_y value is

$$(SD_y) \times (1 + V) \times (1 - TAX) \times (\$10,413)$$
$$\times (1 - 0.05) \times (1 - 0.45) = \$5,441$$

That is 52 percent of the reported value. In addition, assume a discount rate of 10 percent. If the average tenure of computer programmers in the federal government were just two years, the appropriate discount factor (DF) adjustment would be

Equation 3

$$DF = \sum_{t=1}^{T} [1/(1 + i)^t] = 1/(1 + 0.10)^1 + 1/(1 + 0.10)^2 = 1.74$$

Over 10 years, $DF = 6.14$, but the average tenure of computer programmers in the federal government was computed to be 9.69 years (Schmidt et al. 1979). Hence, the appropriate adjustment needed to discount the computed utility values is $6.14 \div 9.69$, or 0.634.

When all three of those factors—variable costs, taxes, and discounting—are considered, the utility values per selectee reported by Schmidt et al. (1979) and shown in Exhibit 10–1 range from $2,987 ($5.6 million $\div 618 = \$9,061$ per selectee $\times 0.634 \times 0.52$) to $51,853 ($97.2 million $\div 618 = \$157,282$ per selectee $\times 0.634 \times 0.52$).

Those values are substantial, but they are 67 percent lower than the values reported. Thus, $97,200,000 \div 618 = \$157,282$; $51,853 \div \$157,282 = 33$ percent.

Effects of Employee Flows on Utility Estimates

Failure to consider the combined effects of variable costs, taxes, and discounting may produce utility estimates that are *overstated* considerably. On the other hand, failure to consider the effect of employee flows may produce utility estimates that are *understated* considerably. That is, most utility analyses assume that a selection program is applied to one group of applicants. Hence, they express the utility of adding one treated cohort to the existing workforce. In practice, however, valid selection programs tend to be reapplied year after year as employees flow into and out of the workforce; that is, selection programs are applied to entering employee cohorts of size N, and the program's benefits are reflected in that cohort for T periods. Often a program's effects on subsequent cohorts will occur in addition to its lasting effects on previously treated cohorts. Boudreau (1983b) called those *additive cohort effects,* and proposed that the terms N and T be altered in equation 2 to account for the effect of employee flows. The derivation is as follows.

Employee flows generally affect utility through the period-to-period changes in the number of treated employees in the workforce. The number of treated employees in the workforce k periods in the future (N_k) may be expressed as

Equation 4

$$N_k = \sum_{t=1}^{k} (N_{at} - N_{st})$$

where N_{at} is the number of treated employees added to the workforce in period t, and N_{st} is the number of treated employees subtracted from the workforce in period t. For example, suppose that at the end of the fourth year a new selection procedure is applied ($k = 4$) and the following results are observed from the inception of the program ($t = 1$) to year 4 ($t = 4$):

$$N_4 = (100 - 0) + (100 - 10) + (100 - 15) + (100 - 20)$$
$$N_4 = 355$$

Thus, the term N_k reflects both the number of employees treated in previous periods and their expected tenure. The formula for the utility (ΔU_k) occurring in the kth future period that includes the economic considerations of equation 2 may be written:

Equation 5

$$\Delta U_k = \left[\sum_{t=1}^{k} (N_{at} - N_{st}) \right] \{[1/(1+i)^k](r_{x,sv}) \times (\bar{Z}_x)(SD_{sv})(1+V)(1-TAX)\}$$
$$- C_k(1-TAX)[1/(1+i)^{(k-1)}]$$

Note that for the sake of simplicity, the utility parameters $r_{x,sv}$, V, SD_{sv}, and TAX are assumed to be constant over time. That assumption is not critical to this utility model, and the factors may vary. Note also that the cost of treating the N_{ak} employees added in period k (C_k) is now allowed to vary over time. However, C_k is not simply a constant multiplied by N_{ak}. Some programs (for example, assessment centers) have high startup costs of development, but those costs do not vary with the number treated in future periods. Also, the discount factor for costs $[1/(1+i)^{(k-1)}]$ reflects the exponent $k - 1$, assuming that such costs are incurred one period prior to receiving benefits. Where costs are incurred in the same period as benefits are received, k is the proper exponent (Boudreau 1983b).

To continue with our previous example, assume the following values in order to compute the dollar gain in productivity to an organization during the fourth year of a new selection program: $N_k = 355$; the discount rate is 10 percent; the validity of the procedure is 0.40; the *SR* is 0.50 (and therefore the average score of those selected is $0.3989 \div 0.50 = 0.80$); SD_y is \$5,000; variable costs $= -0.05$; taxes $= 0.45$; and C_k, the cost of treating the 100 employees added in year 4, is $100 \times \$10 = \$1,000$.

$$\Delta U_4 = 355 \times [(1/1.10^1 + 1/1.10^2 + 1/1.10^3 + 1/1.10^4)$$
$$\times 0.40 \times 0.80 \times \$5,000 \times 0.95 \times 0.55] - \$1,000$$
$$\times 0.55 \,(1/1.10^1 + 1/1.10^2 + 1/1.10^3)$$

$$\Delta U_4 = 355 \times [(3.17) \times \$836] - \$550 \,(2.49)$$
$$= \$940,793 - \$1,370$$
$$= \$939,423$$

To express the utility of a program's effects over F periods, the one-period utility estimates (ΔU_k) are summed. Thus, the complete utility model reflecting employee flow through the workforce for a program affecting productivity in F future periods may be written:

Equation 6

$$\Delta U = \sum_{k=1}^{F} \left[\sum_{t=1}^{k} (N_{at} - N_{st}) \right] \{[1/(1 + i)^k](r_{x,sv}) \times (\bar{Z}_x)(SD_{sv})(1 + V)(1 - TAX)\}$$
$$- \sum_{k=1}^{F} \{C_k(1 - TAX)[1/(1 + i)^{(k-1)}]\}$$

The duration parameter F in equation 6 is not simply a function of employee tenure, but also depends on how long a program is applied. For example, Boudreau (1983b) assumed that the PAT evaluated by Schmidt et al. (1979) is applied for 15 years, or 5 years after the first cohort separates. If 618 programmers are added each year, then for the first 10 future periods N_k will increase by 618 in each period. That is:

$$N_{10} = \sum_{t=1}^{10} (618 - 0)$$

By year 10, therefore, 6,180 programmers selected by the PAT have been added to the workforce, and none have left. Beginning in future period 11, however, one PAT-selected cohort leaves in each period ($N_{st} = 618$). However, by continuing to apply the PAT to select 618 new replacements, the employee inflow is maintained (that is, $N_{at} = 618$). Thus, in future periods 11 through 15, N_{at} and N_{st} offset each other and N_k remains unchanged. Beginning in future period 16, the PAT no longer is used (C_k and N_{at} become zero, assuming the organization returns to random selection). However, the treated portion of the workforce does not disappear immediately. Earlier-selected cohorts continue to separate (that is, $N_{st} = 618$), and N_k falls by 618 each period until the last-treated cohort (selected in future period 15) separates in future period 25. N_k for each of the 25 periods is shown in Exhibit 10–2.

EXHIBIT 10-2   *Hypothetical Employee Flows Resulting from the PAT*

Period (k)	N_k
1	618
2	1,236
3	1,854
4	2,472
5	3,090
6	3,708
7	4,326
8	4,944
9	5,562
10	6,180
11	6,180
12	6,180
13	6,180
14	6,180
15	6,180
16	5,562
17	4,944
18	4,326
19	3,708
20	3,090
21	2,472
22	1,854
23	1,236
24	618
25	0

Note: N_k = number of employees receiving a given treatment who remain in the workforce; PAT = programmer aptitude test.
Source: Adapted from Boudreau, J. W. (1983b). Effects of employee flows on utility analysis of human resource productivity improvement programs. *Journal of Applied Psychology 68*, 400. Copyright © 1983 by the American Psychological Association. Reprinted with permission.

In Exhibit 10–2, $F = 25$ periods. Assuming, as we did in our earlier example, that $V = -0.05$, $TAX = 0.45$, and the discount rate is 10 percent, Boudreau (1983b) showed that the total expected utility of the 15-year selection program (the sum of the 25 one-period utility estimates, ΔU_k in equation 5) is $105.01 million ($207.9 million in 1998 dollars). That amount is considerably higher than the Schmidt et al. (1979) estimate of $37.6 million ($94 million in 1998 dollars), even after considering variable costs, taxes, and discounting. Perhaps the most important lesson to learn from those results is that one-cohort utility models often will *understate* actual utility because they reflect only the first part of a larger series of outcomes (Boudreau 1983b).

At this point, you may be tempted to conclude that the actual dollar payoff from valid selection programs is two or three times higher than one-cohort models predict. Be careful! All existing utility models contain parameters that must be estimated, and in most cases we simply have no way to measure the accuracy of our estimates. Beyond that, as noted earlier, utility values often are based on the assumption that variable costs, SD_y, and the SR are constant over time, and that may be unrealistic. Equation 6 permits those parameters to vary, but until our measurement systems begin to assess multi-period variations in those parameters, we will not know just how unrealistic the assumptions are. Research in utility analysis has produced some exciting new developments, but we have a long way to go in refining our measurements of the parameters of the model.

UTILITIES OF COMPETING PREDICTORS THAT DIFFER IN ADVERSE IMPACT

Two of the most popular classes of predictors used in personnel selection are the assessment center and cognitive ability tests. Ever since pioneering studies by Bray (1964) at American Telephone and Telegraph in the 1950s, the assessment center (AC) approach to personnel selection has been an extremely popular technique. The method's attractiveness is not surprising for it is rooted firmly in sound psychometric principles. By using multiple assessment techniques, by standardizing methods of making inferences from such techniques, and by pooling the judgments of multiple assessors in rating each candidate's behavior, the likelihood of successfully predicting performance is enhanced considerably. Reviews of the predictive validity of AC ratings and subsequent job performance consistently have been positive (Howard & Bray 1989; Gaugler et al. 1987; Hunter & Hunter 1984). ACs predict performance, and they do it well. Over all types of criteria and over 50 studies containing 107 validity coefficients, meta-analysis indicates an average validity for ACs of 0.37, with lower and upper bounds of the 95 percent confidence interval of 0.11 and 0.63, respectively (Gaugler et al. 1987).

With respect to measures of cognitive abilities (for example, verbal and numerical skills, reasoning and comprehension), if job analysis shows that such abilities are important for successful job performance, the tests are among the most valid predictors currently available, with an average validity across hundreds of studies of 0.53 (Hunter & Hunter 1984). Both ACs and cognitive ability tests are used widely in practice, although ACs typically show considerably less adverse impact (Cascio 1998). In terms of scores on cognitive ability tests, African Americans typically score about one *SD* lower than do white Americans, Hispanic Americans score about one-half *SD* lower than do white Americans, and Asian Americans typically perform about as well as do white Americans (Hartigan & Wigdor 1989).

Regardless of how many validity studies are conducted using these predictors, however, their overall worth as selection devices cannot be established definitively in the absence of utility analyses that consider more than just differences in validity and testing costs. The objective of the study by Hoffman and Thornton (1997) was to examine the roles of validity, cut-score choice, and adverse impact on selection system utility using data from two concurrent validity studies. To evaluate two competing systems of predictors, while allowing for differences in cut scores, the authors used the Brogden-Cronbach-Gleser continuous variable utility model. They computed utilities relative to random selection (gross utilities), rather than computing the utility of one predictor relative to the other (net utilities). The net utility model allowed both predictors to be compared in the same equation (see equation 1 in this chapter), but it required the use of the same cut score for each predictor. If the predictors differ in adverse impact, then the lowest cut score at which adverse impact appears also will differ. In that context, therefore, it makes more sense to compute gross rather than net utilities for that allows researchers to apply a series of possible cut scores and to determine utility at the point where adverse impact appears for each system.

Methodology

Data in the Hoffman and Thornton (1997) study came from two concurrent validity studies with non-overlapping samples. One sample comprised 118 supervisors (85 whites, 17 Hispanic Americans, 10 Asian Americans, and 6 African Americans) who attended a one-day developmental AC. The authors calculated an average AC score for each individual across all dimensions that were rated in four exercises: in-basket, budget analysis, employee counseling, and leaderless group discussion.

The second sample completed an aptitude test, the Professional Employment Test (PET), short form, a 20-item multiple-choice test. It was administered for research purposes to a sample of 104 people, 60 of whom had been promoted from nonexempt job classifications, and 44 of whom were still in nonexempt job classifications. Adverse impact calculations were based on the full sample of 104 people.

Both studies used the same criterion measure for purposes of validation, namely, each individual's current administrative performance appraisal. The time lag between collection of predictor and criterion data was similar in both samples (one year or less).

Analyses

The authors correlated AC and PET scores with the criterion, calculated gross utility for each selection system over a range of possible cut scores, and calculated adverse impact (*AI*) for the same cut scores. They calculated *AI* using the four-fifths rule of thumb recommended in the federal *Uniform Guidelines on Employee Selection Procedures* (1978). To do so, they determined the point in the predictor distribution where the nonwhite selection rate would be less than 80 percent of the white selection rate. Because both samples were relatively small, it was not possible to calculate *AI* separately for each minority subgroup. Therefore, the authors calculated white/nonwhite pass rates for each assumed cut score.

To calculate utilities, Hoffman and Thornton (1997) used the Brogden-Cronbach-Gleser gross utility model (equation 8 in chapter 8):

$$\Delta U = r_{xy}SD_y\lambda/\phi - C/\phi$$

where ΔU is gross utility; r_{xy} is validity; SD_y is the dollar-valued criterion; λ is the ordinate of the normal curve associated with the cut score; C is the cost of testing; and ϕ is the selection ratio.

The authors made the following assumptions: PET testing costs were $50 per candidate; the AC cost either $500 or $1,000; and SD_y was

$20,000 using the 40 percent rule (40 percent of a $50,000 annual salary).

Results

The observed validity of the AC was 0.26, and the observed validity of the PET was 0.30. Correcting both of those values for unreliability in the criterion (assuming a criterion reliability of 0.60) yielded estimated corrected validities of 0.34 (AC) and 0.39 (PET). Exhibit 10–3 shows the gross utilities per selectee for one year for the AC and the PET. As noted earlier, the authors computed utilities assuming costs of both $500 and $1,000 for the AC (hereafter reported as AC$500 or AC$1000). Gross utility for AC$500 ranged from $770 (10th-percentile cut score) to $6,934 (90th-percentile cut score). AC$1000 gross utility ranged from $215 (10th-percentile cut score) to $1,934 (90th-percentile cut score). Under either cost scenario, AC utility peaked and then decreased at the 90th-percentile cut score.

PET gross utility ranged from $1,465 (10th-percentile cut score) to $13,189 (90th-percentile cut score). All utility estimates were for one year. The authors did not include tenure in the utility equation to provide conservative estimates.

EXHIBIT 10–3 *Gross Per Selectee Utility in Dollars (One Year) for Assessment Center and Aptitude Test*

Selection Ratio	Cut-Score Percentile	Assessment Center Cost		Aptitude Test
		$500	$1,000	
0.1	0.9	6,934	1,934	13,189
0.2	0.8	7,054	4,554	10,707
0.3	0.7	6,221	4,555	8,881
0.4	0.6	5,312[a]	4,062[a]	7,402
0.5	0.5	4,440	3,440	6,140
0.6	0.4	3,353	2,719	4,948
0.7	0.3	2,652	1,937	3,790
0.8	0.2	1,755	1,130	2,668[b]
0.9	0.1	770	215	1,465

[a] Point where AC produced adverse impact.
[b] Point where PET produced adverse impact.
Notes: AC = assessment center; PET = Professional Employment Test.
Source: Adapted from Hoffman, C. C., Thornton, G. C. III. (1997). Examining selection utility where competing predictors differ in adverse impact. *Personnel Psychology 50,* 464.

The AC produced *AI* at the 60th percentile; the PET produced *AI* at the 20th percentile. Gross utility per selectee for the respective cut scores is \$5,312 (AC$_{\$500}$), \$4,062 (AC$_{\$1000}$), and \$2,668 (PET). Because the validity of the aptitude test was somewhat lower than what the literature would suggest, Hoffman and Thornton also calculated the validity needed for PET utility to match AC utility, assuming that the PET cut score at the 20th percentile was maintained. The PET would have to provide a validity of 0.5982 with a 20th-percentile cut score to match the AC$_{\$1000}$ utility with a 60th-percentile cut score, and a validity of 0.7678 to match AC$_{\$500}$ utility at the same cut score.

Conclusion

If the utility of the AC and the PET had been examined using the net utility model, most researchers would probably have concluded that they should not use the AC for selection. It has lower validity, costs more, and always produces lower utility at comparable cut scores. The AC produces higher utility than the aptitude test, however, when cut scores on each are set to eliminate adverse impact. At the 60th percentile, where the AC just started to produce *AI*, no African Americans in this admittedly small sample would pass the PET. Such an outcome might be unacceptable in some organizations.

The choice of which cut score to apply remains a qualitative judgment, as always, and rests on issues like "how valid" the test is, how extreme the level of *AI*, the type of organization involved, labor market conditions, the relative value an organization places on performance and diversity, and the expected productivity gains or losses associated with different cut scores.

As usually conducted, most utility comparisons simply favor the most valid predictor (Guion & Gibson 1988). The utility analysis conducted here expands our understanding of how selection systems work *as systems*. Reviewing validity evidence without considering adverse impact would lead to conclusions different from those of this study, a fact that illustrates the need to consider multiple outcomes and trade-offs in assessing the relative usefulness of selection systems.

Breakeven Analysis

An additional tool that can aid in the assessment of the relative usefulness of competing selection systems is breakeven analysis. Instead of estimating the *level* of expected utility for each expected alternative (AC or interview), suppose that decision makers focus on the *breakeven values* that are critical to making the decision. In other words, what is the smallest value of any given parameter that will permit a choice of one selection technique over another or over random selection?

To illustrate this approach, we will focus on the parameter SD_y in the general utility equation (equation 10 in chapter 8), and we will use parameter estimates provided by Cascio and Silbey (1979): N is 50, T is 5 (but because year-to-year performance correlates 0.70, this has the effect of multiplying the yearly SD_y estimates by 4.36 rather than by 5); SR is 0.50 (therefore, the average score of selectees is 0.80); validity of assessment is 0.35; validity of a pre-employment interview is 0.25; the direct cost per applicant assessed is $403.28; and the direct cost per applicant interviewed is $290. Substituting those values into the general utility equation produces two utility formulas. For the AC, utility may be expressed as:

Equation 8

$$\Delta U_{ac} = 50 \times 4.36 \times 0.35 \times 0.80 \times SD_y - 100 \times \$403.28$$
$$\Delta U_{ac} = 61.04 \times SD_y - \$40,328$$

For the interview, these values are:

Equation 9

$$\Delta U_{int} = 50 \times 4.36 \times 0.25 \times 0.80 \times SD_y - 100 \times \$290$$

$$\Delta U_{int} = 43.6 \times SD_y - \$29,000$$

As Boudreau (1984) has noted, the determination of critical SD_y values requires answers to only three questions:

1. Above what value of SD_y does the interview break even?
2. Above what value of SD_y does the AC break even?
3. Above what value of SD_y does one option dominate the other?

The minimum value of SD_y that will justify using either alternative is computed by setting $\Delta U = \$0.00$. For the AC it is $40,328 \div 61.04 = \$661$. For the interview it is $29,000 \div 43.6 = \$665$. Those values of SD_y guarantee that the costs of the AC or the interview will be matched by equivalent benefits—no more, no less. Thus the term "breakeven" analysis.

Both options produce equal payoff ($\Delta U_{ac} - \Delta U_{int} = \$0.00$) when SD_y is $650. As might be expected, that payoff is slightly negative, as can be seen from Exhibit 10–4. The decision rules in this case are the following: If SD_y is less than \$661, do not use the AC or the interview; if SD_y is \$662 or more, use the AC because it yields a higher payoff than the interview (that is, it "dominates" the interview) at all values of SD_y greater than \$661.[2]

Cascio and Silbey reported a mean SD_y value of \$9,500 using the global estimation procedure (\$23,740 in 1998 dollars). At this SD_y value, the AC was the preferred option. However, the breakeven analysis shows that any SD_y value above \$661 (\$1,652 in 1998 dollars) would have produced the same decision.

At a broader level, Boudreau (1991) computed breakeven values for 42 studies that estimated SD_y. Without exception, the breakeven values fell at or below 60 percent of the estimated value of SD_y. In many cases, the breakeven value was less than 1 percent of the estimated value of SD_y. As Weekley et al. (1985) noted, however, although the breakeven

EXHIBIT 10–4 *Breakeven Analysis: The Effect of Variations in* SD$_y$ *on the Relative Payoffs of the Assessment Center and the Interview*

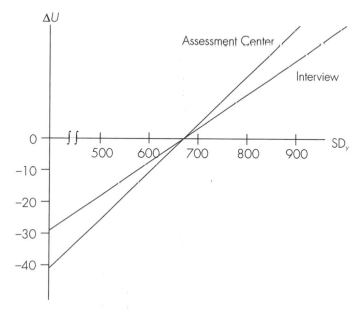

Source: Data for this example were drawn from Cascio, W. F., Silbey, V. (1979). Utility of the assessment center as a selection device. *Journal of Applied Psychology 64*, 107–118.

value might be low when deciding whether to implement an HRM program, comparing HRM programs to other organizational investments might produce decision situations where differences in SD_y estimates do affect the ultimate decision. (For more on research needs when estimating SD_y, see Bobko, Karren, & Kerkar [1987].) Furthermore, as the Hoffman and Thornton (1997) study showed, decision makers may also consider parameters other than or in addition to SD_y in making capital budgeting decisions. Breakeven analysis still can be used under those circumstances.

Breakeven analysis seems to provide two important advantages:

1. It allows practicing managers to appreciate how little variability in job performance is necessary before valid selection procedures begin to pay positive dividends.
2. Even if decision makers cannot agree on an exact point estimate of SD_y, they probably can agree that it is higher than the breakeven value.

Dealing with Risk and Uncertainty in Utility Analysis

Many factors might act to increase or decrease expected payoffs from utility analysis. Exhibit 10–5 summarizes them. Taking such factors into account will make utility estimates more realistic, but in actually conducting utility analyses, researchers have tended to assume away or not even to consider many of those factors. Realistically, even if we could take all of the factors into account, there probably still would be uncertainty in our estimates of expected dollar payoffs.

Researchers have developed three techniques to deal with such uncertainty. The first is breakeven analysis, as we have just seen. That analysis is useful, but its overall validity hinges on the assumption that the relationship between performance and payoff is described best by a straight line. In many if not most cases, that assumption is tenable. If it is not, however, then one should use an alternative procedure such as Monte Carlo simulation (Rich & Boudreau 1987) to assess the extent of variability of utility values, and thus to provide a sound basis for decision making.

A third approach is to compute a standard error of the utility estimate and then to derive a 95% confidence interval around the estimate (SE_u).

Equation 10

$$U - 1.96 \times SE_u \leq U \leq U + 1.96 \times SE_u$$

EXHIBIT 10-5 *Some Key Factors That Affect Economic Payoffs from Selection Programs*

Generally Increase Payoffs	Generally Decrease Payoffs	May Increase or Decrease Payoffs
Low selection ratios	High selection ratios	Changes in the definition of the criterion construct
Multiple employee cohorts	Discounting	Changes in validity
Start-up costs[a]	Variable costs (materials + wages)	Changes in the variability of job performance
Employee tenure	Taxes	
Loose labor markets	Tight labor markets	
	Time lags to fully competent performance	
	Unreliability in performance across time periods	
	Recruitment costs	

[a] Start-up costs decrease payoffs in the period incurred, but they act to increase payoffs thereafter because only recurring costs remain.
Source: Cascio, W. F. (1993). Assessing the utility of selection decisions: Theoretical and practical considerations. In N. Schmitt and W. C. Borman (eds.), *Personnel Selection in Organizations* (p. 330). San Francisco: Jossey-Bass. Used with permission.

Alexander and Barrick (1987) developed a procedure for estimating the standard error of utility estimates. Myors (1998) noted that although there are problems with their method, especially the assumption that all components in the equation are independent and normally distributed, research suggests that it provides a serviceable approximation. To illustrate their method, Alexander and Barrick (1987) applied it to the Schmidt et al. (1979) data and found that the values of SE_u were very large, about half the size of the utility estimate itself—larger than most researchers might have expected. As Myors (1998) noted, "Ironically, the impressively large size of utility estimates per se have [sic] been almost overemphasized . . . while the standard error of utility has been largely ignored. If we are to be impressed by the size of utility, we must similarly be impressed by the size of the uncertainty in these estimates" (pp. 47, 48). To date, we have tended to view utility estimates as point rather than interval estimates. Given the uncertainty of many of the parameters of the utility model, interval estimates are probably more appropriate and they should be reported routinely.

The Impact of Utility Analyses on Decision Makers

In two provocative studies, Latham and Whyte (1994) and Whyte and Latham (1997) showed that presentation of utility results can reduce practicing managers' support for implementing a valid selection procedure, even though the net benefits of the procedure are substantial. Two subsequent studies failed to replicate those findings (both reported in Carson, Becker, & Henderson 1998), and their conclusions and implications have been challenged (Cronshaw 1997; Hoffman & Thornton 1997), but the Latham and Whyte (1994) and Whyte and Latham (1997) studies have stimulated the field to ponder its communication strategies.

Until we begin to develop and share information on how we can improve the way we communicate the results of our analyses; until we learn where the weaknesses in our presentations to managers are; until we begin the painstaking process of soliciting feedback from our audiences, taking constructive steps to respond to it, soliciting more feedback, and repeating the process over and over again, we cannot expect to have the kind of impact on organizations that we desire (Cascio 1996). Boudreau (1998, 1996) argued that utility analysts need to shift their focus, for the fundamental question is not, "How do we construct the best HR measure?" Rather it is, "How do we induce changes through HR measurement systems?" HR measurement is not an end in itself, but rather a decision-support system that can have powerful effects if researchers pay careful attention to the sender, the receivers, the strategy they use to transmit their message, and the organization of their message. In short, because research is not complete until it is communicated to interested parties, the field should change its focus from an emphasis on measures to an emphasis on effects. Hoffman (1996) showed that managers were quite receptive to utility analysis when analysts presented conservative estimates, illustrated the trade-offs involved, did not overload their presentation with technical details, and emphasized things of interest to managers of operating departments (for example, reducing the overall cycle time of the staffing process and reducing costs while maintaining the validity of the overall staffing process). Clearly, the "framing" of the message is critical and has a direct effect on the ultimate acceptability of the message (Carson et al. 1998; Hazer & Highhouse 1997). That is strategic HRM in action, and it illustrates how utility analysis can serve as a useful guide to decision making. In this sense, utility analysis is more than one or several equations; it is a stimulating way of thinking.

EXERCISES

1. You are given the following information regarding the CAP test for clerical employees (clerk-2s) at the Berol Corporation:

   - average tenure as a clerk-2: 7.26 years
   - number selected per year: 120
   - validity of the CAP test: 0.61
   - validity of previously used test: 0.18
   - cost of CAP per applicant: $15
   - cost of old test per applicant: $8
   - *SR:* 0.50
   - ordinate at *SR:* 0.399
   - *SD* in first year: $24,000

   Use equation 1 in this chapter to determine (a) the total utility of the CAP test, (b) the utility per selectee, and (c) the per-year gain in utility per selectee.

2. Referring to exercise 1, suppose that after consulting with the chief financial officer at Berol, you are given the following additional information: variable costs are –0.08, taxes are 40 percent, and the

discount rate is 8 percent. Use equation 2 in this chapter to recompute (a) the total utility of the CAP test, (b) the utility per selectee, and (c) the utility per selectee in the first year.

3. The Top Dollar Co. is trying to decide whether to use an AC to select middle managers for its consumer products operations. The following information has been determined: variable costs are –0.10; corporate taxes are 44 percent; the discount rate is 9 percent; the ordinary selection procedure costs $500 per candidate; the AC costs $2,000 per candidate; the *SD* of job performance is $35,000; the validity of the ordinary procedure is 0.30; the validity of the AC is 0.40; the *SR* is 0.20; the ordinate at that *SR* is 0.2789; and the average tenure as a middle manager is three years. The program is designed to last six years, with 20 managers added each year. Beginning in year 4, however, one cohort separates each year until all of those hired from the program leave.

Use equation 6 in this chapter to determine if Top Dollar Co. should adopt the AC to select middle managers. What payoffs can be expected (a) in total, (b) per selectee, and (c) per selectee in the first year?

REFERENCES

Alexander, R. A., Barrick, M. R. (1987). Estimating the standard error of projected dollar gains in utility analysis. *Journal of Applied Psychology 72*, 475–479.

Becker, B. E. (1989). The influence of labor markets on human resources utility estimates. *Personnel Psychology 42*, 531–546.

Bobko, P., Karren, R., Kerkar, S. P. (1987). Systematic research needs for estimating supervisory-based estimates of *SD_y* in utility analysis. *Organizational Behavior and Human Decision Processes 40*, 69–95.

Boudreau, J. W. (1983a). Economic considerations in estimating the utility of human resource productivity improvement programs. *Personnel Psychology 36*, 551–576.

Boudreau, J. W. (1983b). Effects of employee flows on utility analysis of human resource productivity improvement programs. *Journal of Applied Psychology 68*, 396–406.

Boudreau, J. W. (1984). Decision theory contributions to HRM research and practice. *Industrial Relations 23*, 198–217.

Boudreau, J. W. (1991). Utility analysis for decisions in human resource management. In M. D. Dunnette and L. M. Hough (eds.), *Handbook of Industrial and Organizational Psychology* (Vol. 2, 2nd ed., pp. 621–745). Palo Alto, CA: Consulting Psychologists Press.

Boudreau, J. W. (1996). The motivational impact of utility analysis and HR measurement. *Journal of Human Resource Costing and Accounting 1*(2), 73–84.

Boudreau, J. W. (1998). Strategic human resource management measures: Key linkages and the Peoplescape model. *Journal of Human Resource Costing and Accounting 3*(2), 21–40.

Bray, D. W. (1964). The management progress study. *American Psychologist 19*, 419–420.

Brogden, H. E. (1949). When testing pays off. *Personnel Psychology 2*, 171–185.

Burke, M. J., Frederick, J. T. (1986). A comparison of economic utility estimates for alternative rational SD_y estimation procedures. *Journal of Applied Psychology 71*, 334–339.

Carson, K. P., Becker, J. S., Henderson, J. A. (1998). Is utility really futile? A failure to replicate and an extension. *Journal of Applied Psychology 83*, 84–96.

Cascio, W. F. (1993). Assessing the utility of selection decisions: Theoretical and practical considerations. In N. Schmitt and W. C. Borman (eds.), *Personnel Selection in Organizations* (pp. 310–340). San Francisco: Jossey-Bass.

Cascio, W. F. (1996). The role of utility analysis in the strategic management of organizations. *Journal of Human Resource Costing and Accounting 1*(2), 85–95.

Cascio, W. F. (1998). *Applied Psychology in Human Resource Management* (5th ed.). Upper Saddle River, NJ: Prentice Hall.

Cascio, W. F., Silbey, V. (1979). Utility of the assessment center as a selection device. *Journal of Applied Psychology 64*, 107–118.

Cronbach, L. J. (1965). Comments on "A dollar criterion in fixed-treatment employee selection." In L. J. Cronbach and G. C. Gleser (eds.), *Psychological Tests and Personnel Decisions* (2nd ed., pp. 266, 267). Urbana: University of Illinois Press.

Cronshaw, S. F. (1997). Lo! The stimulus speaks: The insider's view of Whyte and Latham's "The futility of utility analysis." *Personnel Psychology 50*, 611–615.

Gaugler, B. B., Rosenthal, D. B., Thornton, G. C. III, Bentson, C. (1987). Meta-analysis of assessment center validity. *Journal of Applied Psychology 72*, 493–511.

Guion, R. F., Gibson, W. M. (1988). Personnel selection and placement. *Annual Review of Psychology 39*, 349–374.

Hartigan, J. A., Wigdor, A. K. (eds.). (1989). *Fairness in Employment Testing*. Washington, DC: National Academy Press.

Hazer, J. T., Highhouse, S. (1997). Factors influencing managers' reactions to utility analysis: Effects of SD_y method, information frame, and focal intervention. *Journal of Applied Psychology 82*, 104–112.

Hoffman, C. C. (1996). Applying utility analysis to guide decisions on selection system content. *Journal of Human Resource Costing and Accounting 1*(2), 9–17.

Hoffman, C. C., Thornton, G. C. III. (1997). Examining selection utility where competing predictors differ in adverse impact. *Personnel Psychology 50*, 455–470.

Howard, A., Bray, D. W. (1989). *Managerial Lives in Transition*. New York: Guilford.

Hunter, J. E., Hunter, R. F. (1984). Validity and utility of alternative predictors of job performance. *Psychological Bulletin 97*, 72–98.

Latham, G. P., Whyte, G. (1994). The futility of utility analysis. *Personnel Psychology 47*, 31–46.

Murphy, K. R. (1986). When your top choice turns you down: Effects of rejected offers on the utility of selection tests. *Psychological Bulletin 99*, 133–138.

Myors, B. (1998). Utility analysis based on tenure. *Journal of Human Resource Costing and Accounting 3*(2), 41–50.

Rich, J. R., Boudreau, J. W. (1987). The effects of variability and risk on selection utility analysis: An empirical simulation and comparison. *Personnel Psychology 40*, 55–84.

Roche, W. J. Jr. (1961). The Cronbach-Gleser utility function in fixed-treatment employee selection. *Dissertation Abstracts International 22*, 4413. (University Microfilms No. 62-1570). Portions reproduced in L. J. Cronbach and G. C. Gleser (eds.), *Psychological Tests and Personnel Decisions* (2nd ed., pp. 254–266). Urbana: University of Illinois Press.

Schmidt, F. L., Hunter, J. E., McKenzie, R. C., Muldrow, T. W. (1979). Impact of valid selection procedures on work-force productivity. *Journal of Applied Psychology 64,* 609–626.

Schmidt, F. L., Hunter, J. E., Outerbridge, A. N., Trattner, M. H. (1986). The economic impact of job selection methods on size, productivity, and payroll costs of the federal workforce: An empirically based demonstration. *Personnel Psychology 39,* 1–30.

Schmidt, F. L., Mack, M. J., Hunter, J. E. (1984). Selection utility in the occupation of U.S. park ranger for three modes of test use. *Journal of Applied Psychology 69,* 490–497.

Uniform guidelines on employee selection procedures. (1978). *Federal Register 43,* 38290–38315.

Weekley, J. A., O'Connor, E. J., Frank, B., Peters, L. W. (1985). A comparison of three methods of estimating the standard deviation of performance in dollars. *Journal of Applied Psychology 70,* 122–126.

Whyte, G., Latham, G. P. (1997). The futility of utility analysis revisited: When even an expert fails. *Personnel Psychology 50,* 601–610.

ENDNOTES

1. Assuming a 6 percent inflation rate from 1979 to 1990, and a 3.5 percent inflation rate from 1990 to 1998, this value is $26,029 in 1998 dollars.

2. Boudreau (1984) used parameters identical to those of Cascio and Silbey (1979) for illustrative purposes, but a mathematical error in computing the total cost of the AC led him to an erroneous conclusion regarding the decision rules to be used in this case. The error, however, does not affect Boudreau's conclusion that even very low SD_y estimates that may be subject to disagreement among experts often are sufficient to justify investing in improved selection.

Estimating the Costs and Benefits of Human Resource Development Programs

O rganizations in the United States spend billions of dollars each year on employee training (Noe 1999). Those outlays reflect the aggregate cost of keeping abreast of technological and social changes; the extent of managerial commitment to achieving a competent, productive workforce; and the broad array of opportunities available for individuals and teams to improve their productive and social skills. Indeed, the large amount of money spent on training in both public and private organizations is likely to *increase* in the coming years for at least three reasons:

1. Demographic projections suggest that large numbers of skilled people will be needed for entry-level jobs but the available pool of young workers will comprise large numbers of unskilled and undereducated people.
2. The increasing sophistication of technological systems will require greater emphasis on training workers to use the new technology.
3. The growing numbers of service jobs; the inclusion of more women, minorities, and older workers in the workforce; and increasingly complex national and international competition among all sizes and types of firms will make training in interpersonal skills a high priority in the development of managers (Goldstein & Gilliam 1990; Thayer 1997).

Mills (1975) coined the term *human resource development* (HRD) to represent the wide range of behavioral science and management technologies intended to improve both the operating effectiveness of an organization and the quality of working life experienced by its employees. Topics covered by HRD range from basic skills training to job enrichment and training in interpersonal skills, team building, and decision making for individuals or teams. Technologies used run the full gamut from lectures to CD-ROMs, to Internet-based training, intranet-based training, laser discs, interactive video, and intelligent tutoring systems (see Noe 1999 and Quinones & Ehrenstein 1997 for reviews). Unfortunately, billions will be spent providing training and development programs, but little will be spent assessing their social and financial outcomes. As a result, scant comparative evidence exists by which to generalize or to evaluate the impact of the various technologies. Decision makers thus remain unguided by systematic evaluations of past experiments and uninformed about the costs and benefits of alternative HRD programs when considering training efforts in their own organizations. "Billions for training, but not one cent for evaluation" is an exaggerated but not entirely false characterization of present training practice in many organizations.

The intent in this chapter is not to present true experimental or quasi-experimental designs for evaluating HRD programs (for those, see Cascio 1998; Goldstein 1993; Arvey & Cole 1989; or Cook & Campbell 1979). Rather, it is to illustrate how the economic consequences of HRD programs can be expressed. To do so, the chapter will present three very different examples of efforts to assess the financial impact of specific programs. Let us begin by considering how to determine the true cost of a popular approach to HRD—off-site meetings.

EXAMPLE 1: DETERMINING OFF-SITE MEETING COSTS

Off-site meetings—those conducted away from organizational property—are useful for several purposes: conducting HRD programs, communicating information without the interruptions commonly found at the office, strategic planning, and decision making. In many cases, however, the true dollar costs of an off-site meeting remain unknown as long as attendee costs are not included in the final tally along with the direct and obvious expenses. The method described here enables planners to compute the actual costs of an off-site meeting and offers two advantages:

the identification and the evaluation of the dollars invested in each type of activity included in the program.

The method for costing off-site meetings was developed by McKeon (1981). Let's make the following assumptions about the hypothetical firm Valco Ltd · The firm has 500 employees, including 100 first-line supervisors and managers. Under the general planning and direction of Valco's training department (one manager and one secretary), Valco holds an annual total of 10 days of off-site meetings (either training sessions or various types of managers' gatherings). The firm retains outside speakers and consultants to develop and conduct the meetings. On the average, 20 managers attend each meeting, and the typical meeting lasts two full days.

Costs shown in Exhibit 11–1 are based on those figures. The estimates we are using here are broad averages intended only to create a model for purposes of comparison. Note that in this example there is no attempt to place a dollar value on the loss of productive time from the job. If it is possible to estimate such costs reliably in your organization, include them in the calculations. As with the illustrations in other chapters, the numbers are as realistic as possible, but the primary concern here is with the methodology rather than with the numbers.

As can be seen in Exhibit 11–1, the per-day, per-person cost of Valco's meeting comes to $837. Actually, that figure probably does not represent the true cost of the meeting because no distinction is made between recurring and nonrecurring costs (Mathieu & Leonard 1987). During the development of a program, organizations absorb nonrecurring costs such as equipment purchases and trainers' salaries. Recurring costs absorbed each time a program is presented include such session expenses as facilities and trainers' salaries, and costs that correspond to the number of participants in a program, such as training materials and trainees' salaries.

Separating costs allows each set of costs to be incorporated into utility calculations for the time period in which each expense is incurred. Thus, the high initial expenses associated with a program may indicate that costs exceed benefits for some period of time or over a certain number of groups of trainees. However, at some point an organization may begin to derive program benefits that signal the beginning of a payback period. Separating costs helps decision makers to clarify information about the utility of HR programs and return-on-investment (Mathieu & Leonard 1987).

EXHIBIT 11-1   *Cost Breakdown for an Off-Site Management Meeting*

Cost Element	Subtotal Cost	Total Cost	Cost per Participant per Day
A. Development of programs (figured on an annual basis)			
1. training department overhead			
2. training staff salaries			
3. use of outside consultants			
4. equipment and materials for meeting (videos, supplies, workbooks)		205,000	205.00[a]
B. Participant cost (figured on an annual basis)			
1. salaries and benefits of participants (figured for average participant)	40,900		
2. capital investment in participants (based on an average of various industries from *Fortune* magazine)	51,000	91,900	389.41[b]
C. Delivery of one meeting for 20 people			
1. facility costs			
a. sleeping rooms	2,042		
b. three meals daily	1,634		
c. coffee breaks	122		
d. miscellaneous tips, telephone	408		
e. reception	408	4,614	115.35[c]
2. meeting charges			
a. room rental			
b. audiovisual equipment rental			
c. secretarial services			
3. transportation to the meeting		5,107	127.66[d]

Summary: Total Cost per Participant per Day

A. Development of programs   205
B. Participant cost   389
C. Delivery of one meeting (hotel and transportation)   243

Total $837

Note: Meeting duration: two full days. Number of attendees: 20 people. Costs do not reflect a figure for the productive time lost by the people in the program. If that cost were added—and it would be realistic to do so—the above cost would increase dramatically. All costs are expressed in terms of 1999 dollars assuming an average 5 percent inflation rate from 1981 through 1990, and 3.5 percent from 1991 to 1998.

[a] To determine per-day cost, divide $205,000 by number of meeting days held per year (10). Then divide answer ($20,500) by total number of management people (100) attending all programs = $205 per day of a meeting.

[b] To determine per-day cost, divide total of $91,900 by 236 (average number of work days in a year) = $389.41 per day of work year.

[c] To determine per-day, per-person cost, divide group total ($4,614) by number of participants (20) and then divide resulting figure ($230.70) by number of meeting days (2) = $115.35 per day.

[d] To determine per-day, per-person cost, divide group total ($5,107) by number of participants (20) and then divide resulting figure ($255.33) by number of meeting days (2) = $127.66 per day.

Source: Adapted from McKeon, W. J. (1981). How to determine off-site meeting costs. *Training and Development Journal 35*(May), p. 117.

The influence of the environment in training is the chief reason cited for selecting an outside facility for a meeting. A professionally designed and operated meeting facility can make a meeting both more productive and more enjoyable. The task for decision makers is to consider whether facility costs—as a percentage of the total of the true meeting costs identified—will be offset by a corresponding increase in learning effectiveness. In the example shown in Exhibit 11–1, the cost per person per day was $837. If an additional $45, $55, or even $65 were added per person per day to cover the cost of meeting in a superior facility, the extra cost would be 5 to 8 percent. But if those surroundings increased learning effectiveness by a factor of greater than 10 percent—and over 20 percent is a realistic possibility—the desirability of the trade-off is obvious. In short, only by considering all of the factors that have an impact on learning effectiveness—program planning and administration, the quality of the trainer, program delivery, and learning environment—can we derive the greatest return, in time and dollars spent, on this substantial investment in people.

EXAMPLE 2: THE VALUE OF STRUCTURED VERSUS UNSTRUCTURED TRAINING IN BASIC SKILLS

In broad terms, industrial training may be structured or unstructured. The term *structure* implies a systematically developed educational program designed to train a new worker in a logical progression from no job competency to a specified mastery of the job. The trainee is the focal point of the training effect. Unstructured training, on the other hand, implies on-the-job training of a new worker, without a specific program, by an experienced worker who continues to perform his or her regular duties while the training occurs. Ongoing production output rather than the trainee's learning experience is the focal point of the worker-trainer, and mastery is not defined.

Structured job skills training is widely assumed to be more effective than unstructured training, although little controlled research on that has been done. To some extent this is understandable because the variables in ongoing plant operations are so complex, and controlling them in a simulation is, in itself, very difficult. Nevertheless, failure to conduct controlled studies is the most serious shortcoming of industrial training programs for there is no empirical linkage of the training results to improved productivity. In the absence of such a connection, training activities often are the first to go when corporate profits tumble. That need not be the case, as a 14-month study in a university industrial manufacturing laboratory indicates (Cullen et al. 1976). The origins of the study and its financial support came from the Johns-Manville Corporation.

The Experiment

The purpose of the study was to conduct an experimental comparison of the structured versus unstructured training of semiskilled production workers. The job studied was the Rainville plastics extruder. This job was selected because it was representative of Johns-Manville (J-M) operations and because of its general difficulty of operation. The job involved processing raw materials into quality plastic pipe from a plastic extrusion machine.

There were six major steps in the development of the extruder operator structured-training program:

1. job and task analysis
2. general training-design decisions
3. specific training-design decisions
4. production of the training program
5. pilot test
6. revision of the training program

Subjects responded to recruitment methods either by telephoning about the position or by applying in person. As part of the selection procedure, subjects were asked to complete an application form and the Bennett Mechanical Comprehension Test. Forty subjects were selected, matched on characteristics such as age, education, community background, and test scores (to help ensure pre-experimental equivalence), and then assigned randomly to the structured and unstructured groups (20 in each group). Measures of product quantity and quality, worker competence, cost–benefit, and worker attitudes are presented below.

Measures of Quantity and Quality

Quantity was measured by count and weight. The quality of pipe production was based on visual and dimensional criteria. To aid visual judgments, samples of defective pipe were used as standards. The dimensional criteria of pipe roundness and concentricity required the development and validation of a mechanical test device.

Worker Competence

Worker competence was defined as the ability to start up production, to develop quality pipe, and to recover from two production problems (remotely manipulated machine variables) without a loss of production rate. A concealed closed-circuit television system was set up to monitor the extruder operator's work area and the image was broadcast to the project office some 100 feet away. In addition, all production rates and observation logs were time-referenced systematically.

Cost–Benefit

Actual expenditures were used as inputs to a cost–benefit model for the two industrial training methods. The hourly rate of the research assistant performing as the industrial trainer was used, as were all the project costs, even to the point of costing out the paper on which the job analysis was written.

Worker Attitudes

A worker-attitude inventory was developed to assess the attitudes of trainees toward their training and jobs. Content-oriented evidence of validity was established through the development of questions about attitudes toward the job, the training, the trainer, and the equipment.

Subjects in both groups were trained individually because most new workers at a J-M plant enter singly, to replace workers who have left, and not in groups. Methods for collecting and recording data depended on the type of data needed. The times a trainee reported for work and ended work, the hours a subject was a trainee, and the hours a subject was a worker-trainer were recorded in a log.

To compare the material efficiency of one group to another, data were collected on production rates, production weight, and material waste (scrap). Production rate was recorded as the number of acceptable pieces of pipe extruded per hour of work. At the end of each hour the researcher collected and counted the production, and recorded the production count and weight in the log. At the end of each hour the researcher also collected, weighed, and recorded the plastic determined as scrap. Scrap was defined as plastic extruded not as pipe and pipe not meeting the dimensional and visual standards. The researchers also compared the production weight and scrap weight across training groups.

The subjects recorded their attitudes on a questionnaire at the end of the employment period.

Study Results

Time to Achieve Competence

Mean training time for people in the unstructured group was 16.3 hours, compared with an average 4.6 hours for those in the structured group. This difference is statistically significant ($p < 0.005$), and indicates a 72 percent savings in training time using the structured method.

Level of Job Competence

Subjects in the structured training group achieved significantly higher ($p < 0.01$) job competence after four hours of training. Although statistically significant differences were not found at 8- and 12-hour intervals, there were substantial differences in training times. Certainly, statistical power would have been greater with a larger sample size.[1]

Costs of Training

The average cost of $56.25 ($167 in 1998 dollars) to train a group of 20 extruder operators by the structured method was not significantly different ($p > 0.05$) from the average $57.25 ($170 in 1998 dollars) to train an identical-size group by the unstructured method. Such a conclusion is probably an artifact of group size in this study; a firm normally would use an industrial training program to train far more than 20 workers. As the number of trainees increases under a structured training program, the average cost per trainee is reduced because the cost to develop a structured program is fixed even as the number of trainees increases. In an unstructured approach, however, the entire cost varies directly with the number of trainees. Exhibit 11–2 illustrates that breakeven concept. For the extruder operator experiment, the breakeven point was about 18 people.

Production Losses

As might be expected, training under both the structured and unstructured methods resulted in reductions from standard minimum production rates. The average 2.91 pounds of production loss resulting from structured training was significantly less ($p < 0.01$) than the average 9.35 pounds of production loss resulting from the unstructured training. That represents approximately a 70 percent difference in production losses between structured and unstructured training. Such a comparison can be useful in projecting the potential returns for very specific training programs.

EXHIBIT 11-2 *Cost Comparisons of Structured and Unstructured Training for 1–20 Semiskilled Workers*

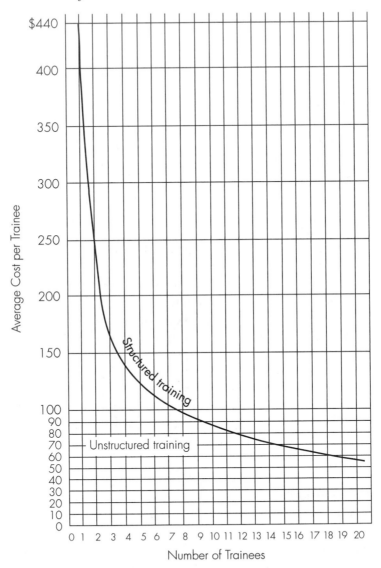

Source: Cullen, J. G., Sawzin, S. A., Sisson, G. R., and Swanson, R. A. (1976). Training: What's it worth? *Training and Development Journal 30*(8), p. 17.

Resolution of Production Problems

The 80 percent rate of success in production troubleshooting by the structured program trainees was significantly higher ($p < 0.025$) than the 33 percent rate of success by unstructured program trainees. That represents a 130 percent increase in solved production problems when structured training is used. Industrial situations characterized by expensive production downtime or difficult start-up procedures would make the reported differences an even greater concern.

Job Attitudes

Trainees in the structured and unstructured groups displayed no significant difference ($p > 0.8$) in their attitudes toward the pipe-extrusion job.

The Economics of Training: A Cost–Benefit Model

To estimate accurately the resources that should be allocated to industrial training, management must know the expected gains of that training. Controversy over training often is fueled by inadequate knowledge of its economic returns. Taken at face value, training costs appear to be an economic burden that reduces company profits; but because some form of training is necessary to maintain worker productivity, a cost–benefit model is needed to determine the relative economic returns of alternative training strategies.

At the most basic level, the lesson from the comparison of structured to unstructured training is that money spent for structured training will be returned many times over. A company can, therefore, view training as an investment to further its objectives. It can consider the gains or losses derived from training as returns, and comparing returns to investment results in the subsequent cost–benefit or cost effectiveness of the training.

Exhibit 11–3 is a cost–benefit model developed by Cullen et al. (1978) for assessing the outcomes of industrial training programs. To illustrate how the model works, let us use as an example the previous comparison of structured versus unstructured training for plastic extruder operators.

Training Costs

For the cost–benefit model, the costs for training are classified as either fixed or variable. Fixed costs do not vary with numbers of trainees, training time, or training program development. Variable costs change

EXHIBIT 11-3 *Industrial Training Cost–Benefit Model*

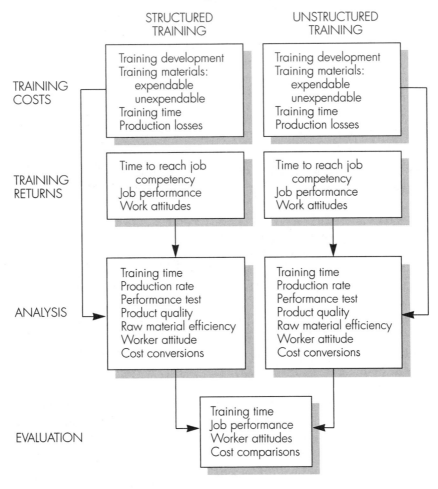

Source: Cullen, J. G., Sawzin, S. A., Sisson, G. R., and Swanson, R. A. (1978). Cost-effectiveness: A model for assessing the training investment. *Training and Development Journal 32*(1), p. 27.

as the number of trainees, training time, and training program development vary. For example, if a firm uses regular production equipment (which is a fixed cost for production) for training, the losses in production are considered a variable cost.

Training costs in the top left box of Exhibit 11–3 include the following elements:

1. Training development
   a. analysis time: total staff hours to analyze the job
   b. design time: total staff hours to design the training program
   c. material costs: all material costs incurred from onset through completion of one training program, including supplies to facilitate program development (secretarial services, graphics work, travel, duplicating, display boards, training aids, and so on)
2. Training materials (expendable): cost of reproducing copies of developed training program
3. Training materials (unexpendable)
   a. instructional hardware: shelf items purchased for the training program (such as production machine to be used just for training, videocassette recorder, or tape recorder)
   b. instructional software: shelf items of instructional content purchased for the training program (such as manufacturer's operating manual, videotapes, CD-ROMs, or transparencies)
4. Training time
   a. trainee: total hours and resulting salary incurred for trainee to reach competency
   b. trainer: total hours and resulting salary incurred for trainee to reach competency
5. Production losses resulting from training
   a. production rate losses
   b. material losses

Training Returns

The resulting return of a structured or unstructured training program is a competent production worker. To evaluate a competent production worker, one must specify the competencies required in each situation. The sum of the components then determines the total evaluation. For the plastic extruder operator training program, production task performance included the following components:

1. Trainee can perform job start-up successfully.
2. Trainee can maintain set standard of plastic tubing.
3. Trainee can perform successfully in production malfunction performance tests.
4. Trainee can perform job shutdown successfully.

Analyses of Training Returns

Measurements of actual task performance for purposes of assessing training returns included:

1. measurement of task performance
   a. time: to reach competency, to deal successfully with deliberately induced machine malfunctions, to follow start-up procedures
   b. production rate: number of three-foot lengths of acceptable pipe per hour of production
   c. performance test: reaction to induction of machine malfunctions via performance test (downtime, loss of tubing, time of malfunction injection versus time to respond to malfunction, time to correct malfunction)
   d. product quality: measured by visual and dimensional criteria (comparison to samples of defective and nondefective pipe)
   e. raw material usage: weight of raw material supplied to the machine versus weight of scrap and amount of acceptable product produced (weight of raw material supplied, scrap, and bundles of acceptable tubing per hour)
2. trainee attitudes toward training and the job measured by the worker-attitude inventory described earlier in the chapter
3. monetary value of returns
   a. trainee performance data converted to a monetary value
   b. total returns of structured and unstructured training programs

Evaluation

Evaluation is the final phase of assessing costs and benefits. As Exhibit 11–3 demonstrated, the structured and unstructured training methods should be compared on all of the points just mentioned. Each variable under training costs and training returns should be quantified. For those variables that are expressed in nonmonetary indexes (for example, time), monetary equivalents should be calculated whenever possible. As chapter 6 showed, the financial impact of employee attitudes also can be estimated, and those figures then can be used for the analysis and evaluation stages.

The general approach to cost–benefit comparison of alternative training strategies is to analyze the training variables, to convert them to monetary equivalents, and then to compare costs. If desired, individual variables such as time taken to reach competency also can be compared and reported as separate indexes of effectiveness.

The cost–benefit model just described has been used successfully in several industrial training situations. Although in some types of HRD programs (such as programs to change attitudes or improve decision-making skills) components of the model may be inappropriate, the general model or approach to cost–benefit analysis should guide evaluation in these circumstances. Evaluation isn't always easy, but failure to establish empirically the links between HRD and improvements in productivity will ensure that in many organizations training is viewed as a cost rather than as an investment.

EXAMPLE 3: ESTIMATING THE COSTS AND BENEFITS OF PROPOSED OR ONGOING HRD PROGRAMS

As is true of all functional areas of business that have to operate within budgetary limits, the key question HR decision makers must answer is, How can we best allocate our scarce resources toward the most cost-effective undertakings? Faced with a bewildering array of alternatives, decision makers must select the programs that will improve productivity and profits, and allocate staff resources only to those programs. Utility analysis—a powerful tool used to evaluate selection programs and such other types of organizational decisions as downsizing options (Mabon 1996; Mabon & Westling 1996)—also can be used to evaluate proposed or ongoing HRD programs. In the Brogden-Cronbach-Gleser model, the only difference between the basic equation for calculating selection utility (equation 10 in chapter 8) and that for calculating utility from HRD programs is that the term d_t is substituted for the product $r_{xy} \times \bar{Z}_x$ (that is, the validity coefficient multiplied by the average standard score on the predictor achieved by selectees) (Schmidt, Hunter & Pearlman 1982). The resulting utility formula is

Equation 1

$$\Delta U = (N)(T)(d_t)(SD_y) - C$$

where ΔU is the gain to the firm in dollars resulting from the program; N is the number of employees trained; T is the expected duration of benefits in the trained group; d_t is the true difference in job performance between the trained and untrained groups in SD units; SD_y is the standard deviation of dollar-valued job performance among untrained employees; and C is the total cost of training N employees.

The parameter d_t is the *effect size*. Like *r*, it describes the degree of departure from the null hypothesis. In the case of HRD programs, the null hypothesis is that training had no effect—after training, the job performance of the trained group is no different from that of the untrained group.

To illustrate that idea graphically we'll plot the (hypothetical) distribution of job performance outcomes of the trained and untrained groups on the same baseline (expressed in *Z*-units, with a mean of zero and a standard deviation of 1.0) as shown in Exhibit 11–4. In that exhibit, *d* represents the size of the effect of the training program—the degree of departure from the null hypothesis. How is *d* computed? It is simply the difference between the mean job performance of the trained and untrained groups in standard (*Z*)-score units. Thus,

Equation 2

$$d = \overline{X}_t - \overline{X}_u / SD_y$$

where *d* is the effect size; $\overline{X}_t$ is the average job performance score of the trained group; $\overline{X}_u$ is the average job performance score of the untrained group; and SD_y is the standard deviation of the job performance scores of the total group, trained and untrained. If the *SD*s of the two groups are unequal, then the *SD* of the untrained group should be used because it is more representative of the incumbent employee population.

EXHIBIT 11–4 *Standard Score Distributions of Job Performance Outcomes Among Trained and Untrained Groups*

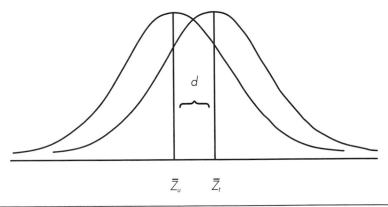

Note: $\overline{Z}_u$ is the average job performance score of the untrained group; $\overline{Z}_t$ is the average job performance score of the trained group; and *d* is the effect size.

Hypothetically, suppose that we are evaluating the impact of a training program for quality control inspectors. Job performance is evaluated in terms of a work sample; that is, the number of defects identified in a standard sample of products with a known number of defects (for example, 10). Suppose the average job performance score of employees in the trained group is 7, for those in the untrained group it is 6.5, and the standard deviation of the job performance scores is 1.0. The effect size is therefore

$$d = 7 - 6.5/1 = 0.5 \; SD$$

In other words, the performance of the trained group is half a standard deviation better than that of the untrained group. Because a perfectly reliable, objective measure of job performance was used in this case, the estimate of d need not be corrected for unreliability. In many if not most cases, managers will be using criteria that are less than perfectly reliable, such as supervisory ratings of the job performance of subordinates. In such cases, d must be corrected statistically for unreliability or measurement error in the criterion. Failure to do so would produce a biased (conservative) estimate of d.

If supervisory ratings are used as job performance criteria, then reliability probably will be estimated in terms of the extent of interrater agreement. A large-sample study that investigated the reliability of ratings of first-level supervisors found that average interrater reliabilities were 0.69 and 0.64, respectively, for ratings of supervisory abilities and ratings of the performance of specific job duties (Rothstein et al. 1990). Regardless of how the reliability of job performance measures is estimated, the formula for computing the true difference in job performance between the trained and untrained groups is

Equation 3

$$d_t = d/\sqrt{r_{yy}}$$

Alternatively, *Equation 4*

$$d_t = (\bar{X}_t - \bar{X}_u) / (SD_y)(\sqrt{r_{yy}})$$

where all terms are as defined above, and $\sqrt{r_{yy}}$ is the square root of the reliability of the job performance measure. As Sackett (1991) indicated, to express that difference as a percentage change in output, assuming that performance is measured on a ratio scale, it is necessary to multiply d_t by the ratio of the pretest standard deviation to the pretest performance mean (*SD/M*) times 100. Thus, the percentage change in output equals

Equation 5

$$d_t \times 100 \times SD_{pretest}/\overline{X}_{pretest}$$

Issues in Estimating d_t

If an organization already has conducted a training program and possesses the necessary data, then it can compute d_t on the basis of an empirical study. Pre- and postmeasures of job performance in the trained and untrained groups should be collected systematically, with special care taken to prevent the ratings or other measures from being influenced by knowledge of who has or has not been trained. Those are the same kinds of problems that bedevil all HRD evaluation research, not just research on d_t. For more about those problems, see Cascio (1998), Goldstein (1993), or Cook and Campbell (1979).

When several studies are available, or when d_t must be estimated for a proposed HRD program, d_t is best estimated by the cumulative results of all available studies, using the methods of meta-analysis. Such studies are available in the literature (Morrow, Jarrett, & Rupinski 1997; Burke & Day 1986; Guzzo, Jette, & Katzell 1985). As studies accumulate, managers will be able to rely on cumulative knowledge of the expected effect sizes associated with proposed HRD programs. Such a "menu" of effect sizes for HRD programs will allow HR professionals to compute the expected utilities of proposed HRD programs before the decision is made to allocate resources to such programs.

Sometimes, the results of evaluation research are presented in terms of statistics such as *r*, *t*, or *F*. Each of these can be transformed into *d* by means of the following formulas (Schmidt et al. 1982). When two groups are compared (and therefore $df = 1$),

Equation 6

$$t = \sqrt{F}$$

The *t*-statistic then can be converted into the point-biserial correlation (r_{pb}) between the dichotomous variable (training versus no training) and rated performance by the following formula:

Equation 7

$$r_{pb} = t/\sqrt{t^2 + (N_t - 2)}$$

where N_t is the total number of persons in the study, the sum of the trained and untrained groups. To transform r_{pb} into d, use the following formula:

Equation 8

$$d = \frac{1}{\sqrt{pq}} \sqrt{\frac{N_t - 2}{N_t}} \times \frac{r}{\sqrt{1 - r^2}}$$

where p and q are the proportions of the total group in the trained and untrained groups, respectively. For example, suppose 100 employees are trained and 100 serve in a control group. Results of training are expressed as $F = 6.0$, using supervisors' ratings as criteria ($r_{yy} = 0.60$). Using equation 6,

$$t = 2.45$$

Using equation 7,

$$r_{pb} = 2.45/\sqrt{6.0 + (200 - 2)}$$

$$r_{pb} = 0.17$$

Using equation 8,

$$d = 1/0.5 \ (0.9950)(0.17/0.985)$$

$$d = 0.\ 34$$

Therefore, d_t is

$$0.34/\sqrt{0.60} = 0.44$$

Estimating *d* in the Raju-Burke-Normand Utility Model

Assuming that the criterion measure used to assess employee performance (for example, performance ratings), denoted as R, is related in a linear fashion to the economic value of employee performance, denoted as y, then the Raju-Burke-Normand (1990) model can be used to calculate the total marginal utility of a training program (ΔU) as follows:

Equation 9

$$\Delta U = A\sigma_{Rp}dN_t - CN_t$$

where A is the factor used to linearly transform measured performance (R) into a metric that represents the economic value of employee performance (y); σ_{Rp} is the pooled SD of employee performance in the trained and untrained groups; d is the standardized difference between the performance of the trained and untrained groups (that is, $d = \bar{X}_t - \bar{X}_u/\sigma_{Rp}$); N_t is the total number of employees trained; and C is the per-person cost of the training program.

In Raju et al.'s (1990) derivations, d represents the change in measured performance (R) in terms of σ_R. Thus both d and σ_R are parameters that represent the distribution of R. Because they represent the same construct measured with the same instrument, any modification of d should also be completed on σ_R. For example, if one corrects d for unreliability, one must also correct σ_R for unreliability. Similarly, as Morrow et al. (1997) have shown, when d is estimated using analysis of covariance (ANCOVA) or repeated-measures analysis of variance (ANOVA), σ_R must be corrected to reflect the same distribution as d. To modify equation 9 above for use with ANCOVA-based effect sizes, replace σ_{Rp} with the product of σ_{Rp} and $\sqrt{1 - r_{pre-post}}$, where r is the correlation between pre- and posttraining measures. Use the same product in the denominator of the ratio used to compute d.

To modify equation 9 above for use with effect sizes based on repeated-measures analysis of variance, replace σ_{Rp} with the product of σ_{Rp} and $\sqrt{2(1 - r_{pre-post})}$ (Morrow et al. 1997). Again, use the same product in the denominator of the ratio used to compute d.

For example, assume that the correlation between pre- and posttest scores is 0.70, that the pooled SD of the trained and untrained groups (σ_{Rp}) is 6, and that repeated-measures ANOVA is used to assess the effect of the training. Assume also that the difference between the means of the trained and untrained groups is 2.4, and therefore the uncorrected value of d is 0.40. Using the formula shown above, the corrected value of d is $2.4/6(0.77) = 0.516$. In equation 9, the product of $\sigma_{Rp}d$ (uncorrected) is $6(0.4) = 2.4$. The same product using σ_{Rp} and the corrected value of d is $6(0.516) = 3.096$. ΔU will therefore be overestimated unless σ_{Rp} is corrected to reflect the same distribution as d. The result using the corrected value of σ_{Rp} and the corrected value of d is $6(0.7746) = 4.64 \times 0.516 = 2.4$, and ΔU will not be overestimated. Note the difference between the uncorrected and corrected values of σ_{Rp}, 6 and 4.64, respectively.

Unless those modifications are made, the Raju-Burke-Normand model can yield large inaccuracies. Thus Morrow et al. (1997) reported that the uncorrected σ_R used to calculate the utility of a training program in hazardous energy control was 0.27, although the corrected σ_R was 0.20. Without the correction, the estimated utility of the program would have been \$339,274 (ROI = 445 percent), but with the correction it was \$232,739 (ROI = 306 percent).

Criterion-Related Issues in Assessing Effect Sizes

Alternative types of training may demonstrate different effect sizes because the criteria used in the evaluations differ in breadth of coverage of the total job. To be methodologically precise, evaluation should measure only training-related performance (Campbell 1988). Training programs in first-level supervisory skills may encompass a large portion of the supervisor's job, whereas training programs designed to affect sales of a specific product may influence only a few tasks of a sales representative's job. As Morrow et al. (1997) noted, effect sizes measured using specific criteria should be larger than those based on overall job performance criteria because of increased precision of measurement. If the content of training is very narrowly defined, a large effect size may be unimportant in a decision-making context, and differences in the breadth of training and criteria may prevent meaningful comparisons of effect sizes. In short, the value of a change in performance will vary according to the percentage of job-relevant tasks measured by the criteria.

To adjust the overall utility estimate for this inflation, Morrow et al. (1997) calculated the valuation base in the Raju-Burke-Normand model, *A*, as the product of the percentage of job skills affected by training and the average full cost of employment. Thus the utility estimate represents the value of performance only on specific job elements. From a practical perspective, that adjustment was suggested and deemed critical by the managers of the training function in the large U.S.-based multinational firm studied by Morrow et al. (1997).

Breakeven Analysis Applied to Proposed HRD Programs

Having determined an expected value of d_t, we can use the Brogden-Cronbach-Gleser model (equation 1 of this chapter) to compute a breakeven value of SD_y—the value at which benefits equal costs and $\Delta U =$ \$0.00. For example, suppose 300 employees are trained, the duration of the training effect is expected to be two years, $d_t = 0.55$, and the per-person cost of training is \$800. Setting $\Delta U =$ \$0.00 yields:

$$\$0.00 = 2(300)(0.55)(SD_y) - 300(\$800)$$
$$SD_y = \$727$$

Even if d_t is as low as 0.10, SD_y is still only $4,000—well below the observed values of SD_y (for example, $10,000 to $15,000) typically reported in the literature. To the extent that precise estimates of d_t and SD_y are unavailable, breakeven analysis still allows a decision maker to use the general utility model to assess the impact of a proposed HRD program. If estimates of d_t and SD_y are available, then utility can be computed, and the *expected* payoff from the program can be compared with the breakeven values for d_t or SD_y. The comparison of "expected-case" and "worst-case" scenarios thus provides more complete information for purposes of decision making.

Duration of the Effects of an HRD Program

A key parameter in equation 1 is *T,* the duration of the effect of a training or HRD program. In most cases, this parameter is difficult to estimate. One approach that has proven useful is the Delphi method, often used in long-range forecasting. With this method, a group of subject matter experts is asked to judge the duration of the training effect. Each expert responds individually and anonymously to a neutral third party (called an "intermediary"). The intermediary's task is to collect and summarize the experts' opinions and redistribute that information to the experts for another round of judgment. The cycle continues until the experts reach a consensus, often after three or four rounds of judgments.

In practice, we have little knowledge about the maintenance of training effects. To deal with that issue, Morrow et al. (1997) computed breakeven values in terms of time. Such values represent the amount of time that the training effect must be maintained in order for the training investment to be equal to the value of the gain resulting from training. Across 18 training programs (managerial, sales, and technical) they found great variability in results, with breakeven periods ranging from a few weeks to several years. In the extreme, two management training courses were never expected to break even or to yield a financial gain, because they produced slight decreases in performance (effect sizes were negative). The lesson to be learned from those results is that if we do not understand the maintenance of training, we do not really understand the effect of training on organizational performance.

Economic Considerations and Employee Flows Applied to Proposed or Ongoing HRD Programs

Boudreau (1983) pointed out that because training activities lead to diminishing returns over time (that is, training effects dissipate over time), a utility model incorporating employee flows should be used to assess the net payoff of the program over time. Beyond that, variable costs, taxes, and discounting must be considered in order to assess correctly the true impact of a proposed or ongoing HRD program. We covered those issues in chapter 10, so here we need consider only the summary model that incorporates all of those factors. Then we will present a worked example to demonstrate how the utility analysis proceeds. The model is shown in equation 10.

Equation 10

$$\Delta U = \sum_{k=1}^{F} \left[\sum_{t=1}^{k} (N_{at} - N_{st}) \right] \{[1/(1 + i)^k] \times (d_t)(SD_{sv})(1 + V)(1 - TAX)\}$$
$$- \sum_{k=1}^{F} \{C_k(1 - TAX)[1/(1 + i)^{k-1}]\}$$

For purposes of illustration let us adopt the d_t value we computed earlier, 0.44. Assume that 100 employees are trained each year for five years, and that for each cohort the training effect dissipates gradually at the rate of 25 percent annually. No employees separate during this period (and therefore $N_{st} = 0$). That information allows us to compute a weighted average d_t value for the trained group each year as a new cohort of trainees is added. Exhibit 11–5 shows the weighted average d_t values.

In order to use equation 10, assume that $SD_y = \$10,000$, variable costs ($V$) = –0.10, the tax rate is 45 percent, and the discount rate is 8 percent. Because costs ($\$500$ per person) are incurred in the same period that benefits are received, we will use k as the exponent in the cost term in equation 10. The total payoff of the HRD program is the sum of the utilities of each of the five periods:

$\Delta U_1 = 100(0.926)(0.44)(\$10,000)(0.90)(0.55) - \$50,000(0.55)(0.926)$
$\Delta U_1 = \$176,218$
$\Delta U_2 = 200(0.857)(0.385)(\$10,000)(0.90)(0.55) - \$50,000(0.55)(0.857)$
$\Delta U_2 = \$303,078$
$\Delta U_3 = 300(0.794)(0.33)(\$10,000)(0.90)(0.55) - \$50,000(0.55)(0.794)$
$\Delta U_3 = \$367,265$
$\Delta U_4 = 400(0.735)(0.275)(\$10,000)(0.90)(0.55) - \$50,000(0.55)(0.735)$

$\Delta U_4 = \$379,995$
$\Delta U_5 = 500(0.681)(0.22)(\$10,000)(0.90)(0.55) - \$50,000(0.55)(0.681)$
$\Delta U_5 = \$352,077$

The sum of those one-period utility estimates is \$1,578,633—the total expected payoff of the HRD program over the five-year period.

The utility analysis concepts discussed thus far were well illustrated in a study of the utility of a supervisory skills training program applied in a large commercial bank (Mathieu & Leonard 1987). The study incorporated the following features:

- Training costs were tabulated using cost-accounting techniques.
- The Schmidt-Hunter global estimation procedure was used to estimate SD_y.
- Pre- and posttraining ratings of the job performance of (nonrandomly assigned) experimental and control group subjects were compared in order to determine d_t.
- Utility analysis results that included adjustments for economic factors (variable costs, taxes, and discounting) were compared with utility results that did not include such adjustments.

EXHIBIT 11-5 *Diminishing Returns of an HRD Program over Five Years*

Year	N_k	Weighted Average
1	100	100(0.44)/100
2	200	100(0.44) + 100(0.44 − 25%)/200
3	300	100(0.44) + 100(0.44 − 25%) + 100(0.44 − 50%)/300
4	400	100(0.44) + 100(0.44 − 25%) + 100(0.44 − 50%) + 100(0.44 − 75%)/400
5	500	100(0.44) + 100(0.44 − 25%) + 100(0.44 − 50%) + 100(0.44 − 75%) + 100(0.44 − 100%)/500

Year	d_t
1	0.44
2	0.385
3	0.33
4	0.275
5	0.22

Notes: d_t = the true difference in job performance between the trained and untrained groups in standard deviation units; HRD = human resources development; N_k = number of employees receiving training who remain in the workforce.

- Breakeven analysis was used to assess the minimum change in SD_y required to recoup the costs invested in the program.
- The effect on estimated payoffs of employee flows, decay in training effects, and employee turnover were considered explicitly.

Results showed that the training program paid off handsomely over time, even under highly conservative assumptions. Training 65 bank managers in supervisory skills produced an estimated net payoff (after adjustment for the economic factors noted earlier) of $34,627 in year 1 ($53,306 in 1998 dollars), and $148,465 by year 5 ($228,555 in 1998 dollars). Not surprisingly, differences between adjusted and unadjusted estimates of payoff tended to become greater the further in time they were projected. In general, however, utility figures adjusted for economic factors were 60 percent to 80 percent smaller than were unadjusted figures.

When breakeven analysis was used, even assuming a 25 percent yearly reduction in the strength of the training effect, breakeven values of SD_y still were less than 50 percent of the values used in the utility analysis. Finally, in terms of employee flows, the economic impact of training additional groups was also considerable. For example, the estimate for the tenth year of the utility of training 225 employees in the first five years was more than $364,300 ($560,800 in 1998 dollars) even after adjustment for economic factors. Data like those are useful to decision makers, whether their focus is on the broad allocation of organizational resources across functional lines or on the choice of specific HR programs from a larger menu of possible programs.

Enhancing Managerial Acceptance of Utility Estimates

In the multinational firm that Morrow et al. (1997) studied, the total cost of the evaluation of 18 training programs was approximately $500,000. That number may seem large until you consider that, during the time of the study, the organization spent more than $240 million on training. The cost of training evaluation, therefore, was roughly 0.2 percent of the training budget during that time period. Given expenditures of such magnitude, some sort of accountability is prudent.

To enhance managerial acceptance, the researchers presented the utility model and the procedures that they proposed to use to the CEO as well as to senior strategic planning and HR managers *before* conducting their research. They presented the model and procedures as fallible but reasonable estimates. As Morrow et al. (1997) noted, management approval prior to actual application and consideration of utility results in a decision-making context is particularly important when you consider that nearly any field application of utility analysis will rely upon an effect size calculated with an imperfect quasi-experimental design.

One of the important lessons to be learned from the material presented in this chapter is that methods are available now for estimating the costs and benefits of HRD programs, whether proposed, ongoing, or completed. Instead of depending on the power of persuasion to convince decision makers of the value of HRD programs, HR professionals can use cost–benefit models to join with the other functional areas of business in justifying the allocation of scarce organizational resources on the basis of evidence, rather than on the basis of beliefs.

EXERCISES

1. Pilgrim Industries, a 2,000-employee firm with 400 managers, holds 40 days of off-site meetings per year. Outside consultants develop and conduct the meetings and, on the average, 20 managers attend each meeting. The typical meeting lasts two full days. Last year, total program development costs consumed $250,000. The average attendee's salary (plus benefits) was $50,000, and Pilgrim's capital investment in each attendee was, on the average, an additional $50,000. To deliver each two-day meeting for 20 people, with sleeping accommodations, food, telephone, and a cocktail reception, cost the company $6,000. In addition, transportation, secretarial services, meeting room, and audiovisual equipment rental totaled another $7,000. Determine the total per-day, per-person cost of one off-site meeting.

2. Soclear, Inc., a janitorial services firm, wants to conduct a controlled study of structured versus unstructured training for window washers of office buildings. How would you design the structured and unstructured training programs? In order to use the cost–benefit model shown in Exhibit 11–3, what criteria of job performance might you use? How will you collect and record data? How might you make cost comparisons?

3. Jane Burns, an HR analyst for Standard City, USA, knows that SD_y for firefighters in her city is $18,000. The fire department has asked the city to provide training in team building for 500 of its employees, at a

cost of $1,500 per employee. The effects of that organizational development effort are expected to last for two years. Using equation 1, compute the breakeven d_t value necessary for the city to recoup the costs of the program.

4. Suppose, in exercise 3, that you have just read a meta-analysis of team-building studies and you know that the cumulated estimate of d_t is 0.45. Compute an expected utility for the program, and compare it to the breakeven value you identified earlier. How might that affect the chances that the project will be funded?

5. With regard to exercise 4, suppose that the discount rate is 10 percent, and variable costs are –0.10. The city is not taxed. How do those factors affect the estimate of expected utility that you developed in exercise 4?

6. Your firm has just completed a training program in project management in which 50 individuals were trained and another 50 (who will be trained at a later time) served as a control group. To assess the effect of training, you use ANCOVA to compare the posttest scores of the trained and untrained groups, holding constant the effects of the pretest scores. Supervisors rate each individual's project management skills six months after the training. The mean score of the trained group is 18, the mean score of the untrained group is 15, and the pooled SD of the ratings in the trained and untrained groups is 4.5. The correlation between pre- and posttest scores is 0.65. Compute both corrected and uncorrected estimates of the effect size (d) of the training. What do you conclude? To use the corrected value of d to estimate the utility of the training using the Raju-Burke-Normand model, what must you do to σ_{Rp}?

REFERENCES

Arvey, R. D., Cole, D. A. (1989). Evaluating change due to training. In I. L. Goldstein (ed.), *Training and Development in Organizations* (pp. 89–117). San Francisco: Jossey-Bass.

Boudreau, J. W. (1983). Effects of employee flows on utility analysis of human resource productivity improvement programs. *Journal of Applied Psychology 68*, 396–406.

Burke, M. J., Day, R. R. (1986). A cumulative study of the effectiveness of managerial training. *Journal of Applied Psychology 71*, 232–246.

Campbell, J. P. (1988). Training design for performance improvement. In J. P. Campbell and R. J. Campbell (eds.), *Productivity in Organizations* (pp. 177–216). San Francisco: Jossey-Bass.

Cascio, W. F. (1998). *Applied Psychology in Personnel Management* (5th ed.). Englewood Cliffs, NJ: Prentice Hall.

Cook, T. D., Campbell, D. T. (1979). *Quasi-Experimentation: Design and Analysis Issues for Field Settings.* Chicago: Rand-McNally.

Cullen, J. G., Sawzin, S. A., Sisson, G. R., Swanson, R. A. (1976). Training: What's it worth? *Training and Development Journal 30*(8), 12–20.

Cullen, J. G., Sawzin, S. A., Sisson, G. R., Swanson, R. A. (1978). Cost effectiveness: A model for assessing the training investment. *Training and Development Journal 32*(1), 24–29.

Goldstein, I. L. (1993). *Training in Organizations* (3rd ed.). Pacific Grove, CA: Brooks/Cole.

Goldstein, I. L., Gilliam, P. (1990). Training system issues in the year 2000. *American Psychologist 45*, 134–143.

Guzzo, R. A., Jette, R. D., Katzell, R. A. (1985). The effects of psychologically based intervention programs on worker productivity: A meta-analysis. *Personnel Psychology 38*, 275–291.

Mabon, H. (1996). The cost of downsizing in an enterprise with job security. *Journal of Human Resource Costing and Accounting 1*(1), 35–62.

Mabon, H., Westling, G. (1996). Using utility analysis in downsizing decisions. *Journal of Human Resource Costing and Accounting 1*(2), 43–72.

Mathieu, J. E., Leonard, R. L. Jr. (1987). Applying utility concepts to a training program in supervisory skills: A time-based approach. *Academy of Management Journal 30*, 316–335.

McKeon, W. J. (1981). How to determine off-site meeting costs. *Training and Development Journal 35*(May), 116–122.

Mills, T. (1975). Human resources—Why the new concern? *Harvard Business Review* (Mar.-Apr.) 120–134.

Morrow, C. C., Jarrett, M. Q. Rupinski, M. T. (1997). An investigation of the effect and economic utility of corporate-wide training. *Personnel Psychology 50*, 91–119.

Noe, R. A. (1999). *Employee Training and Development.* Burr Ridge, IL: Irwin/McGraw-Hill.

Quinones, M. A., Ehrenstein, A. (eds.). (1997). *Training for a Rapidly Changing Workplace*. Washington, DC: American Psychological Association.

Raju, N. S., Burke, M. J., Normand, J. (1990). A new approach for utility analysis. *Journal of Applied Psychology 75*, 3–12.

Rothstein, H. R., Erwin, F. W., Schmidt, F. L., Owens, W. A., Sparks, C. P. (1990). Biographical data in employment selection: Can validities be made generalizable? *Journal of Applied Psychology 75*, 175–184.

Sackett, P. R. (1991). On interpreting measures of change due to training or other interventions: A comment on Cascio (1989, 1991). *Journal of Applied Psychology 76*, 590, 591.

Schmidt, F. L., Hunter, J. E., Pearlman, K. (1982). Assessing the economic impact of personnel programs on workforce productivity. *Personnel Psychology 35*, 333–347.

Thayer, P. W. (1997). A rapidly changing world: Some implications for training systems in the year 2001 and beyond. In M. A. Quinones and A. Ehrenstein (eds.), *Training for a Rapidly Changing Workplace* (pp. 15–30). Washington, D. C.: American Psychological Association.

ENDNOTE

1. Statistical power is the probability of detecting a significant effect, given that the effect is present.

C H A P T E R   1 2

Linking Effective Human Resources Management to Profits

The preceding 11 chapters have shared a common objective: to quantify in financial terms the outcomes associated with a set of common topics in human resource management. Traditionally, and more often, such outcomes have been expressed only in terms of behavior or performance. Topics presented in chapters 1 through 5 focused on reducing controllable costs. Topics presented in chapters 6 through 11 focused on improving productivity. Both reduction of costs and improvement of productivity enhance corporate profits—an important objective in almost all for-profit enterprises.

We need to integrate those approaches so that HR professionals can develop a financial reporting system for HR activities related most directly to the strategic thrust of the business or business unit that they serve. That was a major objective of the intellectual capital framework presented in chapter 1. As we noted there, a radar chart, called an "intellectual capital navigator," creates a coherent picture that integrates measures of human, structural, and customer capital. Its purpose is to focus management decisions and investments into areas that will have the greatest payoff for the firm. In this book we have emphasized the development of some measures of human capital. A key assumption is that any attempt to assess the outcomes associated with activities of the HR function must focus on outcomes that are regarded as most important to the various constituencies that the HR function serves. The objective of chapter 12 is to develop a broad set of guidelines for determining which outcomes to consider.

The chapter will begin by showing the relationship between effective HRM and profits; and by explaining why the assessment of HR activities must take into account specific types of outcomes (quantitative and qualitative), the management level at which those outcomes are most important, and the strategic nature of HRM activities. We will discuss strategic HRM in some detail, focusing on the role of HR professionals as strategic partners along with line managers. The chapter text will emphasize the important linkage between HR strategy and general business (competitive) strategy, and show how the HR function is linked closely to achieving the competitive strategic goals of the broader organization or organizational units.

The scope here will be limited to the topics addressed in this book, with no attempt made to identify the myriad potential measures of HR quality or quantity of HR services that are available. For an excellent treatment of those issues, see Tsui and Gomez-Mejia (1988).

THE CASE FOR HUMAN RESOURCES MANAGEMENT AS A PROFIT CONTRIBUTOR

The HR function derives power from its ability to help line managers solve business-related problems. Unfortunately, the perception in some companies is that the HR function is exclusively a cost center, that it makes no contribution to profits. To change that perception, HR professionals must be able to answer the question, How much more product can be sold or services delivered because of your efforts? Many HR contributions are not related directly to the bottom line, but HR activities are related to the purposes of the organization. Some possible responses to questions from senior management in six key areas (Sheley 1996) include:

- Here's what we did for you (for example, in recruiting), here's what it cost, and here's what you would have done without us and what it would have cost you.
- Here's how much money we saved you by changing insurers in our benefits package.
- Here's an idea that workers developed in a training program we lead. It's now working and saving you $50,000 per year.

- If you had not asked us to do this executive search, you would have had to hire an outside consultant at a cost of $30,000. We did it for $5,000.
- You used to have an unhappy person doing this job for $45,000 per year. As a result of our job redesign efforts, you now have a motivated person doing the same work for $25,000.
- In working with the union on a new contract, we found a way to reduce grievances by 30 percent and saved the company 6,429 hours per year in management time.

To be most useful, however, the responses should be tailored to address three key considerations: types of outcomes, level of analysis, and the focus of HR activities.

Types of Outcomes

Outcomes may be expressed in quantitative terms (as in the preceding responses) or in qualitative terms (such as indicators of overall morale, individual job satisfaction, or reactions to a training program). Alone, each type of outcome is incomplete because both quantitative and qualitative outcomes are important in describing the rich results of HR programs. Although we have emphasized quantitative outcomes, qualitative measures are no less useful or important.

Attitude surveys are good examples of qualitative research tools. To a great extent, the growing popularity of attitude surveys is the result of an idea stressed in many popular books on management: It is important to listen to employees. That idea has taken on added significance as more companies endure the organizational trauma of mergers and restructurings or attempt to adopt supportive organizational cultures.

As employee surveys become more common, the range of issues on which opinions are solicited is expanding considerably. At Wells Fargo & Co. in San Francisco, for example, employees have been asked about such things as the effectiveness of the bank's advertising, the quality of product innovation, and its responsibility to the community.

Surveys are most effective when they are aligned with competitive strategy—that is, when they tap issues that are important to strategy implementation at all levels and when managers commit at the outset to take action based on survey findings. Doing so helps to build bridges between survey feedback and existing change strategies such as total quality management, reengineering, or continuous improvement (Kraut 1996).

Level of Analysis

As Tsui and Gomez-Mejia (1988) noted, most attempts to evaluate the HR function have not distinguished HR activities performed at the corporate level from those performed at the management level or at the operating level. At the corporate level, HR decisions involve the design of policies that meet the organization's strategic challenges, such as business objectives, corporate values or culture, technology, structure, and responses to constraints posed by the external environment.

At the management level, key HR decisions involve systems or program designs that are consistent with policy guidelines and that will facilitate the cost-effective achievement of business goals. The objective at this level is management control, and it is accomplished by assessing the cost-effectiveness of HR programs.

At the operating level, managers implement HR policies and programs and make decisions that affect the attraction, retention, and motivation of employees. This level includes the hands-on HR practices of line managers (for example, in reducing absenteeism or controllable turnover) and the day-to-day services provided by the HR function (for example, recruiting, staffing, and training) that directly affect HR outcomes.

Focus of Human Resources Activities

Such activities may be tactical or strategic. Tactical decisions, which are short range in nature, may involve deploying staff for a temporary project, to conduct a recruitment program, or to conduct or respond to an investigation by an agency of the federal government. Because tactical issues demand attention from HR professionals in the short run, it is easy to avoid considering issues such as the long-term fit of HR activities and programs with the strategic objectives of the larger organization.

Unless HR professionals can look at both short- and long-term issues, they will not meet a fundamental challenge: to discard low-payoff activities while they focus on activities that will yield the highest payoffs. That kind of thinking is strategic and long-range in nature. It is known as *strategic human resource management,* and we will examine it more fully in the following sections.

STRATEGIC HUMAN RESOURCE MANAGEMENT

CEOs need HR executives who have a clear sense of strategic direction, know the services required by the business, and understand the initiatives it should be taking toward organizational change (Ulrich 1998). They need HR executives who can implement strategic HRM.

In practical terms, strategic HRM means getting everybody, from the top of the organization to the bottom, doing things to implement the business's strategy effectively. The idea is to use people most wisely with respect to the strategic needs of the organization. That doesn't just happen on its own. An integrative framework that systematically links HR activities with strategic business needs can help. Consider one such approach, the "Human Resources Strategic Blueprint" (Advisory Board Company 1995).

The goal of the approach is to develop a map and a timeline to ensure alignment between HR strategy and general business strategy. To make that happen, the imaginary Perez Corporation takes the following steps:

1. Representatives from HR and line managers from the business unit generate key business strategies for the coming year. To do so, they identify major external and internal factors that may affect the future of the business, together with future customer requirements. As a result, they develop a business unit annual plan that outlines

   • major driving forces in the business unit.
   • major business initiatives in the business unit.
   • primary directions.
   • major priorities for key executives of the business unit.

2. The HR manager at Perez assembles a cross-functional team (for example, a finance analyst, a staffing expert, a quality manager, and an organization development consultant, and an operations training manager) whose members will be instrumental in leading the business unit toward its productivity goals.

3. Beginning with the business needs identified in the business unit plan, the objective of the cross-functional team is to identify HR implications. For example, if the business objective is to increase production by 50 percent in six months, major implications for HR include all workers developing fully competent skill sets, additional staffing, and team development (that is, better communication among production teams and design teams).

4. With the problem diagnosed (at Perez, 80 percent of the manufacturing unit's managers have fewer than 18 months' tenure so are ill prepared to increase productivity by 50 percent in six months), the cross-functional team brainstorms possible options for solving the

problem. Those options include: a training program for new managers on how to produce during peak periods; on-the-job observations of managers to assess their weaknesses; a mandatory mentoring program for all novice managers; and the hiring of managers (either from internal or external sources) who have the requisite skills.

5. A designated team member returns to his or her unit to research the feasibility of each option, and then makes the case for the best option with the cross-functional team. (In this case, the best option is establishing the mentoring program because it can be developed quickly.)

6. HR presents the first draft of its blueprint to senior managers who either agree or disagree on substance with each element of the blueprint. Where there is disagreement on substance, senior managers return those items to the cross-functional team for reconsideration or reworking. Thus the blueprint emerges through multiple iterations with managers responsible for operations.

7. The critical element in the blueprint process is assigning to individuals responsibility for specific actions that have target completion dates (for example, in the areas of management development, employee development, staffing, and the drafting of new competency profiles for various grade levels of workers).

8. Every six months, the HR manager meets with the business-unit manager to consider two key questions: How important is the strategy we are pursuing? and How well are we executing that strategy? If business conditions have changed, HR needs to adjust or redirect its priorities and change its blueprint. If conditions have not changed, then management assesses the extent to which strategies being pursued are aligned properly with business-unit objectives and decides if HR's delivery of services is complete and timely. HR receives a grade for delivery.

9. To provide an incentive for superior performance, business-unit management at Perez (managers in marketing, operations, finance, product development, and manufacturing) rigorously assess HR's performance against its blueprint objectives. If HR meets its goals by year's end, all HR managers receive additional bonus compensation.

Managers who have used the strategic blueprint process emphasize that its single greatest benefit is this: *it forces HR managers to concentrate solely on critical, value-adding activities.* Such an approach is sorely needed, as an American Management (1995) survey of 1,500 HR managers found.

When asked how well HR strategy is linked to business results, 6 out of 10 respondents said it was either not effective or just somewhat effective. Only 3 percent characterized the linkage as "world class."

Earlier we identified strategic HRM as a process of getting everybody from the top of the organization to the bottom to do things to implement the strategy of the business effectively—to use people most wisely with respect to the organization's strategic needs. In the following sections, we'll describe some alternative competitive strategies and then link HR processes to each one. Let's begin by describing the concept of competitive strategy.

COMPETITIVE STRATEGY

The means that firms use to compete for business in the marketplace and to gain competitive advantage are known as *competitive strategies* (Porter 1985). Competitive strategies can differ in a number of ways, including the extent to which firms emphasize innovation, quality enhancement, cost reduction, or speed (Vinton 1992; Schuler & Jackson 1987). Although it might appear logical that the different types of strategies require different types of HR practices (Jackson & Schuler 1990), the research evidence on the issue is mixed (Becker & Gerhart 1996; Gerhart, Trevor, & Graham 1996). That has led some authors to recommend that firms adopt a set of "best practices" regardless of their competitive strategy (Pfeffer 1994). Other authors emphasize the need to focus on activities that are most crucial to implementing the competitive strategy chosen (Cappelli & Crocker-Hefter 1996). Those two perspectives are not necessarily mutually exclusive, however, because a firm's performance may be enhanced further when best practices are matched to the requirements inherent in a firm's competitive strategy (Youndt et al. 1996). The important lesson for managers is that *human resources represent a competitive advantage that can increase profits when managed wisely.*

Because different types of HR practices are important in different organizations or units of organizations, assessing the outcomes associated with HR activities should focus on those activities that are most crucial to implementing the competitive strategy the organization has chosen. Later, we will map the HR topics discussed in this book to alternative competitive strategies. To begin, we'll define each strategy.

Alternative Competitive Strategies

Innovation strategy is used to develop products or services that differ from those of competitors; its primary objective is to offer something new and different. Enhancing product or service quality is the major objective of the *quality-enhancement strategy,* and the objective of a *cost-reduction strategy* is to gain competitive advantage by being the lowest-cost producer of goods or provider of services. Finally, the objective of a time-based or *speed strategy* is to be the fastest innovator, producer, distributor, and responder to customer feedback. Innovation strategy emphasizes managing people so that they work *differently,* quality-enhancement strategy emphasizes managing people so that they work *smarter,* cost-reduction strategy emphasizes managing people so that they work *harder;* and speed strategy emphasizes managing people so they work more *efficiently* by changing the way that work is done.

Although it is convenient to think of those four competitive strategies as pure types applied to entire organizations, business units, or even functional specialties, reality is more complex. Various combinations of the strategies can be observed in practice.

Consider an initial statement of employee involvement strategy at the Ford Motor Company. According to Banas (1988), in October 1978 Philip Caldwell, then president of Ford, made the following statement at a meeting of the top executives of the company: "Our strategy for the years ahead will come to nothing unless we ask for greater participation of our workforce. Without motivated and concerned workers, we're not going to lower our costs as much as we need to—and we aren't going to get the product quality we need" (p. 391). Elements of cost-reduction as well as quality-enhancement strategies are evident in Caldwell's statement.

Employee Behaviors Appropriate to Each Competitive Strategy

Innovation Strategy

The implications of pursuing a competitive strategy of innovation for managing people may include selecting highly skilled individuals, giving employees more discretion, using minimal controls, making a greater investment in human resources, providing more resources for experimentation, allowing and even rewarding occasional failure, and appraising performance for its long-term implications. Successful innovative firms such as Sun Microsystems, Hewlett-Packard, 3M, Raytheon, and PepsiCo illustrate this strategy (Brown 1999; Schuler & Jackson 1987).

Because the innovation process depends heavily on individual expertise and creativity, employee turnover can have disastrous consequences (Kanter 1985). Also, firms pursuing an innovation strategy are more likely to emphasize long-term needs in their training programs for managers and to offer training to more employees throughout the organization (Jackson, Schuler, & Rivero 1989). Otherwise, turnover is likely to increase, as a recent survey revealed. Among employees who said their company offered poor training, 41 percent planned to leave within a year, versus only 12 percent of those who rated training opportunities as excellent. Likewise, 35 percent of employees who did not receive regular mentoring planned to look for another job within 12 months, versus just 16 percent of those with regular mentoring (Reingold 1999). The same survey found the cost of losing a typical worker to be $50,000. So a 1,000-worker company with poor training could lose as much as $14.5 million, and nonexistent mentoring could cost $9.5 million (not all dissatisfied employees will actually leave).

Desired role behaviors of employees suggest that any assessment of the HR function's contributions should focus attention primarily on the utility of selection and training programs and on reducing controllable turnover, especially among high performers who are not easy to replace. Because innovation strategy requires a long-term orientation that emphasizes the personal and professional development of employees, HR activities that involve work–life programs, employee assistance programs, or wellness programs could help achieve success. Supportive organizational cultures that underlie each of those approaches are critical components of retention efforts (Shellenbarger 1997).

Quality-Enhancement Strategy

The profile of behaviors appropriate for a quality-enhancement strategy includes relatively repetitive and predictable behaviors; a longer-term focus; a modest amount of cooperative, interdependent behavior; a high concern for quality with a modest concern for quantity of output; a high concern for how goods or services are made or delivered; low risk-taking activity; and commitment to the goals of the organization (Schuler & Jackson 1987).

Because quality enhancement typically involves greater employee commitment and fuller use of employees' abilities, fewer employees are needed to produce the same level of output. This phenomenon has been observed at such firms as L. L. Bean, Corning Glass, Honda, and Toyota (Taylor 1990).

It is well known that productivity gains resulting from improved selection or training can be expressed in various ways: in dollars, in increases in output, in decreases in hiring needs, or in savings in payroll costs (Cascio 1989). Because fewer workers may be needed after valid selection programs are implemented, the change in staffing requirements may be useful for assessing behavioral and performance outcomes associated with implementing a quality-enhancement strategy.

Another objective of this strategy is to minimize absenteeism, tardiness, and turnover because reliable and predictable behavior is important to its implementation. Cost savings associated with any HR programs designed to control those undesirable behaviors should therefore be documented carefully. Moreover, opportunities to participate in formal and informal training programs tend to promote employees' long-term commitment to the goals of the organization and their flexibility to change. Another way to signal concern for the long-term welfare of employees is to promote work–life programs, diversity programs, EAPs, and wellness programs actively.

Finally, commitment to the organization's goals can be assessed by measuring employee attitudes over multiple time periods. As we have seen, methods are also available to assess the financial consequences associated with improvements (or decrements) in their attitudes.

In summary, to link effective HR management to profits in the context of a quality-enhancement strategy, focus on assessing the utility of selection and training programs, on the financial gains associated with promoting positive changes in employees' attitudes and in their lifestyles, and on the cost savings associated with decreasing absenteeism and turnover.

Cost-Reduction Strategy

Given the highly competitive markets that firms confront everyday, cost control has become a mantra for organizations everywhere. Firms pursuing a cost-reduction strategy are characterized by tight fiscal and management controls, minimization of overhead, and pursuit of economies of scale. Their primary objective is to increase productivity by decreasing the unit cost of output per employee. Strategies for reducing costs include reducing the number of employees; reducing wage levels; using part-time workers, subcontractors, or automation; changing work rules; and permitting flexibility in job assignments (Schuler & Jackson 1987).

The profile of role behaviors in the context of a cost-reduction strategy includes relatively repetitive and predictable behaviors, a relatively short-term focus, primarily autonomous or individual activity, a modest concern for quality coupled with a high concern for quantity of output (goods or services), emphasis on results, low risk-taking, and stability In addition, there is minimal use of training and development.

Sometimes managers adopt cost-reduction strategies in rather desperate situations, as their firms struggle to survive (Richman 1993). More commonly, cost reduction is used in combination with other strategies to keep companies prosperous. As an example, Ford Motor Company assigns managers to "100-day" projects to attack costs or other problems. At Ford's Escort factory in Wayne, Michigan, for example, one group studied how to reduce the $585,000 the plant spent each year on Kevlar gloves to protect workers who handle sheet metal and glass. By figuring out how to have the $4.72-a-pair gloves washed so they could be worn more than once, the group saved 50 cents a car, or $115,000 a year (Simison 1999).

The profile of role behaviors for employees and managers under a cost-reduction strategy suggests that an assessment of the contributions of the HR function should emphasize the control of labor costs associated with dysfunctional turnover and unscheduled employee absenteeism, and consider implementing and assessing the outcomes of low-cost options associated with the control of health care costs and dependent care.

Speed Strategy

"The computer, the fax, and the microwave are not going to go away; they are going to get faster or be replaced by new technologies that do even more than they do and are faster yet. Demands by consumers for more choices, and faster, more comprehensive services . . . would seem to underline the need for speed in development, production, and delivery of products and services" (Vinton 1992, p. 14).

The first imperative under such a strategy is to hire highly skilled people who are committed to speed management and whose beliefs, attitudes, and values related to time are consistent with those the organization is seeking. Both workers and managers must embrace change, rather than resist it; company culture must support their efforts; and both work groups and cross-functional teams must share the same norms about time. A fluid, networked organizational structure, rather than the old "command, control, and compartmentalization" system, is most appropriate. Finally, all HR systems, including staffing, training, reward, and performance management, must support the speed-management philosophy.

As an example of speed strategy in action, consider Dell Computer's approach to business-to-business elctronic commerce. Dell applies its customer-obsessed direct-sales practices and enhances them using the World Wide Web to take care of annoying details. The company's main weapon is its Premier Page Program, which serves over 5,000 U.S. companies. When Dell wins a corporate customer with more than 400 employees, it will build that customer a Premier Page. The Page is little more than a set of smaller Web pages, often linked to the customer's intranet, which let approved employees go online to configure personal computers (PCs), pay for them, and track their delivery status. About $5 million of Dell PCs are ordered this way every day. Premier Pages provide access to instant technical support and Dell sales representatives. There is no more waiting on hold. The Pages reduce ordering errors, and they free Dell employees to do things only they can do—such as talking face-to-face with customers and selling merchandise. One corporate customer, Bayer Corporation, had the following to say about Dell's sales representative: "He solicits input. He knows the heartbeat of Bayer. He's there to solve our problems, not just get commissions" (Brown 1999, p. 114). That's speed strategy in action, but it's also innovation, quality enhancement, and cost control. People are essential ingredients of Dell's hybrid strategy, for they are the sources of innovation and renewal.

CONCLUSION

Exhibits 12–1 and 12–2 summarize the ideas discussed thus far. In presenting these exhibits, we add the following cautions:

- Treatment is limited to the topics discussed in this book. In practice, a broader mix of qualitative and quantitative measures should be used to assess the HR function's contribution to achieving strategic business goals.
- the range of competitive strategies (and HR strategies to support them) should not be limited to the four discussed here: innovation, quality enhancement, cost reduction, and speed. In practice, others will likely be found, along with hybrid versions of the four covered here. Nevertheless, careful mapping of HR strategies onto long-term business strategies will produce meaningful contributions from the HR function.

- The mapping of outcomes onto strategies, as shown in Exhibit 12–2, should be regarded only as a rough taxonomy. As research evidence accumulates, a more comprehensive classification scheme can be developed, and that remains an important challenge in HRM research.

EXHIBIT 12–1 *Primary and Secondary Objectives of Topics Examined in Chapters 2 through 11*

	Objectives	
Topic	Reduce Costs	Increase Productivity
Turnover (ch. 2)	1	2
Absenteeism (ch. 3)	1	2
HR mismanagement (ch. 4)	1	2
EAPs/wellness programs (ch. 5)	1	2
Attitudes (ch. 6)	2	1
Work–life programs (ch. 7)	2	1
Utility (selection) (chs. 8–10)	2	1
Utility (training) (ch. 11)	2	1

Notes: 1 = primary objective; 2 = secondary objective.

EXHIBIT 12–2 *Relationship Between Competitive Strategy and Measures of Outcomes That Are Most Appropriate Under Each Strategy*

	Measures of Outcomes	
Competitive Strategy[a]	Primary	Secondary
Innovation	Increase productivity	Reduce costs
Quality enhancement	Increase productivity	Reduce costs
Cost reduction	Reduce costs	Increase productivity
Speed	Increase productivity	Reduce costs

[a] The mix of HR strategies designed to increase productivity and to decrease costs is likely to be somewhat different under innovation, quality-enhancement, and speed strategies (see the text for a fuller discussion).

EXERCISES

1. As senior vice-president for human resources, you have received the following memo from top management: "Please join the Top Executive Group for three days of strategic planning beginning one month

from today. As you know, the major item under consideration is our possible involvement in developing the Eastern European market for our products." In order to assume the role of "strategic partner," what specific issues will you raise? Further, assuming that the company does decide to exploit that new market, outline a set of strategic HR initiatives that will guide your activities as the company's strategy unfolds over time.

2. Your company, E-Mart, is a "big-box" retailer that sells a wide variety of items to consumers electronically. E-Mart has embarked on an aggressive strategy of innovation across all of its product and service lines. What specific HR activities will you recommend that the company adopt over short- as well as long-range horizons?

3. Describe the HR implications of electronic shopping malls. How might Internet-based commerce affect the competitive strategies of innovation, quality enhancement, cost control, and speed?

4. You work for an airline that is caught up in the consolidation of that industry. Unless you can control costs in the short run, the airline's long-run viability may be in jeopardy. What specific HR strategies would you recommend in order to achieve that objective?

REFERENCES

Advisory Board Company. (1995). Human resources strategic blueprint. In *Vision of the Future: Role of Human Resources in the New Corporate Headquarters* (pp. 193–210). Washington, DC: Author.

American Management Association. (1995). *Business Goals and Strategies: The Human Resources Perspective.* New York: Author.

Banas, P. A. (1988). Employee involvement: A sustained labor/management initiative at the Ford Motor Company. In J. P. Campbell and R. J. Campbell (eds.), *Productivity in Organizations* (pp. 388–416). San Francisco: Jossey-Bass.

Becker, B., Gerhart, B. (1996). The impact of human resource management on organizational performance: Progress and prospects. *Academy of Management Journal 39,* 779–801.

Brown, E. (1999). Nine ways to win on the Web. *Fortune* (May 24), pp. 112–125.

Cappelli, P., Crocker-Hefter, A. (1996). Distinctive human resources are firms' core competencies. *Organizational Dynamics 24*(3), 7–22.

Cascio, W. F. (1989). Using utility analysis to assess training outcomes. In I. L. Goldstein (ed.), *Training and Development in Organizations* (pp. 63–88). San Francisco: Jossey-Bass.

Gerhart, B., Trevor, C., Graham, M. (1996). New directions in employee compensation research. In G. R. Ferris (ed.), *Research in Personnel and Human Resources Management* (pp. 143–203). Greenwich, CT: JAI Press.

Jackson, S. E., Schuler, R. S. (1990). Human resource planning. *American Psychologist 45*, 223–239.

Jackson, S. E., Schuler, R. S., Rivero, J. C. (1989). Organizational characteristics as predictors of personnel practices. *Personnel Psychology 42*, 727–736.

Kanter, R. M. (1985). Supporting innovation and venture development in established companies. *Journal of Business Venturing 1* (Winter), 47–60.

Kraut, A. I. (1996). *Organizational Surveys.* San Francisco: Jossey-Bass.

Pfeffer, J. (1994). *Competitive Advantage Through People.* Boston: Harvard Business School Press.

Porter, M. E. (1985). *Competitive Advantage.* New York: Free Press.

Reingold, J. (1999). Why your workers might jump ship. *Business Week* (Mar. 1), 8.

Richman, L. S. (1993). When will the layoffs end? *Fortune* (Sept. 20), 54–56.

Schuler, R. S., Jackson, S. E. (1987). Linking competitive strategies with human resource management practices. *Academy of Management Executive 1*(3), 207–219.

Sheley, E. (1996). Share your worth: Talking numbers with the CEO. *HRMagazine 41*(6), 86–95.

Shellenbarger, S. (1997). For keeping employees, money isn't everything. *San Francisco Chronicle* (Dec. 21), J1.

Simison, R. L. (1999). Ford rolls out new model of corporate culture. *The Wall Street Journal* (Jan. 13), B1, B4.

Taylor, A. III. (1990). Why Toyota keeps getting better and better and better. *Fortune* (Nov. 19), 66–79.

Tsui, A. S., & Gomez-Mejia, L. R. (1988). Evaluating human resource effectiveness. In L. Dyer and G. W. Holder (eds.), *Human Resource*

Management: Evolving Roles and Responsibilities (pp. 1-187–1-227). Washington, DC: Bureau of National Affairs.

Ulrich, D. (1998). A new mandate for human resources. *Harvard Business Review* (Jan.-Feb.), 124–134.

Vinton, D. E. (1992). A new look at time, speed, and the manager. *Academy of Management Executive* 6(4), 7–16.

Youndt, M. A., Snell, S. A., Dean, J. W. Jr., Lepak, D. P. (1996). Human resource management, manufacturing strategy, and firm performance. *Academy of Management Journal* 39(4), 836–866.

A P P E N D I X   A

The Taylor-Russell Tables

These are tables of the proportion of employees who will be satisfactory among those selected (success ratio) for given values of the proportion of present employees considered satisfactory (base rate), the selection ratio, and *r*.

Proportion of Employees Considered Satisfactory = 0.05

	Selection Ratio										
r	0.05	0.10	0.20	0.30	0.40	0.50	0.60	0.70	0.80	0.90	0.95
0.00	0.05	0.05	0.05	0.05	0.05	0.05	0.05	0.05	0.05	0.05	0.05
0.05	0.06	0.06	0.06	0.06	0.06	0.05	0.05	0.05	0.05	0.05	0.05
0.10	0.07	0.07	0.07	0.06	0.06	0.06	0.06	0.05	0.05	0.05	0.05
0.15	0.09	0.08	0.07	0.07	0.07	0.06	0.06	0.06	0.05	0.05	0.05
0.20	0.11	0.09	0.08	0.08	0.07	0.07	0.06	0.06	0.06	0.05	0.05
0.25	0.12	0.11	0.09	0.08	0.08	0.07	0.07	0.06	0.06	0.05	0.05
0.30	0.14	0.12	0.10	0.09	0.08	0.07	0.07	0.06	0.06	0.05	0.05
0.35	0.17	0.14	0.11	0.10	0.09	0.08	0.07	0.06	0.06	0.05	0.05
0.40	0.19	0.16	0.12	0.10	0.09	0.08	0.07	0.07	0.06	0.05	0.05
0.45	0.22	0.17	0.13	0.11	0.10	0.08	0.08	0.07	0.06	0.06	0.05
0.50	0.24	0.19	0.15	0.12	0.10	0.09	0.08	0.07	0.06	0.06	0.05
0.55	0.28	0.22	0.16	0.13	0.11	0.09	0.08	0.07	0.06	0.06	0.05
0.60	0.31	0.24	0.17	0.13	0.11	0.09	0.08	0.07	0.06	0.06	0.05
0.65	0.35	0.26	0.18	0.14	0.11	0.10	0.08	0.07	0.06	0.06	0.05

Source: Taylor, H. C., Russell, J. T. (1939). The relationship of validity coefficients to the practical effectiveness of tests in selection: Discussion and tables. *Journal of Applied Psychology 23*, 565–578.

Proportion of Employees Considered Satisfactory = 0.05 (continued)

r	0.05	0.10	0.20	0.30	0.40	0.50	0.60	0.70	0.80	0.90	0.95
						Selection Ratio					
0.70	0.39	0.29	0.20	0.15	0.12	0.10	0.08	0.07	0.06	0.06	0.05
0.75	0.44	0.32	0.21	0.15	0.12	0.10	0.08	0.07	0.06	0.06	0.05
0.80	0.50	0.35	0.22	0.16	0.12	0.10	0.08	0.07	0.06	0.06	0.05
0.85	0.56	0.39	0.23	0.16	0.12	0.10	0.08	0.07	0.06	0.06	0.05
0.90	0.64	0.43	0.24	0.17	0.13	0.10	0.08	0.07	0.06	0.06	0.05
0.95	0.73	0.47	0.25	0.17	0.13	0.10	0.08	0.07	0.06	0.06	0.05
1.00	1.00	0.50	0.25	0.17	0.13	0.10	0.08	0.07	0.06	0.06	0.05

Proportion of Employees Considered Satisfactory = 0.10

r	0.05	0.10	0.20	0.30	0.40	0.50	0.60	0.70	0.80	0.90	0.95
						Selection Ratio					
0.00	0.10	0.10	0.10	0.10	0.10	0.10	0.10	0.10	0.10	0.10	0.10
0.05	0.12	0.12	0.11	0.11	0.11	0.11	0.11	0.10	0.10	0.10	0.10
0.10	0.14	0.13	0.13	0.12	0.12	0.11	0.11	0.11	0.11	0.10	0.10
0.15	0.16	0.15	0.14	0.13	0.13	0.12	0.12	0.11	0.11	0.10	0.10
0.20	0.19	0.17	0.15	0.14	0.14	0.13	0.12	0.12	0.11	0.11	0.10
0.25	0.22	0.19	0.17	0.16	0.14	0.13	0.13	0.12	0.11	0.11	0.10
0.30	0.25	0.22	0.19	0.17	0.15	0.14	0.13	0.12	0.12	0.11	0.10
0.35	0.28	0.24	0.20	0.18	0.16	0.15	0.14	0.13	0.12	0.11	0.10
0.40	0.31	0.27	0.22	0.19	0.17	0.16	0.14	0.13	0.12	0.11	0.10
0.45	0.35	0.29	0.24	0.20	0.18	0.16	0.15	0.13	0.12	0.11	0.10
0.50	0.39	0.32	0.26	0.22	0.19	0.17	0.15	0.13	0.12	0.11	0.11
0.55	0.43	0.36	0.28	0.23	0.20	0.17	0.15	0.14	0.12	0.11	0.11
0.60	0.48	0.39	0.30	0.25	0.21	0.18	0.16	0.14	0.12	0.11	0.11
0.65	0.53	0.43	0.32	0.26	0.22	0.18	0.16	0.14	0.12	0.11	0.11
0.70	0.58	0.47	0.35	0.27	0.22	0.19	0.16	0.14	0.12	0.11	0.11
0.75	0.64	0.51	0.37	0.29	0.23	0.19	0.16	0.14	0.12	0.11	0.11
0.80	0.71	0.56	0.40	0.30	0.24	0.20	0.17	0.14	0.12	0.11	0.11
0.85	0.78	0.62	0.43	0.31	0.25	0.20	0.17	0.14	0.12	0.11	0.11
0.90	0.86	0.69	0.46	0.33	0.25	0.20	0.17	0.14	0.12	0.11	0.11
0.95	0.95	0.78	0.49	0.33	0.25	0.20	0.17	0.14	0.12	0.11	0.11
1.00	1.00	1.00	0.50	0.33	0.25	0.20	0.17	0.14	0.13	0.11	0.11

Proportion of Employees Considered Satisfactory = 0.20

r	0.05	0.10	0.20	0.30	0.40	0.50	0.60	0.70	0.80	0.90	0.95
0.00	0.20	0.20	0.20	0.20	0.20	0.20	0.20	0.20	0.20	0.20	0.20
0.05	0.23	0.23	0.22	0.22	0.21	0.21	0.21	0.21	0.20	0.20	0.20
0.10	0.26	0.25	0.24	0.23	0.23	0.22	0.22	0.21	0.21	0.21	0.20
0.15	0.30	0.28	0.26	0.25	0.24	0.23	0.23	0.22	0.21	0.21	0.20
0.20	0.33	0.31	0.28	0.27	0.26	0.25	0.24	0.23	0.22	0.21	0.21
0.25	0.37	0.34	0.31	0.29	0.27	0.26	0.24	0.23	0.22	0.21	0.21
0.30	0.41	0.37	0.33	0.30	0.28	0.27	0.25	0.24	0.23	0.21	0.21
0.35	0.45	0.41	0.36	0.32	0.30	0.28	0.26	0.24	0.23	0.22	0.21
0.40	0.49	0.44	0.38	0.34	0.31	0.29	0.27	0.25	0.23	0.22	0.21
0.45	0.54	0.48	0.41	0.36	0.33	0.30	0.28	0.26	0.24	0.22	0.21
0.50	0.59	0.52	0.44	0.38	0.35	0.31	0.29	0.26	0.24	0.22	0.21
0.55	0.63	0.56	0.47	0.41	0.36	0.32	0.29	0.27	0.24	0.22	0.21
0.60	0.68	0.60	0.50	0.43	0.38	0.34	0.30	0.27	0.24	0.22	0.21
0.65	0.73	0.64	0.53	0.45	0.39	0.35	0.31	0.27	0.25	0.22	0.21
0.70	0.79	0.69	0.56	0.48	0.41	0.36	0.31	0.28	0.25	0.22	0.21
0.75	0.84	0.74	0.60	0.50	0.43	0.37	0.32	0.28	0.25	0.22	0.21
0.80	0.89	0.79	0.64	0.53	0.45	0.38	0.33	0.28	0.25	0.22	0.21
0.85	0.94	0.85	0.69	0.56	0.47	0.39	0.33	0.28	0.25	0.22	0.21
0.90	0.98	0.91	0.75	0.60	0.48	0.40	0.33	0.29	0.25	0.22	0.21
0.95	1.00	0.97	0.82	0.64	0.50	0.40	0.33	0.29	0.25	0.22	0.21
1.00	1.00	1.00	1.00	0.67	0.50	0.40	0.33	0.29	0.25	0.22	0.21

Proportion of Employees Considered Satisfactory = 0.30

r	0.05	0.10	0.20	0.30	0.40	0.50	0.60	0.70	0.80	0.90	0.95
0.00	0.30	0.30	0.30	0.30	0.30	0.30	0.30	0.30	0.30	0.30	0.30
0.05	0.34	0.33	0.33	0.32	0.32	0.31	0.31	0.31	0.31	0.30	0.30
0.10	0.38	0.36	0.35	0.34	0.33	0.33	0.32	0.32	0.31	0.31	0.30
0.15	0.42	0.40	0.38	0.36	0.35	0.34	0.33	0.33	0.32	0.31	0.31
0.20	0.46	0.43	0.40	0.38	0.37	0.36	0.34	0.33	0.32	0.31	0.31
0.25	0.50	0.47	0.43	0.41	0.39	0.37	0.36	0.34	0.33	0.32	0.31
0.30	0.54	0.50	0.46	0.43	0.40	0.38	0.37	0.35	0.33	0.32	0.31
0.35	0.58	0.54	0.49	0.45	0.42	0.40	0.38	0.36	0.34	0.32	0.31
0.40	0.63	0.58	0.51	0.47	0.44	0.41	0.39	0.37	0.34	0.32	0.31
0.45	0.67	0.61	0.55	0.50	0.46	0.43	0.40	0.37	0.35	0.32	0.31
0.50	0.72	0.65	0.58	0.52	0.48	0.44	0.41	0.38	0.35	0.33	0.31
0.55	0.76	0.69	0.61	0.55	0.50	0.46	0.42	0.39	0.36	0.33	0.31

Proportion of Employees Considered Satisfactory = 0.30 (continued)

					Selection Ratio						
r	0.05	0.10	0.20	0.30	0.40	0.50	0.60	0.70	0.80	0.90	0.95
0.60	0.81	0.74	0.64	0.58	0.52	0.47	0.43	0.40	0.36	0.33	0.31
0.65	0.85	0.78	0.68	0.60	0.54	0.49	0.44	0.40	0.37	0.33	0.32
0.70	0.89	0.82	0.72	0.63	0.57	0.51	0.46	0.41	0.37	0.33	0.32
0.75	0.93	0.86	0.76	0.67	0.59	0.52	0.47	0.42	0.37	0.33	0.32
0.80	0.96	0.90	0.80	0.70	0.62	0.54	0.48	0.42	0.37	0.33	0.32
0.85	0.99	0.94	0.85	0.74	0.65	0.56	0.49	0.43	0.37	0.33	0.32
0.90	1.00	0.98	0.90	0.79	0.68	0.58	0.49	0.43	0.37	0.33	0.32
0.95	1.00	1.00	0.96	0.85	0.72	0.60	0.50	0.43	0.37	0.33	0.32
1.00	1.00	1.00	1.00	1.00	0.75	0.60	0.50	0.43	0.38	0.33	0.32

Proportion of Employees Considered Satisfactory = 0.40

					Selection Ratio						
r	0.05	0.10	0.20	0.30	0.40	0.50	0.60	0.70	0.80	0.90	0.95
0.00	0.40	0.40	0.40	0.40	0.40	0.40	0.40	0.40	0.40	0.40	0.40
0.05	0.44	0.43	0.43	0.42	0.42	0.42	0.41	0.41	0.41	0.40	0.40
0.10	0.48	0.47	0.46	0.45	0.44	0.43	0.42	0.42	0.41	0.41	0.40
0.15	0.52	0.50	0.48	0.47	0.46	0.45	0.44	0.43	0.42	0.41	0.41
0.20	0.57	0.54	0.51	0.49	0.48	0.46	0.45	0.44	0.43	0.41	0.41
0.25	0.61	0.58	0.54	0.51	0.49	0.48	0.46	0.45	0.43	0.42	0.41
0.30	0.65	0.61	0.57	0.54	0.51	0.49	0.47	0.46	0.44	0.42	0.41
0.35	0.69	0.65	0.60	0.56	0.53	0.51	0.49	0.47	0.45	0.42	0.41
0.40	0.73	0.69	0.63	0.59	0.56	0.53	0.50	0.48	0.45	0.43	0.41
0.45	0.77	0.72	0.66	0.61	0.58	0.54	0.51	0.49	0.46	0.43	0.42
0.50	0.81	0.76	0.69	0.64	0.60	0.56	0.53	0.49	0.46	0.43	0.42
0.55	0.85	0.79	0.72	0.67	0.62	0.58	0.54	0.50	0.47	0.44	0.42
0.60	0.89	0.83	0.75	0.69	0.64	0.60	0.55	0.51	0.48	0.44	0.42
0.65	0.92	0.87	0.79	0.72	0.67	0.62	0.57	0.52	0.48	0.44	0.42
0.70	0.95	0.90	0.82	0.76	0.69	0.64	0.58	0.53	0.49	0.44	0.42
0.75	0.97	0.93	0.86	0.79	0.72	0.66	0.60	0.54	0.49	0.44	0.42
0.80	0.99	0.96	0.89	0.82	0.75	0.68	0.61	0.55	0.49	0.44	0.42
0.85	1.00	0.98	0.93	0.86	0.79	0.71	0.63	0.56	0.50	0.44	0.42
0.90	1.00	1.00	0.97	0.91	0.82	0.74	0.65	0.57	0.50	0.44	0.42
0.95	1.00	1.00	0.99	0.96	0.87	0.77	0.66	0.57	0.50	0.44	0.42
1.00	1.00	1.00	1.00	1.00	1.00	0.80	0.67	0.57	0.50	0.44	0.42

Proportion of Employees Considered Satisfactory = 0.50

						Selection Ratio					
r	*0.05*	*0.10*	*0.20*	*0.30*	*0.40*	*0.50*	*0.60*	*0.70*	*0.80*	*0.90*	*0.95*
0.00	0.50	0.50	0.50	0.50	0.50	0.50	0.50	0.50	0.50	0.50	0.50
0.05	0.54	0.54	0.53	0.52	0.52	0.52	0.51	0.51	0.51	0.50	0.50
0.10	0.58	0.57	0.56	0.55	0.54	0.53	0.53	0.52	0.51	0.51	0.50
0.15	0.63	0.61	0.58	0.57	0.56	0.55	0.54	0.53	0.52	0.51	0.51
0.20	0.67	0.64	0.61	0.59	0.58	0.56	0.55	0.54	0.53	0.52	0.51
0.25	0.70	0.67	0.64	0.62	0.60	0.58	0.56	0.55	0.54	0.52	0.51
0.30	0.74	0.71	0.67	0.64	0.62	0.60	0.58	0.56	0.54	0.52	0.51
0.35	0.78	0.74	0.70	0.66	0.64	0.61	0.59	0.57	0.55	0.53	0.51
0.40	0.82	0.78	0.73	0.69	0.66	0.63	0.61	0.58	0.56	0.53	0.52
0.45	0.85	0.81	0.75	0.71	0.68	0.65	0.62	0.59	0.56	0.53	0.52
0.50	0.88	0.84	0.78	0.74	0.70	0.67	0.63	0.60	0.57	0.54	0.52
0.55	0.91	0.87	0.81	0.76	0.72	0.69	0.65	0.61	0.58	0.54	0.52
0.60	0.94	0.90	0.84	0.79	0.75	0.70	0.66	0.62	0.59	0.54	0.52
0.65	0.96	0.92	0.87	0.82	0.77	0.73	0.68	0.64	0.59	0.55	0.52
0.70	0.98	0.95	0.90	0.85	0.80	0.75	0.70	0.65	0.60	0.55	0.53
0.75	0.99	0.97	0.92	0.87	0.82	0.77	0.72	0.66	0.61	0.55	0.53
0.80	1.00	0.99	0.95	0.90	0.85	0.80	0.73	0.67	0.61	0.55	0.53
0.85	1.00	0.99	0.97	0.94	0.88	0.82	0.76	0.69	0.62	0.55	0.53
0.90	1.00	1.00	0.99	0.97	0.92	0.86	0.78	0.70	0.62	0.56	0.53
0.95	1.00	1.00	1.00	0.99	0.96	0.90	0.81	0.71	0.63	0.56	0.53
1.00	1.00	1.00	1.00	1.00	1.00	1.00	0.83	0.71	0.63	0.56	0.53

Proportion of Employees Considered Satisfactory = 0.60

						Selection Ratio					
r	*0.05*	*0.10*	*0.20*	*0.30*	*0.40*	*0.50*	*0.60*	*0.70*	*0.80*	*0.90*	*0.95*
0.00	0.60	0.60	0.60	0.60	0.60	0.60	0.60	0.60	0.60	0.60	0.60
0.05	0.64	0.63	0.63	0.62	0.62	0.62	0.61	0.61	0.61	0.60	0.60
0.10	0.68	0.67	0.65	0.64	0.64	0.63	0.63	0.62	0.61	0.61	0.60
0.15	0.71	0.70	0.68	0.67	0.66	0.65	0.64	0.63	0.62	0.61	0.61
0.20	0.75	0.73	0.71	0.69	0.67	0.66	0.65	0.64	0.63	0.62	0.61
0.25	0.78	0.76	0.73	0.71	0.69	0.68	0.66	0.65	0.63	0.62	0.61
0.30	0.82	0.79	0.76	0.73	0.71	0.69	0.68	0.66	0.64	0.62	0.61
0.35	0.85	0.82	0.78	0.75	0.73	0.71	0.69	0.67	0.65	0.63	0.62
0.40	0.88	0.85	0.81	0.78	0.75	0.73	0.70	0.68	0.66	0.63	0.62
0.45	0.90	0.87	0.83	0.80	0.77	0.74	0.72	0.69	0.66	0.64	0.62
0.50	0.93	0.90	0.86	0.82	0.79	0.76	0.73	0.70	0.67	0.64	0.62
0.55	0.95	0.92	0.88	0.84	0.81	0.78	0.75	0.71	0.68	0.64	0.62

Proportion of Employees Considered Satisfactory = 0.60 (continued)

	Selection Ratio										
r	0.05	0.10	0.20	0.30	0.40	0.50	0.60	0.70	0.80	0.90	0.95
0.60	0.96	0.94	0.90	0.87	0.83	0.80	0.76	0.73	0.69	0.65	0.63
0.65	0.98	0.96	0.92	0.89	0.85	0.82	0.78	0.74	0.70	0.65	0.63
0.70	0.99	0.97	0.94	0.91	0.87	0.84	0.80	0.75	0.71	0.66	0.63
0.75	0.99	0.99	0.96	0.93	0.90	0.86	0.81	0.77	0.71	0.66	0.63
0.80	1.00	0.99	0.98	0.95	0.92	0.88	0.83	0.78	0.72	0.66	0.63
0.85	1.00	1.00	0.99	0.97	0.95	0.91	0.86	0.80	0.73	0.66	0.63
0.90	1.00	1.00	1.00	0.99	0.97	0.94	0.88	0.82	0.74	0.67	0.63
0.95	1.00	1.00	1.00	1.00	0.99	0.97	0.92	0.84	0.75	0.67	0.63
1.00	1.00	1.00	1.00	1.00	1.00	1.00	1.00	0.86	0.75	0.67	0.63

Proportion of Employees Considered Satisfactory = 0.70

	Selection Ratio										
r	0.05	0.10	0.20	0.30	0.40	0.50	0.60	0.70	0.80	0.90	0.95
0.00	0.70	0.70	0.70	0.70	0.70	0.70	0.70	0.70	0.70	0.70	0.70
0.05	0.73	0.73	0.72	0.72	0.72	0.71	0.71	0.71	0.71	0.70	0.70
0.10	0.77	0.76	0.75	0.74	0.73	0.73	0.72	0.72	0.71	0.71	0.70
0.15	0.80	0.79	0.77	0.76	0.75	0.74	0.73	0.73	0.72	0.71	0.71
0.20	0.83	0.81	0.79	0.78	0.77	0.76	0.75	0.74	0.73	0.71	0.71
0.25	0.86	0.84	0.81	0.80	0.78	0.77	0.76	0.75	0.73	0.72	0.71
0.30	0.88	0.86	0.84	0.82	0.80	0.78	0.77	0.75	0.74	0.72	0.71
0.35	0.91	0.89	0.86	0.83	0.82	0.80	0.78	0.76	0.75	0.73	0.71
0.40	0.93	0.91	0.88	0.85	0.83	0.81	0.79	0.77	0.75	0.73	0.72
0.45	0.94	0.93	0.90	0.87	0.85	0.83	0.81	0.78	0.76	0.73	0.72
0.50	0.96	0.94	0.91	0.89	0.87	0.84	0.82	0.80	0.77	0.74	0.72
0.55	0.97	0.96	0.93	0.91	0.88	0.86	0.83	0.81	0.78	0.74	0.72
0.60	0.98	0.97	0.95	0.92	0.90	0.87	0.85	0.82	0.79	0.75	0.73
0.65	0.99	0.98	0.96	0.94	0.92	0.89	0.86	0.83	0.80	0.75	0.73
0.70	1.00	0.99	0.97	0.96	0.93	0.91	0.88	0.84	0.80	0.76	0.73
0.75	1.00	1.00	0.98	0.97	0.95	0.92	0.89	0.86	0.81	0.76	0.73
0.80	1.00	1.00	0.99	0.98	0.97	0.94	0.91	0.87	0.82	0.77	0.73
0.85	1.00	1.00	1.00	0.99	0.98	0.96	0.93	0.89	0.84	0.77	0.74
0.90	1.00	1.00	1.00	1.00	0.99	0.98	0.95	0.91	0.85	0.78	0.74
0.95	1.00	1.00	1.00	1.00	1.00	0.99	0.98	0.94	0.86	0.78	0.74
1.00	1.00	1.00	1.00	1.00	1.00	1.00	1.00	1.00	0.88	0.78	0.74

Proportion of Employees Considered Satisfactory = 0.80

| | | | | | Selection Ratio | | | | | | |
r	0.05	0.10	0.20	0.30	0.40	0.50	0.60	0.70	0.80	0.90	0.95
0.00	0.80	0.80	0.80	0.80	0.80	0.80	0.80	0.80	0.80	0.80	0.80
0.05	0.83	0.82	0.82	0.82	0.81	0.81	0.81	0.81	0.81	0.80	0.80
0.10	0.85	0.85	0.84	0.83	0.83	0.82	0.82	0.81	0.81	0.81	0.80
0.15	0.88	0.87	0.86	0.85	0.84	0.83	0.83	0.82	0.82	0.81	0.81
0.20	0.90	0.89	0.87	0.86	0.85	0.84	0.84	0.83	0.82	0.81	0.81
0.25	0.92	0.91	0.89	0.88	0.87	0.86	0.85	0.84	0.83	0.82	0.81
0.30	0.94	0.92	0.90	0.89	0.88	0.87	0.86	0.84	0.83	0.82	0.81
0.35	0.95	0.94	0.92	0.90	0.89	0.89	0.87	0.85	0.84	0.82	0.81
0.40	0.96	0.95	0.93	0.92	0.90	0.89	0.88	0.86	0.85	0.83	0.82
0.45	0.97	0.96	0.95	0.93	0.92	0.90	0.89	0.87	0.85	0.83	0.82
0.50	0.98	0.97	0.96	0.94	0.93	0.91	0.90	0.88	0.86	0.84	0.82
0.55	0.99	0.98	0.97	0.95	0.94	0.92	0.91	0.89	0.87	0.84	0.82
0.60	0.99	0.99	0.98	0.96	0.95	0.94	0.92	0.90	0.87	0.84	0.83
0.65	1.00	0.99	0.98	0.97	0.96	0.95	0.93	0.91	0.88	0.85	0.83
0.70	1.00	1.00	0.99	0.98	0.97	0.96	0.94	0.92	0.89	0.85	0.83
0.75	1.00	1.00	1.00	0.99	0.98	0.97	0.95	0.93	0.90	0.86	0.83
0.80	1.00	1.00	1.00	1.00	0.99	0.98	0.96	0.94	0.91	0.87	0.84
0.85	1.00	1.00	1.00	1.00	1.00	0.99	0.98	0.96	0.92	0.87	0.84
0.90	1.00	1.00	1.00	1.00	1.00	1.00	0.99	0.97	0.94	0.88	0.84
0.95	1.00	1.00	1.00	1.00	1.00	1.00	1.00	0.99	0.96	0.89	0.84
1.00	1.00	1.00	1.00	1.00	1.00	1.00	1.00	1.00	1.00	0.89	0.84

Proportion of Employees Considered Satisfactory = 0.90

| | | | | | Selection Ratio | | | | | | |
r	0.05	0.10	0.20	0.30	0.40	0.50	0.60	0.70	0.80	0.90	0.95
0.00	0.90	0.90	0.90	0.90	0.90	0.90	0.90	0.90	0.90	0.90	0.90
0.05	0.92	0.91	0.91	0.91	0.91	0.91	0.91	0.90	0.90	0.90	0.90
0.10	0.93	0.93	0.92	0.92	0.92	0.91	0.91	0.91	0.91	0.90	0.90
0.15	0.95	0.94	0.93	0.93	0.92	0.92	0.92	0.91	0.91	0.91	0.90
0.20	0.96	0.95	0.94	0.94	0.93	0.93	0.92	0.92	0.91	0.91	0.90
0.25	0.97	0.96	0.95	0.95	0.94	0.93	0.93	0.92	0.92	0.91	0.91
0.30	0.98	0.97	0.96	0.95	0.94	0.94	0.94	0.93	0.92	0.91	0.91
0.35	0.98	0.98	0.97	0.96	0.95	0.95	0.94	0.93	0.93	0.92	0.91
0.40	0.99	0.98	0.98	0.97	0.96	0.95	0.95	0.94	0.93	0.92	0.91
0.45	0.99	0.99	0.98	0.98	0.97	0.96	0.95	0.94	0.93	0.92	0.91
0.50	1.00	0.99	0.99	0.98	0.97	0.97	0.96	0.95	0.94	0.92	0.92
0.55	1.00	1.00	0.99	0.99	0.98	0.97	0.97	0.96	0.94	0.93	0.92

Proportion of Employees Considered Satisfactory = 0.90 (continued)

r	\multicolumn{11}{c}{Selection Ratio}
	0.05	0.10	0.20	0.30	0.40	0.50	0.60	0.70	0.80	0.90	0.95
0.60	1.00	1.00	0.99	0.99	0.99	0.98	0.97	0.96	0.95	0.93	0.92
0.65	1.00	1.00	1.00	0.99	0.99	0.98	0.98	0.97	0.96	0.94	0.92
0.70	1.00	1.00	1.00	1.00	0.99	0.99	0.98	0.97	0.96	0.94	0.93
0.75	1.00	1.00	1.00	1.00	1.00	0.99	0.99	0.98	0.97	0.95	0.93
0.80	1.00	1.00	1.00	1.00	1.00	1.00	0.99	0.99	0.97	0.95	0.93
0.85	1.00	1.00	1.00	1.00	1.00	1.00	1.00	0.99	0.98	0.96	0.94
0.90	1.00	1.00	1.00	1.00	1.00	1.00	1.00	1.00	0.99	0.97	0.94
0.95	1.00	1.00	1.00	1.00	1.00	1.00	1.00	1.00	1.00	0.98	0.94
1.00	1.00	1.00	1.00	1.00	1.00	1.00	1.00	1.00	1.00	1.00	0.95

The Naylor-Shine Table for Determining the Increase in Mean Criterion Score Obtained by Using a Selection Device

USING THE TABLE

The following definitions are used in the table:

r_{xy} = validity coefficient

Z_{xi} = cutoff point (score) on the predictor in standard-score units

ϕ_i = selection ratio

$\bar{Z}_{yi}$ = mean criterion score (in standard-score units) of all cases above cutoff

λ_i = ordinate of normal distribution at Z_{xi}

and the table is based on the following equation:

$$\bar{Z}_{yi} = r_{xy}\frac{\lambda_i}{\phi_i}$$

Note: The use of the table may differ slightly in the case where r_{xy} is really a multiple regression coefficient. The major difference occurs in the Z_{xi} column. With a single predictor there is no difficulty in expressing a cutoff score in terms of a particular value of X, the predictor variable (thus we use Z_{xi}). However, in the case of multiple predictors, it is no longer feasible to do so, since there are several X variables. The easiest procedure, therefore, is to reduce conceptually the multivariate case to the bivariate case by treating the multiple correlation coefficient as the correlation coefficient between the observed criterion scores (Z_y) and the predicted criterion scores (Z_y'). Thus it becomes possible to talk about cutoff values for the multiple predictor case, but these cutoff scores are expressed in terms of Z_{yi}' values, rather than Z_{xi} values. The only difficulty this creates is that $s_{z'y}^2 \neq 1$, but will always be equal to R_{xy}^2, the squared multiple correlation coefficient. Thus, in order to use the tables when r_{xy} is actually a multiple correlation coefficient, it is necessary to transform Z_{yi}' values by

$$Z_{xi} = \frac{Z_{yi}'}{R_{xy}}$$

A Table for Computing the Mean Criterion Score (Z_{yi}) for the Group Falling Above Some Cutoff Score (Z_{xi})

ϕ_i	Z_{xi}	λ_i	λ_i/ϕ_i	ϕ_i	Z_{xi}	λ_i	λ_i/ϕ_i	ϕ_i	Z_{xi}	λ_i	λ_i/ϕ_i
0.9987	-3.00	0.0044	0.00	0.9974	-2.79	0.0081	0.01	0.9951	-2.58	0.0143	0.01
0.9986	-2.99	0.0046	0.00	0.9973	-2.78	0.0084	0.01	0.9949	-2.57	0.0147	0.01
0.9986	-2.98	0.0047	0.00	0.9972	-2.77	0.0086	0.01	0.9948	-2.56	0.0151	0.02
0.9985	-2.97	0.0048	0.00	0.9971	-2.76	0.0088	0.01	0.9946	-2.55	0.0154	0.02
0.9985	-2.96	0.0050	0.01	0.9970	-2.75	0.0091	0.01	0.9945	-2.54	0.0158	0.02
0.9984	-2.95	0.0051	0.01	0.9969	-2.74	0.0093	0.01	0.9943	-2.53	0.0163	0.02
0.9984	-2.94	0.0053	0.01	0.9968	-2.73	0.0095	0.01	0.9941	-2.52	0.0167	0.02
0.9983	-2.93	0.0055	0.01	0.9967	-2.72	0.0099	0.01	0.9940	-2.51	0.0171	0.02
0.9982	-2.92	0.0056	0.01	0.9966	-2.71	0.0101	0.01	0.9938	-2.50	0.0175	0.02
0.9982	-2.91	0.0058	0.01	0.9965	-2.70	0.0104	0.01	0.9936	-2.49	0.0180	0.02
0.9981	-2.90	0.0060	0.01	0.9964	-2.69	0.0107	0.01	0.9934	-2.48	0.0184	0.02
0.9981	-2.89	0.0061	0.01	0.9963	-2.68	0.0110	0.01	0.9932	-2.47	0.0189	0.02
0.9980	-2.88	0.0063	0.01	0.9962	-2.67	0.0113	0.01	0.9931	-2.46	0.0194	0.02
0.9979	-2.87	0.0065	0.01	0.9961	-2.66	0.0116	0.01	0.9929	-2.45	0.0198	0.02
0.9979	-2.86	0.0067	0.01	0.9960	-2.65	0.0119	0.01	0.9927	-2.44	0.0203	0.02
0.9978	-2.85	0.0069	0.01	0.9959	-2.64	0.0122	0.01	0.9925	-2.43	0.0208	0.02
0.9977	-2.84	0.0071	0.01	0.9957	-2.63	0.0126	0.01	0.9922	-2.42	0.0213	0.02
0.9977	-2.83	0.0073	0.01	0.9956	-2.62	0.0129	0.01	0.9920	-2.41	0.0219	0.02
0.9976	-2.82	0.0075	0.01	0.9955	-2.61	0.0132	0.01	0.9918	-2.40	0.0224	0.02
0.9975	-2.81	0.0077	0.01	0.9953	-2.60	0.0136	0.01	0.9916	-2.39	0.0229	0.02
0.9974	-2.80	0.0079	0.01	0.9952	-2.59	0.0139	0.01	0.9913	-2.38	0.0235	0.02
0.9911	-2.37	0.0241	0.02	0.9834	-2.13	0.0413	0.04	0.9706	-1.89	0.0669	0.07

Notes: ϕ_i = proportion above cutoff (selection ratio); Z_{xi} = predictor cutoff value in standard-score form; λ_i = normal curve ordinate at Z_{xi}.
Source: Naylor, J. C., Shine, L. C. (1965). A table for determining the increase in mean criterion score obtained by using a selection device. *Journal of Industrial Psychology* 3, 33–42.

A Table for Computing the Mean Criterion Score (Z_{yi}) for the Group Falling Above Some Cutoff Score (Z_{xi}) (continued)

ϕ_i	Z_{xi}	λ_i	λ_i/ϕ_i	ϕ_i	Z_{xi}	λ_i	λ_i/ϕ_i	ϕ_i	Z_{xi}	λ_i	λ_i/ϕ_i
0.9909	-2.36	0.0246	0.02	0.9830	-2.12	0.0422	0.04	0.9699	-1.88	0.0681	0.07
0.9906	-2.35	0.0252	0.03	0.9826	-2.11	0.0431	0.04	0.9693	-1.87	0.0694	0.07
0.9904	-2.34	0.0258	0.03	0.9821	-2.10	0.0440	0.04	0.9686	-1.86	0.0707	0.07
0.9901	-2.33	0.0264	0.03	0.9817	-2.09	0.0449	0.05	0.9678	-1.85	0.0721	0.07
0.9898	-2.32	0.0270	0.03	0.9812	-2.08	0.0459	0.05	0.9671	-1.84	0.0734	0.08
0.9896	-2.31	0.0277	0.03	0.9808	-2.07	0.0468	0.05	0.9664	-1.83	0.0748	0.08
0.9893	-2.30	0.0283	0.03	0.9803	-2.06	0.0478	0.05	0.9656	-1.82	0.0761	0.08
0.9890	-2.29	0.0290	0.03	0.9798	-2.05	0.0488	0.05	0.9649	-1.81	0.0775	0.08
0.9887	-2.28	0.0297	0.03	0.9793	-2.04	0.0498	0.05	0.9641	-1.80	0.0790	0.08
0.9884	-2.27	0.0303	0.03	0.9788	-2.03	0.0508	0.05	0.9633	-1.79	0.0804	0.08
0.9881	-2.26	0.0310	0.03	0.9783	-2.02	0.0519	0.05	0.9625	-1.78	0.0818	0.08
0.9878	-2.25	0.0317	0.03	0.9778	-2.01	0.0529	0.05	0.9616	-1.77	0.0833	0.09
0.9875	-2.24	0.0325	0.03	0.9772	-2.00	0.0540	0.06	0.9608	-1.76	0.0848	0.09
0.9871	-2.23	0.0332	0.03	0.9767	-1.99	0.0551	0.06	0.9599	-1.75	0.0863	0.09
0.9868	-2.22	0.0339	0.03	0.9761	-1.98	0.0562	0.06	0.9591	-1.74	0.0878	0.09
0.9864	-2.21	0.0347	0.04	0.9756	-1.97	0.0573	0.06	0.9582	-1.73	0.0893	0.09
0.9861	-2.20	0.0355	0.04	0.9750	-1.96	0.0584	0.06	0.9573	-1.72	0.0909	0.09
0.9857	-2.19	0.0363	0.04	0.9744	-1.95	0.0596	0.06	0.9564	-1.71	0.0925	0.10
0.9854	-2.18	0.0371	0.04	0.9738	-1.94	0.0608	0.06	0.9554	-1.70	0.0940	0.10
0.9850	-2.17	0.0379	0.04	0.9732	-1.93	0.0620	0.06	0.9545	-1.69	0.0957	0.10
0.9846	-2.16	0.0387	0.04	0.9726	-1.92	0.0632	0.06	0.9535	-1.68	0.0973	0.10
0.9842	-2.15	0.0396	0.04	0.9719	-1.91	0.0644	0.07	0.9525	-1.67	0.0989	0.10
0.9838	-2.14	0.0404	0.04	0.9713	-1.90	0.0656	0.07	0.9515	-1.66	0.1006	0.11
0.9505	-1.65	0.1023	0.11	0.9192	-1.40	0.1497	0.16	0.8749	-1.15	0.2059	0.24

ϕ_i	Z_{xi}	λ_i		ϕ_i	Z_{xi}	λ_i		ϕ_i	Z_{xi}	λ_i	
0.9495	-1.64	0.1040	0.11	0.9177	-1.39	0.1518	0.17	0.8729	-1.14	0.2083	0.24
0.9484	-1.63	0.1057	0.11	0.9162	-1.38	0.1539	0.17	0.8708	-1.13	0.2107	0.24
0.9474	-1.62	0.1074	0.11	0.9147	-1.37	0.1561	0.17	0.8686	-1.12	0.2131	0.25
0.9463	-1.61	0.1092	0.12	0.9131	-1.36	0.1582	0.17	0.8665	-1.11	0.2155	0.25
0.9452	-1.60	0.1109	0.12	0.9115	-1.35	0.1604	0.18	0.8643	-1.10	0.2179	0.25
0.9441	-1.59	0.1127	0.12	0.9099	-1.34	0.1625	0.18	0.8621	-1.09	0.2203	0.26
0.9429	-1.58	0.1145	0.12	0.9082	-1.33	0.1647	0.18	0.8599	-1.08	0.2227	0.26
0.9418	-1.57	0.1163	0.12	0.9066	-1.32	0.1669	0.18	0.8577	-1.07	0.2251	0.26
0.9406	-1.56	0.1182	0.13	0.9049	-1.31	0.1691	0.19	0.8554	-1.06	0.2275	0.27
0.9394	-1.55	0.1200	0.13	0.9032	-1.30	0.1714	6.19	0.8531	-1.05	0.2299	0.27
0.9382	-1.54	0.1219	0.13	0.9015	-1.29	0.1736	0.19	0.8508	-1.04	0.2323	0.27
0.9370	-1.53	0.1238	0.13	0.8997	-1.28	0.1753	0.19	0.8485	-1.03	0.2347	0.28
0.9357	-1.52	0.1257	0.13	0.8980	-1.27	0.1781	0.20	0.8461	-1.02	0.2371	0.28
0.9345	-1.51	0.1276	0.14	0.8962	-1.26	0.1804	0.20	0.8438	-1.01	0.2396	0.28
0.9332	-1.50	0.1295	0.14	0.8944	-1.25	0.1826	0.20	0.8413	-1.00	0.2420	0.29
0.9319	-1.49	0.1315	0.14	0.8925	-1.24	0.1849	0.21	0.8389	-0.99	0.2444	0.29
0.9306	-1.48	0.1334	0.14	0.8907	-1.23	0.1872	0.21	0.8365	-0.98	0.2468	0.30
0.9292	-1.47	0.1354	0.15	0.8888	-1.22	0.1895	0.21	0.8340	-0.97	0.2492	0.30
0.9279	-1.46	0.1374	0.15	0.8869	-1.21	0.1919	0.22	0.8315	-0.96	0.2516	0.30
0.9265	-1.45	0.1394	0.15	0.8849	-1.20	0.1942	0.22	0.8289	-0.95	0.2541	0.31
0.9251	-1.44	0.1415	0.15	0.8830	-1.19	0.1965	0.22	0.8264	-0.94	0.2565	0.31
0.9236	-1.43	0.1435	0.16	0.8810	-1.18	0.1989	0.23	0.8238	-0.93	0.2589	0.31
0.9222	-1.42	0.1456	0.16	0.8790	-1.17	0.2012	0.23	0.8212	-0.92	0.2613	0.32
0.9207	-1.41	0.1476	0.16	0.8770	-1.16	0.2036	0.23	0.8186	-0.91	0.2637	0.32
0.8159	-0.90	0.2661	0.33	0.7454	-0.66	0.3209	0.43	0.6628	-0.42	0.3653	0.55
0.8133	-0.89	0.2685	0.33	0.7422	-0.65	0.3230	0.44	0.6591	-0.41	0.3668	0.56

Notes: ϕ_i = proportion above cutoff (selection ratio); Z_{xi} = predictor cutoff value in standard-score form; λ_i = normal curve ordinate at Z_{xi}.

A Table for Computing the Mean Criterion Score (Z_{yi}) for the Group Falling Above Some Cutoff Score (Z_{xi}) (continued)

ϕ_i	Z_{xi}	λ_i	λ_i/ϕ_i	ϕ_i	Z_{xi}	λ_i	λ_i/ϕ_i	ϕ_i	Z_{xi}	λ_i	λ_i/ϕ_i
0.8106	-0.88	0.2709	0.33	0.7389	-0.64	0.3251	0.44	0.6554	-0.40	0.3683	0.56
0.8078	-0.87	0.2732	0.34	0.7357	-0.63	0.3271	0.44	0.6517	-0.39	0.3697	0.57
0.8051	-0.86	0.2756	0.34	0.7324	-0.62	0.3292	0.45	0.6480	-0.38	0.3712	0.57
0.8023	-0.85	0.2780	0.35	0.7291	-0.61	0.3312	0.45	0.6443	-0.37	0.3725	0.58
0.7995	-0.84	0.2803	0.35	0.7257	-0.60	0.3332	0.46	0.6406	-0.36	0.3739	0.58
0.7967	-0.83	0.2827	0.35	0.7224	-0.59	0.3352	0.46	0.6368	-0.35	0.3752	0.59
0.7939	-0.82	0.2850	0.36	0.7190	-0.58	0.3372	0.47	0.6331	-0.34	0.3765	0.59
0.7910	-0.81	0.2874	0.36	0.7157	-0.57	0.3391	0.47	0.6293	-0.33	0.3778	0.60
0.7881	-0.80	0.2897	0.37	0.7123	-0.56	0.3410	0.48	0.6255	-0.32	0.3790	0.61
0.7852	-0.79	0.2920	0.37	0.7088	-0.55	0.3429	0.48	0.6217	-0.31	0.3802	0.61
0.7823	-0.78	0.2943	0.38	0.7054	-0.54	0.3448	0.49	0.6179	-0.30	0.3814	0.62
0.7794	-0.77	0.2966	0.38	0.7019	-0.53	0.3467	0.49	0.6141	-0.29	0.3825	0.62
0.7764	-0.76	0.2989	0.38	0.6985	-0.52	0.3485	0.50	0.6103	-0.28	0.3836	0.63
0.7734	-0.75	0.3011	0.39	0.6950	-0.51	0.3503	0.50	0.6064	-0.27	0.3847	0.64
0.7704	-0.74	0.3034	0.39	0.6915	-0.50	0.3521	0.51	0.6026	-0.26	0.3857	0.64
0.7673	-0.73	0.3056	0.40	0.6879	-0.49	0.3538	0.51	0.5987	-0.25	0.3867	0.65
0.7642	-0.72	0.3079	0.40	0.6844	-0.48	0.3555	0.52	0.5948	-0.24	0.3876	0.65
0.7611	-0.71	0.3101	0.41	0.6808	-0.47	0.3572	0.52	0.5910	-0.23	0.3885	0.66
0.7580	-0.70	0.3123	0.41	0.6772	-0.46	0.3589	0.53	0.5871	-0.22	0.3894	0.66
0.7549	-0.69	0.3144	0.42	0.6736	-0.45	0.3605	0.54	0.5832	-0.21	0.3902	0.67
0.7517	-0.68	0.3166	0.42	0.6700	-0.44	0.3621	0.54	0.5793	-0.20	0.3910	0.67
0.7486	-0.67	0.3187	0.43	0.6664	-0.43	0.3637	0.55	0.5753	-0.19	0.3918	0.68
0.5714	-0.18	0.3925	0.69	0.4721	0.07	0.3980	0.84	0.3745	0.32	0.3790	1.01
0.5675	-0.17	0.3932	0.69	0.4681	0.08	0.3977	0.85	0.3707	0.33	0.3778	1.02

ϕ_i	Z_{xi}	λ_i	Z_{xi}	ϕ_i	Z_{xi}	λ_i	Z_{xi}	ϕ_i	Z_{xi}	λ_i	Z_{xi}
0.5636	-0.16	0.3939	0.70	0.4641	0.09	0.3973	0.86	0.3669	0.34	0.3765	1.03
0.5596	-0.15	0.3945	0.70	0.4602	0.10	0.3970	0.86	0.3632	0.35	0.3752	1.03
0.5557	-0.14	0.3951	0.71	0.4562	0.11	0.3965	0.87	0.3594	0.36	0.3739	1.04
0.5517	-0.13	0.3956	0.72	0.4522	0.12	0.3961	0.88	0.3557	0.37	0.3725	1.05
0.5478	-0.12	0.3961	0.72	0.4483	0.13	0.3956	0.88	0.3520	0.38	0.3712	1.05
0.5438	-0.11	0.3965	0.73	0.4443	0.14	0.3951	0.89	0.3483	0.39	0.3697	1.06
0.5398	-0.10	0.3970	0.74	0.4404	0.15	0.3945	0.90	0.3446	0.40	0.3683	1.06
0.5359	-0.09	0.3973	0.74	0.4364	0.16	0.3939	0.90	0.3409	0.41	0.3668	1.07
0.5319	-0.08	0.3977	0.75	0.4325	0.17	0.3932	0.91	0.3372	0.42	0.3653	1.08
0.5279	-0.07	0.3980	0.75	0.4286	0.18	0.3925	0.92	0.3336	0.43	0.3637	1.08
0.5239	-0.06	0.3982	0.76	0.4247	0.19	0.3918	0.92	0.3300	0.44	0.3621	1.09
0.5199	-0.05	0.3984	0.77	0.4207	0.20	0.3910	0.93	0.3264	0.45	0.3605	1.10
0.5160	-0.04	0.3986	0.77	0.4168	0.21	0.3902	0.94	0.3228	0.46	0.3589	1.10
0.5120	-0.03	0.3988	0.78	0.4129	0.22	0.3894	0.94	0.3192	0.47	0.3572	1.11
0.5080	-0.02	0.3989	0.79	0.4090	0.23	0.3885	0.95	0.3156	0.48	0.3555	1.12
0.5040	-0.01	0.3989	0.79	0.4052	0.24	0.3875	0.96	0.3121	0.49	0.3538	1.13
0.5000	0.00	0.3989	0.80	0.4013	0.25	0.3867	0.96	0.3085	0.50	0.3521	1.13
0.4960	0.01	0.3989	0.80	0.3974	0.26	0.3857	0.97	0.3050	0.51	0.3503	1.14
0.4920	0.02	0.3989	0.81	0.3936	0.27	0.3847	0.98	0.3015	0.52	0.3485	1.15
0.4880	0.03	0.3988	0.82	0.3897	0.28	0.3835	0.98	0.2981	0.53	0.3467	1.16
0.4840	0.04	0.3986	0.82	0.3859	0.29	0.3825	0.99	0.2946	0.54	0.3448	1.16
0.4801	0.05	0.3984	0.83	0.3821	0.30	0.3814	1.00	0.2912	0.55	0.3429	1.17
0.4761	0.06	0.3982	0.84	0.3783	0.31	0.3802	1.01	0.2877	0.56	0.3410	1.18
0.2843	0.57	0.3391	1.19	0.2090	0.81	0.2874	1.38	0.1459	1.05	0.2299	1.57
0.2810	0.58	0.3372	1.20	0.2061	0.82	0.2850	1.38	0.1446	1.06	0.2275	1.57
0.2776	0.59	0.3352	1.21	0.2033	0.83	0.2827	1.39	0.1423	1.07	0.2251	1.58

Notes: ϕ_i = proportion above cutoff (selection ratio); Z_{xi} = predictor cutoff value in standard-score form; λ_i = normal curve ordinate at Z_{xi}.

A Table for Computing the Mean Criterion Score (Z_{yi}) for the Group Falling Above Some Cutoff Score (Z_{xi}) (continued)

ϕ_i	Z_{xi}	λ_i	λ_i/ϕ_i	ϕ_i	Z_{xi}	λ_i	λ_i/ϕ_i	ϕ_i	Z_{xi}	λ_i	λ_i/ϕ_i
0.2743	0.60	0.3332	1.21	0.2005	0.84	0.2803	1.40	0.1401	1.08	0.2227	1.59
0.2709	0.61	0.3212	1.22	0.1977	0.85	0.2780	1.41	0.1379	1.09	0.2203	1.60
0.2676	0.62	0.3292	1.23	0.1949	0.86	0.2756	1.41	0.1357	1.10	0.2179	1.61
0.2643	0.63	0.3271	1.24	0.1922	0.87	0.2732	1.42	0.1335	1.11	0.2155	1.61
0.2611	0.64	0.3251	1.25	0.1894	0.88	0.2709	1.43	0.1314	1.12	0.2131	1.62
0.2578	0.65	0.3230	1.25	0.1867	0.89	0.2685	1.44	0.1292	1.13	0.2107	1.63
0.2546	0.66	0.3209	1.26	0.1841	0.90	0.2661	1.45	0.1271	1.14	0.2083	1.64
0.2514	0.67	0.3187	1.27	0.1814	0.91	0.2637	1.45	0.1251	1.15	0.2059	1.65
0.2483	0.68	0.3166	1.28	0.1788	0.92	0.2613	1.46	0.1230	1.16	0.2036	1.66
0.2451	0.69	0.3144	1.28	0.1762	0.93	0.2589	1.47	0.1210	1.17	0.2012	1.66
0.2420	0.70	0.3123	1.29	0.1736	0.94	0.2565	1.48	0.1190	1.18	0.1989	1.67
0.2389	0.71	0.3101	1.30	0.1711	0.95	0.2541	1.49	0.1170	1.19	0.1965	1.68
0.2358	0.72	0.3079	1.31	0.1685	0.96	0.2516	1.49	0.1151	1.20	0.1942	1.69
0.2327	0.73	0.3056	1.31	0.1660	0.97	0.2492	1.50	0.1131	1.21	0.1919	1.70
0.2296	0.74	0.3034	1.32	0.1635	0.98	0.2468	1.51	0.1112	1.22	0.1895	1.70
0.2266	0.75	0.3011	1.33	0.1611	0.99	0.2444	1.52	0.1093	1.23	0.1872	1.71
0.2236	0.76	0.2989	1.34	0.1587	1.00	0.2420	1.52	0.1075	1.24	0.1849	1.72
0.2206	0.77	0.2966	1.34	0.1562	1.01	0.2396	1.53	0.1056	1.25	0.1826	1.73
0.2177	0.78	0.2943	1.35	0.1539	1.02	0.2371	1.54	0.1038	1.26	0.1804	1.74
0.2148	0.79	0.2920	1.36	0.1515	1.03	0.2347	1.55	0.1020	1.27	0.1781	1.75
0.2119	0.80	0.2897	1.37	0.1492	1.04	0.2323	1.56	0.1003	1.28	0.1758	1.75
0.0985	1.29	0.1736	1.76	0.0618	1.54	0.1219	1.97	0.0367	1.79	0.0804	2.19
0.0968	1.30	0.1714	1.77	0.0606	1.55	0.1200	1.98	0.0359	1.80	0.0790	2.20
0.0951	1.31	0.1691	1.78	0.0594	1.56	0.1182	1.99	0.0351	1.81	0.0775	2.21

ϕ_i	Z_{xi}	λ_i	λ_i/ϕ_i	ϕ_i	Z_{xi}	λ_i	λ_i/ϕ_i	ϕ_i	Z_{xi}	λ_i	λ_i/ϕ_i
0.0934	1.32	0.1669	1.79	0.0582	1.57	0.1163	2.00	0.0344	1.82	0.0761	2.21
0.0918	1.33	0.1647	1.79	0.0571	1.58	0.1145	2.01	0.0336	1.83	0.0748	2.23
0.0901	1.34	0.1626	1.80	0.0559	1.59	0.1127	2.02	0.0329	1.84	0.0734	2.23
0.0885	1.35	0.1604	1.81	0.0548	1.60	0.1109	2.02	0.0322	1.85	0.0721	2.24
0.0869	1.36	0.1582	1.82	0.0537	1.61	0.1092	2.03	0.0314	1.86	0.0707	2.25
0.0853	1.37	0.1561	1.83	0.0526	1.62	0.1074	2.04	0.0307	1.87	0.0694	2.26
0.0838	1.38	0.1539	1.84	0.0516	1.63	0.1057	2.05	0.0301	1.88	0.0681	2.26
0.0823	1.39	0.1518	1.84	0.0505	1.64	0.1040	2.06	0.0294	1.89	0.0669	2.28
0.0808	1.40	0.1497	1.85	0.0495	1.65	0.1023	2.07	0.0287	1.90	0.0656	2.29
0.0793	1.41	0.1476	1.86	0.0485	1.66	0.1006	2.07	0.0281	1.91	0.0644	2.29
0.0778	1.42	0.1456	1.87	0.0475	1.67	0.0989	2.08	0.0274	1.92	0.0632	2.31
0.0764	1.43	0.1435	1.88	0.0465	1.68	0.0973	2.09	0.0268	1.93	0.0620	2.31
0.0749	1.44	0.1415	1.89	0.0455	1.69	0.0957	2.10	0.0262	1.94	0.0608	2.32
0.0735	1.45	0.1394	1.90	0.0446	1.70	0.0940	2.11	0.0256	1.95	0.0596	2.33
0.0721	1.46	0.1374	1.91	0.0436	1.71	0.0925	2.12	0.0250	1.96	0.0584	2.34
0.0708	1.47	0.1354	1.91	0.0427	1.72	0.0909	2.13	0.0244	1.97	0.0573	2.35
0.0694	1.48	0.1334	1.92	0.0418	1.73	0.0893	2.14	0.0239	1.98	0.0562	2.35
0.0681	1.49	0.1315	1.93	0.0409	1.74	0.0878	2.15	0.0233	1.99	0.0551	2.36
0.0668	1.50	0.1295	1.94	0.0401	1.75	0.0863	2.15	0.0228	2.00	0.0540	2.37
0.0655	1.51	0.1276	1.95	0.0392	1.76	0.0848	2.16	0.0222	2.01	0.0529	2.38
0.0643	1.52	0.1257	1.95	0.0384	1.77	0.0833	2.17	0.0217	2.02	0.0519	2.39
0.0630	1.53	0.1238	1.97	0.0375	1.78	0.0818	2.18	0.0212	2.03	0.0508	2.40
0.0207	2.04	0.0498	2.41	0.0113	2.28	0.0297	2.63	0.0059	2.52	0.0167	2.84
0.0202	2.05	0.0488	2.42	0.0110	2.29	0.0290	2.64	0.0057	2.53	0.0163	2.85
0.0197	2.06	0.0478	2.43	0.0107	2.30	0.0283	2.64	0.0055	2.54	0.0158	2.86
0.0192	2.07	0.0468	2.44	0.0104	2.31	0.0277	2.65	0.0054	2.55	0.0154	2.87

Notes: ϕ_i = proportion above cutoff (selection ratio); Z_{xi} = predictor cutoff value in standard-score form; λ_i = normal curve ordinate at Z_{xi}.

A Table for Computing the Mean Criterion Score (Z_{yi}) for the Group Falling Above Some Cutoff Score (Z_{xi}) (continued)

ϕ_i	Z_{xi}	λ_i	λ_i/ϕ_i	ϕ_i	Z_{xi}	λ_i	λ_i/ϕ_i	ϕ_i	Z_{xi}	λ_i	λ_i/ϕ_i
0.0188	2.08	0.0459	2.44	0.0102	2.32	0.0270	2.66	0.0052	2.56	0.0151	2.88
0.0183	2.09	0.0449	2.45	0.0099	2.33	0.0264	2.67	0.0051	2.57	0.0147	2.89
0.0179	2.10	0.0440	2.46	0.0096	2.34	0.0258	2.68	0.0049	2.58	0.0143	2.90
0.0174	2.11	0.0431	2.48	0.0094	2.35	0.0252	2.68	0.0048	2.59	0.0139	2.90
0.0170	2.12	0.0422	2.48	0.0091	2.36	0.0246	2.69	0.0047	2.60	0.0136	2.91
0.0166	2.13	0.0413	2.49	0.0089	2.37	0.0241	2.71	0.0045	2.61	0.0132	2.92
0.0162	2.14	0.0404	2.49	0.0087	2.38	0.0235	2.71	0.0044	2.62	0.0129	2.93
0.0158	2.15	0.0396	2.51	0.0084	2.39	0.0229	2.72	0.0043	2.63	0.0126	2.94
0.0154	2.16	0.0387	2.51	0.0082	2.40	0.0224	2.73	0.0041	2.64	0.0122	2.95
0.0150	2.17	0.0379	2.53	0.0080	2.41	0.0219	2.74	0.0040	2.65	0.0119	2.96
0.0146	2.18	0.0371	2.54	0.0078	2.42	0.0213	2.74	0.0039	2.66	0.0116	2.97
0.0143	2.19	0.0363	2.54	0.0075	2.43	0.0208	2.76	0.0038	2.67	0.0113	2.98
0.0139	2.20	0.0355	2.55	0.0073	2.44	0.0203	2.76	0.0031	2.68	0.0110	2.99
0.0136	2.21	0.0347	2.55	0.0071	2.45	0.0198	2.77	0.0036	2.69	0.0107	3.00
0.0132	2.22	0.0339	2.57	0.0069	2.46	0.0194	2.79	0.0035	2.70	0.0104	3.01
0.0129	2.23	0.0332	2.57	0.0068	2.47	0.0189	2.80	0.0034	2.71	0.0101	3.01
0.0125	2.24	0.0325	2.60	0.0066	2.48	0.0184	2.80	0.0033	2.72	0.0099	3.02
0.0122	2.25	0.0317	2.60	0.0064	2.49	0.0180	2.82	0.0032	2.73	0.0096	3.03
0.0119	2.26	0.0310	2.61	0.0062	2.50	0.0175	2.82	0.0031	2.74	0.0093	3.04
0.0116	2.27	0.0303	2.61	0.0060	2.51	0.0171	2.83	0.0030	2.75	0.0091	3.05
0.0029	2.76	0.0088	3.06	0.0022	2.85	0.0069	3.14	0.0016	2.94	0.0053	3.23
0.0028	2.77	0.0086	3.07	0.0021	2.86	0.0067	3.15	0.0016	2.95	0.0051	3.24
0.0027	2.78	0.0084	3.08	0.0021	2.87	0.0065	3.16	0.0015	2.96	0.0050	3.25
0.0026	2.79	0.0081	3.09	0.0020	2.88	0.0063	3.17	0.0015	2.97	0.0048	3.26

ϕ_i	Z_{xi}	λ_{xi}	
0.0026	2.80	0.0079	3.10
0.0025	2.81	0.0077	3.11
0.0024	2.82	0.0075	3.12
0.0023	2.83	0.0073	3.13
0.0023	2.84	0.0071	3.13
0.0019	2.89	0.0061	3.18
0.0019	2.90	0.0060	3.19
0.0018	2.91	0.0058	3.20
0.0018	2.92	0.0056	3.21
0.0017	2.93	0.0055	3.22
0.0014	2.98	0.0047	3.26
0.0014	2.99	0.0046	3.27
0.0013	3.00	0.0044	3.28

Notes: ϕ_i = proportion above cutoff (selection ratio); Z_{xi} = predictor cutoff value in standard-score form; λ_{xi} = normal curve ordinate at Z_{xi}.

I N D E X